THE NEW GROVE GUIDE TO
Mozart and His Operas

Praise for *The New Grove Dictionary of Opera*

"The last word on opera."—The *Washington Post*

"Opera buffs need look no further."—The *Observer*, London

"A monument of enlightened scholarship."
—The *Sunday Telegraph*, London

THE NEW GROVE GUIDE TO

MOZART

and His Operas

Julian Rushton

OXFORD
UNIVERSITY PRESS

2007

OXFORD
UNIVERSITY PRESS

Oxford University Press, Inc., publishes works that
further Oxford University's objective of excellence
in research, scholarship, and education.

Oxford   New York
Auckland   Cape Town   Dar es Salaam   Hong Kong   Karachi
Kuala Lumpur   Madrid   Melbourne   Mexico City   Nairobi
New Delhi   Shanghai   Taipei   Toronto

With offices in
Argentina   Austria   Brazil   Chile   Czech Republic   France   Greece
Guatemala   Hungary   Italy   Japan   Poland   Portugal   Singapore
South Korea   Switzerland   Thailand   Turkey   Ukraine   Vietnam

Published by Oxford University Press, Inc.
198 Madison Avenue, New York, NY 10016
www.oup.com

Library of Congress Cataloging-in-Publication Data
Rushton, Julian.
    The New Grove guide to Mozart and his operas / Julian Rushton.
        p. cm. — (New Grove operas)
    Rev. ed. of: Mozart and his operas / edited by Stanley Sadie, c2000.
    Includes bibliographical references and index.
    ISBN: 978-0-19-531318-5 (pbk.)
    ISBN: 978-0-19-531317-8 (cloth)
    1. Mozart, Wolfgang Amadeus, 1756–1791. Operas.   2. Opera—18th century.
    I. Title.
    ML410.M9.R876 2007
    782.1092—dc22   2006035186

Printed in the United States of America
on acid-free paper

Contents

{ The Performers

{ The Cities

Preface

For the purposes of this edition, the editor has lightly revised his own texts on Mozart and his individual operas from the original dictionary. The sections on librettists, performers, and cities are rewritten, to replace the alphabetical organization appropriate to a dictionary by a chronological narrative, but much of this remains the work of the original authors, whose work is acknowledged, as before.

The book begins with a life of Mozart slanted towards his production of opera. There follows a chronological catalogue of his stage works. This does not include oratorios (*Die Schuldigkeit des ersten Gebotes*; *Betulia liberata*; *Davidde penitente*), which despite their at least metaphorically dramatic structure are not stage works, nor does it include Mozart's exceptional ventures into ballet and incidental music, with the exception of *Der Schauspieldirektor*, which is sometimes categorized as an opera, but which merits inclusion primarily because it was commissioned for the Habsburg court, and because of the involvement of singers who were significant for Mozart in other ways.

Within the chronological narratives on authors and performers, I have taken the opportunity to mention a number of figures who were not entered into the dictionary in their own right. Among the literary figures these include a few not personally known to Mozart, or dead before his birth, but who contributed to the wider literary culture of which the opera librettos form a part (the earlier edition already included Beaumarchais, whose work lies behind *Le nozze di Figaro*, and Metastasio, whose words Mozart frequently set, although neither wrote anything specifically for Mozart). Among the performers, there is little to be done on those of whom (as Stanley Sadie wrote) 'we are almost totally ignorant', but we know enough about some others for it to be worth mentioning them in connection with Mozart premieres. I have also mentioned some cities where he saw operas performed, but which were not the scene of his own opera premieres.

I am immeasurably indebted to the authors of the relevant articles in *The New Grove Dictionary of Opera*. Sections taken directly from them are in some cases lightly edited and a little cut, so that what remains is slanted more towards Mozart than would have been appropriate for the dictionary. These sections are identified by starting with the relevant article name in bold type—as it might be, **Lorenzo da Ponte**—and concluding with the initials of the author of the dictionary article in square brackets—for instance [**T.C.**]. These entries are included in the table of contents, and a key to authors' initials is given on p. xiii. Any editorial insertion within what is essentially another author's work is also in brackets. I have put a number of names in bold and added my own initials where the material seemed of sufficient importance to warrant inclusion in the table of contents. The glossary of terms is also considerably revised from the earlier edition, and I have added a personal recommendation of a selection of the vast recorded repertoire of Mozart's operas.

References to musical pitch use Helmholtz's notation: $C–B$ covers the octave beginning on C below the bass clef, the lowest string of the cello; $c–b$ is an octave higher, with c' as middle C on the piano. Thus c''' is a very high note for a soprano, and f''' the highest note in the role of the Queen of Night in *Die Zauberflöte*, while the low bass Osmin in *Die Entführung* sings down to D.

Julian Rushton
Golcar, West Yorkshire
2006

List of Illustrations

Contributors

A.H.K.	Alec Hyatt King
B.A.B.	Bruce Alan Brown
B.D.M.	Barbara Dobbs Mackenzie
B.M.	Betty Matthews
C.H.	Clemens Höslinger
C.R.	Christopher Raeburn
D.E.M.	Dale E. Monson
D.H.	Daniel Heartz
D.L.	Dorothea Link
D.N.	Don Neville
G.C.	Gerhard Croll
H.G.	Harald Goertz
H.J.-W.	Harrison James Wignall
H.S.	Herbert Seifert
J.A.R.	John A. Rice
J.L.	Jitka Ludov
J.R.	Julian Rushton
K.J.S.	Klaus J. Seidel
K.K.H.	Kathleen Kuzmick Hansell
L.T.	Linda Tyler
M.C.	Mosco Carner
M.D.	Mariangela Donà
P.B.	Peter Branscombe
P.C.	Paul Corneilson
P.L.G.	Patricia Lewy Gidwitz
P.W.	Piero Weiss
R.K.	Rudolf Klein
R.W.	Roland Würz
T.B.	Thomas Bauman
T.C.	Tim Carter
W.E.R.	Walter E. Rex

THE NEW GROVE GUIDE TO

Mozart and His Operas

Chronology
of Mozart's Life and Operas

{ 1756
27 JAN — Born in Salzburg, the son of Leopold Mozart and Anna Maria Mozart (née Pertl)

{ 1763–66
Travels with his family to Vienna, France, England, and the Netherlands

{ 1767
Dramatic debut in Salzburg with Part 1 of the oratorio *Die Schuldigkeit des ersten Gebotes* (the rest by Michael Haydn and Cajetan Adlgasser)
13 MAY — *Apollo et Hyacinthus* performed, Salzburg, Benedictine University

{ 1768
Composes *La finta semplice* in Vienna. *Bastien und Bastienne* performed, Vienna, at Mesmer's home

{ 1769
1 MAY ? — *La finta semplice*, Salzburg, Archbishop's palace

{ 1770
Mozart's first visit to Milan
26 DEC — *Mitridate, re di Ponto*, Milan, Regio Ducal Teatro

{ 1771
17 OCT   *Ascanio in Alba*, Milan, Regio Ducal Teatro

{ 1772
MAY   *Il sogno di Scipione*, Salzburg, Archbishop's palace
26 DEC   *Lucio Silla*, Milan, Regio Ducal Teatro

{ 1775
13 JAN   *La finta giardiniera*, Munich, Salvatortheater
23 APR   *Il re pastore*, Salzburg, Archbishop's palace

{ 1777–78
                Mozart's stay in Paris; death of Maria Anna Mozart there

{ 1779/80
                Zaide composed; not performed in Mozart's lifetime

{ 1781
29 JAN   *Idomeneo, re di Creta*, Munich, Residenztheater

{ 1782
16 JUL   *Die Entführung aus dem Serail*, Vienna, Burgtheater
4 AUG   Marries Constanze Weber

{ 1783
                Starts composition of *L'oca del Cairo* (abandoned
                early 1784)

{ 1783–84
                Lo sposo deluso begun, but unfinished

{ 1786
7 FEB   *Der Schauspieldirektor*, Schönbrunn, Orangery
1 MAY   *Le nozze di Figaro*, Vienna, Burgtheater

{ 1787
28 MAY   Leopold Mozart dies in Salzburg
29 OCT   *Don Giovanni*, Prague, National Theatre

{ **1788**
　　7 MAY　　　　*Don Giovanni*, Vienna, Burgtheater

{ **1789**
　　29 AUG　　　*Le nozze di Figaro* revived, Vienna, Burgtheater

{ **1790**
　　26 JAN　　　*Così fan tutte*, Vienna, Burgtheater

{ **1791**
　　6 SEP　　　*La clemenza di Tito*, Prague, National Theatre
　　30 SEP　　　*Die Zauberflöte*, Vienna, Freihaus-Theater auf der
　　　　　　　　Wieden
　　6 DEC　　　Mozart dies in Vienna

Life

Joannes Chrysostomus Wolfgangus Theophilus (or Gottlieb) Mozart, who usually signed himself Wolfgang Amadè Mozart, was born in Salzburg on 27 January 1756; he died in Vienna on 5 December 1791. He was the son of Leopold Mozart, Chamber Composer and Deputy Kapellmeister to successive Prince-Archbishops of Salzburg.

Mozart's comprehensive mastery of three genres, Italian (*opera seria* and *opera buffa*) and German (*Singspiel*), is unmatched in operatic history. Although he wrote no operas in French, French texts are represented in translation: *opéra comique* by *Bastien und Bastienne* and *tragédie lyrique* by *Idomeneo*. This achievement is founded on his genius for assimilation and in the circumstances of his life and early experience of operatic genres. He is also the first operatic composer some of whose works have been established in the repertory without serious interruption since his lifetime.

Although Mozart's principal formative experiences in opera lay away from home, the musical life of Salzburg included serenata performances (operatic, although not necessarily fully staged); plays with music at the University and Gymnasium; and *opera buffa* and plays from visiting troupes. The Mozart family were keen theatre-goers. Mozart composed three operatic works for Salzburg, as well as his only incidental music to a spoken drama. His earliest travels with his family to Vienna, France, England, and the Netherlands (1763–6) displayed him and his sister Nannerl as keyboard prodigies, and in due course Wolfgang as a composer, but mainly of instrumental music. Nevertheless he was soon exposed to opera, which in Austria and Germany was mostly sung in Italian. In Paris the Académie Royale de Musique, or Opéra, bastion of a tradition extending back to Lully and a musical style particularly disliked by Leopold Mozart, contrasted with the more modern and Italian-influenced *opéra comique*, dominated by Duni, Philidor, and Monsigny. In England Mozart met J. C. Bach and imitated his instrumental works, but Bach was also at the centre of London's almost entirely Italian operatic culture and his operatic influence on Mozart was no less significant in the longer run. In London, Mozart took singing lessons from the castrato Giovanni Manzuoli and the family was befriended by another famous castrato, Ferdinando Tenducci. In London and The Hague Mozart composed his first arias, including his earliest settings of poetry by Metastasio (K21/19c and 23). His precocious understanding of the idioms of Italian opera is documented in Daines Barrington's report (published 1769) to the Royal Society in London, reprinted in Deutsch's Documentary Biography, and in the reports from the music historian Dr Charles Burney. According to Barrington Mozart at the age of nine could already improvise recitatives and arias, aping operatic styles suited to love and anger, emotions he could hardly yet have experienced personally.

Back in Salzburg, Mozart made his dramatic debut in 1767 with the first act of an oratorio, *Die Schuldigkeit des ersten Gebotes* (K35: the other acts, by Adlgasser and Michael Haydn, are lost). He began his lifelong practice of inserting numbers into other composers' operas, and wrote his first complete dramatic work, the Latin intermezzo *Apollo et Hyacinthus*.

From September 1767 the Mozarts spent 15 months based in Vienna, apart from a journey into Moravia in an unsuccessful attempt to evade smallpox. In Vienna they may have met the young Antonio Salieri, a protégé of the music director of the court theatres, Florian Gassmann. Among other operas they heard Gluck's *Alceste*; its profound impact emerged later, in *Lucio Silla* and especially *Idomeneo* and *Don Giovanni*. Mozart's first real operas, written in Vienna during 1768, inaugurate the two principal categories within his output, operas in Italian with recitatives and operas in German with spoken dialogue. The *opera buffa La finta semplice*, written in the mistaken belief that the Emperor had ordered it, was tried over but not performed in Vienna, much to Leopold Mozart's chagrin; this apparent snub added fuel to Leopold's ever smouldering distrust of the Italian musicians in favour at the Habsburg and Salzburg courts. The opera may have received a single performance in Salzburg in 1769. In Vienna, some pride was recovered by the performance of a Mass by imperial command, and with the Singspiel *Bastien und Bastienne*, given privately in 1768 at the Vienna home of Dr Franz Anton Mesmer, who later developed the 'magnetism therapy' pilloried in *Così fan tutte*.

Whereas many contemporaries specialized in opera, sometimes writing over a hundred, Mozart spent much of his career until 1780 in the employment of the church and court of Salzburg, meanwhile developing his unmatched inventiveness in instrumental music. As a result his production of operas is punctuated by gaps, resulting from circumstances rather than inclination. The early 1770s seemed to promise a more conventional career in opera: experience in Italy, followed by relative security in Germany or (as Mozart sometimes hoped) England. Between 1770 and 1773 he was commissioned to write five serious Italian works, one of them an oratorio. Three of the operas were produced in Milan, then under Austrian rule like much of North Italy: when Leopold and Wolfgang Mozart undertook their tour of Italy at the end of 1769, it was a considerable time before they left lands controlled by the Habsburgs. Naturally they took advantage of the chance to see Italian opera in the land of its origin: Guglielmi's *Ruggiero* in Verona, a setting of *Demetrio* in Mantua, and Valentini's *La clemenʒa di Tito* in Cremona. They also saw operas by Piccinni and Paisiello, and some including comedies which are impossible to identify; all would have been modern works.

In Milan they were welcomed by the Austrian governor, Count Firmian, and obtained a serious opera commission for next Carnival season (see Milan), the confidence of those involved being obtained by performance of new settings of scenes (recitatives and arias) from two of Metastasio's most popular librettos, *Artaserse* and *Demofoonte*. Once the commission for an *opera seria* for Carnival 1771 was settled they travelled on. In Parma they met the virtuoso singer Lucrezia Agujari whose range extended considerably higher than Mozart ever required any soprano to go (to c''''); Mozart wrote out some of her feats to impress his sister (letter of 24 March 1770). After visiting Bologna and meeting the learned Padre Martini, they went on to Florence, ruled by Leopold, Grand Duke of Tuscany, who was eventually to succeed his brother Joseph to the Habsburg Empire in 1790. In Florence they met again Mozart's London singing teacher Manzuoli, and the English prodigy Thomas Linley. After a stay in Rome they visited Naples, and saw Jommelli's new opera *Armida*. Mozart reported home that it was 'beautiful, but much too elaborate and old-fashioned for the theatre' (letter of 5 June 1770). The blow is directed at the structure, and particularly the 'pompous' ballets, rather than Jommelli's music; to some extent, however, Mozart had to conform to similar tastes in Milan.

They returned northwards during the late summer, and Mozart was knighted by the Pope on a return visit to Rome. In October, having received the libretto for *Mitridate, re di Ponto*, Mozart complained that his fingers were aching from writing recitatives. Composition of the arias had to await his arrival in Milan, where he could discuss them with the singers, some of whom had not been in Milan on his previous visit and were new to him. Several arias had to be revised, some more than once, a circumstance that does not seem to have recurred with later Mozart operas, or not to such an extent. Yet with *Mitridate* Mozart achieved mastery of *opera seria* in a single stride, a fact recognized by its immediate success and the commission for another two years later. In the meantime, he gained further experience with an oratorio to a libretto by Metastasio, *La Betulia liberata* (K118/74c), commissioned for Padua; there is, however, no record of its performance. Its musical forms are those typical of Italian opera, with the addition of choruses.

Meanwhile another commission came from the Habsburgs for Milan. This was for a short opera, or serenata, *Ascanio in Alba*, for the marriage of Archduke Ferdinand in October 1771. Ferdinand seemed keen to employ Mozart, but was advised against it by his mother, the Empress Maria Theresia, in terms suggesting a measure of hostility directed at Leopold ('useless people who go about like beggars . . . besides, he has a large family'). The Mozarts returned to Salzburg in December to find the tolerant Archbishop Schrattenbach on the verge of death. His successor, Archbishop Colloredo, proved far less generous with leave of absence. Mozart, however, may have helped inaugurate his reign with the performance of another serenata, *Il sogno di Scipione*, originally intended for Schrattenbach's anniversary and thus written before *Ascanio*. With Colloredo reliant upon the friendship of the Habsburgs, Mozart could hardly be denied leave to present *Lucio Silla* in Milan (Carnival 1773), scoring another triumph, but one upon which he never had the opportunity to capitalize.

It was not for over a year that an opportunity arose to write another opera. Count Seeau, theatre Intendant to the Elector of Bavaria, commissioned an *opera buffa*, *La finta giardiniera*, performed in Munich early in 1775. It occupies a special place in Mozart's output, as it became his first opera to enter the German repertory; the version adapted as a Singspiel received far more performances than the Italian original. It is the first of his operas whose musical and dramatic qualities have encouraged more than an occasional and respectful modern revival. It is an example of the sentimental genre of comedy, like Haydn's *La fedeltà premiata*, which was also translated into German and performed in Vienna in 1784. Almost immediately afterwards, in Salzburg, Mozart set a cut-down version of Metastasio's *Il re pastore* as a serenata for the visit of a younger Habsburg. Then, apart from concert arias, he wrote no more Italian dramatic music for five years, the longest operatic hiatus of his career.

His next journey began with a fruitless attempt to obtain employment in Germany. During his traumatic stay in Paris (1777–8), the *opéra comique* provided themes for instrumental variations, and Mozart experienced the repertory of the Opéra (Académie Royale de Musique) following its regeneration by Gluck. But the 'Querelle des Gluckistes et Piccinnistes' preoccupied the public and the management. Piccinni's first French opera, *Roland*, was the newest opera in the repertory, and J. C. Bach came over to discuss his own commission (*Amadis*, 1779), renewing his friendship with the younger composer. Mozart's only theatrical music was part of a ballet, *Les petits riens*, commissioned by Jean-Georges Noverre. Yet the period between *Il re pastore* and *Idomeneo* was not entirely wasted for him as a dramatic composer. He worked out dramatic ideas in his first great concertos. On the way to Paris, affected by his love for Aloysia Weber, whom he had met in Mannheim, he composed substantial scenas, usually known as concert arias, preceded by recitative. Their texts are taken from operas, including one from *Alceste*. He also composed arias for Dorothea Wendling and Anton Raaff. Knowledge of the Mannheim and Paris orchestras, and of these two singers, was seminal in the development of the instrumental aspect of his later operas, notably *Idomeneo*.

In 1778, on the return journey from Paris, he had become interested in melodrama, words spoken to instrumental music: of Benda's *Medea* he wrote 'nothing has ever surprised me so much, for I had always imagined that such a piece would be quite ineffective! . . . I think that most operatic recitatives should be treated in this way—and only sung occasionally, when the words *can be perfectly expressed by the music*' (letter of 12 November 1778). He may have composed a melodrama *Semiramis* (1778), but if so it is lost. Back in Salzburg, he used melodrama in adding more incidental music to Gebler's *Thamos, König in Ägypten* (K345/366a), probably composed in 1779, and in his unfinished opera of this period, *Zaide*. The latter resulted from an interest in German opera kindled in Mannheim, but must have been undertaken in the hope of production by Emperor Joseph II's recently established National Singspiel company in Vienna. The neglect of melodrama in his later German works may represent disenchantment with the medium, or it may reflect the need to conform to Viennese tastes.

Carl Theodor, Elector Palatine at Mannheim, admired Mozart's music, but never went so far as to offer him employment. He became Elector of Bavaria in 1778 and took most of his Kapelle—some of the singers and his unrivalled orchestra—with him to Munich. Thus when Count Seeau commissioned *Idomeneo* (1781) it was certainly with the Elector's approval, and perhaps following urging from musicians who knew Mozart, including the distinguished elderly tenor Raaff and the musical director Christian Cannabich. It is Mozart's first undoubted operatic masterpiece, and marks a watershed in his career. After this close approach to Gluck's development of *tragédie lyrique*, he never again had the chance to write so dramatically for chorus, and so pictorially for the orchestra, nor to provide so extended a ballet. The solo arias and especially the ensembles banish display for its own sake, and their dramatic impact arises directly from their stylistic, as well as merely poetical, relevance to the action. The composition of *Idomeneo* gave rise to a fascinating correspondence while Leopold Mozart remained in Salzburg, liaising with the librettist, Gianbattista Varesco. This and subsequent letters from Vienna about *Die Entführung* give us the clearest indication of Mozart's opera aesthetic, and demonstrate his acute dramatic intelligence and his determination to ensure that the success of his opera was not jeopardized by the libretto. Although comparable documentary evidence is lacking for the Da Ponte operas and *Die Zauberflöte*, it seems legitimate to assume that Mozart took a guiding role in the dramatic construction of all his later operas: after *Die Entführung*, with only qualified exceptions, his librettos were written specially for him.

Mozart's absence from Salzburg tested Colloredo's patience to the limit. He was summoned to Vienna, where he was happy to go and still happier to stay when dismissed from the archbishop's service (June 1781). His remaining operas were composed for the Austrian capital or for Prague, capital of Bohemia and also a major city within the Habsburg Empire. In Vienna Mozart was quick to make theatrical friends, among them Gottlieb Stephanie the younger, director of the National Singspiel. Instead of accepting *Zaide*, however, he offered Mozart a similar libretto, *Die Entführung aus dem Serail*. The original intention was to put on a production at the National Singspiel during the visit of the Russian Archduke Paul in September 1781, but some of Gluck's operas were revived instead, in one case translated into German. Mozart's opera could thus take longer to gestate; it was eventually performed two weeks before his marriage, on 4 August 1782, to Constanze Weber (sister of Aloysia, now married to Joseph Lange). This opera became popular throughout Germany, was taken on tour (in Salzburg it was seen by a delighted Leopold Mozart), and was revived in Vienna itself, in the Kärntnertortheater. Had there been royalties on performances, Mozart's subsequent financial problems would have greatly eased.

Despite its success, *Die Entführung* was the last new production for the National Singspiel, which was replaced by an Italian *opera buffa* troupe. This move, popular with the aristocratic end of the spectrum of Viennese audiences, led to the last serious hiatus in Mozart's operatic output. He was eager to contribute to the Italian repertory, and studied it avidly; he acquainted himself with the performers and was impressed by several of them, notably the *buffo* Francesco Benucci and the English soprano Nancy Storace, later the first Figaro and Susanna. The Italian composer most performed in Vienna during the mid-1780s was Giovanni Paisiello; the repertory included his *Il barbiere di Siviglia* (1783), and a newly commissioned work for Vienna, *Il re Teodoro in Venezia* (1784). The repertory included several operas brought in from Italy and elsewhere, but some composers, at least for a time, concentrated their output in Vienna, notably Salieri, Vincenzo Righini, the English Stephen Storace, and the Spanish Vicente Martín y Soler, all of whom wrote new operas with librettos by Lorenzo da Ponte. Martín's operas were particularly successful, but he and Mozart were on amicable terms. Mozart certainly benefited by studying Salieri's works, such as *La fiera di Venezia* (1772: revived in the 1780s), where the ballroom scene anticipates the complex central finale to *Don Giovanni*. Salieri's intrigues against Mozart have been exaggerated, but as musical director of the Italian company, he wielded considerable influence. Mozart had inherited something of his father's distrust of foreigners, and his initial perception of the situation is clear (letter of 7 May 1783):

> [Da Ponte] has promised to write an entirely new libretto for me. But who knows whether he will be able to keep his word—or will want to? For, as you are aware, these Italian gentlemen are very civil to your face. Enough: we know them! If he is in league with Salieri, I shall never get anything out of him.

Mozart was encouraged by the Emperor's favourable response to him as a pianist, and by Count Rosenberg-Orsini, the theatre intendant, who urged him to contribute something to the *opera buffa* repertoire. He read more than a hundred librettos without finding anything suitable, and in the same letter asks his father to persuade Varesco to write an original comedy:

> The most essential thing is that on the whole the story should be really *comic*: and, if possible, he ought to introduce *two equally good female parts*, one of these to be *seria*, the other *mezzo carattere*. . . . The third female character may be entirely *buffa*, and so may all the male ones.

The prescription for three contrasted female roles is fulfilled in varying degrees in the Da Ponte operas, especially *Don Giovanni*.

Varesco began work on *L'oca del Cairo*, and Mozart, who may have discussed it with him on what proved to be his last visit to Salzburg, in 1783, drafted several numbers, including a finale, before abandoning it. He then turned to *Lo sposo deluso*, a libretto of uncertain authorship; this too remains fragmentary. In 1783 he honed his skills by writing three arias for Anfossi's *Il curioso indiscreto* (K418–20), two of them in the two-tempo rondò form which he later put to significant use in his own operas. Two of these arias were for Lange and one for Valentin Adamberger, the first Belmonte in *Die Entführung*, but his was not performed. In 1785 Mozart composed two ensembles for Bianchi's *La villanella rapita*, a trio and a quartet (K479–80) that mingle sentiment, comedy, rage, and accents of a heroine near to despair.

Early in 1786 *Der Schauspieldirektor* was commissioned for performance at the palace of Schönbrunn alongside Salieri's *Prima la musica*: Mozart's work was buffoonery about German theatre folk, Salieri's a sophisticated consideration of the relation of music and poetry. The contrast might have been galling, and Salieri had the pick of the *opera buffa* singers, but by this time Mozart had already composed most of *Le nozze di Figaro* in which his mastery of the Italian genre is complete. According to Da Ponte, Mozart himself suggested following up the success of Paisiello's *Il barbiere di Siviglia* by basing the libretto on Beaumarchais' sequel, *Le Mariage de Figaro*. Despite an initially good reception *Figaro* was not a runaway success in Vienna, and was soon outstripped by Martín's *Una cosa rara*. *Figaro*, however, marks the last watershed in Mozart's career; from now on he was a recognized opera composer, and in his remaining five years he produced four major works. The second production of *Figaro* took place in Prague. It was perhaps his greatest triumph, and it led directly to the commission for *Don Giovanni*, first performed there in October 1787. The longest remaining interval in Mozart's operatic output separates *Don Giovanni* from *Così fan tutte* (Vienna, January 1790), but it was bridged by the Viennese production of the former (1788) and the successful 1789 revival of *Figaro*, both requiring new music to accommodate a changed cast of singers. Adapted as a Singspiel, *Don Giovanni* soon joined *Die Entführung* in the German repertory.

Figaro has lost nothing of its freshness in 220 years. The preparation for this epiphany in operatic history naturally included Mozart's previous operas, but also, typically and perhaps more importantly, local conditions including the presence of a group of expert singers, and Vienna's recent experience of *opera buffa*: Paisiello's *Il barbiere*, a model for 'really *comic*' opera with a fast-moving, realistic plot and precise characterization, operas by Salieri and other Italians not resident in Vienna, and Martín's operas, which display the virtues of a popular, song-like idiom. Memories of *opéra comique*, some of whose descendants were still part of the Viennese operatic diet at the other official theatre, the Kärntnertor, may have contributed to the masterly action ensembles. The long finales are the culmination of an *opera buffa* tradition associated with Goldoni's Venice. Yet Mozart's own genius is needed to account for the radical nature of the transition from the uncompromisingly extended musical developments of *Die Entführung*; from now on, the symbiotic harmony between music and drama is complete.

The last phase of Mozart's career marks a climax in three genres, each transformed by his dramatic insight. *Opera buffa* reached an unsurpassable peak in the three Da Ponte operas, *Figaro*, *Don Giovanni* and *Così fan tutte*. Their length and intensity, although there is no shortage of humour and even farce, make them unique in the literature of 18th-century comedy, and it is no exaggeration to call them the foundation of the modern repertory. Mozart also wanted to display his strength in *opera seria* and, contrary to an opinion often expressed, the commission for *La clemenza di Tito* (for the Prague coronation of Leopold II) was far from unwelcome; it enabled him to produce a concise and serious drama that, despite the speed at which it had to be composed, had considerable success over the next 20 years, and has proved its worth in several modern revivals.

La clemenza was his last opera in order of composition, but the last to reach performance was *Die Zauberflöte*. This was Mozart's only opera since *Bastien und Bastienne* not composed for a court theatre; it was written for Schikaneder's suburban Theater auf der Wieden. In it Mozart transformed the comic and magical Singspiel into an allegory which alludes to his own serious commitment to freemasonry, while sacrificing nothing in the way of humour and popular appeal. The loss opera suffered by his early death is incalculable; the level and range of his achievement is rivalled only by specialists in the genre such as Verdi and Wagner.

Works: An Overview of Mozart's Operas

Mozart's stylistic development in opera parallels that of his instrumental music, but because of the intervals within his output and the variety of genres exploited, it may appear less consistent. Until *Il re pastore* his aims and methods were representative of his time; thereafter he composed individual masterpieces whose qualities have affected operatic composition ever since they became widely known. While the excellence in relation to prevailing standards of all but his earliest operas should be emphasized, the following observations refer mainly to his mature work.

In both *opera seria* and *Singspiel* Mozart's masterpieces stand in direct opposition. The musical riches of *Idomeneo* contrast with the austerity of *La clemenza di Tito*, as does the profuse invention of *Die Entführung*, redolent of court opera, with the expressive concentration and the mixture of styles (from the religious to the demotic) in *Die Zauberflöte*. The earlier pair displays the exuberance of invention found in his instrumental works up to about 1785—the Vienna piano concertos and wind serenades, the quartets dedicated to Haydn. The first Da Ponte operas, *Figaro* and *Don Giovanni*, share the riper mastery of the 1786 piano concertos, the last four symphonies (1786–8), and the string quintets of 1787; the style of *Così fan tutte* moves towards the operas of 1791 which share the effortless lucidity, the virtual concealment of actual complexity, in the late instrumental works (the 'Prussian' quartets, the last quintets and concertos).

While insisting on the primacy of music in opera, Mozart never lost sight of its dramatic context. He intended his arias to suit both the available voices and the dramatic situation, and fed the appetites and expectations of his audiences rather than defying them. If his greatest works did not immediately conquer audiences, it was not because their forms or dramatic content were unacceptable, but because of the elaboration of his musical language. Mozart explained his priorities in a letter to Leopold (26 September 1781) concerning 'Solche hergelaufne Laffen' (*Die Entführung*):

> Osmin's rage is rendered comical by the use of the Turkish music. In working out the aria I have . . . allowed Fischer's beautiful deep notes to glow. The passage 'Drum beim Barte des Propheten' is indeed in the same tempo, but with quick notes; and as Osmin's rage gradually increases, there comes (just when the aria seems to be at an end) the Allegro assai, which is in a totally different metre and in a different key; this is bound to be very effective. For just as a man in such a towering rage oversteps all the bounds of order, moderation and propriety and completely forgets himself, so must the music too forget itself. But since passions, whether violent or not, must never be expressed to the point of exciting disgust, and as music, even in the most terrible situations, must never offend the ear, but must please the listener, or in other words must never cease to be *music*, so I have not chosen a key foreign to F major (in which the aria is written) but one related to it—not the nearest, D minor, but the more remote A minor.

Mozart adds the 'Turkish' percussion to entertain the Viennese, but also to render Osmin both comical and alien, and a serious threat to the sympathetic (European) characters. To convey this, Mozart takes advantage of instrumental possibilities and the capabilities of his singer, and acknowledges the right of expressive exigencies to overrule musical decorum. The resulting blend of serious purpose and comedy is one of his most characteristic dramatic achievements.

His discussion of Belmonte's aria, in the same letter, is hardly less revealing. It is written 'expressly to suit Adamberger's voice'; Belmonte's 'throbbing heart' is represented by violins in octaves; 'you see the trembling—the faltering—we see his heaving breast begin to swell—this I have expressed by a crescendo—you hear the whispering and sighing—which I have indicated by muted first violins and a flute in unison'. It is tempting to assume that principles of this kind lie behind other arias, but it is noteworthy that the features Mozart selects for illustration either concern motion—literally, with Belmonte, the movements of rage with Osmin—or actual sounds (sighing, whispering). It cannot be assumed, therefore, that every feature of his later orchestral accompaniments requires interpretation on these lines.

Perhaps unwittingly, Mozart followed Gluck's precepts on overtures, even in comedies; as early as *La finta semplice* he joined the last movement to the first scene, and from *Idomeneo* onwards he abandoned the three-movement sinfonia. A slow central section interrupts the Allegro in *Die Entführung* and *Lo sposo deluso*, and a similar one was planned for *Figaro* and rejected. Three later overtures have slow introductions. Except in the two works of 1786 (*Figaro* and *Der Schauspieldirektor*), the overtures go beyond mere appropriateness to incorporate important musical ideas from the opera. Instrumental expression reaches its zenith in orchestral recitatives (and in the melodramas of *Zaide*), enhancing the expressive penetration of instrumental sounds by harmonic daring and, notably, an increased use of wind instruments. Obbligato recitative was conventionally reserved for soliloquy (for instance, Donna Elvira's 'In quali eccessi' in the Vienna version of *Don Giovanni*), or soliloquy overheard (Susanna's 'Giunse al fin il momento'), but it was also used for long dialogues in *Idomeneo* (notably the sacrifice scene) and *Così fan tutte*, where it also gives rise to measured music in a recitative context (arioso). Mozart was also imaginative in his use of *recitativo semplice*. Occasionally, but not so often as to become predictable, the bass line has a pertinent shape; a descending scale over a diminished 4th is characteristic of *Idomeneo* (ex.1a: Ilia contrasts the woes of Troy with the gods' defence of Greece; ex.1b: Idamante sings of Arbace's approach bearing evil tidings). Even ostensibly conventional declamation sometimes makes use of shapes related to formal numbers. Before 'Là ci darem la mano', Don Giovanni makes repeated allusions to the pitch-contour a–c–f (preceding recitative, bars 1–4, extending f–b by bar 7; bar 10; bars 14–16), ending with a direct anticipation of the melody (ex.2); similarly, b–d–b in recitative immediately precedes 'Fin ch'an dal vino' (the main motif, b–b–b–d'–b repeated, appears at 'voglio divertir').

Mozart's choice of musical forms was dictated by dramatic requirements, ensuring that the musical numbers emerge from the inner drama of character or the outer drama of action. His ensembles and finales are usually considered more original or significant than the arias, but even in the late comedies solo expression remains of paramount importance. Mozart always found a place for arias that explore a character's mental state and contribute to dramatic understanding by changing our perception of a personality; such arias occur even in his fastest-moving comedies, although beside comparable scenes in *opera seria* they gain intensity through their relative brevity and absence of display.

Writing for a Viennese *buffo* troupe, or for Schikaneder's company, Mozart not only eschewed the formal cadenzas in arias that are a regular feature of his earlier *opera seria*, but developed a precision and conciseness of expression that may be gauged by comparing *La finta giardiniera* with

Ex. 1

(a) Act 1 scene ii

ILIA

Non te - mer.   Di - fe - sa di Mi - ner - va è la Gre - cia

['Fear not. Defended by Minerva and Greece']

(b) Act 1 scenes iv-v

IDAMANTE

Ar - ba - ce vie - ne   Ma qual pian - to ch'an - nun - zia?

['Arbace approaches. But what complaint does he announce?']

Ex.2 Mozart: *Don Giovanni*, Act 1

GIOVANNI

Quel ca - si - net - to è mi - o,   so - li - sa - re - mo

GIOVANNI

Là ci da - rem la   ma - no

['You see that little house there? Well that is my house']

['You'll lay your hand in mine']

Figaro, or Belmonte's love song in E♭ (*Die Entführung*: 'Ich baue ganz') with Tamino's (*Die Zauberflöte*: 'Dies bildnis'). Yet he can still indulge the voice: Susanna's 'Deh vieni, non tardar' (*Figaro*), Zerlina's arias (*Don Giovanni*), or in a tragic context Pamina's 'Ach ich fühl's' (*Die Zauberflöte*) penetrate to the core of feeling partly because they are so grateful to sing. Virtuosity—the grotesque depths of Osmin, the fireworks of the Queen of Night, the *coloratura* of Konstanze, Fiordiligi, or Vitellia—also plays a part in characterization. Shorter arias may be highly dramatic without recourse to structural modulation; often they only briefly visit the dominant before returning to the tonic, a tonal 'flatness' also found in some of the late chamber music. Mozart prolongs pieces by obsessive repetition (Figaro: 'Aprite un po'), alluring melodic extension (Zerlina: 'Vedrai, carino'), or sensitive play on expectations by cadential postponement, which can be comical and satirical (Don Alfonso's 'Vorrei dir', Dorabella's 'Smanie implacabili'), or project the most intense pathos ('Ach, ich fühl's').

Most arias are composed in close correspondence with the lyrical verse forms (usually two strophes of three or four lines each) supplied by the librettist, but they also take forms peculiar to a dramatic situation. In 'Aprite un po' quegl'occhi', Da Ponte provided Figaro with 26 lines. Mozart worked through two quatrains in tonic and dominant sections (to bar 48); then, assisted by changes in verse metre, he ran through the remaining 18 lines in a mere 21 bars (from bar 49), largely on tonic harmony. The first quatrain returns on dominant harmony (bar 71); the incomplete repetition of the remaining text is punctuated by the nagging 'il resto nol dico' (in which Figaro bitterly invites us to imagine what his beloved Susanna might be getting up to with the Count). The whole cadential period (57–70) is repeated exactly, with a mocking coda (85–102). Such a form, although perhaps modelled on an aria in Paisiello's *Barbiere* ('Veramente, ho torto in vero'), resists formal classification; yet it is unlikely to be experienced as unorthodox, since it combines musical solidity with dramatic directness.

The question of verse metre is too complicated to be broached here, but a change in metre devised by the librettist often coincides with a dramatic change, or in an aria or ensemble with a change in tempo. It is sometimes implied that Mozart's choice of musical metre was determined by the poet, but clearly this is not the case. Compare Figaro's 'Se vuol ballare / Signor Contino, / Il chitarrino / Le suonerò' and Giovanni's 'Fin ch'an dal vino / Calda la testa / Una gran festa / Va preparar'; they have identical syllabification, lines of five syllables, *versi piani*, with the fourth line a *verso tronco* (end accented). But the former is set as a fast minuet (3/4 time) and the latter as a fast contredanse (2/4 time). Later Figaro (at 'L'arte schermendo, / L'arte adoprando') changes to a contredanse metre without a change in syllabification, except that the penultimate line ('Tutte le macchine') is a *verso sdrucciolo*, a line accented on the antepenultimate syllable. Thus poetic metre does not determine musical metre which is, indeed, a very different concept. Nevertheless the poetic metres, and particularly the changes introduced in longer texts such as finales, will have had considerable suggestive power in determining Mozart's compositional choices.

Mozart used all available forms, selecting the simplest such as the single-section cavatina or sectional rondo for single states of mind. 'Cavatina' implies an aria that is short but not always simple in feeling (*Figaro*: Countess Almaviva's 'Porgi amor'; *Così*: Ferrando's 'Tradito, schernito'). Simple rondos appear for sentiment (Zaide's 'Trostlos schlutzet Philomele'), unalloyed delight (*Die Entführung*: Blonde's 'Welche Wonne, welche Lust'), and—with a faster coda—a pretended optimism (*Così*: Ferrando's 'Ah lo veggio'). Ternary form, descended from the da capo, is appropriate to the controlled fury of Donna Anna's 'Or sai chi l'onore' (*Don Giovanni*). Binary arias, in design resembling sonata form and equivalent to the first section of a full da capo aria, represent a complex of feelings unresolved at the end; this type, prevalent in *Idomeneo* (including Ilia's 'Padre, germani, addio!'), also appears in comedies (*Così*: 'Smanie implacabile'). Additional text may be accommodated in a middle section, sometimes a complete contrast (Titus's 'Se 'all'impero'), sometimes a modulating section like a sonata 'development' (Idomeneus's 'Fuor del mar') (Webster in Eisen, 1991).

Complex feelings modified in the course of the aria give rise to additive structures, for which Gluck provided an obvious model in Mozart's earlier operas (*Il re pastore*: Elisa's 'Barbaro! oh Dio'). Less conventionally, Fiordiligi ('Come scoglio') accelerates to a third tempo, her single-minded rejection of the invitation to be unfaithful paradoxically demanding such emphasis; musical coherence resides largely in continuity of key. A similar plan is used in Sextus's 'Parto, parto' (*La clemenza di Tito*). Leporello, however, proceeds from fast (numerical) to slow (taxonomic) cataloguing of Giovanni's conquests; the model may have been an aria for Figaro ('Scorsi già molti paesi') in Paisiello's *Barbiere*. In his Vienna operas, Mozart favoured the modern design known as 'rondò' (the spelling is important to distinguish it from simple rondos which remain in their original tempo). The essential design of the rondò lies in the alternation of tonic areas and episodes, a system spanning the succession of slow and fast tempi even where the mood of the Allegro supersedes that of the preceding slow movement. Examples: in *Figaro* the countess's 'Dove sono'; in *Don Giovanni*, Anna's 'Non mi dir'; in *Così*, Fiordiligi's 'Per pietà'; and in *La clemenza*, Sesto's and Vitellia's final arias.

Similarly additive forms commonly occur in ensembles where the final tempo, almost invariably faster, corresponds to a concluding phase in the action which brings the voices together. A simple device of musical form in the duet 'Ah guarda, sorella' (*Così*), this procedure marks Zerlina's complete acquiescence to Giovanni's seductive blandishment in 'Là ci darem la mano'. The slower sections usually contrast tonic and dominant areas, but (unlike the rondò) the faster music is a single section entirely in the tonic, requiring no thematic reprise. The unusual fast-slow pattern is used wittily in Leporello's 'catalogue' aria ('Madamina'), tragically in the first finale of *La clemenza* (activity: bad news: despair), and turns from humour to numinous beauty in the first-act quintet of *Die Zauberflöte*. Such progressive schemes, developed in the quartet-finale of Act 2 of *Die Entführung*, reach a pitch of complexity in the chain finales, which both in action and musical duration (sometimes over 600 bars) bulk hugely in the Da Ponte operas and *Die Zauberflöte*.

Mozart's welding of action to musical continuity is usually most appreciated in ensembles and finales, but an action aria can also develop a situation as well as characterization (Figaro's 'Non più andrai', Susanna's 'Venite, inginocchiatevi'; in *Don Giovanni*, Masetto's 'Ho capito', and especially Giovanni's 'Metà di voi quà vadano'). Mozart certainly exploited the necessities of musical language for dramatic ends, but where character and feelings rather than action are concerned careful analysis is required to define what is really happening— or to resist that definition, since Mozart's own position frequently appears ambiguous, and allows interpretative scope to the singers and director.

In the often-cited first duet of *Le nozze di Figaro* (ex. 3), a marked opposition appears between Figaro's theme and Susanna's gracious melody; he is counting measurements of the room, she is admiring her hat. Figaro moves towards the dominant, sufficiently established by the perfect cadence (bar 30) for the music to continue there; instead Susanna enters in the tonic. Figaro resumes counting, and articulates the dominant more decisively (underlining its dominant, A, in bars 45–6). Susanna develops this tonal situation but forgets her melody, resorting to pettish repetition over the pedal A. Figaro then sings her tune in the dominant (bar 50), but her insistent 'guarda un pò' (bars 55, 57) suggests that his attention is elsewhere. Susanna leads the music back to the tonic for restatements of her melody, which Figaro now dutifully doubles. These musical processes are usually held to demonstrate Susanna's greater force of personality and intelligence. Yet, in conventionally musical terms, strength is considered to reside in the establishment of the dominant, here accomplished only by Figaro: Susanna's music twice relaxes back to the tonic. Is Figaro, after all, the stronger? Hardly, since Susanna finally seduces him away from his work. The rest of the opera tends to support Susanna's claim to superior wit, but the duet itself may be read as striking a balance emblematic of the compromises that make a successful marriage.

Action may be less ambiguously wedded to musical events than character, but even in Mozart's busiest ensembles it does not develop at a rate comparable to recitative. In the *Figaro* sextet, a 24-bar ensemble expands the situation reached at the end of the previous recitative; 16 bars of dialogue follow Susanna's entry, half of them mingled with further ensemble. Susanna sees Figaro embracing Marcellina and slaps him; this takes 14 bars, reaction to it 20. From bar 74 (reprise of the opening) the misunderstanding is explained (with humorous repetitions); from bar 102 the rest is commentary, embodying contrasted views (Count Almaviva and Don Curzio are angered by what rejoices the others, and show it by inflections from the minor mode). Commentary exceeds action in a proportion of about 3:2. In such frozen tableaux, the music is extended before the next event, or to

Ex.3 Mozart: *Le nozze di Figaro*, Act 1

[Figaro: 'Five...ten...twenty...thirty...thirty-six...forty-three...' Susanna: 'Now like this I'm happy']

make a decisive conclusion; the final situation may be still more extended in the closing (and paradoxically the fastest) sections of finales.

The relationship of certain ensembles to sonata form has often been described (notably in the trios and sextets of *Figaro* and *Don Giovanni*: on the *Don Giovanni* trio, see Kerman, 1956). These undoubtedly represent a remarkable synthesis of instrumental and operatic styles. But additive designs are also common (*Die Entführung*: quartet-finale to Act 2; *Così*: sextet in Act 1). Comparing the sextet in *Don Giovanni* (Act 2) to a finale, Rosen (1971) justifies the huge closing section (147 bars entirely in E♭) by the need for tonal resolution of the extreme modulations of the first part. Here sonata form is merely an analogy; unlike the *Figaro* sextet, there is no thematic reprise, and the dramatic effect would be the same if it ended in C rather than E♭, a licence the harmonic situation before the Allegro (a dominant of C minor) would certainly permit (though such a procedure would have been exceptional, even indecorous, in this period, as Mozart's comments on Osmin's rage aria make clear).

Mozart started with primitive chain finales (*La finta semplice*), and enriched their musical and dramatic content in *La finta giardiniera* where, however, the action remains slow and the tonal architecture primitive. The realistic *opera buffa* produced swifter action, and Mozart devised appropriate tonal schemes, beginning and ending in the same key and moving between sections by a 5th or 3rd. Landon (1989) postulates influence from the key-changes by a third in Haydn's *La fedeltà premiata*. In *Figaro* and *Don Giovanni* Mozart used this device more efficiently than Haydn, because more sparingly: 5th-progressions are normal and shifts down a 3rd mark a peripeteia (entries of Figaro, Act 2: B♭ to G, and the masked trio, *Don Giovanni* Act 1: E♭ to C). A more complicated scheme lies behind the first finale of *Così* (see Table 1). It begins with the ladies alone in the garden (*A*). The men rush in, taking poison (*B*); Alfonso and Despina go for the doctor (*C*), leaving the frightened ladies to tend the 'dying' men (*D*). Despina disguised as the doctor 'cures' them (*E*). Feigning to believe they are in paradise (a delusion explained as 'the effect of the medicine'), the men make amorous approaches to the ladies (*F*), who reject them with renewed energy (*G*).

In sections *A* to *E*, each key-change also involves a change of mode; in *E* to *G* the shifts are chromatic. The still more active second-act finale is tonally almost eccentric: the overall tonality is C, but at one point the key-sequence is A♭, E, D, E♭. A tonal architecture ostensibly weaker than in *Figaro* and *Don Giovanni* perhaps reflects the deceptiveness of the dramatic situation.

TABLE 1: *Così fan tutte* Act 1 finale

section	A	B	C		D	E	F	G
key	D	g	E♭		c	G	B♭	D
tempo	Andante	Allegro	(continued)			Allegro	Andante	Allegro
metre	2/4	¢	(continued)			3/4	C	¢

Mozart's key-schemes can never be completely systematized as signs of character, social class, affect, or even musical form. For every proposition concerning affective key-symbolism there is an exception. 'Regal' and 'heroic' D major (besides being available for trumpets and drums, it is particularly brilliant on strings) can embody the tenderest feelings (*Così*, opening of the first finale). F major as 'pastoral' is belied by Donna Anna's 'Non mi dir'; the more convincingly rustic G (peasant choruses in *Figaro* and *Don Giovanni*; Papageno) is used in *Idomeneo* for Elektra's 'Idol mio' and (in comedy) for arias of Marcellina and Despina, who are far from bucolic. E major is used for gentle breezes in *Zaide, Idomeneo* (twice) and the trio in *Così*, but also for deep introspection (*Così*: Fiordiligi's 'Per pietà') and for a *buffo* duet in a graveyard (*Don Giovanni*).

Instrumentation and tempo, harmony, melody, and rhythm, contribute more to mood and characterization than tonality or absolute pitch (Allanbrook, 1983). Social structures may partly be encoded through metre and association with dance. The contredanse in the Act 1 finale of *Don Giovanni* is the meeting-point between an aristocratic minuet and a plebeian waltz, all three eventually being heard together. Figaro's 'Se vuol ballare' turns from minuet to contredanse as his mimicry of the count explodes into an expression of his own fury; Susanna mocks the count by emerging from the closet (Act 2 finale) to a minuet. This system has less applicability in *Così* or *opera seria*, where distinctions of social class play a lesser role, but a parallel hierarchy of musical types (including counterpoint) governs the complex society of *Die Zauberflöte*.

It is certainly interesting that 14 Mozart operas begin and end in the same key (the last exception is *Il re pastore*). Eight are 'in' D and five in another key accessible to trumpets and timpani. But to relate all the other keys to this 'tonic' proposes a scheme spread over a time-scale too huge to be grasped. Even secondary evidence such as thematic reprise or instrumentation may deceive: in *Don Giovanni*, during the first finale, music is heard in F but recurs in G; in the Act II sextet, the trumpets enter in D, a semitone below the tonic. The claims of affective key symbolism and tonal architecture are virtually irreconcilable, and it is not self-evident that such systematic structures are appropriate to dramatic forms; they are best understood as an aspect of Mozart's musical language, and as a rhetorical resource. Dramatic criticism is more appropriately founded on the interaction of these and other elements, rather than upon single cohesive theories.

The statue music in *Don Giovanni*, the folkishness and solemnity of *Die Zauberflöte*, resonated throughout the 19th century; even the gaiety of *Figaro* was occasionally evoked, as in Berlioz's *Béatrice et Bénédict*. But while

Mozart's influence was widespread, composers took what they needed. Because Mozart's operas were still seen and heard, aspects of opera were attributed to his inventiveness that in fact he borrowed, and improved upon. For instance the dance scene in *Don Giovanni* was surely in Verdi's mind at the opening of *Rigoletto*, but he was probably unaware of its origins in a forgotten opera by Salieri; other composers, including Gluck and Salieri, exploited colourful instrumentation in their operas; Mozart's rondò aria form has been credited as the ancestor of the 19th-century double aria (cantabile and cabaletta), which is, however, an entirely different form, and requires quite different preparation by the librettist to be effective. From a modern perspective, there seems to have been surprisingly little imitation of Mozart's dramatic methods. His transmutation of the sonata into a vehicle for drama may appear his most radical achievement; yet it was not much developed even by Beethoven in the vocal numbers of *Fidelio*. The chain finale (already established a quarter-century before Mozart composed the definitive examples) may seem to anticipate 19th-century continuous opera. Nowhere is this more evident than in *Die Zauberflöte*; the first finale is tonally simple, using only the closest relations to C major, but it includes obbligato recitative building to expressive arioso (Tamino and the Orator), lyrical song (Tamino with the flute), action ensembles, and choruses. The second finale incorporates popular and learned styles as well as spectacular scenic effects. Nevertheless the operatic styles engendered by the French Revolution, and the continuity of Italian traditions, played at least as great a role in forming Romantic opera. The musical languages of Rossini's and Weber's operas were not sonata-based; Wagner had more immediate models than Mozart; Verdi's *Falstaff*, Strauss's *Der Rosenkavalier*, and Stravinsky's *The Rake's Progress* are spiritual descendants, but are too diverse and remote in time to be regarded as a continuation of Mozart.

In every genre Mozart built on existing conventions to point a new way. His last Singspiel accommodates heroism and religious quest, as well as a huge musical expansion; in *La clemenza*, *opera seria* is purged of artificiality and humanized; *opera buffa* provided the framework for serious explorations of society and sexuality. His influence on the next century's opera is perhaps the victim of the very perfection of his works. Yet from Goethe and E. T. A. Hoffmann he affected the minds of poets and philosophers as well as musicians. He is the first composer whose operas have never been out of the repertory and whose work as a whole has never needed to be revived. It is likely to remain the touchstone of operatic achievement.

The Operas

Apollo et Hyacinthus

('Apollo and Hyacinth')

Intermezzo in three acts, K38, to a Latin libretto by Father Rufinus Widl; first performed in Salzburg, at the Benedictine University, on 13 May 1767, with the five-act Latin tragedy *Clementia Croesi* by Widl.

Mozart's first stage work is an intermezzo, written to a text by the Gymnasium (school) teacher of syntax, for performance by students, some of them as young as the composer. The god Apollo (boy alto) and the wind god Zephyrus (boy alto) are rivals in love with Melia (boy soprano), daughter of Oebalus (tenor), King of Lacedonia—sanitizing the Greek myth in which Apollo is homosexually attracted to Hyacinth. In Widl's version Hyacinthus (boy soprano), the son of Oebalus, is fatally wounded by Zephyrus to incriminate his rival and win Melia for himself. Melia denounces Apollo, but the dying Hyacinthus reveals the truth. Zephyrus is banished, Apollo and Melia marry, and the god turns Hyacinthus into the flower that bears his name.

The musical idiom is not yet characteristic, but within the conventions of the time it is competent and never less than expressive, doing its best to animate a slender plot. Although the singers were aged between 12 and 23, the solo numbers (an aria for each character, two duets and a trio) are neither short nor particularly easy. There is a single-movement overture and an opening chorus. Melia's fury at Apollo and his attempts to exonerate himself form a duet that would be truly dramatic if it were not so long; it immediately precedes the recitative for the dying Hyacinthus whose broken phrases show Mozart already well able to manipulate the gestures that moved audiences of his time.

Bastien und Bastienne

('Bastien and Bastienne')

Singspiel in one act, K50/46b, to a libretto by Friedrich Wilhelm Weiskern and Johann Müller, after Charles-Simon and Marie-Justine-Benoîte Favart and Harny de Guerville's *opéra comique Les amours de Bastien et Bastienne*. It was first performed during September or October 1768, in F. A. Mesmer's house in Vienna (not as sometimes stated in his garden theatre, which had not yet been constructed). The singers are unknown, and may have been amateurs.

Favart and Guerville's realistic parody of Rousseau's *Le devin du village* (1753) reached Vienna in 1755 and was translated in 1764. It was used in children's theatre and may have been performed in Salzburg in 1766. Following the Vienna performance, the libretto was revised by Johann Andreas Schachtner, whose alterations included versification of the dialogue; Mozart set some of Schachtner's text as recitative, possibly for a revival in Salzburg in 1774.

Bastien (tenor) and Bastienne (soprano) are betrothed, but Bastien has shown signs of fickleness. Bastienne (soprano), advised by the 'magician' Colas (bass), wins him back by feigning indifference, even encouraging him to drown himself. The overture (Intrada) is a short allegro made famous by its fortuitous anticipation of the opening theme of Beethoven's *Eroica* symphony. There is no chorus and the orchestration is appropriately simple, with oboes, horns, and strings.

The action unfolds in sixteen musical numbers. Pastoral innocence is reflected in a profusion of short melodious arias; comparison with *La finta semplice* shows that their unsophisticated style derives from appropriate treatment of the subject, not from Mozart's youthfulness. Variety is given by Colas's pseudo-magical invocation; by dividing a two-section aria between the angry lovers; and by a short recitative-arioso at the crux (the threat of suicide). A longer duet, a comic equivalent to the one in *Apollo et Hyacinthus*, opens with the feigned anger of Bastienne, continues with Bastien's plaintive response, and includes their reconciliation. It leads without a break into the multi-sectioned trio finale.

La finta semplice

('The Pretended Simpleton')

Opera buffa in three acts, K51/46a, to a libretto by Carlo Goldoni with alterations by Marco Coltellini; probably first performed in Salzburg, in the Archbishop's Palace, on 1 May 1769.

Coltellini's revisions tighten the intrigue and provide for a better third-act finale than in Goldoni's original version (an *opera buffa* third act was often somewhat perfunctory). *La finta semplice* was rehearsed in Vienna in 1768 but not performed. There were doubts about whether a mere boy could have written it, but Mozart overcame them by composing an aria unaided, before distinguished witnesses including Hasse. Other intrigues were indignantly, but not circumstantially, outlined by Leopold, who may have misunderstood the extent of the Emperor's interest in having the opera composed, and he persisted in his complaints, as a matter of honour, beyond what was likely to be acceptable to an Imperial court. One performance may have taken place in Mozart's lifetime, in Salzburg the following year, but no date is known. The evidence is a surviving libretto, naming the singers: Maria Magdalena Haydn, née Lipp (Rosina), Maria Anna Braunhofer (Giacinta), Maria Anna Fesemayr (Ninetta), Joseph Hornung (Cassandro), Franz Anton Spitzder (Polidoro), Joseph Nikolaus Meissner (Fracasso), and Felix Winter (Simone).

The three-movement *sinfonia* K45 became the overture, its final cadence elided with the opening *coro*. *La finta semplice* is a comedy of love overcoming obstacles through deceit, a plot with roots in the Italian popular theatre, *commedia dell'arte*. Cassandro (bass) and Polidoro (tenor) forbid their sister Giacinta (soprano) to marry the nobleman Fracasso (tenor), and also ban their maid Ninetta (soprano) from marrying Fracasso's servant Simone (bass). Fracasso's sister Rosina (soprano) commands this variant of a traditional plot in which the solipsistic folly of somewhat older males leads to them being tricked by the young lovers. Rosina is accordingly the major role. Her range of sentiment is wider than for the other characters, her role including the longest and most serious arias. She wins over Cassandro by her feigned simplicity (which gives the opera its title), and Polidoro by instructing him in how to woo. The brothers' resistance is finally broken by the threat of a duel and the theft of their gold. The lovers succeed in forcing assent to their marriages, and Rosina marries Cassandro, leaving Polidoro on the shelf.

By Mozart's own later standards, a certain rhythmic squareness and monotony of key in the long finales are signs of immaturity. The libretto is to blame for a lack of good opportunities for other ensembles. The characterization, by Mozart's later standards, is weak; the music fails fully to reflect distinctions of class among the dramatis personae. Nevertheless *La finta semplice* shows a sound grasp of the idiom, and, no doubt following discussion with the Vienna singers, Mozart produced an appropriately wide variety of formal types and conventional musical imagery. Overall it can withstand comparison with most contemporary *opera buffa* by experienced composers such as Lattila or Piccinni.

Mitridate, re di Ponto

('Mithridates, King of Pontus')

Dramma per musica in three acts, K87/74a, to a libretto by Vittorio Amedeo Cigna-Santi after Giuseppe Parini's translation of Jean Racine's *Mithridate*. Its first performance was at the Regio Ducal Teatro in Milan, on 26 December 1770.

Mitridate was commissioned for the opening night of Carnival 1771. Mozart wrote the recitatives and sinfonia (overture) on his return from southern Italy in 1770. Reaching Milan on 18 October, he was forced to write the arias quickly and rewrite some of them as well. The castrato Benedetti caused anxiety by delaying his arrival to 1 December. All the singers required changes to their arias, and even the duet; the prima donna Antonia Bernasconi, however, nobly refused to introduce arias from Gasparini's *Mitridate* (1767, Turin: with the same libretto). The tenor Guglielmo d'Ettore was less accommodating; Mozart had to rewrite one aria four times, and d'Ettore still introduced Gasparini's setting of 'Vado incontro' into Act 3; it was long assumed to be Mozart's, and appears as his in published scores. Mozart was, however, well supported by the resident maestro, the distinguished composer Giovanni Battista Lampugnani, who directed the opera after the third performance. As in Vienna in 1768 there were those who condemned the work in advance because of Mozart's extreme youth, but they were silenced by the quality of the music. The performance lasted six hours, with the addition of a ballet not composed by Mozart, but this was in accordance with local custom, and *Mitridate* was repeated 21 times. Besides the inclusion of some music not by Mozart, a few lines of recitative are missing in every source. No further performances are known until the 20th century.

The setting is at Nymphaeum, in 63 BC. The scenes, for which designs by the brothers Galliani were applauded, include the palace, a temple, the port, hanging gardens, and a military encampment. Mithridates, who long defended his kingdom against the Roman empire, and his son Pharnaces (who in Racine's play remains treacherous to the end) are historical personages; but the plot is fiction. The original cast was Guglielmo d'Ettore (Mithridates, tenor), Pietro Benedetti (Xiphares, soprano castrato), Giuseppe Cicognani (Pharnaces, alto castrato), Antonia Bernasconi (Aspasia, soprano), Gaspare Bassano (Marcius, tenor), Anna Francesca Varese (Ismene, soprano), Pietro Muschietti (Arbates, soprano castrato).

* * *

ACT 1 Mithridates, betrothed to Aspasia (Racine's Monime), is reported to be dead after a battle with the Romans under Pompey the Great. Twice married, he has two sons, Farnace [Pharnaces] and the younger, Sifare [Xiphares]. Both are in love with Aspasia; she reciprocates the love of Xiphares, a situation explored in four of the first five arias. Thwarted love and ambition lead Pharnaces to conspire against his father with the Roman Marzio [Marcius]; his aria follows. But Mithridates is not dead; the report was a ruse, to test the others' fidelity. He returns unexpectedly, his entrance aria (called 'Cavata': 'Se di lauri il crine adorno') following a march. He brings with him Ismene, a Parthian Princess betrothed to Pharnaces (this character does not appear in Racine; her aria is with strings only, indicating her secondary status). Mithridates fears he has returned to two ungrateful sons, but he is reassured by his lieutenant, the governor of Nymphaeum, Arbate [Arbates], at least as far as Xiphares is concerned. Mithridates' second aria ('Quel ribelle e quell'ingrato') ends the first act in a regal D major.

ACT 2 Pharnaces spurns Ismene ('Va, l'error mio palesa'). She complains to Mithridates, who condemns Pharnaces as worthy of death. The king now doubts Aspasia's fidelity. He must leave to resume the war with Pompey, but he proposes to marry her first. His aria ('Tu, che fedel mi sei') alternately thanks loyal Xiphares (andante) and hurls accusations at Aspasia (allegro). Xiphares decides to escape the situation by leaving Pontus, and he bids Aspasia a moving farewell ('Lungi da te, mio bene': one of the three extant versions has an obbligato horn part). Aspasia laments her fate in a soliloquy (aria in two tempi, 'Nel grave tormento'). Ismene has a second aria accusing Pharnaces, and Mithridates now accuses his elder son of treachery; he admits his guilt ('Son reo: l'error confesso'), but meanly betrays Xiphares's love for Aspasia. Enraged (aria, 'Già di pietà mi spoglio'), Mithridates imprisons both his sons; the lovers bid a last farewell, a scene conveniently arising in the conventional position for a duet in an opera seria, the end of the second act; it is the only such ensemble in *Mitridate*.

ACT 3 Mithridates prepares for his final battle ('Vado incontro al fato'). Spurned by Aspasia, he sends her poison, which she prepares to take (monologue: recitative framing a cavatina). Xiphares prevents her from drinking it, and prepares for his own worthy death in battle ('Se il rigor d'ingrata sorte', a noble *Sturm und Drang* aria in C minor). As the Romans attack, Marcius (here given an aria with strings only in the orchestra) frees Pharnaces; in a magnificent *scena* (aria, 'Già dagli occhi') Pharnaces resolves to support his father after all, and sets off to burn the Roman fleet. Mithridates is victorious but mortally wounded in the battle; he unites Xiphares with Aspasia, and forgives Pharnaces, who marries Ismene.

*   *   *

Fitting the arias for demanding singers did not prevent Mozart from introducing ample variety of expression. Aspasia's second aria is a powerful lament in G minor; Xiphares's second combines short *andante* sections with vehement *allegro* passages. All his, Aspasia's, and Ismene's music is characterized by extreme virtuosity. Mozart skilfully abbreviated the required ternary forms and used a large number of arias in which contrasting affections are expressed by alternating tempi. The overture is a three-movement sinfonia in D major and the finale a very short 'coro' of soloists. Characterization is perhaps easier in *opera seria* than in comedy, as all the characters are of high social class and the sentiments expressed include those Mozart had shown, in his interview with Daines Barrington, that he could ape even as a child: sentiment and anger (in London he used the words 'affetto' and 'perfido'). His prior experience was also considerable for his age, as it included his Salzburg opera and oratorio, and numerous arias set to words by Metastasio, and drawn from the repertoire of *opera seria*. Nevertheless *Mitridate* is an astonishing achievement for a boy of 14; it makes the best use of conventional forms of expression and presents a drama which, if artificial, contains scenes of real intensity.

Ascanio in Alba

Festa teatrale in two acts, K111, to a libretto by Giuseppe Parini; first performed in Milan at the Regio Ducal Teatro on 17 October 1771.

Mozart's second Milan opera is in the courtly genre beloved of the Habsburgs. Following the success of *Mitridate*, it was commissioned to celebrate the wedding of Archduke Ferdinand, who was to take up the reins of government in Milan, to Maria Ricciarda Berenice d'Este. According to Leopold Mozart, it 'killed' the opera seria commissioned for the occasion, Hasse's last opera *Il Ruggiero*, though it is probably reading too much into the situation to regard this as a turning-point, the new generation replacing the old. *Ascanio* was repeated three or four times, but no revivals are known until the 20th century.

Ascanio (alto castrato, sung by Mozart's former singing instructor, Giovanni Manzuoli) is the son of Aeneas and thus grandson of Venere [the goddess Venus], though the libretto seems to imply he is actually her son. Venus (soprano) represents the Archduke's mother, Maria Theresia, but was sung by the *seconda donna*, Geltrude Falchini. Ascanio is destined to marry Silvia (soprano, the *prima donna* Antonia Maria Girelli-Aguilar). She represents the royal bride and so is a descendant of Hercules, alluding to Duke Ercole d'Este. In an allegory of arranged marriage, Venus contrives to have Silvia fall in love with a dream-image of Ascanio. Meanwhile he in turn is allowed to see her, but may not identify himself. This slender plot develops amid pastoral scenes with shepherds, votaries of Venus led by Fauno (soprano castrato or *secondo uomo*, Adamo Solzi) and the priest Aceste (tenor, Giuseppe Tibaldi). During an entr'acte (a ballet, for which only the orchestral bass parts have survived), the city of Alba Longa miraculously springs up; in Act 2 a little dramatic tension is generated by

Silvia's uncertainty about whether the man she has fallen in love with is really Ascanio, or someone else forbidden to her. Several scenes are structured by repeated choruses; there is one trio. The arias, particularly Fauno's second and those for Ascanio and Silvia, are exceptionally brilliant. Mozart's growing maturity is best revealed by the solo scene for the unhappy Silvia (aria, 'Infelici affetti miei'), and in the skilful blend of counterpoint and homophony in one of the work's most distinctive features, its choral writing. In addition the orchestration available allowed Mozart to make good use of a pair of flutes and sometimes an independent line for bassoons in addition to the standard scoring (oboes, horns, and strings with continuo, plus trumpets and drums in ceremonial scenes) not usually available in *opera seria*.

Il sogno di Scipione

('The Dream of Scipio')

Azione teatrale in one act, K126, to a libretto by Pietro Metastasio; its first performance may have been in Salzburg, in the Archbishop's Palace, in May 1772.

Il sogno di Scipione, Mozart's first full-length setting of a text by Metastasio, was planned for the 50th anniversary of Archbishop Schrattenbach's ordination in 1772, and accordingly was composed before *Ascanio in Alba*. But Schrattenbach died in December 1771, and the opera may have been performed instead, at least in part, as a serenata in the Salzburg palace during the installation ceremonies for Archbishop Colloredo. Otherwise no performances are known in Mozart's lifetime, or until the 20th century.

Il sogno di Scipione belongs to the Viennese court tradition of moral theatre. In his dream Scipio (tenor) is claimed by Fortuna [Fortune] (soprano), promising earthly rewards, and Costanza [Constancy] (soprano), representing unselfish virtue. In Elysium he meets his adopted father Publio [Publius] (tenor) and his real father Emilio [Emilius] (tenor), but they refuse to dictate his choice. Fortune impatiently demands an answer; but despite her threats (in the only *recitativo obbligato*), Scipio elects to follow the gentler persuasion of Constancy. There follows a *licenza* (recitative) in praise of the Archbishop, 'Girolamo' (Colloredo) replacing 'Sigismondo' (Schrattenbach).

The solos are arranged symmetrically round the aria for Emilius, the other singers each having two. The series of abbreviated da capo forms is mitigated by variation of tempo and metre, the brevity of the second aria for Publius, and two choruses. The overture, lacking a third movement, is linked to the first scene; Mozart later added a finale to make a separate symphony, K141a. The decisive *recitativo obbligato* is harmonically and instrumentally adventurous; otherwise, as befits its function, *Scipione* is elegant and brilliant in style rather than dramatic.

Lucio Silla

('*Lucius Sulla*')

Dramma per musica in three acts, K135, to a libretto by Giovanni de Gamerra; first performed in Milan at the Regio Ducal Teatro on 26 December 1772.

The original cast was Bassano Morgnoni (Sulla), Venanzio Rauzzini (Cecilius), Anna de Amicis-Buonsolazzi (Junia), Felicità Suardi (Cinna), Daniella Mienci (Celia), and Giuseppe Onofrio (Aufidius).

Lucius Sulla *dictator of Rome*	tenor
Giunia [Junia] *daughter of Gaius Marius, betrothed to Cecilius*	soprano
Cecilio [Cecilius] *exiled Roman senator*	soprano castrato
Lucio [Lucius] Cinna *his friend, a conspirator*	soprano
Celia *sister of Sulla*	soprano
Aufidio [Aufidius] *tribune, friend of Sulla*	tenor

Guards; nobles; senators; people of Rome

Setting Rome, 79 BC

The contract for *Lucio Silla*, dated 4 March 1771, required Mozart to deliver the recitatives in October 1772 and to be in Milan by November to compose the arias and rehearse, 'with the usual reservations in case of theatrical misfortunes and Princely interventions (which God forbid)'. The primo uomo Rauzzini (Cecilius) arrived only on 21 November, the prima donna De Amicis (Junia) still later; this did not prevent Mozart from writing for them his most powerful dramatic music to date. Morgnoni was a last-minute replacement for a more experienced tenor, and his role is therefore relatively simple; the dictator loses some of his impressiveness thereby. Mozart had to make alterations in the light of Metastasio's comments on the libretto. Archduke Ferdinand's dilatory letter-writing delayed the premiere two hours; it was immensely long (there were three ballets), but was nevertheless followed by 25 more performances, a major triumph for Mozart. The libretto was set by other composers including J. C. Bach (1775, Mannheim), but Mozart's opera was not revived until 1929 (Prague, in German).

*   *   *

The successful general Lucius Sulla seized total power in Rome but voluntarily laid it down the year before his death. Some of the characters are historical, but the plot is fiction.

ACT I *A neglected grove*   The banished Cecilius reappears secretly in Rome and learns from Cinna that Sulla, declaring him dead, proposes to marry Junia. Cecilius plans to meet her when she goes to the mausoleum to mourn her father Marius, once Sulla's political rival. Love promises a better future ('Vieni ov'amor t'invita'). Cecilius is prey to fear yet filled with joyful anticipation (the first of many fine obbligato recitatives) as well as feelings of tenderness (aria, 'Il tenero momento'): noteworthy is that, whereas the good-hearted, loquacious Cinna enters singing the tune presented by the orchestral ritornello, the more introspective Cecilius enters with a dreamy long note over a gentle, themeless orchestral continuum. Perhaps this was Rauzzini's favoured way of beginning a role, with a *messa di voce*; but the outcome is an early example of Mozart's subtlety in character differentiation, even within the constraints of the style and form of a virtuoso aria.

In Sulla's palace   Celia agrees to try to persuade Junia to accept Sulla (in minuet style, 'Se lusinghiera speme'); no girl will resist him for the sake of a dead man. Junia, however, rejects the tyrant who had deposed her father and banished her lover. Sulla, at first not unkind, says the price of her obstinacy may be death. Junia responds as a true heroine. In an Adagio ('Dalla sponda tenebrosa') she invokes the dead Marius and Cecilius, then in the Allegro she pours scorn on the dictator's love. Sulla decides he must overcome his own weakness of affections and, like a true tyrant, condemn her (*recitativo obbligato* and aria, 'Il desio di vendetta').

The mausoleum of Marius   Very remarkably, the remainder of Act I unfolds without any *recitativo semplice*. In contrast to the fiery D major of Sulla's aria, Mozart sets the new scene by sombre orchestral music, modulating obliquely to C minor. This is a magnificent musical tableau in *ombra* style, which despite the probable impact of Gluck's recent *Alceste* upon Mozart remains an astonishing achievement for a 16-year-old. Cecilius expresses his anxiously mixed feelings to varied orchestral figurations and rapid tempo changes (*recitativo obbligato*, using wind instruments to powerful effect as well as the usual strings). Junia enters with a chorus of mourners; enclosed within their funeral dirge is her powerful G minor lament ('O del padre ombra diletta'). Seeing Cecilius, she at first takes him for a ghost. Their duet ('D'Eliso in sen m'attendi'), a moving Andante and brilliant Allegro, ends the act on a note of hope.

ACT 2 *A military arch*   Aufidius tells Sulla that as Junia has many supporters in Rome, he would do well publicly to declare her his wife ('Guerrier, che d'un acciaro'). Sulla permits Celia's betrothal to Cinna. Cecilius enters intending to attack Sulla with a sword, but Cinna restrains him; rashness will gain nothing. Cecilius mingles hope and despair in snatches of *recitativo obbligato*, but his aria ('Quest' improviso tremito'), a concise Allegro in D, shows his fierce desire for revenge. Celia tries to declare her love for Cinna but is tongue-tied (an appealing Grazioso, 'Se il labbro timido'). Cinna is more concerned with plotting; but Junia refuses to betray her lover by marrying Sulla, even though the plan is that she should murder him in bed. She tells Cinna to care for Cecilius (*recitativo obbligato*), whose danger freezes her heart. Her aria ('Ah se il crudel periglio') is a grandiose Allegro of stunning virtuosity. Cinna decides that he must take communal vengeance upon himself (*recitativo obbligato* and a vigorous aria, 'Nel fortunato istante').

Hanging gardens   Struggling with contradictory feelings, Sulla again assures Junia that refusing his love means death. His aria ('D'ogni pietà mi spoglio') explodes without ritornello. Drained of pity, he will assuage his own pain by murdering those who offend him. In a short middle section he is overcome by tenderness towards Junia, but it is quickly suppressed. Cecilius tells Junia that he must kill the tyrant; if he dies his shade will watch over her ('Ah, se a morir mi chiama'). Exceptionally, the main section is Adagio, nobly arching in wide leaps (up to a 15th), and the middle section a tender Andante. Celia urges Junia to marry Sulla ('Quando sugl'arsi campi'). Her cheerful A major is followed by the tragic D minor of Junia's soliloquy on the conflict of duty and love. She will kill herself rather than submit, and gasps out her despair in an agitated aria ('Parto, m'affretto') with a daring harmonic shift (E♭ from G, the tonic being C) at the reprise.

The Capitol   The chorus hopes that Sulla's glory will be crowned by love ('Se gloria il crin ti cinse'). Sulla publicly claims Junia as the token of civil peace; she is prevented from killing herself when Cecilius again appears, making a vain attack upon Sulla. In a trio ('Quell'orgoglioso sdegno') Sulla declares that he will humble his enemies, Cecilius is defiant, and Junia, joined by Cecilius, anticipates the consolation of their union in death.

ACT 3 *Before the prison*　Cinna excuses his failure to support the futile assassination attempt. He agrees to marry Celia if she can persuade her brother to have mercy; she promises to achieve this whatever storms may arise ('Strider sento la procella'). Cinna expresses optimism, for Cecilius has supporters in Rome, in a heroic aria in D ('De' più superbi il core'). Junia appears for a last farewell; she continues to refuse Sulla even though this is the price of Cecilius's life. Aufidius comes to take Cecilius to public judgment; in a melting, rondo-like aria ('Pupille amate') in minuet tempo he says her tears will make him die too soon; his soul will return, dissolved in a sigh. Junia is left to her premonitions, her *recitativo obbligato* richly scored and anticipating the motif of the aria ('Frà i pensier più funesti') in which she imagines Cecilius dead. Her lament unfolds over a throbbing muted accompaniment; then with a determined Allegro she runs after her lover.

A hall in the palace　The denouement takes place in recitative. Even as Sulla condemns Cecilius, Junia publicly proclaims her betrothal. Baffled, even moved, the tyrant decides to forgive her and permit the two couples to marry. He then unexpectedly retires from public life. In the concerted finale the chorus sycophantically praises his devotion to Rome, while the soloists sing of love and freedom.

*　　　*　　　*

Mozart constructed the first two acts cleverly, gradually abandoning the conventionally formed and very long arias enjoyed by Milan audiences in favour of more flexible designs perhaps suggested by Gluck's *Alceste*. Yet despite this, and the magnificent mausoleum scene, *Lucio Silla* remains in essence an unreformed *opera seria*, albeit a very fine one. Several D major arias with trumpets and drums, needed to bolster the confidence of the dictator (sung by the inexperienced tenor), are contrasted with the remarkable richness of expression in the splendid roles of Cecilius and Junia, while Celia's lightly scored music provides relief. Although its plot is turgid and its denouement unconvincing, *Lucio Silla* is the most important work Mozart wrote in Italy, and ranks with *opera seria* by the greatest masters of the time.

La finta giardiniera

('The Pretended Garden-Girl')

Opera buffa in three acts, K196, of uncertain authorship. First performed at the Munich Salvatortheater on 13 January 1775.

The casting of the first production remains largely unknown. Rosa Manservisi sang Sandrina/Violante and the castrato Tommaso Consoli probably sang Ramiro; the range suits the modern (female) mezzo. Other likely singers include Teresa Manservisi (Serpetta; Leopold called her a 'miserable' singer), Johann Walleshauser (Belfiore), Augustin Sutor (the Mayor), and Giovanni Rossi (Nardo). Unless it was Teresa Manservini, the performer of Arminda is unknown.

Ramiro *a knight*	soprano castrato
Don Anchise *Mayor (Podestà) of Lagonero*	tenor
Marchioness Violante Onesti *disguised as Sandrina, working in the Mayor's garden*	soprano
Roberto *her servant, disguised as Nardo, a gardener*	baritone
Serpetta *the mayor's housekeeper*	soprano
Arminda *a Milanese lady, the Mayor's niece*	soprano
Count (Contino) Belfiore	tenor

Setting The Mayor's estate at Lagonero near Milan

No published libretto of *La finta giardiniera* acknowledges its authorship; the suggested attribution to Petrosellini seems less questionable than earlier attributions to Calzabigi or Coltellini, but remains unproven. The first setting, by Anfossi, was given at Rome during Carnival 1774; Mozart's followed within a year.

The Mozarts left Salzburg for Munich three weeks before the planned first performance (29 December), which was postponed, as Leopold wrote on 28 December, to allow more time for the cast to learn the music and actions. Three performances took place, widely spaced (perhaps because of illness in the cast). The first and third (on 2 March) had great success in the old court theatre; the second, on 2 February in the Redoutensaal, was truncated because one singer was ill.

The first revival was as a Singspiel, *Die verstellte Gärtnerin*. Mozart may have assisted with the adaptation, which was performed by Johann Böhm's company in Augsburg (1 May 1780). Böhm took it to other German centres including Frankfurt (1782; it was the first Mozart opera given in North Germany). After 1797 it was not heard again until 1891, in Vienna. Until recently, 20th-century revivals necessarily used the German form since no source survived of the Italian first act. Its rediscovery (in time for the new edition, the Neue Mozart Ausgabe, in 1978) permitted revival of the original version at Munich and Salzburg in 1979; there have been several subsequent productions. English performances have been given under the title *Sandrina's Secret*.

*   *   *

ACT 1 *The Mayor's garden* In an *Introduzione* the characters present themselves and their situations, and in a set of arias, they develop their initial feelings. Ramiro, spurned by Arminda, finds love a snare ('Se l'augellin sen fugge'). The Mayor compares his love for the garden-maid to a series of musical instruments ('Dentro il mio petto', an aria which had some currency outside the opera). Sandrina (Violante) reminds Nardo (Roberto, pretending to be her cousin) of the background to the story; she is seeking her lover Count Belfiore who a year ago stabbed her during a quarrel. He then fled, assuming he had killed her. The pastoral style of her aria ('Noi donne poverine') maintains her disguise, as Ramiro is present. Nardo ('A forza di martelli') is in love with Serpetta, but she intends to become a *serva padrona* by marrying the Mayor. Arminda clamours for attention until the arrival of her betrothed. He is none other than Belfiore, whose heroic postures comically contrast with his evident weakness in the head. He enters politely singing the praises of female beauty ('Che beltà'). Arminda threatens him with punishment if he should prove unfaithful ('Si promette facilmente'). Belfiore's response ('Da Scirocco a Tramontana') is to trace his pedigree to the heroes of Greece and Rome, a glance at classical antiquity that anticipates a later development in the plot (as well as allusions in the Da Ponte operas). Serpetta engages in banter with Nardo (each singing one verse of an aria); she adds a sprightly aria of her own ('Appena mi vedon').

Hanging gardens   Sandrina bewails her fate in an eloquent cavatina, evoking the fidelity of the turtle-dove ('Geme la tortorella'). She still hopes to find and forgive her lover. On learning the name of Arminda's betrothed she faints. In the extended finale Belfiore recognizes her, but she denies her identity. Nevertheless their behaviour appears compromising to the other characters who observe it. In a brilliantly varied multi-movement 'ensemble of perplexity', Ramiro is pleased at this development, Nardo is concerned, Serpetta and Arminda are jealous, Sandrina is upset, Belfiore, characteristically, is bemused, and the Mayor is vexed by the upset to his household and his and Arminda's marriage prospects.

ACT 2   *Hall of the Mayor's house*   Having again dismissed Ramiro, Arminda turns on Belfiore for his apparent infidelity ('Vorrei punirti indegno', in a vibrantly emotional G minor). Nardo woos Serpetta in Italian, French, and English, but she is too jealous of his 'cousin' (Sandrina) to admit to liking him. Sandrina confuses Belfiore still more by giving an eyewitness account of her own death. His response is an amorous aria ('Care pupille'), but in his confusion he accidentally pays court to the Mayor, from whom Sandrina has then to repel a further advance (aria, 'Una voce sento al core'; he gives vent to his own agitation in the aria 'Una damina, una nipote'). Ramiro, the only character with much initiative, now appears bearing a warrant for Belfiore's arrest, his crime being the murder of Violante. Surely the Mayor will not allow a murderer to marry his niece. Ramiro pleads his cause in the warmest melody of the opera ('Dolce d'amor compagna').

Another room   Belfiore is confronted with the accusation of murder. Sandrina defends him: there was no murder, for she is Violante. The others only half-believe her. Then, turning to Belfiore, she again denies her identity, saying that she spoke only to save him. The poor man's confusion merges into madness, giving rise to the use of an *opera seria* form, the full scena with *recitativo obbligato* before the aria ('Già divento freddo'). It is notable that Mozart had sufficient confidence in the Munich orchestra to introduce wind instruments, to excellent effect, during the recitative, a genre usually confided to strings. Meanwhile we learn that Arminda has caused Sandrina to be abandoned in the wild woods; everyone hastens to her rescue. Serpetta's roguish aria ('Chi vuol godere il mondo') leads without a break into the new scene, and the music is continuous to the end of the act.

A dark wood, with rocks and caves   Sandrina cries out in fear (Agitato in C minor; 'Crudeli, fermate'; cavatina and recitative). She hides in a cave and in the finale the others appear one by one, to pair off in a comedy of mistaken identity. Their confusion is relieved only when the practical Ramiro brings a light. The noble lovers at last find harmony but only in madness, for Violante/Sandrina has also lost contact with reality. Amid general consternation, the two believe themselves persons from classical mythology: at first they are Arcadian shepherds, but when the others intervene they assume the dangerous characters of Medusa and Hercules.

ACT 3 *Interior*   Each of the lunatics mistakes Nardo for his or her lover. He makes his escape, leaving them prey to imaginary disasters. In an ingenious compression unusual in number opera, his aria ('Mirate che contrasto') is bolted onto their confused duet. The Mayor complains that he cannot understand what is going on ('Mio padrone, io odir volevo'). Arminda is still determined to marry Belfiore; Ramiro gives vent to his frustration and rage in a powerful C minor aria ('Va pure ad altri').

The garden   Sandrina/Violante and Belfiore are sleeping. Where the woods represent danger and the house social disorder, the garden represents nature under enlightened control: hence they awake restored to sanity. At first they decide they must part, and take leave of one another in a long recitative and duet before deciding, with ecstatic finality, that they must after all marry. This determination reconciles Arminda with Ramiro; Serpetta, seeing that the Mayor will always sigh for Sandrina, agrees to marry Nardo. Only the Mayor is left single. In a short finale all sing Sandrina's praises.

*   *   *

La finta giardiniera is Mozart's first mature *opera buffa*, but it is a far cry from the swiftly unfolding, ensemble-driven plots of the Da Ponte operas. Its ancestry lies in Goldoni's librettos, mingling high, middle, and lower social classes and contrasting serious emotions with comedy. Apart from the finales it consists almost entirely of arias. A descent from the subject of Pergolesi's popular *La serva padrona* survives in the Serpetta—Nardo—Mayor intrigue, and the disguised noblewoman, nearly killed by a jealous rival, descends from Piccinni's immensely successful *La buona figliuola* (1760). While the count is both comic and pathetic, Ramiro is entirely serious, while Arminda in her exaggerated posturing adopts the high style of *opera seria*—and thereby anticipates a weapon Mozart wielded skilfully in *Così fan tutte*.

The music is almost too elaborate for the intrigue, but is an astounding achievement for an 18-year-old: richly coloured, distinctive in characterization, alternately good-humoured and searchingly expressive in the arias, and continuously inventive in the finales. The characterization marks out the class distinctions: the nobles (at least when Violante is in her true, not her *finta*, character) employ a developed musical idiom, including *recitativo obbligato* and a greater degree of coloratura than is given to Ramiro and Arminda, despite the vehemence of their minor-mode arias, or to the Mayor. For the servants Mozart provides a simpler melodic style, largely syllabic word-setting, and lighter orchestration. The opera contains an almost wilful variety of emotional entanglements, but its resolution remains obstinately symmetrical. Love-ties across class barriers (Arminda—Belfiore; Serpetta or Violante/Sandrina—Mayor) are not permitted. The restoration of the aristocrats' wits, and the union of social equals in three couples, symbolize restoration of the order threatened by the aftermath of Belfiore's rash attack on Violante.

Il re pastore

('*The Shepherd King*')

Serenata in two acts, K208, to a libretto by Pietro Metastasio; first performed in Salzburg in the Archbishop's Palace, on 23 April 1775.

Il re pastore was written immediately after Mozart's return from Munich, where he had gone to oversee the performance of *La finta giardiniera*. It was one of two short works performed in honour of Archduke Maximilian, who was on his way from Vienna to Italy via Salzburg (the other was *Gli orti esperidi* by the Salzburg Kapellmeister Fischietti). A reduced form of Metastasio's libretto had been devised for a performance in Munich in 1774, with music taken from Pietro Guglielmi's 1767 setting for Venice. This was Mozart's principal source, but there were further alterations, possibly made by Gianbattista Varesco. Metastasio's second and third acts are compressed into the new second act by removing five arias and cutting down recitatives. Thus what was originally a short *opera seria* in a pastoral setting was scaled down to the proportions of a serenata, but *seria* conventions—such as the character leaving the stage after each aria—remain.

The performance is believed to have been semi-staged, without elaborate scenery, as was normal for a serenata. The castrato Tommaso Consoli came from Munich to sing the title role; with him came a friend of Mozart's, the flautist Johann Baptist Becke. The exact disposition of the other roles, taken by members of the Salzburg Hofkapelle, is unknown.

*　　*　　*

Il re pastore is based on an episode in the career of Alexander the Great. Metastasio designed it to flatter the Habsburgs by demonstrating magnanimity and understanding in this imperial archetype. The title role is not Alexander but the shepherd Aminta [Amyntas] (soprano castrato) who,

unknown to himself, is by birth Abdalonimus, legitimate heir to the kingdom of Sidon. Rather surprisingly, he is in love with Elisa (soprano), who
is of noble birth, and she with him.

ACT 1   The first act is almost unchanged from Metastasio's. As in Gluck's
setting (1756), the single-movement overture and Amyntas's first aria are
continuous. The aria ('Intendo amico rio') is really a short song, in a pastoral 6/8; it in turn is interrupted by the arrival of Elisa. Amyntas is wor-
ried by the proximity of Alexander's army; Elisa is sanguine ('Alla selva, al
prato'); the country and her beloved will provide a sanctuary. Alessandro
[Alexander] (tenor) enters in disguise, accompanied by the Sidonian nobleman Agenore [Agenor] (tenor). Alexander questions Amyntas about
his life; the shepherd praises the simplicity and honesty of a pastoral existence (*recitativo obbligato* and aria, 'Aer tranquillo', a replacement text already present in the 1774 Munich libretto).

   Alexander looks forward to restoring this instinctively noble young man
to his rightful station, which apparently requires the shepherd to change his
nature, for Alexander's aria ('Si spande al sole in faccia') is martial in character. Tamiri [Tamyris] (soprano) comes to find Agenor, her betrothed. She
is a friend of Elisa and the daughter of the tyrant Straton whom Alexander
has deposed, and is accordingly in hiding. Agenor assures her of his love
('Per me rispondete'); she, however, fears the wrath of Alexander ('Di
tante sue procelle'). Agenor tells Amyntas of his change in fortune; he fears
parting from his Elisa, but she expresses confidence in their future together
(*recitativo obbligato*). The lovers' duet ends the first act.

ACT 2   In this compressed form of the libretto, the lovers' problems are
sharply increased, then as quickly resolved. First Agenor is obliged to prevent Elisa from seeing Amyntas; her anguish is expressed in her second
aria ('Barbaro, oh Dio!'), a lamenting Andante in which the coloratura is
deeply expressive, leading to a protesting Allegro. Amyntas is likewise
prevented from following Elisa. Alexander commands him to deck himself
like a king. On learning from Agenor that Tamyris is near, Alexander announces his intention to marry her off to Amyntas, thus resolving the dynastic dispute that divided their fathers. He wishes through his conquests
to make people happy (a virtuoso aria in F major, 'Se vincendo vi rendo felici'). Amyntas's next aria ('L'amerò, sarò costante') is the centrepiece of
the act: a ravishing piece in rondo form, with violin obbligato, muted
strings, two flutes, and two cors anglais. The noble arches of his melody
support a declaration of the constancy of his love for Elisa. But he is over-

heard and misunderstood; Elisa and Agenor both assume that he is talking of a new love for Tamyris. Tamyris in turn compounds Agenor's misery by accusing him of infidelity ('Se tu di me fai dono': surprisingly, a Grazioso in A). Agenor's response is expressed in the only minor-mode aria of the opera, a vehement Allegro protesting his constancy ('Sol può dir'). Thus everyone is confused, and none of the couples reconciled.

Alexander enters to sing a final aria ('Voi che fausti ognor donate'), a kingly showpiece in C. Tamyris and Elisa throw themselves on his mercy, and as soon as he understands what his well-meaning interference has achieved, he unites the four lovers and declares that the Shepherd King and Elisa will rule in Sidon, while Agenor and Tamyris will be granted another kingdom. All join in a 'coro' in praise of the virtuous conqueror ('Viva l'invitto Duce').

*   *   *

The second and third arias of Act 2 add two flutes to the standard Salzburg group of two oboes and two horns; the virtuoso flourishes in the first of them ('Se vincendo vi rendo felici') were doubtless intended for Becke. Trumpets appear in Alexander's other arias, so that all three are distinguished instrumentally. So, however, are the crucial arias for the characters facing real dilemmas: Amyntas in his rondo with obbligato violin (presumably for Antonio Brunetti, who played Mozart's violin concertos) and Agenor ('Sol può dir'), where the minor mode acquires its unusual sonority by use of two horns pitched in different keys (something Mozart had previously done in his early G minor symphony). The arias with strings only (Agenor's first and Tamyris's second) act as a foil to these more elaborate movements. Mozart shows equal resource in the handling of the now standard aria design, the 'modified da capo' or small-scale sonata-form aria. If *Il re pastore* is not as strikingly original as *La finta giardiniera*, which is not surprising given the relatively restricted resources of the Salzburg Kapelle, it nevertheless makes the most of its slender dramatic basis, and it surely helped Mozart to develop his powers of characterization in the serious style. But it should not be considered merely a useful preparation for *Idomeneo*, for it has a charm and dramatic integrity of its own, and has proved its worth in modern revivals.

Zaide

Singspiel in two acts, K344/336b, to a libretto adapted by Johann Andreas Schachtner from Franz Josef Sebastiani's *Das Serail*. The work was unfinished, and never performed in Mozart's lifetime.

Mozart wrote *Zaide* in Salzburg between autumn 1779 and mid-1780, perhaps with J. H. Böhm's or Schikaneder's touring companies in mind, but more probably in the hope of production by the National Singspiel in Vienna. The autograph of the unfinished opera is untitled. The source, a Singspiel by Franz Josef Sebastiani, is called *Das Serail*; he probably derived much of it from Voltaire's tragedy *Zaïre*, but Sebastiani avoided ending his opera with a murder and a suicide. Johann Anton André chose the heroine's name for his 1838 publication of Mozart's opera, and it avoids confusion with *Die Entführung aus dem Serail*, an opera with a similar theme composed by Mozart in Vienna because the National Singspiel director, Stephanie, considered *Zaide* too serious.

Schachtner's libretto was probably more than merely a revision, but it is lost apart from the sung text and short cues from the dialogue entered into the autograph score. *Zaide* was first performed at Frankfurt on the 110th anniversary of Mozart's birth, 27 January 1866, with an overture and finale added by André, and new text by Friedrich Carl Gollmick. Other versions followed, in German, French, and English, often with additional music taken from *Thamos, König in Ägypten*, K345/336a. There is no evidence for the missing overture being the one-movement G major Symphony K318 (composed in April 1779), although its date makes it an appropriate choice. The instrumentation does not correspond to anything in the opera, but could have been re-used in the missing finale. However, Mozart was unlikely to have written the overture before completing the vocal numbers.

*   *   *

ACT 1 begins with slaves (tenor solo and unison chorus) finishing work for the day, seemingly in cheerful mood ('Brüder, lasst uns lustig sein'). This serves as a contrast to the first important scene in which Gomatz (tenor), exiled and enslaved, laments his bitter fate in Mozart's finest passage of melodrama ('Unerforschliche Fügung!'). The opening Adagio would have done credit to a composer 50 years later (Weber, Schubert, or Mendelssohn), and other passages display unusual enharmonic daring. Gomatz falls asleep. Unknowingly, he is being watched over by Zaide (soprano), the beautiful favourite of the Sultan. Her aria ('Ruhe sanft') is an image of peacefulness. The tensile melodic line, recurring after each episode, is one of a handful of Mozart passages that fortuitously evoke memories of J. S. Bach (for instance, 'Schlummert ein' from the Anna Magdalena notebook, adapted from Cantata 82). She leaves her portrait beside the sleeping Gomatz. He wakes, finds it, and is inspired to defy the wrath of fate ('Rase, Schicksal'). Zaide reveals herself and they declare their love (duet, 'Meine Seele hüpft von Freuden') in a short and gentle Allegretto.

Allazim (bass) has decided to betray the Sultan by helping the lovers escape. Gomatz ('Herr und Freund') is almost embarrassingly grateful; he returns to the stage during a ritornello designed to cover his exit, offering further thanks. Allazim instils courage into his own heart ('Nur mutig, mein Herze'). The three prepare to escape by boat, singing a ravishing trio ('O selige Wonne', in E major): the sea is calm at sunrise, though Zaide imagines a storm may intervene. The final Allegro is a prayer for their future happiness.

ACT 2 begins as the Sultan Soliman (tenor), assisted by the only appearance of trumpets and drums, rages against these ungrateful subjects. This is the second melodrama, less harmonically adventurous than the first, as befits the mood and characterization. Zaide has spurned his love to fly with a Christian slave, but an officer assures him that they will be recaptured at any moment. Soliman now rails against all women. In his huge aria ('Der stolze Löw'', 246 bars) his anger twice boils over into a headlong Presto: a proud lion may be tamed, but treat him shamefully and he becomes a tyrant. There follows a comic scene for the overseer Osmin (bass) with a laughing aria ('Wer hungrig bei der Tafel sitzt').

Soliman tells the captives that he is capable of being wicked as well as good; he rewards service but punishes treachery ('Ich bin so bös' als gut'). Zaide acknowledges his bounty, but he did not offer her the freedom she craved. The central importance of this scene, with its quasi-feminist implications, is expressed in two consecutive arias. Her aria ('Trostlos schluchzet Philomele') asserts that even the favourite in the harem is no better off than a caged nightingale, who can sing only of her sorrow. This melting rondo fails to move the Sultan, and Zaide turns to attacking his tyrannical ways ('Tiger! wetze nur die Klauen'): 'Tiger, show your claws', a G minor aria of splendid fury. The contrasting middle section ('Ach, mein Gomatz') looks forward to the lovers' release from sorrow through death (later the subject of a duet in *Die Entführung*), but her predominant mood is justifiable anger, and it extends to the last bar, with its final cry of 'Tiger!'

Allazim (whose life is to be spared) now lectures Soliman on the virtues of enlightened rule, for the mighty should recognize slaves as brothers ('Ihr Mächtigen seht ungerührt'). But the Sultan is unmoved. The last number Mozart composed is a fine quartet ('Freundin, stille deine Tränen'). Gomatz asks Zaide to calm her tears, for death will crown their love. Allazim's heart is breaking. Zaide, like Konstanze in *Die Entführung*, tries to take the blame, and pleads for Gomatz's life, but Soliman remains vindictive to the end. This resourceful ensemble worthily anticipates the quartets in *Idomeneo* and *Die Entführung*, and was probably intended as the finale to the second act, functioning like the traditional duet of *opera seria* (as in *Mitridate*).

*   *   *

Thanks to her wonderful arias, Zaide is Mozart's first three-dimensional character, but the portrayal of Gomatz is relatively weak; in *Die Entführung* Belmonte has far more to say and do, for there is no Allazim, the benevolent helper within the Harem walls. We do not know what the outcome of the plot would have been, but surely not the improbable and perfunctory outcome in *Das Serail*, in which Zaide and Gomatz are revealed as siblings (so they cannot marry), and moreover children of Renegat (the source for Allazim)—whose name, as well as the sentiments he displays, suggest that he was once a Christian. Soliman forgives everyone because Renegat once saved his life (this may account for the mercy shown to Allazim in act 2 of *Zaide*). In *Das Serail* Soliman is a spoken role, like Selim in *Die Entführung*. In *Zaide* a few bars within his arias may imply a more compassionate personality, but this is suppressed in the quartet, the only finale we possess.

Mozart's opera therefore consists of two acts of equivalent length. It is possible that after the quartet Soliman was suddenly to relent, like Sulla, allowing the opera to end quickly with a cursory and presumably choral finale, but it seems more likely that a third act was planned. *Zaide* is not viable as it stands, for it requires dialogue or a linking narration, and a conclusion. Nevertheless, in the strength of the feelings, tender and furious, suffering and triumphant, expressed within it, it marks a striking advance on Mozart's previous operas and approaches the power of the next.

Idomeneo, re di Creta

('Idomeneus, King of Crete')

Dramma per musica in three acts, K366, to a libretto by Giovanni Battista [Gianbattista] Varesco after Antoine Danchet's *Idomenée*; first performed in the Munich Residenztheater on 29 January 1781.

The original cast included Anton Raaff (Idomeneus), Dorothea Wendling (Ilia), Elisabeth Wendling (Elektra), Vincenzo dal Prato (Idamantes), and Domenico de Panzacchi (Arbaces).

Idomeneus *King of Crete*	tenor
Idamante [Idamantes] *his son*	soprano castrato
Ilia *Trojan princess, daughter of Priam*	soprano
Elettra [Elektra] *princess, daughter of*	
Agamemnon	soprano
Arbace [Arbaces] *confidant of Idomeneus*	tenor
High Priest of Neptune	tenor
Oracle of Neptune	bass

Trojan prisoners; sailors; people of Crete

Setting Mycenean Crete: the Royal palace at Kydonia (Sidon), by the sea, the harbour, and the temple of Neptune

Mozart received the commission from the Munich Intendant, Count Seeau, during the summer of 1780. Danchet's five-act libretto of 1712 was adapted by Varesco in three acts, on the pattern of the 'reformed' operas of Jommelli and Gluck, and Jean-François Marmontel's adaptations of French *tragédie lyrique*, such as Piccinni's *Roland*, that were entering the Paris repertoire around this time. Like Marmontel, Varesco balanced the need to introduce full-length Italian arias (never a feature of *tragédie lyrique*) with the equal requirement for a strong choral element, dramatically appropriate ballet, scenic effects, and some ensemble writing, as well as a high proportion of *recitativo obbligato* (at the Paris Opéra by this date, all the recitative was orchestrated, as Mozart presumably knew). The influence of Gluck's *Alceste* is felt in hieratic scenes, particularly the speech for the High Priest and the utterance of the oracle, but also in a prevailing seriousness. Besides witnessing Piccinni's synthesis of French forms and Italian music, Mozart knew some operas with similar mixed roots by Jommelli and, with German texts, by Ignaz Holzbauer, whose *Günther von Schwarzburg* he had admired in Mannheim in 1777 (letter of 14 November). The example of Jommelli and Piccinni no doubt encouraged Mozart to pursue what Gluck tended to repress in his more severely neo-classical dramas: highly developed aria forms with the bloom of Italian lyricism, and with due deference to the virtuosity and individuality of the original singers.

Raaff may have been instrumental in obtaining the commission for Mozart, and most of the other singers, as well as the orchestra, were well known from Mozart's stay in Mannheim. He was therefore able to start work before leaving Salzburg on 5 November. His work in Munich is documented by letters home; his father, besides supplying trumpet mutes, had to act as intermediary between composer and librettist. He also offered advice of his own, which Mozart, constantly concerned with effect and timing, and composing during an extended rehearsal period, could call on his greater theatrical experience to ignore. The libretto required severe pruning: the oracle would be ineffective if it makes a long speech and must be cut; the recitatives were too long; there were too many arias (at the last minute, some were omitted from the final act).

Mozart also reported the singers' generally favourable reactions, and the elector's approval of the music. The first performance, which Leopold Mozart and his daughter attended, was well received. The designs were by Lorenzo Quaglio and the ballet-master was Le Grand, who in the absence of the librettist may have acted as stage director. Raaff, by then 66, was tactfully nursed by the composer; Idomeneus's music contrives to be brilliant and expressive without placing exceptional demands on breath-control. The Wendling sisters-in-law were capable and experienced; Dorothea was the prima donna, but Elisabeth must also have been a formidable singer to have inspired Elektra's music. Unfortunately Dal Prato failed to satisfy the composer, who had to teach him his part 'as if he were a child'. The good qualities of Panzacchi as Arbaces led to a dramatically unnecessary but musically rewarding development of his role through a third-act *recitativo obbligato*.

There were probably only three performances in Munich. In September 1781 Mozart wrote to his father from Vienna that he would like to revise *Idomeneo* 'more in the French style', but with a German text, which he hoped might be supplied by J. B. van Alxinger, who was occupied in translating Gluck's *Iphigénie en Tauride*. Mozart hoped to cast the singers who were to shine in *Die Entführung*: Idomeneus would become a bass (Ludwig Fischer) and Idamantes a tenor (Valentin Adamberger), which would have required extensive recomposition. Separate numbers were included in concerts in Mozart's first year in Vienna, as if to prepare the way for a production. But the only other full performance in Mozart's lifetime was at Prince Auersperg's theatre in Vienna, in 1786, and was given by amateurs mainly drawn from the nobility. The chief alteration was to recast Idamantes as a tenor, but the corresponding change of Idomeneus to a bass, intended to balance the ensemble and distinguish the generations, was never made. Mozart carefully rewrote two ensembles (trio and quartet) to accommodate the tenor Idamantes. He also composed a new duet with Ilia, with some musical ideas related to the Munich version, and composed an entirely new aria for Idamantes. He produced a simplified version of Idomeneus's showpiece ('Fuor del mar') fitted for an amateur tenor, and made further cuts including both arias for Arbaces. The recitative was so heavily cut as to become at times barely intelligible.

Idomeneo was not performed again until the 19th century, when various translations appeared in the repertory of German companies. The first was in Kassel (1802), followed by Vienna and Berlin (1806). The music was occasionally employed in 19th-century *pasticcios*, but there were few recognizable performances outside Austria and Germany until the 20th century, the first in Paris (in concert form) being in 1902. It was performed in Britain (Glasgow) in 1934, and in Italy and the USA only in 1947. Prior to that its 150th anniversary (1931) was recognized by productions in German, in forms variously arranged, notably by Richard Strauss whose radically altered version for Vienna undertaken with libretto by Lothar Wallerstein was published in vocal score (Walton, in Rushton, 1993). In the last 30 years most major companies have produced *Idomeneo*, but as an opera in need of perpetual revival rather than a repertory item. Criticism, however, is confident in proclaiming it the first operatic masterpiece of Mozart's maturity.

*   *   *

The legendary misfortunes of the Greek chieftain Idomeneus, returning home after the Trojan war, closely parallel the biblical story of Jephtha. The Trojan princess Ilia and other captives have been sent to Crete ahead

of him. Elektra, the Greek princess from Mycenae, is already there, following the murder of the leader of the Greek forces, Agamemnon, by his
wife Clytemnestra. Both princesses have fallen in love with Idamantes.

The overture, in D major, is a boldly truncated sonata-form movement
replete with majesty and intimations of suffering. It ends with a diminu-
endo making repeated use of a significant motif first heard in the ninth bar,
and which occurs throughout the opera; it has been identified as a 'Sacrifice' or 'Idamantes' motif. Other ideas form a network apparently referring to reconciliation. The overture's cadence prefigures the tonality of the
first aria and allows Ilia to sing without further introduction.

ACT I *Ilia's apartment in the palace*   Ilia bewails her fate: orphaned, a pris-
oner, in love with her captor's son and certain that he must prefer his com-
patriot Elektra to a foreign slave. She explores her dilemma in a subdued
lament in G minor, its moderate tempo as characteristic of her as *Allegro* is
of Elektra (*recitativo obbligato* and aria, 'Padre, germani, addio!'). When Ilia
considers her own disloyalty to her race, in loving a Greek, Mozart introduces the 'Idamantes motif' in the cellos.

Idamantes enters with words of comfort and even affection, but she
proudly rejects him. In a short, majestic Adagio Idamantes protests that he
has committed no fault, and in a driving Allegro he blames the gods for his
suffering ('Non ho colpa'). As evidence of his kindly intentions, he frees
the Trojan prisoners (chorus, 'Godiam la pace'). Elektra protests at this
action and is justifiably suspicious of his motives. Arbaces brings news of
Idomeneus's shipwreck and Idamantes rushes off to attempt a rescue.

In *recitativo obbligato*, Elektra gives vent to her jealousy: with Idomeneus
dead, who will prevent Idamantes from marrying Ilia? Her D minor aria
('Tutte nel cor vi sento') writhes between fury and self-pity. The daring
reprise in C minor not only symbolizes her mental disturbance but anticipates the storm in the next scene; although decorum is restored in that the
aria ends in D, the music continues without interruption or change of speed
into the following chorus, modulating back to C minor; this is a piece of continuity striking in its originality, anticipating the transformations in Wagnerian opera, though little time is allowed for the scene-change.

The sea-shore, strewn with wreckage   A distant chorus of sailors echoes
the chorus on shore ('Pietà! Numi, pietà'). In pantomime Neptune is seen
calming the waters. Idomeneus, whose prayer has persuaded the god to relent, reaches land. He dismisses his followers; he wishes to be alone to
meditate upon the awful vow he has made. The price of survival is that he
must sacrifice the first person he meets to Neptune; in his unhappy aria, he

imagines himself haunted by the innocent victim ('Vedrommi intorno'). The 'Idamantes motif' reappears in the Andantino, as do images of the storm in the Allegro. As this is not an orthodox *opera seria*, Idomeneo remains on stage after this aria, and fate brings the sacrificial victim: it is Idamantes. At the son's ecstatic recognition of his father, *recitativo semplice* gives way to dynamic orchestral figures. But Idomeneus rejects his son and rushes off, leaving Idamantes a prey to fear and longing. The atmosphere of the storm again affects his aria ('Il padre adorato').

In an interlude, customary in this kind of courtly opera, the returning Cretan soldiers are greeted by the populace (ballet sequence with choral chaconne, 'Nettuno s'onori').

ACT 2 *A royal apartment* [1786 only: orchestrated dialogue and aria K490. Ilia yields Idamantes to Elektra but asks not to be forgotten. His reply— 'Ch'io mi scordi di te?': he cannot possibly forget her—leads to the new aria, in rondò form ('Non temer, amato bene'), with obbligato violin.]

[Both versions] Idomeneus tells Arbaces everything; he resolves that Idamantes must escape sacrifice by taking Elektra back to Argos. Arbaces responds sententiously, in an energetic Allegro ('Se il tuo duol', omitted in 1786). Now Ilia approaches the king. In Mozart's most tenderly poised melodic vein, and one of the most beautiful arias he ever wrote, enriched by four obbligato wind instruments, she accepts Idomeneus as a second father ('Se il padre perdei'). He now sees that the sacrifice will ruin two lives as well as the victim; in another strikingly original and effective piece of continuity, his *recitativo obbligato* underlines his concern by referring to motifs from her aria, darkened by changed harmony. His own aria ('Fuor del mar'), majestically cast in the opera's opening and closing tonality, D major, exists in a simplified version (1786) as well as the more flamboyant original destined for Raaff. Freed from the sea, he finds a worse storm in his own heart. In the middle section he asks why he cannot find the shipwreck he now desires; the enharmonic modulation shortly before the reprise of the first section is heart-stopping.

Elektra is transformed by the thought that Idamantes will escort her home; surely, when they are thrown together, he will fall for her instead of Ilia. Her aria is a serene invocation of love ('Idol mio, se ritroso'), accompanied by strings only, and so quite unlike the remainder of her role. A distant march, beginning with muted brass, grows to *fortissimo* to mark the change of scene.

The port of Kydonia Elektra and the chorus welcome the propitious calm ('Placido è il mar, andiamo'). Idomeneus bids farewell to his sorely perplexed son, Elektra joining in a beautiful trio ('Pria di partir, o Dio!'). As the young people are about to embark, a tempest breaks out, represented in music of barely repressed violence, and a terrible sea-monster appears (storm, with chorus, 'Qual nuovo terrore'). The people demand to know who has angered the gods and brought down their wrath. Without naming Idamantes, Idomeneus publicly confesses (*recitativo obbligato*) that he himself is the sinner, for he owes the gods a sacrifice; but he has the temerity to accuse the gods of injustice in demanding innocent blood. Terrified at the revelation that their king is to blame, the crowd flees in confusion ('Corriamo, fuggiamo'). A note in the libretto states that this scene serves as the entr'acte, and indeed at this juncture a ballet sequence would be badly misplaced.

ACT 3 *The palace garden*   In a tender E major aria, Ilia bids the winds bear her message of love to Idamantes ('Zeffiretti lusinghieri'), whom she believes to be far away by now. When he suddenly appears, she is unable to suppress her real feelings, and they declare their love (duet, 'S'io non moro'—omitted at the premiere; replaced in 1786 by a shorter duet with some of the same material, 'Spiegarti non poss'io' K489). Idomeneus and Elektra find them together. The varied emotions of all four are embodied in the harrowingly beautiful harmonic and contrapuntal web of one of Mozart's supreme achievements, the quartet ('Andrò, ramingo e solo'). Ilia's heart is still divided; Elektra is full of suppressed jealousy; Idamantes, again banished without knowing the reason, is deeply saddened, and Idomeneus wishes the gods would kill him instead. Each has reached the limit of suffering; their voices unite at 'soffrir più non si può'. Idamantes repeats his opening phrase, an emblem of loneliness and misery, and leaves the stage. Arbaces begs the king to help his suffering people and laments the condition of his country in a magnificent *recitativo obbligato* ('Sventurata Sidon!'). His aria ('Se colà ne' fati è scritto', omitted in 1786) is more conventional, a broadly conceived piece accompanied only by strings.

A large public place before the palace   The high priest confronts the king (recitative, 'Volgi intorno lo sguardo, o Sire'): the monster has devoured thousands and laid waste the country. Only Idomeneus can save them by naming the victim and completing the sacrifice. To the longest development of the 'Idamantes motif' he confesses the truth. The priest and people are awed and deeply moved. In the C minor chorus 'O voto tremendo' the collision of violin triplet quavers with the duple rhythms of the voices, the ominous fanfares of muted brass, and a melancholy chromatic fragment, form a picture of desolation without scarcely an equal in 18th-century music.

The temple of Neptune, both exterior and interior being visible The king and priests process to the temple (march) and prepare the sacrifice (chorus of priests with Idomeneus, 'Accogli, o re del mar'). A jubilant cry is heard (fanfare); Idamantes has slain the monster. Idomeneus fears this will offend Neptune, and worse will befall them; but Idamantes enters wearing the white robes used for sacrifice, prepared to lay down his life for his father and his country. The dialogue in *recitativo obbligato* is interrupted only by one of the arias Mozart planned to omit before the 1781 performances, but may ultimately have included ('Nò, la morte io non pavento': Idamantes has no fear of death and dies willingly for his father). The orchestrated recitative is of unprecedented length and expressiveness, partly based on the 'reconciliation' network of motives. At the moment of sacrifice Ilia enters and offers herself as an alternative victim; the confusion is ended only when the oracle speaks. It commands the abdication of Idomeneus in favour of his son, who will marry Ilia. The general happiness is not universal. Elektra invokes the Furies in a *recitativo obbligato* and a stupendous rage aria ('D'Oreste, d'Ajace'); although this was omitted by Mozart, the revised recitative is overpowering even by the standards of this opera.

Idomeneus now welcomes his retirement in an elaborate *recitativo obbligato*, as finely organised as Elektra's was manic ('Popoli! a voi l'ultima legge'). His exquisitely beautiful aria ('Torna la pace al core') was also cut in 1781, but its serene glow perfectly reconciles the opera's conflicts. The young lovers have nothing to say at this point, but the brisk final chorus ('Scenda Amor, scenda Imeneo') and the extended ballet essentially celebrate their union.

*   *   *

Idomeneo is divided from its French model by the spread of Enlightenment. Danchet's libretto included another love tangle (Idomeneus loves Ilia) and involved Elektra closely in the plot (jealous of Ilia, she reveals to the priests Idomeneus's scheme to save Idamantes). It also ended tragically, with Idomeneus, driven mad by Nemesis, killing his son. Varesco turned the myth into an allegory of enlightened monarchy; flawed by his vow, rather than his failure to fulfil it, Idomeneus is unfitted to reign, but the god permits the organic transfer of power to the new generation and the reconciliation of former enmities by dynastic marriage. This restoration of harmony is movingly captured in Idomeneus's final aria, so that Mozart's omission of 'Torna la pace', while justifying its omission in modern performances, is particularly regrettable. This theme also reflects the father-son relationship which is considered to have been the source of much creative tension for Mozart, although it should be emphasised that he did not choose the subject of the opera, and that he and Leopold were on good terms at this period.

The letters to his father, and the cuts on which he insisted, demonstrate Mozart's mature theatrical judgment as well as the powers of persuasion he exercised upon the singers. Most remarkable is his willingness at the last moment, following the dress rehearsal, to sacrifice superlative music for a theatrical end. In view of his intended and actual reworking, it seems safe to say that *Idomeneo* never reached a form with which he was completely satisfied. Unfortunately some performances with a tenor Idamantes ignore not only the 1786 aria and duet but also Mozart's careful revision of the trio and quartet, whose texture is ruined by singing the castrato line an octave too low.

Even within the repertory of 'reform' opera (Italian, French, and German), *Idomeneo* is remarkable for its orchestration. Mozart used clarinets here for the first time in an opera, and four horns, but the music for flutes, oboes, bassoons, and trumpets is equally striking as are the brass mutes in the Act 2 march and the scene in which the Cretans learn that the sacrificial victim must be Idamantes. The varied but almost continual use of wind instruments creates an unprecedentedly rich palette, although trombones are confined to the oracle's speech, of which Mozart made four different settings. One of these has no trombones, probably because these instruments were considered by Seeau to be an expense too far. Most remarkable is the deployment of wind instruments during critical passages of recitative, notably those preceding the two final arias. The strings are treated with equal resourcefulness; for instance, the tremolando in the High Priest's recitative, the hammering c''' in 'O voto tremendo', responding to the muted trumpet calls, and the harp-like pizzicato in the invocation to Neptune at the beginning of the last scene.

Instrumental inventiveness is matched by harmonic daring; even the simple recitatives make expressive use of enharmonic progressions and remote tonalities. *Idomeneo* is also notable for its continuity, again beyond what was normal in 'reform' operas. Several numbers have no final cadence but move into the next recitative as if to avoid leaving time for applause; in 1786 Mozart added such an ending to the simpler version of 'Fuor del mar'.

Idomeneo is also the first Mozart opera in which the arrangement of tonalities seems deliberately calculated. Recognition of certain recurring keys is not only assisted by instrumentation but also by the use of distinct motifs; the use of these is more highly developed than in any previous opera. Although it is unlikely that every instance was intentional, Mozart can scarcely have overlooked the 'Idamantes motif': from the overture to the sacrifice scene its most clearly identifiable recurrences nearly all relate to the young hero (it is, however, a figure that crops up regularly in his other works). Nevertheless, most of the opera consists of discrete numbers which reflect Mozart's determination that music should govern the poetry. With this end in view, he did not reject virtuosity, but turned its musical qualities to dramatic ends. Despite detectable influences within it, and from it (for instance in *Don Giovanni* and *La clemenza di Tito*), *Idomeneo* stands on its own, occupying a special place in the affections of its composer who went on to other achievements as vital and significant, but never returned to its dignified, heroic, yet thoroughly human world.

Die Entführung aus dem Serail

('The Abduction from the Seraglio')

Singspiel in three acts, K384, to a libretto by Christoph Friedrich Bretzner (*Belmont und Constanze, oder Die Entführung aus dem Serail*), adapted and enlarged by Gottlieb Stephanie the younger; first performed at the Burgtheater, Vienna, on 16 July 1782.

Caterina Cavalieri was the first Konstanze, with Valentin Adamberger as Belmonte. Osmin was sung by Ludwig Fischer, Blonde by Therese Teyber, and Pedrillo by Johann Ernst Dauer.

Selim *Pasha*	spoken
Konstanze *a Spanish lady, Belmonte's betrothed*	soprano
Blonde *Konstanze's English maid*	soprano
Belmonte *a Spanish nobleman*	tenor
Pedrillo *servant of Belmonte, now supervisor of the Pasha's gardens*	tenor
Osmin *overseer of the Pasha's country house*	bass
Klaas *a sailor*	spoken
Mute *in Osmin's service*	

Chorus of Janissaries; guards

Setting The country house of Pasha Selim, on the Mediterranean coast in an unidentified part of the Ottoman Empire.

Dismissed by the Archbishop of Salzburg, Mozart must have felt satisfaction in being able to write to his father on 1 August 1781: 'the day before yesterday Stephanie junior gave me a libretto to compose'. Gottlieb

Stephanie, director of the National Singspiel, wanted Bretzner's *Belmont und Constanze* set quickly for the visit in September of the Russian Grand Duke Paul Petrovich. Bretzner was a popular librettist, whose name ensured interest (*Belmont und Constanze* had been set in Berlin by Johann André). Yet with the postponement of the royal visit to November and the eventual choice of operas by Gluck, *Die Entführung* might have suffered the fate of *Zaide*, unperformed in Mozart's lifetime, had not Stephanie and, no doubt, the singers maintained their support for the composer. Mozart had already written much of Act 1; he wrote in detail to his father on 26 September about the arias for Belmonte, Osmin, and Konstanze.

The opera soon grew, with alterations and enlargements to Bretzner's dramatic framework. A short aria for Belmonte was added, directly linked to the overture, and Osmin's song was turned into a duet. Thus instead of Bretzner's spoken dialogue, with Osmin's song its only music, there is something like a continuous introduction that drives the action forward, as later in *Don Giovanni* and *Die Zauberflöte*. It was Mozart who decided to establish Osmin as a major force with an additional aria, 'Solche hergelauf'ne Laffen', sending Stephanie the music to which the words must be fitted. His comments to his father concerning 'Solche hergelauf'ne Laffen' and Belmonte's aria 'O wie ängstlich' contain some of his most important recorded views on operatic aesthetics. The Janissary chorus is 'short, lively and written to please the Viennese'; he also admitted that he had 'sacrificed Konstanze's aria ['Ach ich liebte'] a little to the flexible throat of Mlle Cavalieri'.

Mozart and Stephanie recast the remaining two acts more extensively. The women and Osmin each received one additional aria ('Martern aller Arten', 'Welche Wonne' and 'O, wie will ich triumphieren'), while Belmonte received two (the second, opening Act 3, is often cut in modern performances or nonsensically replaced by the first). They devised a new situation for a long ensemble (the quartet finale to Act 2) and a new denouement. If much of the libretto thus remains essentially Bretzner's (he alone was credited on the original playbill and libretto), there are significant structural differences. Mozart began setting a quintet which, in Bretzner, covered the whole elopement scene. The loss of such an extended action ensemble is tantalizing; doubtless it was rejected because, being in the middle of the third act, it could not form a finale. Instead the elopement is in dialogue and its musical climax comes only after its failure, with Osmin's triumphant aria. The enhanced importance of Osmin develops the oriental, alien element in the action and makes him a tangible menace; the change may have resulted from, or merely taken advantage of, Fischer's immense range and full deep notes.

Mozart finished the score in April 1782. Rehearsals began in June and, despite some delays, an alleged cabal, and the difficulty of the music, the first performance was a success. Performances continued until the closure of the National-Singspiel early in 1783; the German company at the Kärntner-tor revived it (1784–5) with Aloysia Lange as Konstanze.

The fame of the new opera spread rapidly. The second production, also in 1782, was in Prague, and the city immediately took Mozart's music to its heart (the first performance in Czech came only in 1829). *Die Entführung* was the foundation of Mozart's reputation outside Austria. In 1783 there were productions in Warsaw, Bonn (under Neefe, the young Beethoven possibly assisting), Frankfurt, and Leipzig. The first translation (into Polish) followed in November, again for Warsaw. In 1784 there were productions in Mannheim, Carlsruhe, Cologne, and Salzburg; Dresden, Munich, and other German cities followed in 1785. It was given in some 40 centres in Germany and the Austrian Empire, and reached Amsterdam in Mozart's lifetime. The second foreign language used was Dutch (1797, Amsterdam), the third French (1798, Paris, in a version by Gluck's librettist Moline); it was also the first opera ever heard in German in Paris (1801). In Moscow it was given in 1810 in Russian (St Petersburg following in 1816) and in 1820 in German.

The first London performance, in English, was at Covent Garden in 1827, the score arranged by C. Kramer with an altered plot; the setting was moved by the translator, W. Dimond, to a Greek island. Such alterations were standard in 19th-century revivals and usually had some topical source (such as the Greek War of Independence). In Paris the 1859 revival to a translation by Prosper Pascal reordered several numbers and gave 'Martern aller Arten' to Blonde (no less a Mozartian than Thomas Beecham removed this aria to Act 3). Later in the 19th century there were London productions in German and Italian, under the title *Il Seraglio*. The American premiere was in New York in 1860, probably in German. An attempt to produce it in 1840 in Milan came to nothing, and the Italian premiere was not until 1935, in Florence, by which time the 20th-century revival of Mozart was under way and *Die Entführung* had already appeared at Glyndebourne.

The background to the story is the territorial and cultural intersection of Islamic lands with the older Christian civilization of Europe, especially Spain; Belmonte's father is Governor of Oran on the coast of North Africa. A major stimulus for artistic interest in things Turkish was the nearly successful siege of Vienna in 1683, but the action evokes an earlier period when piracy was rife and crossing between religions not uncommon; Pasha Selim is a renegade Christian, like Sebastiani's Renegat.

The overture is a bubbling Allegro in C major, its 'Turkish' style martial and colourful yet, in Mozart's hands, subject to abrupt changes of mood; a promising crescendo lurches into the dominant minor, anticipating the confusion of the action to come. A slow middle section in C minor brings a foretaste of sentiment, its melody by turns hesitant and passionate, richly clothed in woodwind sound. The Allegro resumes, ending on a dominant chord to lead directly into the first scene, a proceeding related to that in *Don Giovanni*.

*   *   *

ACT I   *A plaza before Selim's palace, near the sea*   A major-key version of the middle section of the overture ('Hier soll ich dich denn sehen') forms an aria short by the standards of this opera, but after its hesitant start, lyrical cadences convey Belmonte's ardent desire for reunion with Konstanze. Osmin appears with a ladder, and begins picking figs while singing a moral song (Lied and duet, 'Wer ein Liebchen hat gefunden': 'Whoever finds a lover, let him beware'). When Belmonte speaks Osmin refuses to answer, directing the later verses at him instead: plausible strangers bring danger to lovers. Belmonte enquires after Pedrillo, wrenching the tempo to Allegro, but the wrath of the Turk, enraged by mention of the gardener, dominates the duet section. In a furious Presto, the original G minor yielding to D major, he drives Belmonte away.

Pedrillo asks Osmin whether Selim has returned. Still not answering, Osmin fumes about vagabond fops fit only to be hanged ('Solche hergelauf 'ne Laffen'). A full binary exit aria, portentous and often contrapuntal, it flies off the handle in the coda to which Mozart added 'Turkish' music, as he said, for comic effect. Belmonte reveals himself and the delighted Pedrillo assures him that Selim will not force love on Konstanze. But they are in great danger; Osmin watches everything. He goes to find a way of getting Belmonte into the house. Belmonte's heart is beating with anxiety and ardour ('O wie ängstlich, o wie feurig'); both melody and orchestra are suffused with feeling as well as detailed imitation of the lover's symptoms.

A march (possibly cut by Mozart, but restored in the Neue Mozart-Ausgabe) announces the arrival of the pasha in a boat with Konstanze; the Janissaries greet them with a vigorous chorus in 'Turkish' style. Selim asks why Konstanze remains sad, promising that her answer will not anger him. In the aria ('Ach ich liebte, war so glücklich!') Konstanze's Adagio relives her past love; her Allegro compresses the Adagio's melodic outline into a vehement protest, for all her happiness has fled (the Adagio text and mood return in the middle of the Allegro). Mozart's sacrifice for Cavalieri brings coloratura to the text 'Kummer ruht in meinem Schoss' ('sorrow dwells in my heart'), but contrasted with passages of tenderness. Overall, this emphatic utterance makes Konstanze a formidable character. Selim is after all angered, but when she leaves he admits that he loves her all the more for her resistance. Pedrillo introduces Belmonte as an Italian-trained architect; Selim approves his entry into the household. But Osmin has other ideas. A vivacious trio in C minor ('Marsch, marsch, marsch! trollt euch fort!'), ending with a faster major section, forms a comic finale; eventually the Europeans force an entry.

ACT 2 *The palace garden, with Osmin's house to one side* Osmin is pursuing Blonde, whom the pasha has given him as a slave, but she will have none of his Turkish ways; tenderness, not force, wins a girl's heart. This Andante aria ('Durch Zärtlichkeit und Schmeicheln') is the epitome of Mozartian elegance. Osmin indignantly orders her to love him, but she merely laughs, and wards off an assault by threatening his eyes with her nails and reminding him that her mistress is the pasha's favourite (duet, 'Ich gehe, doch rate ich dir'). Osmin warns her not to flirt with Pedrillo; she mocks his low notes with her own (to d'). In a lugubrious Andante Osmin declares that the English are mad to allow their women such liberties; Blonde rejoices in her freedom.

At the nadir of her fortunes, Konstanze turns to the most intense style of *opera seria, recitativo obbligato* ('Welcher Wechsel herrscht in meiner Seele'), before her moving second aria ('Traurigkeit ward mir zum Loose'). In the exquisite Adagio Mozart paints her sighing breaths, her halting steps. The aria, its orchestra enriched by basset-horns, is a sustained lament in G minor, like Ilia's (*Idomeneo*, Act 1), but attaining a new poignancy through its higher tessitura. Blonde tries to comfort her mistress. Then Selim enters, threatening not death, which Konstanze would welcome, but every kind of torture, bringing, as in *Zaide*, another aria from the heroine at the very centre of the opera. 'Marten aller Arten' ('Every kind of torture awaits me; I laugh at pain; death will come in the end') picks up his threat, its grandeur established by a 60-bar ritornello in which the orchestra, with obbligato flute, oboe, violin, and cello, unfolds a rich motivic tapestry founded on a march rhythm (with trumpets and timpani). The closing words are given more emphasis by a faster tempo. This magnificent piece, coming immediately after another long aria for Konstanze, presents a challenge to the actors and the producer; but the expression of noble resistance to coercion, from a woman with no hope of deliverance, is of immense dramatic power. Selim is baffled; affection and force having failed, he wonders if he can use cunning. (This exit line perhaps prefigured a new intrigue intended for Act 3, but eventually not included.)

Pedrillo tells Blonde of Belmonte's arrival. Blonde's unalloyed delight sparks a rondo aria with a melody taken from the oboe/flute concerto K314/271*k* ('Welche Wonne, welche Lust'). Pedrillo musters his courage in a martial D major ('Frisch zum Kampfe!'), but a nagging phrase ('Nur ein feiger Tropf verzagt': 'Only a cowardly fool despairs') shows his underlying lack of confidence. He succeeds in getting Osmin drunk (duet, 'Vivat Bacchus'), and sends him to sleep it off so that the lovers can meet. Tears of joy are love's sweetest reward; Belmonte's aria of *galanterie* ('Wenn der Freude Tränen fliessen') is a slow gavotte, then a serenade-like minuet announced by the wind and embellished with wide-ranging passage-work.

The escape is planned before the finale (quartet, 'Ach Belmonte!'). The first mature Mozart ensemble to incorporate dramatic development begins with a lively D major Allegro. Joy gives way to anxiety (Andante, G minor); the men wonder if the women have yielded to blandishment from their Turkish admirers. In a faster tempo, Konstanze expresses hurt, Blonde slaps Pedrillo's face, and the voices come together in mingled relief and regret. The men ask forgiveness (Allegretto); Blonde pretends to withhold it, singing in compound time against the simple time of the others (a device Mozart might have picked up from *opéra comique*). But eventually misunderstanding is cleared away and the four join in praise of love.

ACT 3 *The scene of Act 1; Osmin's house to one side [midnight]* Pedrillo and Klaas bring two ladders. Belmonte is assured that all is ready, but they must wait for the guards to finish their rounds. Pedrillo advises him to sing; he himself often sings at night and no one will notice the difference. In a long Andante, featuring clarinets and extended coloratura, Belmonte builds his hopes on the power of love ('Ich baue ganz auf deine Stärke'). Pedrillo gives the agreed signal, a romance ('In Mohrenland gefangen war ein Mädchen': 'A maid was captive in Moorish lands'). The opera's second Lied, this too refers obliquely to the dramatic situation. Its haunting melody, to a plucked accompaniment, rests upon harmonic ambiguity and it ends, after dialogue interruptions, with its harmony unresolved after four verses, Pedrillo sees a light, the signal that the women are ready. Belmonte fetches Konstanze; they hurry off as Pedrillo climbs up for Blonde. But the mute has seen them. Suspecting thieves and murderers, the bleary-eyed Osmin sends for the guard and dozes. Blonde and Pedrillo spot him too late; all four Europeans are arrested. In a brilliant rondo ('O, wie will ich triumphieren'), with piccolo but without trumpets or Turkish music, which Mozart keeps in reserve, Osmin, now wide awake, anticipates the delight of torturing and killing his enemies, his lowest bass notes (to D) filled with ghoulish relish.

The interior of the palace Osmin claims credit for the arrest. Selim confronts the lovers. Konstanze admits that in his eyes she must be guilty, but she pleads loyalty to her first lover. She begs to die if only his life can be spared. Belmonte humbles himself; he is worth a fine ransom; his name is Lostados. Selim recognizes the son of the enemy who chased him from his homeland. He bids them prepare for the punishment Belmonte's father would certainly have meted out, and leaves them under guard. Belmonte movingly laments his folly in bringing Konstanze to her doom; she blames herself for his destruction, but death is the path to an eternal union, symbolized by the serenely extended arabesques (recitative and duet, 'Welch ein Geschick! O Qual der Seele!').

Selim asks if they are prepared for judgment. Belmonte says they will die calmly, absolving him from blame. Selim, however, bids him take Konstanze and go. He despises Belmonte's father too much to imitate him; clemency will be his revenge. As he takes dignified leave of them, Pedrillo begs freedom for himself and Blonde. Osmin protests, but is overruled; this way, the pasha says, he should keep the use of his eyes. The finale, a catchy vaudeville, is a frank (and successful) bid for popularity. Each character sings a verse of suitable sentiment, with a moral sung by the ensemble: those who forget kindness are to be despised. Blonde is interrupted by Osmin who is unable to sing the whole tune; instead his rage boils over into a repetition of the litany of torture from his Act 1 aria, complete with 'Turkish' percussion. He rushes off; the others draw the further moral, inspired by the pasha's forgiveness, that nothing is so hateful as revenge. A brief chorus in praise of the pasha, in the principal key, C major, brings back the merry 'Turkish' style of the overture.

*   *   *

The viewpoint of *Die Entführung* is decidedly European. Muslim life-style is crudely represented as luxurious but immoral; the Enlightenment, through Blonde, makes tart observations about the social position of Muslim women. Selim himself, raised to eminence by ability rather than rank, reflects Enlightenment values; he is not moved to clemency by his past or present religion, but contrasts his action with the cruelty of Belmonte's Christian father. This ending is more subtle than Bretzner's denouement, in which Belmonte proves to be Selim's son. Perhaps with the example of Sebastiani's modifications to Voltaire in mind (see *Zaide*), Mozart and his collaborator avoided this complex of sexual and religious affiliation. It is a pity, however, that the denouement, unlike that of *Die Zauberflöte*, was not set to music; it had to accommodate the pasha as a speaking role, and thus a major character is undefined by Mozart's music.

The lavish musical invention of *Die Entführung* perhaps exceeds what the dramatic structure is fit to bear; nor is its design immaculate. Apart from the cluster of arias for Konstanze in Act 2, there is one aria too many for Belmonte, and the length of the individual numbers (if not their forms) suggests *opera seria*, contrasting starkly with the speed of the dialogue. Joseph II's comment 'Too many notes, my dear Mozart' is probably apocryphal, but could have been induced by the opera's length, or its plenitude of instrumentation. Such problems cannot be overcome by making alterations, still less by cutting the dialogue, for Mozart and Stephanie controlled the flow between speech and music, running some numbers closely together but separating others more widely. Mozart's prodigality of invention is a cause of the opera's enduring fascination. Even as it endangers the dramatic whole, the music, paradoxically through its creation for a specific group of remarkable singers, turns the actors in this serious comedy into humans a little larger than life but of universal appeal.

L'oca del Cairo

('The Cairo Goose')

Opera buffa in two acts, K422, to a libretto by Giovanni Battista Varesco; the work remained unfinished.

Mozart requested the libretto from Varesco in May 1783, discussed it in Salzburg during the summer, and by December had composed most of the first act. He abandoned work early in 1784 and in a letter to his father (10 February) he offered sharp criticism of the libretto's detail and design. The story involves an amorous intrigue on the island of Ripasecca, governed by Don Pippo (bass); the Cairo goose was to intervene as a disguise for the young lover Biondello, rather like a mechanical *deus ex machina*. Mozart may have recognised an excessive likeness of plot to an opera which quickly became popular in Vienna, Paisiello's *Il barbiere di Siviglia*.

Full-length musical drafts survive for two duets (one on a text not in the libretto), two arias, a quartet, and a finale; another aria survives complete in the hand of J. S. Mayr. Mozart also set one section of dialogue in simple recitative. The scenes nearest completion are between *buffo* servants, Aurelia (soprano) and Chichibeo (bass). The richly expressive quartet is for two more serious pairs of lovers, Celidora and Lavina (sopranos), Biondello and Calandrino (tenors). The finale of 461 bars promises more action than actually occurs. It includes a chorus of police preventing an elopement, and its tonal scheme anticipates that of the central finale to *Le nozze di Figaro*.

Various attempts have been made to 'realize' the fragments, among them a reconstruction by Nicholas Temperley, staged at Urbana-Champaign, Illinois, in 1991, and a realization of the sketched numbers by Erik Smith for the recording in Philips's Complete Mozart Edition.

Lo sposo deluso

('The Deluded Bridegroom')

Opera buffa, K430/424a, to a libretto after *Le donne rivali*; unfinished.

Lo sposo deluso was composed in 1783–4, probably after Mozart decided to abandon *L'oca del Cairo*. Its libretto, surviving complete with Mozart's idea for casting members of the Italian company resident at the Vienna Burgtheater, was formerly attributed, without evidence, to Lorenzo da Ponte. Campana (1988–9) has shown that the libretto is based on a Roman intermezzo (*Le donne rivali*), possibly written by Giuseppe Petrosellini. The changed title may suggest that Mozart had in mind that the buffo Francesco Benucci would take the title-role.

The first three numbers were drafted and a trio completed. The overture's Allegro begins with a sprightly fanfare to launch a sonata form. There is a central Andante, and then, in a masterstroke, the reprise of the Allegro becomes the opera's first number, a quartet. Pulcherio (tenor or high baritone, intended for Francesco Bussani) laughs at Bocconio, the title role (bass, Benucci) for aspiring to a young bride, Eugenia. Bettina (soprano, Catarina Cavalieri), his niece, and Don Asdrubale (tenor, Stefano Mandini) deride the old man's pretensions. Eugenia (soprano, Nancy Storace) arrives; the sketched aria (the second number) reveals a lady of spirit. Pulcherio's aria is addressed to the ill-matched couple. Eugenia and Asdrubale, former lovers tragically separated, contrast in the trio with the bafflement of Bocconio, expressed in a phrase re-used in Bartolo's aria (*Le nozze di Figaro*, Act 1).

This trio comes closest to the style of the future Da Ponte operas. Some lively invention notwithstanding, the rest, in line with the libretto, may seem conventional in comparison with what Mozart was doing in other genres. But the deliberately simple, even simplistic, style of the opening quartet comes off well in the theatre, as was shown in Paul Griffiths's staged anthology *The Jewel Box*, first presented by Opera North (Leeds) in 1991 and performed subsequently in the United States and Britain.

Der Schauspieldirektor

('The Impresario')

Singspiel in one act, k486, to a libretto by Gottlieb Stephanie the younger; first performed in Schönbrunn, at the Orangery, on 7 February 1786.

Der Schauspieldirektor was performed on 7 February 1786 at Schönbrunn Palace as part of an Imperial entertainment for the Governor-General of the Netherlands. On the same day, but at the opposite end of the room, there followed the premiere of Salieri's *Prima la musica*; there were three subsequent public performances.

Frank (spoken role, originally Stephanie), the impresario, and Puf (bass, Josef Weidmann, more an actor than a singer) are assembling a company of actors and professional singers, who squabble over pre-eminence and pay. There are five other spoken roles, including a banker. Besides Mozart's music, extracts from three plays were used for the 'auditions'.

The overture is a sonata allegro with the full development missing in the overture to *Figaro*. Frank auditions the actors, then Mme Herz ('heart': soprano, Aloysia Lange). In her aria ('Da schlägt des Abschieds Stunde') the pathetic style yields to a brilliant conclusion. Her rival is Mlle Silberklang ('silver sound': soprano, Catarina Cavalieri) who sings an elegant rondò ('Bester Jüngling'). Unfortunately they cannot both be prima donna, and they argue in a hilarious trio ('Ich bin die erste Sängerin'), with Vogelsang, the company's tenor (Johann Valentin Adamberger), trying to keep the peace. During this movement Mme Herz displays her f''' and provides illustrations of types of singing to the words 'adagio' and 'allegro'. Both ladies are promised large salaries and joint star billing; quarrels are ended, nominally for the sake of art (if in reality just to have a quiet life). Puf joins in the finale.

Stephanie's *Gelegenheitsstück* ('pièce d'occasion': Mozart called it 'comedy with music', the singers being minor characters) makes a crude contrast with the short but relatively subtle opera by Salieri and Casti. Revivals in the 19th century tried to enhance the pertinence of the music by changing the plot—a version staged in Berlin includes Mozart and Schikaneder in the cast, preparing *Die Zauberflöte*—and adding more music. In its original form, *Der Schauspieldirektor* is not an opera but a play with musical numbers. Nevertheless this silly farce provided an opportunity, which Mozart seized, to write serious arias which could adorn a real opera or concert programme, to display a talent for musical farce in the trio, and compose an overture of scintillating ingenuity and charm.

Le nozze di Figaro

('The Marriage of Figaro')

Opera buffa in four acts, K492, to a libretto by Lorenzo da Ponte after Pierre-Augustin Beaumarchais' play *La folle journée, ou Le Mariage de Figaro* (1784, Paris); first performed at the Burgtheater, Vienna, on 1 May 1786; revived there, 29 August 1789.

The original cast was Francesco Benucci (Figaro), Nancy Storace (Susanna), Luisa Laschi (Countess), Stefano Mandini (Count), Dorotea Bussani (Cherubino), Maria Mandini (Marcellina), Francesco Bussani (Bartolo and Antonio), Michael Kelly (Basilio and Curzio), and 12-year-old Anna Gottlieb (Barbarina).

Count Almaviva	baritone
Countess Almaviva	soprano
Susanna *her maid, betrothed to Figaro*	soprano
Figaro *valet to Count Almaviva*	bass
Cherubino *the Count's page*	mezzo-soprano, breeches role
Marcellina *housekeeper to Bartolo*	soprano
Bartolo *a doctor from Seville*	bass
Don Basilio *music master*	tenor
Don Curzio *magistrate*	tenor
Barbarina *daughter of Antonio*	child soprano
Antonio *gardener, Susanna's uncle*	bass

Villagers, peasants, servants

Setting Aguasfrescas near Seville, the Almaviva's country house; the action is almost contemporary with the play.

The operatic version of Beaumarchais' *Le Mariage de Figaro* may have been a timely notion of Mozart's own. Although the play was banned from the Viennese stage, it was available in print and Paisiello's opera on the earlier play, *Le Barbier de Séville*, had triumphed in Vienna in 1783 (and all over Europe). Mozart evidently studied Paisiello's handling of the same personalities and included deliberate references to his predecessor's work (their admiration was mutual). Composition began in the second half of 1785 and the opera may have been drafted in only six weeks. After some opposition attributed to the Italians, and (if Da Ponte is to be believed) after the librettist had overcome the emperor's objections, it was produced in May with an outstanding cast whose character and skills, as well as their performance in Paisiello's *Barbiere*, contributed to its conception. Michael Kelly discussed the event in his reminiscences, with a vivid account of Mozart rehearsing Benucci in 'Non più andrai'. Mozart may have expected Storace to sing the Countess; he rearranged the Act 2 trio and other passages so that Susanna took the upper line, presumably after the transfer of Storace to the larger role.

Contrary to what is often stated, *Figaro* was generally liked, as is indicated by the emperor's ban on encores of ensembles (arias could still be repeated). There were, however, only nine performances in 1786. The Viennese perhaps preferred lighter works in revival, and Martín y Soler's *Una cosa rara* later in 1786 became their favourite among new operas. Early in 1787 important members of the original cast (Storace and Kelly) left Vienna for good; Mandini soon followed. But *Figaro* was soon staged in Prague, where according to Mozart's report (letter of 15 January 1787) it created a furore. Certainly it led to the commission for *Don Giovanni*. The successful Vienna revival (nearly 30 performances from August 1789 to early 1791) preceded the commission for *Così fan tutte*: Susanna was confirmed as the prima donna's role when Mozart wrote two new arias for Adriana Ferrarese del Bene, Da Ponte's mistress and in 1790 the first Fiordiligi. He made a number of minor alterations, some to accommodate the new Countess, Cavalieri.

By this time *Figaro* had received isolated performances in Italy (Acts 1 and 2, the rest composed by Angelo Tarchi, Monza, autumn 1787; Florence, spring 1788), and had been translated into German for performances in Prague (June 1787), Donaueschingen (1787), Leipzig, Graz and Frankfurt (1788), followed by other German centres over the next few years. These performances used spoken dialogue, as did the first performance in France (Paris Opéra, 1793, using Beaumarchais' original dialogue). The London premiere in 1812 was in Italian, and followed interpolation by Storace, Martín, and Benucci of various numbers from *Figaro* into other operas; in 1819 it was given in English, reduced to three acts and arranged by Henry Bishop. Glyndebourne opened with *Figaro* in 1934. In New York the first performances were in 1824, in English, and 1858, in Italian. Numerous translations have been used during the 19th and 20th centuries. *Figaro* is perhaps Mozart's most popular opera, displacing *Don Giovanni*, and no major company allows it to fall out of the repertory for long.

In production, the vein of rococo nostalgia which inspired its epigone, *Der Rosenkavalier*, was displaced by the greater realism of Visconti (1963, Rome) and Hall (1973, Glyndebourne); it has become customary to emphasize the socio-political tensions in Beaumarchais, which Da Ponte had necessarily suppressed, although some productions go in the contrary direction and, failing to understand the power of one such as Count Almaviva over his dependents, present him as a foolish man easily deceived. Undoubtedly there are elements of farce, but they only incidentally concern the Count; and a good balance between comedy and danger can be achieved in an intelligent presentation of the work. Fortunately there have been many.

*   *   *

For the overture Mozart abandoned a planned middle section, leaving an electrifying sonata without development which perfectly sets the scene for the 'crazy day'. In the first part of Beaumarchais' trilogy, *Il barbiere*, Almaviva wooed Bartolo's ward Rosina with the aid of Figaro, now his valet. He has also, despite his Don Juanesque tendencies, abolished the *droit de Seigneur* whereby he had the right to deflower every bride among his feudal dependants.

ACT I *An antechamber*   The pacing motif and lyrical response in the opening duet ('Cinque, dieci') belong respectively to Figaro, who is measuring the room, and Susanna, who is trying on a new hat for their forthcoming wedding. She finally entices him from his work to admire it, and to sing her motif (see ex. 3, p. 23). Figaro tells her that the Count has offered them this room, conveniently placed between those of the Count and Countess, but she reacts with alarm. In the ensuing duet ('Se a caso madama') she mocks Figaro's imitation of the high and low bells of their employers: the room's convenience will also make it easy for the Count to visit Susanna when Figaro has been sent on an errand. Figaro's confidence is shaken, but if the Count wants to dance, he, Figaro, will pick the tune (cavatina, 'Se vuol ballare'), first offering a minuet, then a Presto contredanse.

Figaro has obtained a loan from Marcellina, and, never imagining he will have to keep the bargain, has agreed to marry her if he defaults. Bartolo offers Marcellina his help in enforcing the contract; he will thus avenge himself on Figaro (who thwarted his plans to marry Rosina in *Il barbiere*) and rid himself of an embarrassment (Marcellina). His exit aria ('La vendetta') has a full orchestra with trumpets, in the opera's principal key, D major. His vaunted legal knowledge brings formal counterpoint, but his fury also vents itself in comically undignified patter. Susanna, aware of Marcellina's interest in Figaro, hustles her out, the music poised, the exchange of compliments venomous (duettino, 'Via resti servito'), with Susanna victorious when she insists Marcellina's age entitles her to preference.

Cherubino enters and in a lyrical melodic arch over a sensuously muted accompaniment, he impulsively confides his love for all women; the aria 'Non so più' enchantingly evokes his adolescent longing. The Count is heard approaching; Susanna hides Cherubino behind a chair. Believing himself alone with Susanna, the Count makes amorous proposals, but when interrupted by the sound of Basilio's voice, he in turn hides behind the chair, not seeing Cherubino who nips onto the chair; Susanna covers him with a dress. Basilio's malicious (but accurate) observation that Cherubino adores the Countess rouses the Count and he breaks cover. Gruffly, in an ascending line, he demands an explanation (trio, 'Cosa sento!'); Basilio disclaims knowledge; his unctuously descending motif, however, is a transformation of Cherubino's 'Non so più'. Susanna, turning to the minor dominant, threatens to faint. The men officiously come to her aid (a new, ardent motif with a chromatic cadence) but, rather than sit on Cherubino, she flings them off with reproaches. The Count demonstrates his discovery of Cherubino in Barbarina's room, hidden under a cloth (and using an inversion of Basilio's descending motif). The page is again revealed, to the Count's self-righteous indignation, Basilio's delight, and Susanna's horror. Sonata form perfectly matches the action, the recapitulation fraught with irony (or, from Basilio, sarcasm: Mozart took the music set to his 'Così fan tutte le donne'—thus all women behave—into the overture to *Così fan tutte*). Figaro ushers in a rustic chorus praising the Count's magnanimity in renouncing his extra-marital right, but the Count, who is after Susanna's virginity, refuses to be trapped into marrying the couple then and there. He banishes Cherubino to his regiment with an officer's commission. Figaro makes a great show of sending the boy on his way to a bold march rhythm ('Non più andrai': no more frolicking and flirting; he is off to death or glory), but in fact detains the page for purposes of his own.

ACT 2 *The Countess's chamber*   In an achingly tender Larghetto, the neglected Countess prays to the god of love to restore her husband's affections (cavatina, 'Porgi, Amor'). But she listens eagerly to Susanna and Figaro's plotting: Cherubino is to be dressed as a girl, take Susanna's place, and compromise the Count. The Count is to be unsettled by an anonymous let-. ter saying that his wife is entertaining a lover—a mistake on Figaro's part, as will appear. The over-confident Figaro leaves singing a fragment of 'Se vuol ballare'. Cherubino's ardour is formalized, in a canzona of his own composition, 'Voi che sapete', sung to Susanna's 'guitar' accompaniment; in composing it Mozart miraculously suggests, but evades, the clumsiness of youthful composition. Susanna tries to dress Cherubino but he keeps gazing at the Countess ('Venite, inginocchiatevi', an action aria replaced in 1789 by the strophic 'Un moto di gioia'). Left alone with the Countess, Cherubino is close to winning her heart when the Count demands admittance: he has returned precipitately from the hunt because of an anonymous letter (part of Figaro's ill-laid plot). In confusion the Countess thrusts Cherubino into her closet; the Count demands an explanation for her evident agitation. At this juncture Susanna enters unseen. The Countess says it is Susanna in the closet. The Count's jealous fury, his wife's terror, and Susanna's anxiety again outline a sonata form, although the action does not advance (trio, 'Susanna, or via sortite'). When the Count leaves to fetch tools to break down the door, forcing the Countess to go with him and locking the bedroom door behind them, Susanna thrusts Cherubino through the window (duettino, 'Aprite, presto aprite') and enters the closet.

When they return, the Countess confesses that Cherubino is in the closet, half-dressed. She protests his innocence; the Count is ready to kill him. Mozart's most consummate comic finale begins by resuming the fury and anxiety of the trio (E♭, 'Ecci omai, garzon malnato'). But it is Susanna who emerges, mocking the nobles' consternation by a simple minuet. Explanations and further confusion occupy an extended Allegro which deploys its thematic wealth with marvellous inventiveness. Although puzzled, the Count has to ask forgiveness. At the only abrupt key-change of the finale (B♭ to G), Figaro enters, again asking for an immediate wedding. Recovering his sang-froid (C major, gavotte tempo), the Count poses questions about the anonymous letter; Figaro prevaricates. Antonio charges in to complain of damage to his garden caused by Cherubino (Allegro molto, F major). The Count senses more chicanery when Figaro claims it was he who jumped from the window. The tempo slows to Andante (in B♭) and with measured calm the Count questions Figaro about a paper the page has dropped: the music emerges from a harmonic cloud to a shining recapitulation as Figaro (prompted by the women) identifies it as the page's commission, left with him (he claims) to be sealed. The Count is baffled, for indeed it is not sealed, but he revives when Marcellina, Basilio, and Bartolo rush in demanding justice (E♭).

ACT 3 *A large room decorated for a marriage-feast* The Countess urges Susanna to make an assignation with the Count; they will exchange cloaks and his own wife will compromise him. Susanna approaches the Count, explaining her previous reticence as delicacy, and offering to meet him that evening. In a rare outburst in the minor (duet, 'Crudel! perchè finora') the Count reproaches her; changing to major, he sings of his coming happiness with exuberant syncopation. She tries to join in but trips over the replies (saying 'yes' for 'no', and vice versa), correcting herself at a melodic high point. Leaving, she encounters Figaro and carelessly shows her satisfaction: 'without a lawyer we've won the case'. The Count overhears and is again suspicious and angry (*recitativo obbligato* and aria, 'Vedrò, mentre io sospiro'). Must he sigh in vain while a mere servant wins the prize? The martial orchestration and key, even the contrapuntal language, recall Bartolo's aria, but the music snarls with aristocratic jealousy rather than pompous self-importance: a truly menacing utterance.

At the trial of Marcellina's case Curzio has found for the plaintiff. Figaro protests that he cannot marry Marcellina without his parents' consent. He shows a birthmark on his arm, which shows that he is the lost son of Marcellina, and Bartolo reluctantly admits paternity. Marcellina embraces Figaro and the three express delight while the Count and Curzio mutter their annoyance in a sextet, 'Riconosci in questo amplesso'. The sixth singer is Susanna who enters after the sextet has begun. Misinterpreting the situation, she boxes Figaro's ears. The comical explanation leads to a satisfied reprise for the quartet coupled with the angry interjections of the baffled Count and Curzio.

The Countess, waiting for Susanna, muses on the past and wonders if there is hope for her marriage (*recitativo obbligato* and rondò, 'Dove sono i bei momenti'). The aria shows her to be profoundly tender yet impulsive, and reaches a glowing *a"* at the climax. Antonio tells the Count that Cherubino is still in the castle. The Countess dictates a letter from Susanna to the Count confirming their rendezvous (duettino, 'Che soave zeffiretto'), their voices mingling in an expression of the love they feel, each for her own; the honeyed music shows none of the deviousness of their intentions.

During a choral presentation to the Countess, Cherubino is unmasked, but allowed to stay for the wedding when Barbarina innocently implies that she could make revelations embarrassing to the Count. Throughout the finale, the necessary action is cunningly woven into the sequence of dances. During the march the two couples (Marcellina and Bartolo having decided to regularize their union) are presented to the Count and Countess. The bridesmaids' duet and chorus (contredanse) precede the alluring fandango, during which Susanna slips the letter to the Count, sealed with a pin (to be returned as a sign of agreement to the rendezvous); Figaro notices with amusement that the Count has pricked himself.

ACT 4 *The garden, at night; pavilions on either side*   Barbarina, the go-between, has lost the pin (a mock-tragic cavatina in F minor, 'L'ho perduta'). Figaro, hearing her tale, concludes that Susanna is after all unfaithful, and an abyss seems to open beneath him. He confides in his parents, but Marcellina is inclined to warn Susanna; she must have a good reason for meeting the Count, and women should stick together (aria, 'Il capro e la capretta'). Barbarina is preparing to meet Cherubino in one of the pavilions. Figaro summons Basilio and Bartolo as witnesses to his wife's infidelity. Basilio moralizes that it is wiser not to resist one's superiors, adding a tale of his own hot youth (aria, 'In quegl'anni').

Figaro's monologue (*recitativo obbligato* and aria, 'Aprite un po' quegl'occhi') uses raw musical gestures to convey the terror, for a clever but emotionally simple man, of sexual betrayal. Disconnected phrases witness to his anxiety, and at the end horn fanfares mock him unmercifully. He overhears Susanna but cannot see that she is disguised as the Countess (*recitativo obbligato* and aria, 'Deh vieni, non tardar'). The floating line and titillating woodwind cadences with which she confides her amorous longing to the night perfectly capture the blended love and mischief with which she deliberately rouses Figaro's passion (in 1789 Mozart replaced the aria with the elaborate rondò, 'Al desio').

From now on all is confusion; the characters mistake identities and blunder into each other in the dark, receiving kisses and blows intended for others, before nearly all of them end up in the pavilions (finale). Cherubino begs Susanna (actually the disguised Countess) for a kiss; Susanna watches anxiously as the Count and Figaro drive the pest away. The Count begins to woo 'Susanna', who responds shyly; Figaro's impotent rage is highlighted in the orchestral bass. He contrives a temporary interruption. As the key changes from G to E♭ a serenade-like melody ironically evokes the peace of the night. Believing he has found the Countess (it is actually Susanna), Figaro tells her what is going on; then recognizing Susanna's voice, he decides to avenge his own humiliation and pays 'the Countess' passionate court. Enraged, Susanna boxes his ears again, blows he greets with rapture as signs of love. This scene unfolds in a frantic allegro, replaced at the reconciliation by pastoral 6/8. Now the pair do a little play-acting together, for the benefit of the Count. Figaro pleads passionate love, apparently to the Countess; on cue, with a second abrupt key-change (B♭ to G), the Count bursts in, calling witnesses, dragging everyone including the false Countess from the pavilion, and shouting accusations. The pair apparently caught in the act plead for mercy, joined by the other characters, but the Count is inexorable until the plea is reinforced by a new voice: the real Countess (in Susanna's clothes). There is a moment of shock before the humbled Count kneels, asking forgiveness. Her loving response is to pardon him again; it is built into a radiant hymn before the brilliant conclusion brings down the curtain on the crazy day.

*   *   *

Figaro is generally accepted as the most perfect and least problematic of Mozart's great operas. The libretto, despite its complication, is founded on a carefully constructed intrigue and Mozart draws musical dividends even from a hat, an anonymous letter, and a pin. The advance on the sketched *opere buffe* of the immediately preceding years is astonishing, and must be attributed to the effect on his imagination of the play, ably seconded by Da Ponte's adaptation, as well as his intervening experience in other genres and his trial runs in unfinished operas, and in writing ensembles in 1785 for Bianchi's *La villanella rapita*.

The originality of the ensembles (including finales and numerous duets, all involving Susanna) has often and rightly been considered the chief glory of *Figaro*. Many of them carry the action forward, not at the 'natural' tempo of recitative but under musical control; this makes such moments as the revelation of Figaro's parentage to Susanna (the Act 3 sextet) both touching and funny, and creates palpable tension when the Count comes near to murdering his wife's 'lover' in Act 2, although we know the unseen Susanna will enable the page to escape, and again in Act 4. The arias are no less original for their brevity and directness. They convey, economically and unforgettably, the essential characterization of Bartolo, Cherubino, the Countess and Count. Figaro and Susanna are most characteristically presented in ensembles and action arias (his Act 1 cavatina, although it is a kind of soliloquy, and 'Non più andrai'; her 'Venite, inginocchiatevi'). Their central place in the intrigue is confirmed in the last act, when each has a *recitativo obbligato*, normally a sign of high rank, particularly when this serious design is inserted into a comedy. These recitatives precede their final arias, soliloquies which deepen Figaro's character (his cynical denunciation of women, while not endearing, is understandable in the circumstances and born of love) and reveal the subtlety and tenderness of Susanna. Mozart's replacement of 'Deh vieni' in 1789 by 'Al desio' is perhaps a case of his damaging his own work by pandering to a singer's needs, although the new aria is beautiful in its own fashion.

Modern performances often omit Marcellina's aria, a stately minuet and melodious Allegro of deliberately old-fashioned cut (with coloratura and orchestra of strings only), and Basilio's, an elaborate and inventively composed narration in three sections (andante, minuet, allegro). Despite their virtues these pieces of moralizing by minor characters produce an excess of minuet tempo and, more seriously, a sequence of four arias, with Figaro's and Susanna's, and slow the action prior to the denouement. The only other critical reservation about *Figaro* concerns the episodic structure of Act 3, the point where Da Ponte departed decisively from Beaumarchais by omitting the trial. A reordering of scenes has been proposed (with the Countess's recitative and aria before the sextet, thus avoiding two entries for the Countess in quick succession); it certainly does not represent Mozart's intentions, but is effective in the theatre. But the non-sequiturs count for little in performance, and throw into greater relief the ingenious management of the Act 3 finale. In the great finales of Acts 2 and 4, Mozart reached a level even he could never surpass; indeed, he was hardly to equal the B♭ Allegro of the second act finale for its mercurial motivic play, and the subsequent Andante for its synchronization of dramatic revelation with the demands of musical form.

1 The opening scene of *Don Giovanni* as performed in 1890.

2 Michael Yeargan's set for the final scene of the 2004 production of *Don Giovanni* at the Metropolitan Opera, New York.

3 Act II of the Vienna Freihaustheater production of *Die Zauberflöte*, 1791.

4 Design by Karl Friedrich Schinkel for Act I of the 1815 production of *Die Zauberflöte*, The Starlit Hall of the Queen of Night.

5 George Tsypin's set for the final scene of the 2004 production of *Die Zauberflöte* at the Metropolitan Opera, New York.

6 Angelica Catalani as Susanna and Giuseppe Naldi as Figaro in *Le nozze di Figaro* at the King's Theatre, London, 1812; anonymous drawing.

7 Engraving of Act II of
Le nozze di Figaro by J.-P.-J
de Saint-Quentin, from the
first authentic edition of
Beaumarchais' 'La folle journée,
ou Le marriage de Figaro' (Paris,
1785).

8 Peter J. Davison's set and James Acheson's costumes for the Countess and
Cherubino in the 2005 production of *Le nozze di Figaro* at the Metropolitan
Opera, New York.

9 Colored rendering of the Old Burgtheater in Vienna, 1783, by Carl Scheutz.

10 Unfinished portrait of Mozart at the piano, 1789, by Joseph Lange.

Don Giovanni

[*Il dissoluto punito, ossia Il Don Giovanni*
('The Libertine Punished, or Don Giovanni')]

Opera buffa in two acts, K527, to a libretto by Lorenzo da Ponte; first performed at the National Theatre, Prague, on 29 October 1787. First Vienna performance, Burgtheater, 7 May 1788.

Don Giovanni *a young and extremely licentious nobleman*	baritone
Commendatore	bass
Donna Anna *his daughter*	soprano
Don Ottavio *her betrothed*	tenor
Donna Elvira *a lady from Burgos*	soprano
Leporello *Giovanni's servant*	bass
Masetto *a peasant, betrothed to Zerlina*	bass
Zerlina *a peasant girl*	soprano

Peasants, servants, demons

Setting A Spanish city (traditionally Seville), in the 16th century

Although commissioned by the Prague theatre, Mozart surely had in mind production in Vienna with the remaining personnel of the 1786 *Figaro*. The original and Vienna casts are listed together.

	Prague, 1787	*Vienna, 1788*
Giovanni	Luigi Bassi	Francesco Albertarelli
Commendatore/Masetto	Giuseppe Lolli	Francesco Bussani
Anna	Teresa Saporiti	Aloysia Lange

Ottavio	Antonio Baglioni	Francesco Morella
Elvira	Caterina Micelli	Caterina Cavalieri
Leporello	Felice Ponziani	Francesco Benucci
Zerlina	Caterina Bondini	Luisa Mombelli/
		Theresa Teyber

The commission for *Don Giovanni* followed the triumphant production of *Figaro* in Prague (December 1786). The impresario Guardasoni proposed a new version of Bertati's one-act *Don Giovanni*, set by Gazzaniga for Venice in February 1787, and probably asked for it to be expanded to a full evening's entertainment. In one version of his memoirs, Da Ponte claimed to have suggested the subject, suppressing his indebtedness to Bertati, whom he affected to despise and whose work he improved in every respect. He drew on other sources, notably Molière's *Dom Juan* and versions from popular theatre. About half the libretto, between the Act 1 quartet and the graveyard scene, is essentially original.

Mozart began work during the summer, leaving for Prague on 1 October. This season in the Bohemian capital has the flavour of legend; but there is no reason to suppose that Mozart's compositional processes were out of the ordinary, even in the late composition of the overture (on the eve of the performance, already twice postponed, or of the final rehearsal). He may have had to resist Bassi's demand for a big aria, and it is not clear that he knew Baglioni when he composed 'Il mio tesoro', although it is possible that they met in Vienna. A new triumph in Prague ensued. When staged in Vienna in the summer of 1788 *Don Giovanni* was less enthusiastically received, although there were more performances than *Figaro* had . had in 1786. Mozart wrote a replacement aria for the new tenor, Morella, an additional scena for Cavalieri, enlarging Elvira's role to be approximately equal to Anna's, and a buffo duet for Mombelli and Benucci. The final scene was probably omitted, at least at some performances, so that the opera ended with the departure of the walking statue and Giovanni's disappearance into the underworld.

Don Giovanni acquired a reputation for exceptional difficulty, thanks to the superimposed dance metres of the first finale and the unprecedented harmonic richness of the second. Nevertheless, Guardasoni gave it in Warsaw in 1789, and it made rapid progress in Germany as a Singspiel, second only to *Die Entführung* as the opera most performed in Mozart's lifetime. At least three translations were made, and it was sometimes adapted to the four-act design of *Figaro*. German was used in Prague in 1791, Vienna in 1792, and in Amsterdam (1793) and St Petersburg (1797). *Don Giovanni* became popular in France, often in adapted versions (in French, arranged by C. Kalkbrenner, 1805; in Italian, 1811). An attempt at Florence in 1805 seems to have been frustrated by the first finale; the Italian premiere was at Bergamo in 1811, followed by Rome the same year. In London there is some doubt over the earliest performances, which may have been partly amateur affairs. In 1817 it appeared at rival theatres in Italian and in English, and it remained popular in both languages. The first American performances, in 1826, by Manuel García's company, were attended and quite possibly assisted by Da Ponte. Nearly every opera singer of note has been associated with one or other of the main roles.

* * *

The overture begins with the imposing music for the entrance of the 'stone guest'. Its emergence into the D major Allegro establishes the ambivalence of the opera, its perilous balance of humour and tragedy. The full sonata form has been interpreted as a portrait of Giovanni, or as justice (the heavy five-note figure) pursuing the mercurial seducer. There is no final cadence; the coda modulates to a new key (F major) for the opening scene (Mozart did supply an orthodox ending in D, perhaps for concert performance; presumably unaware of this, Johann André composed a longer one).

ACT I *Courtyard of the Commendatore's house; night* Leporello is on guard as usual (Introduzione, 'Notte e giorno faticar'), and wishes he were the gentleman and in Giovanni's place ('Voglio far il gentiluomo'). He hides at the approach of Anna, who is pursuing Giovanni; he is hiding his face. The music is still formal despite its growing intensity, and becomes a trio with Leporello commenting in the background. Anna rushes off to fetch help, and her father emerges to confront Giovanni; musical formality yields to disordered gestures as they fight. The old man dies at a rare moment of stillness, even Giovanni apparently being moved (in the short trio in F minor, he uses a melody formerly sung by Anna in a faster tempo). With the first *recitativo secco*, Giovanni and Leporello run off before Anna returns with Ottavio. She sees her father's body and faints (*recitativo obbligato* and duet, 'Fuggi, crudele'); reviving, she responds to Ottavio's tender invitation to take him as husband and father by demanding that he wreak vengeance on the murderer. Their voices unite in the powerful D minor cadences that form the first decisive closure of the opera.

A street; dawn Elvira, in travelling clothes, is pursuing her betrayer (aria, 'Ah, chi mi dice mai'); her sincere, slightly ridiculous pose is conveyed by a sweeping melodic line and formal orchestral gestures. Giovanni scents adventure; mutual recognition comes too late to forestall his unctuous advance, which overlaps the cadence of the aria. He escapes from her reproaches, leaving Leporello to show her his catalogue (aria, 'Madamina, il catalogo è questo'). Giovanni's conquests total 640 in Italy, 230 in Germany, 100 in France, 91 in Turkey, and in Spain, 1003. Bubbling patter is succeeded by a luscious minuet as Leporello classifies the women who have yielded; although willing to seduce anybody, Giovanni prefers the young beginner (an orchestral and tonal shiver underlines this depravity).

[*Mid-morning*] Peasants invade the stage (a bucolic G major chorus). Attracted to the bride, Zerlina, Giovanni invites everyone to his house. He dismisses the jealous Masetto, who upbraids Zerlina in an action aria ('Ho capito, signor, sì') before being dragged away by Leporello. Giovanni flatters Zerlina with an offer of marriage (duettino, 'Là ci darem la mano'). 'Vorrei, e non vorrei', she sings: I would, yet I would not. Held by the hand, and following his melodic lead, Zerlina still worries about Masetto, but her impending submission is not in doubt, and their voices join in a pastoral 6/8 ('Andiam, andiam mio bene'). Elvira intervenes with a homily to Zerlina. 'Ah fuggi il traditor' is a very short aria of Baroque vigour and formality, ending with strident coloratura.

Anna and Ottavio greet Giovanni as a friend, who will help in their quest for vengeance; murmuring that the devil is frustrating all his plans, he offers his assistance with exaggerated courtesy. Elvira interrupts again; recognizing a social equal in Anna, she tells her in measured tones not to trust Giovanni (quartet, 'Non ti fidar, o misera'). Anna and Ottavio are perplexed; Giovanni tries to hush Elvira, explaining to the others that she is mad. In the course of this finely wrought ensemble her denunciation grows more vehement, even shameless. She leaves and Giovanni makes an excuse to follow, but something in his farewell tells Anna that this was the man who had tried to seduce her the previous night. The harrowing description of her ordeal (*recitativo obbligato*) revives the turbulent spirit of the first scene; her aria in D major ('Or sai chi l'onore') embodies both steely determination and lamentation which nearly disrupts an unusually symmetrical form. Ottavio can hardly believe Giovanni's villainy, but his role is to support Anna. The exquisite aria, 'Dalla sua pace' K540a, added for the Vienna production, is well placed here.

Giovanni congratulates Leporello on disposing of Elvira, and prepares for a good afternoon's work (aria, 'Fin ch'han dal vino'); wine will warm up the guests, they will mix the minuet, follia and allemande, and ten names will be added to the catalogue.

Giovanni's garden [afternoon]   In Mozart's most enchanting melodic vein, with cello obbligato, Zerlina wins Masetto back in her aria 'Batti, batti' (like 'Là ci darem' it begins in 2/4 and ends in a honeyed 6/8). Yet when she hears Giovanni's voice she is obviously aroused. The finale begins as Giovanni gives orders to his servants. Espying Zerlina as she tries to hide, he resumes his blandishments. Masetto pops out of hiding to interrupt the scene, and is greeted with amused irony by Giovanni. To the sound of a contredanse they go inside. Elvira leads Anna and Ottavio, masked, towards Giovanni's lair. Leporello sees them (a minuet is now heard from the window), and they are invited in. Their short prayer ('Protegga il giusto ciel') is a moment of stillness at the heart of one of Mozart's most active finales.

The ballroom   To music resembling the earlier bucolic chorus, Giovanni and Leporello entertain the peasants. Masetto urges prudence on his bride. The central key-change from E♭ to C, resplendent with trumpets, greets the masked trio with the acclamation 'Viva la libertà!'. Now in G major, in a tour de force using three small stage bands, the ball resumes. The minuet already heard is danced by Anna and Ottavio; on it are superimposed the contredanse (also already heard), which is in 2/4 with the same pulse, three bars to every two of the minuet; this is the 'follia' of Giovanni's prescription and is danced by Giovanni and Zerlina. Finally the 'teitsch' (Allemande) begins in bars of 3/8 superimposed upon each beat of the other dances. At this point Leporello forces Masetto to dance with him, and Giovanni drags Zerlina out. She screams; Masetto rushes after them; G major is destroyed by flat keys, and then an ascent via F to the tonic C as Giovanni complacently blames Leporello and offers to kill him on the spot. The masked trio reveal themselves and with Zerlina and Masetto denounce Giovanni, who is momentarily nonplussed before outfacing them all in a whirlwind conclusion.

ACT 2 *A street*   Giovanni scorns Leporello's furious attempts to resign (duet, 'Eh via buffone'). A purse changes hands, but when Leporello asks his master to give up women, he claims to need them 'as much as the food I eat and the air I breathe'. His love is universal; faithfulness to one women betrays the rest. Leporello is forced to change clothes for the seduction of Elvira's maid. It is twilight; Elvira, on a balcony, tries to repress her desire for Giovanni but her fluttering heart betrays her (trio, 'Ah taci, ingiusto core'). Giovanni adopts her melody, but in the more intense dominant (sonata form perfectly matches Mozart's dramatic requirements). In the middle section his ardour is extreme; exploring a remote key (C within the

dominant region of A), he anticipates the melody of his serenade. She denounces him; he presses her; she weakens; though he pities her, Leporello
can hardly help laughing aloud. She comes down and the disguised Leporello, told to keep her occupied, begins to enjoy wooing her. Giovanni
chases them away and to a mandolin accompaniment serenades the maid
(canzonetta, 'Deh vieni alla finestra'). But Masetto and a group of peasants, bearing crude weapons, are after his blood. The false Leporello pretends to sympathize, and in an action aria ('Metà di voi quà vadano') he
gives instructions on how to search the streets and recognize the villain—
in reality himself, described with narcissistic relish. He keeps Masetto with
him and then beats him up. Hearing his groans, Zerlina offers the balm
only she can provide; a heart-easing melody in a gentle 3/8 invites Masetto
to lay his hand on her bosom (aria, 'Vedrai, carino').

A courtyard at Anna's house   Leporello, seeing lights, retreats with Elvira
into the darkness, intent on abandoning her. She begs him not to leave
her; he gropes for the exit (sextet, 'Sola in buio loco'; in E♭). A moment of
magic—soft trumpets and drums mark a key-change from the dominant
(B♭) to D—brings Anna and Ottavio with servants and lights, the others
being concealed. His renewed plea for marriage, and her prevarication, un-
fold in long melodic spans which draw the tonality down to C minor.
Elvira resumes her search for 'Giovanni', and Leporello his for the gate,
but on the way out he is caught by Zerlina and Masetto. All denounce the
betrayer, in a scene of unreality (for the true villain is absent) made pathetic by Elvira's plea for mercy, and comic by Leporello's terror and ab-
ject submission when his identity is revealed. The sextet resembles a short
finale, ending with a huge ensemble of consternation, but the action continues. They all turn on Leporello, who babbles excuses as he escapes (aria,
'Ah pietà, Signori miei'). Ottavio decides to go to the authorities; he asks
the others to watch over Anna. His aria, 'Il mio tesoro', is a full-length virtuoso piece accompanied by muted strings and clarinets.

[In the Vienna version, after the sextet, Leporello escapes in a recitative,
using a motif from the Prague aria; Ottavio decides to go to the authorities, but has no aria. Zerlina drags Leporello back and ties him up, threatening dire punishment (duet, 'Per queste tue manine'); Leporello again
escapes. Masetto claims to have prevented another of Giovanni's crimes.
Elvira vents her mixed feelings (*recitativo obbligato*, 'In quali eccessi' and
aria, 'Mi tradì'), a piece of vertiginous emotion embodied in perpetual-
motion quavers, and one of Mozart's most compelling and moving arias.]

A graveyard [*night*]   Giovanni escapes an unspecified adventure by leap-
ing over the wall into the churchyard. Leporello joins him, complaining

that once again he has nearly been killed. Giovanni heartlessly narrates his conquest of Leporello's girl; his laughter is rebuked by the statue of the Commendatore (an oracular utterance, with trombones). They locate the statue and Leporello is forced to read the inscription: 'I await vengeance on the villain who slew me'. Giovanni forces Leporello to invite the statue to supper. This sinister situation is handled as a *buffo* duet ('O statua gentilissima') mainly reflecting the fear of Leporello as he approaches and retreats. The statue nods, then sings its acceptance; even Giovanni is puzzled and subdued, but he leads Leporello off to prepare the meal.

A darkened room in Anna's house   Ottavio is again pressing his suit; he calls Anna cruel. She protests at the word (*recitativo obbligato*, 'Crudele! Ah nò, mio bene'): but society would frown on an immediate wedding. The recitative anticipates the Larghetto of the aria ('Non mi dir'), an undulating melody of great sweetness. In the Allegro she hopes that heaven will take pity on her; the blossoming coloratura corresponds to the strength of her resolve. In a brief recitative Ottavio determines to share her martyrdom.

A dining-room in Giovanni's house (finale)   Giovanni is enjoying a meal without waiting for his guest; Leporello is envious, and astonished at his appetite. A sequence of popular tunes (from Martín y Soler's *Una cosa rara*, Sarti's *Fra i due litiganti*, and 'Non più andrai' from *Figaro*) is played by an onstage wind band during a passage of farce: Leporello steals food and is caught with his mouth full. Elvira bursts in, making a last appeal to Giovanni to reform. He laughs at her, invites her join him, and in a flowing melody drinks a toast to wine and women, 'Sostegno e gloria d'umanità'. Recognizing that he is incorrigible, Elvira runs off in despair. From outside, she utters a piercing scream; Leporello, sent to investigate, returns in terror, babbling of the white statue taking giant strides. Knocking is heard and Leporello hides under the table. Giovanni opens the door.

The opening of the overture is heard, reinforced by trombones, as the statue enters to music which remains the apogee of the *ombra* style. His slow utterance, solemn and grand, Giovanni's responses, at first polite, then impatient, and Leporello's terrified asides, are musically characterized but subsumed to harmonic development of unparalleled complexity. The statue says he cannot take mortal food, but he invites Giovanni to sup with him. With admirable fearlessness and in a phrase of marked dignity, Giovanni accepts; but on grasping the statue's hand he is frozen and senses his impending doom. Offered a last chance to repent, he proudly refuses. The statue releases him into engulfing flames, with a chorus of demons that replicates the cadences of the vengeance duet in Act I. [*Scena ultima,*

probably cut in Vienna, 1788, and certainly in several later productions]
The other characters rush on with the police, but find only Leporello, who
stammers out enough for them to understand what has happened. In an extended Larghetto, Ottavio again pleads with Anna, but she tells him to
wait a year for their wedding. Elvira will go to a convent, Zerlina and
Masetto will marry, Leporello will find a better master. All join to point the
moral in a bright fugato: 'This is the end of the evil-doer: his death befits
his life'.

$$*\qquad*\qquad*$$

There are two authentic versions of *Don Giovanni*, the differences mainly
in the distribution of arias. Each version has only one tenor aria: when including a new aria for Elvira (Cavalieri) in Act 2, Mozart omitted 'Il mio
tesoro' as well as a short aria for Leporello. The concentration of arias in
Act 2 which results from the common practice of including those for Leporello, Ottavio, and Elvira was never the authors' intention. The additional duet for Zerlina and Leporello, its coarseness perhaps designed to
humour the Viennese, is generally omitted, but Elvira's scene with the aria
'Mi tradì' is too good to lose; some 19th-century performances, including
one in America that may have had Da Ponte's approval, removed it to Act 1.

In musical form and dramatic technique, particularly the proportion and
design of arias and ensembles, *Don Giovanni* is partly modelled on *Figaro*.
Exceptions include the 'catalogue' aria, with its fast-slow tempo pattern;
the central finale which besides the unique dance sequence covers a change
of location; and the introduction, embedded in a vast structure extending
from the overture to the end of the duet 'Fuggi, crudele'. The harmonic
language associated with Don Giovanni's fall, including that duet and the
second finale, marks a decisive departure from *buffo* norms (certainly not
anticipated by Gazzaniga, whose setting, if Mozart knew it, might have influenced Anna's first entry, but nothing else).

The designation 'dramma giocoso' by Da Ponte (not by Mozart, who
called it 'opera buffa') has no particular significance; the serious characters
are as much embroiled in the intrigue as they are in *Figaro*. The tragic elements nevertheless enabled Mozart to forge a new synthesis of *buffo* and
serious styles, and explain why *Don Giovanni* has gripped the imagination
of writers and philosophers. In particular they have been attracted by the
daemonic in Giovanni, and by the impossibility of grasping the humanity
of so mercurial a character, whose music says so little about his motivation; even 'Fin ch'han dal vino' is a set of instructions to Leporello, though
also an explosion from his joyous daemon. Whereas the other characters

are remarkably three-dimensional, Giovanni adapts the style of each of his victims, including the Commendatore who brings out the heroic in him and Leporello whom he chaffs in pure *buffo* style. He woos Anna by courtly flattery, Zerlina by condescension, Elvira's maid in the disguise that also deceives Masetto; Elvira herself he evades or mocks, or woos with false ardour (in the trio at the beginning of Act 2).

Elvira, the *mezzo carattere*, ignored in the 19th century, now seems the most interesting of the women because psychologically she is the most complex. Though the greatest singers, such as Patti, sometimes sang the *buffo* role of Zerlina, Anna, the *seria* role, attracted most interest from the romantics; E. T. A. Hoffmann suggested that she had after all been seduced by Giovanni and was in love with him rather than Ottavio, a fantasy which received comic treatment in Shaw's *Man and Superman* and which influences interpretation and production to this day. Stendhal and Kierkegaard used Giovanni to illustrate aspects of love and the erotic. Significantly Kierkegaard was aware of earlier dramatic treatments but derived his views from the music, not the libretto or the historical evolution of the character (B. Williams, in Rushton, 1981).

Don Giovanni is governed by a single idea, Giovanni's flouting of society in pursuit of sexual pleasure, which binds together a disparate set of ambivalent or comic incidents. The libretto has been unfairly criticized; its episodic nature is a condition of the subject, in which respect it differs from *Figaro* and *Così*. Divine retribution appears like an act of God, or a different life-force personified in the statue; what in previous treatments had been comic, perfunctory, or merely gruesome is raised to the sublime by Mozart's music.

Così fan tutte

[*Così fan tutte, ossia La scuola degli amanti*]

('All Women Do the Same, or The School for Lovers')

Opera buffa in two acts, K588, to a libretto by Lorenzo da Ponte; first performed in the Burgtheater, Vienna, on 26 January 1790.

The first cast consisted of Adriana Ferrarese del Bene (Fiordiligi), Luisa Villeneuve (Dorabella), Vincenzo Calvesi (Ferrando), and three stalwarts from the 1786 *Figaro*, Dorotea Bussani (Despina), Francesco Benucci (Guglielmo), and Francesco Bussani (Alfonso).

Fiordiligi	*ladies from Ferrara, sisters living*	soprano
Dorabella	*in Naples*	soprano
Guglielmo *an officer, Fiordiligi's lover*		bass
Ferrando *an officer, Dorabella's lover*		tenor
Despina *maidservant to the sisters*		soprano
Don Alfonso *an elderly philosopher*		baritone/bass

Soldiers, servants, sailors, wedding guests

Setting Naples, in the 18th century

Così fan tutte was commissioned following the successful revival of *Le nozze di Figaro* in 1789. The libretto is original, and was intended for Salieri who abandoned it after setting the first two ensembles (Brown, 1995). There is no basis for the legend that it was based on a recent Viennese scandal, but it has mythological and literary ancestry in the Procris story, and in Boccaccio, Shakespeare (*Cymbeline*), and Cervantes, all of whom anticipate the driving motif of the plot: the wager that leads to a trial of female constancy and, at least potentially, to distrust and disaster.

Così fan tutte was rehearsed at Mozart's apartment on 31 December, and in January with Haydn present. It received five performances before the death of Joseph II on 20 February closed the theatres; five more followed from June to August. There is little information about its early reception. Performances followed in 1791 in Prague, Leipzig, and Dresden, and in German in Frankfurt (as *Liebe und Versuchung*), Mainz, and Amsterdam. At Leipzig in 1794 and in other centres it appeared as *Weibertreue, oder Die Mädchen sind von Flandern*, translated by C. F. Bretzner, author of the source of *Die Entführung*. No opera of Mozart received such frequent 'improvement' or so many alternative titles, but the standard German became *So machen es alle*. The alleged immorality of the libretto encouraged such treatment. One variant had the ladies learn of the plot from Despina and avenge themselves by pretending to yield, thus turning the tables on their lovers. Critical opinion in the 19th century branded it one of Mozart's weaker pieces, and the music appeared in pasticcios or with a completely different story. The 20th century, thanks partly to Richard Strauss, revived it in its original form and began to take it seriously; nowadays even Mozart's own cuts are sometimes restored. *Così* was the second opera performed at Glyndebourne (1934), and productions since World War II are too numerous to mention; it is by now as much a staple of the repertory as the other Mozart-Da Ponte operas.

*   *   *

The short introduction to the overture concludes with a motto, a double cadence of striking simplicity (*piano*, interrupted, then *forte*, perfect), later sung to the words of the title. The sonata-form Presto mockingly tosses a figure among the woodwinds, and its cadence is taken from Basilio's line 'Così fan tutte le belle' from the Act 1 trio in *Figaro*. The motto reappears just before the end.

ACT 1 *A coffee-house*   Ferrando and Guglielmo proclaim the virtues of the sisters Dorabella and Fiordiligi, to whom, respectively, they are betrothed; Alfonso is sceptical (trio, 'La mia Dorabella'). The young men prepare to defend the ladies' honour with swords, but the diatonic brilliance of music shared by all three argues no great discord. Alfonso declines to fight, but calls them simpletons to trust female constancy: a faithful woman is like a phoenix; all believe in it but none has seen it (trio, 'È la fede delle femmine': his mocking *pianissimo* unison cadence resembles the motto). The lovers insist that the phoenix is Dorabella/Fiordiligi. Alfonso wagers 100 zecchini that fidelity will not endure a day of the lovers' absence; he will prove it if they promise to obey him while wooing each other's betrothed in disguise. Ferrando plans to spend his winnings on a serenade, Guglielmo (the first division between them) on a meal; Alfonso listens politely (trio, 'Una bella serenata'). An extended orchestral coda closes a scene of purely *buffo* electricity.

A garden by the sea [*morning*]   Fiordiligi and Dorabella sing rapturously to the portraits of their lovers (duet, 'Ah guarda sorella'); Dorabella (surprisingly, in view of the sequel) touches a note of melancholy before they launch into voluptuous coloratura in 3rds, united in loving the idea of loving. Alfonso appears, the prolonged F minor cadences of his tiny aria ('Vorrei dir') choking back the awful news: their lovers are to leave for active service. The men take solemn leave with only hints at lyricism (quintet, 'Sento, o Dio'). The girls' agitation is coloured by the dominant minor; Alfonso quells any premature delight at this evidence of love. Ferrando's lyricism (to a motif from the trio, 'Una bella serenata') now matches the girls'; Guglielmo sings with Alfonso (this inevitable consequence of differences in tessitura continually invites differentiation of character). The girls declare they will die; in a prepared speech (duettino, 'Al fato dan legge', usually omitted) their lovers promise to return. A march is heard (chorus, 'Bella vita militar'). The lovers embrace, promising a daily letter, their rapturous indulgence in misery (particularly intense in the melodic line, taken by Fiordiligi) counterpointed by Alfonso's efforts not to laugh (quintet, 'Di scrivermi ogni giorno'). The men embark (reprise of the chorus); Alfonso joins a moving prayer for their safety (trio, 'Soave sia il vento'), the orchestra evocative yet sensuous, in the E major also used for such scenes in *Zaide* and *Idomeneo*. Alfonso prepares for action (arioso); 'He ploughs the waves, sows in sand, traps the wind in a net, who trusts the heart of a woman'.

A furnished room   Despina has prepared the ladies' chocolate and is sampling it when they burst in. Dorabella explains their despair, but extravagant grief renders her barely coherent (*recitativo obbligato* and the first real aria, 'Smanie implacabili'). Despina cannot take them seriously; surely they can find other lovers. In the teeth of their protests she inverts Alfonso's creed (aria, 'In uomini'): men, especially soldiers, are not expected to be faithful; women should also use love to enjoy themselves. Alfonso bribes Despina to assist him, without revealing the plot. The men enter as 'Albanians', their bizarre disguise impenetrable even to the sharp-witted Despina (sextet, 'Alla bella Despinetta'). The ladies hear men's voices and come to investigate (Alfonso meanwhile concealing himself). Despina helps the lovers plead for a moment's kindness; they are rejected in a furious Allegro, ending the sextet which, like that in *Don Giovanni*, resembles a miniature finale.

Alfonso, emerging, claims the 'Albanians' as old friends, but after the men's voices unite, turning recitative towards arioso, Fiordiligi articulates her constancy in a powerful recitative and aria ('Come scoglio'); she stands firm as a rock in tempestuous seas. The three sections grow in brilliance and versatility; near the start, after leaps of a 10th and 12th, she ascends majestically over two octaves (the total range is *a-c'''*); near the end she doubles the bass line. Guglielmo's patter-song in praise of his own appearance (especially the moustaches) finds no favour ('Non siate ritrosi'; the original longer aria, 'Rivolgete a lui lo sguardo', K584, was jettisoned). As the outraged girls depart, the men bubble with delight (trio, 'E voi ridete?'), ignoring Alfonso's insistence that the more girls protest, the surer they are to fall. Guglielmo wonders when they can get lunch; Ferrando enjoys the atmosphere of love ('Un' aura amorosa'), muted violins and (at the reprise) clarinets supporting his ardently extended line.

The garden [afternoon] Finale.   The girls unwittingly share Ferrando's mood of longing, spinning a tender D major melody to a gently ironic rococo decoration of flutes and bassoons. How their fate has changed! Their sighs are displaced by fear when the men rush in drinking poison, to music (in G minor) suggestive of impending tragedy. Alfonso and Despina go for help, instructing the ladies to nurse the men, who are thoroughly enjoying themselves pretending to be about to die; yet minor modes prevail as never before in Mozart's finales. Despina, to a pompous G major minuet, appears disguised as the doctor, invoking Mesmer as she magnetizes the poison away. The key abruptly changes to B♭: the men profess to believe they are in paradise. In the final Allegro (in D) the men request a kiss and are again rebuffed.

ACT 2 *A room*   Despina tries to persuade her shocked employers that there is no harm in a little flirtation. In Mozart's slyest *buffa* aria for soprano ('Una donna a quindici anni'), she explains that a young girl who knows the arts of attracting men can have them at her mercy. The girls agree that there can be nothing wrong in enjoying the men's company, and they select partners (duet, 'Prenderò quel brunettino'). Dorabella will take the brown-haired one (Guglielmo), Fiordiligi the blond (Ferrando), thus falling in with the men's plan.

Furnished garden by the sea [early evening]   The serenade on wind instruments, repeated by the lovers and chorus ('Secondate, aurette amiche'), is a prayer for success in love. The four meet but are tongue-tied; Alfonso and Despina give a lesson in etiquette, and join their hands (quartet, the sisters present but silent, 'La mano a me date'). The couples separate to tour the garden. Guglielmo is all too successful in winning Dorabella's heart and a mark of her favour, replacing Ferrando's portrait by his own gift, a pendant heart (duet, 'Il core vi dono'). The gently bantering 3/8, in F major, matches Dorabella's innocent flirtatiousness; Guglielmo can hardly believe his own success, but falls comfortably in with her mood. As they leave, Fiordiligi rushes in, pursued by Ferrando: she has seen in him temptation, a serpent, a basilisk; he is stealing her peace of mind. He protests that he wants only her happiness and asks for a kindly glance, notes when she looks at him, and sighs. Her lovely soul will not long resist his pleading; otherwise her cruelty will kill him ('Ah lo veggio quell'anima bella'). As in 'Un'aura amorosa', clarinets are added at the reprise of this aria, a lightly flowing rondo with an ending of unexpected intensity. It is traditionally omitted, but without it Ferrando's exit is inexplicable. Fiordiligi wrestles with her conscience, her *recitativo obbligato* ('Ei parte') running a gamut of feeling while traversing tonal space from B♭ to E. Her searching rondò ('Per pietà, ben mio') expresses her despair and desire for forgiveness from her absent lover. The elaborate wind parts (notably the horns) recall the obbligato groupings in earlier arias, while the wide vocal range and coloratura again evoke the formal beauty of arias in *opera seria*. There has been no *recitativo secco* since before the duet for Guglielmo and Dorabella; the symmetry of the couplings breaks down in an unparalleled 400 bars of orchestrated music.

The men compare notes. When he learns of Dorabella's fickleness Ferrando is roused to fury (*recitativo obbligato*, 'Il mio ritratto! Ah perfida!'). Guglielmo tries to console him by adopting Alfonso's philosophy (aria, 'Donne mie la fate a tanti'); he is fond of women and defends their honour, but their little habit of deceiving men is reprehensible. The restless perpetual motion conveys Guglielmo's confidence that no such tragedy will befall him. Ferrando's feelings are in turmoil (*recitativo obbligato*, 'In qual fiero contrasto'). An obsessive orchestral figure projects his shame ('Alfonso! how you will laugh!') and anger ('I will cut the wretch out of my heart') to a degree beyond the decorum of comedy. In a cavatina ('Tradito, schernito') he denounces Dorabella's treachery but admits (clarinets entering as C minor turns to E♭ major) that he still loves her. Alfonso and Guglielmo overhear the reprise in which the E♭ melody recurs in C, oboes replacing clarinets: this new instrumental colour (his previous arias used no oboes) may be prophetic. His pride piqued, he agrees to a further attack on Fiordiligi.

A room, with several doors, a mirror, and a table Despina praises Dorabella's good sense; Dorabella answers Fiordiligi's protests in a graceful 6/8 aria ('È amore un ladroncello') which despite its sophisticated instrumentation shows her conversion to Despina's easy virtue; love is a thief, a serpent, but if you let him have his way, he brings delight. Alone, Fiordiligi resolves to repel her new suitor. Sadistically observed by the men, she prepares to join her lover at the front, and orders Despina to bring Guglielmo's uniform. She launches what she clearly means to be an aria ('Fra gli amplessi'), but as she quickens the tempo from Adagio Ferrando joins her, turning it into a duet. Her anguished plea holds a striking allusion to Ferrando's first phrase in the Act 1 trio for the men, 'Una bella serenata', and the key-scheme (reaching C major from A) parallels the seduction trio in *Don Giovanni*. Ferrando's lyricism now outdoes Fiordiligi's, striking a note of true ardour when the acceleration of tempo is halted by a Larghetto (back in A); it is hard not to believe that Ferrando is sincere. Despite a high a'' on 'crudel', Fiordiligi's responses are tremulous; the solo oboe rises above her voice, speaking for her, as she admits defeat ('hai vinto'). The fourth (Andante) section of this greatest of Mozart's duets combines their voices in an intimacy never vouchsafed to the other couple.

Guglielmo is enraged; Ferrando responds with irony; Alfonso tells them their only revenge is to marry their 'plucked crows'. Women are always accused of fickleness, but he forgives them; they are not responsible for their own nature ('Tutti accusan le donne'). All three sing the motto from the overture: 'Così fan tutte'.

A reception room prepared for a wedding Finale.   In an Allegro, resembling the opera's opening number, Despina orders the servants to a prepare a feast (there is a brief choral response), and Alfonso applauds their work. The chorus greets the couples; in their carefree response, an accident of casting matches the composer's dramatic insight by bringing Fiordiligi and Ferrando together in expansive coloratura. With Dorabella they sing the toast, a ravishing canon of a type made popular in Viennese opera, particularly by Martín y Soler. Guglielmo, whose vocal range prevents him from singing the melody, mutters curses instead, whereas Ferrando appears reconciled to his new situation.

Alfonso enters with Despina disguised as a notary. Coughing formally, she reads out a marriage contract, and the ladies sign it. At that moment the Act 1 march, associated with the officers' departure, is heard. Consternation: their original lovers must be returning. The 'Albanians' are bundled into hiding, but Ferrando and Guglielmo soon reappear jauntily, as their old selves, pretending puzzlement at their reception. They discover the notary, who reveals herself as Despina in fancy dress, but then find the marriage contract: indignation, confession, blame (on Alfonso). Threatening revenge, the men go to seek the Albanians, and return half-changed back.

Ferrando greets Fiordiligi, apparently quoting earlier music subsequently abandoned, Guglielmo greets Dorabella, quoting their duet, and both address the flabbergasted Despina as the doctor, quoting the first finale. Alfonso calms them down; the girls beg pardon; the men condescend to forgive, and all agree to follow Alfonso's idea of reason: to laugh when there is cause to weep, and so find equilibrium.

*   *   *

Così fan tutte was long considered a heartless farce clothed in miraculous music, a view supported by its obvious artificiality (the lovers' disguises, the 24-hour time-scale). A number of cuts, particularly of second-act arias, became customary. Recently directors and critics have sought deeper meanings, and even questioned the restoration of the original pairing of lovers, which may reasonably be assumed from the conventionality of the conclusion, but which is not specified in the libretto or confirmed by anything in the music.

Così has been seen as revealing a misogynist dark side to the Enlightenment, even sadism (Ford, 1991). Yet by any showing the most admirable character is Fiordiligi, and the women develop more than the men. Dorabella learns to understand her own lightness; and 'Fra gli amplessi' suggests that Fiordiligi has matured through learning the power of sexuality. There is little sign that Guglielmo learns anything, even that those who set traps deserve to get caught, although his vanity is wounded as deeply as his purse. Ferrando, however, comes to live as intensely as Fiordiligi, and may appear to have fallen in love with her. To suggest that they should marry (leaving Guglielmo for Dorabella) is, however, still less satisfactory than reversion to the original pairings. The conclusion represents not a solution but a way of bringing the action to a close; its artificiality is so evident that the outcome of the imbroglio cannot be predicted. The music creates this enigma, but cannot resolve it.

By standards other than Mozart's, the instrumentation in *Così* would be of novel richness. The inclusion of B♭ trumpets, not previously used in the Vienna operas, allows their substitution for horns in 'Come scoglio' and 'Ah lo veggio', divorced from their usual companions, the timpani; three other numbers also use trumpets without horns. The resourceful use of woodwinds, application of string mutes, and exploration of a wider than usual range of keys and key relations create an unprecedentedly voluptuous colouring (E major and A♭ major are juxtaposed in the second finale, and the former is used in three other numbers, a concentration unusual in Mozart).

Much of the style of *Così* has been attributed to parody, but stylistic mixture had long been a feature of *opera buffa*. Guglielmo sings pure *buffo* arias, but Ferrando's strike serious notes reflected in the variety of their forms. The girls' first arias overplay feelings which will not endure: Dorabella's prolonged cadences in 'Smanie implacabili' recall Alfonso's mock-seriousness in 'Vorrei dir'. 'Come scoglio' is sometimes considered pure parody, Fiordiligi's second aria 'Per pietà' essentially serious; yet the latter has equally wide leaps and even more florid instrumentation, the differences in perception of them being explicable by the fact that one administers a rebuff to the 'Albanian' strangers, and the other, following the dangerous attack on her loyalty to Guglielmo, is an internal monologue. Both are distinct in style from the over-the-top parody of a virtuoso soprano in *Die Schauspieldirektor*.

There are fewer arias in *Così* than in the other Da Ponte operas, but they are correspondingly more important in unfolding the inner drama. The increased number of ensembles is balanced by the brevity of several, not only the sparkling *buffo* trios for the men but also 'Soave sia il vento', a gem that bids farewell to innocence as well as to the lovers. There is a marked increase in the amount of *recitativo obbligato*, which with the tone of some of the arias (notably Fiordiligi's) brings *Così* closer to *opera seria* than the other Da Ponte operas.

Così fan tutte is likely to remain an unsettling experience because of, rather than despite, its aesthetic attractions. Since the libretto was originally destined for Salieri, we do not know exactly what form it would have taken had he decided to set all of it; even in the final version, its superb pacing cannot disguise the potential to fall back on triviality, and, prior to the modern feminist interpretation, that was a common approach in productions. Mozart found in it ways to seek out hitherto unplumbed depths in the human psyche, making the uncut whole, for an increasing audience, the most disturbing of his Italian comedies.

La clemenza di Tito

('The Clemency of Titus')

Opera seria in two acts, K621, to a libretto by Pietro Metastasio, some situations derived from Pierre Corneille's *Cinna, ou la Clémence d'Auguste*, and adapted by Caterino Mazzolà. It was first performed in the National Theatre, Prague, on 6 September 1791.

The first cast was Antonio Baglioni (Titus), Maria Marchetti-Fantozzi (Vitellia), Domenico Bedini (Sextus), Carolina Perini (Annius), Gaetano Campi, well known as a *buffo* singer (Publius), and 'Signora Antonini' (Servilia).

Tito [Titus Flavius Vespasianus] *Roman Emperor*	tenor
Vitellia *daughter of the deposed Emperor Vitellius*	soprano
Servilia *sister of Sextus, in love with Annius*	soprano
Sesto [Sextus] *friend of Titus, in love with Vitellia*	soprano castrato
Annio [Annius] *friend of Sextus, in love with Servilia*	soprano, breeches role
Publio [Publius] *prefect of the praetorian guard*	bass

Senators, ambassadors, praetorian guards, lictors, Roman people

Setting Rome, AD *c*.80

Although mostly composed after *Die Zauberflöte*, *La clemenza di Tito* was performed first. The impresario Guardasoni obtained an open commission from the Bohemian Estates in July 1791, for an opera designed to celebrate Leopold II's coronation as King of Bohemia, and to some degree adapted to his particular taste. The commission was offered to Salieri, who declined it, after which it came to Mozart. Contrary to received opinion, the commission was far from unwelcome; Mozart wanted to impress the new regime and one way to do so might be to show his strength in *opera seria.*

Metastasio's libretto, already set by more than 40 composers, was 'ridotta a vera opera' ('reduced to a proper opera'), as Mozart wrote in his catalogue. Only seven arias and one chorus (designated 'Metastasio' below) were unchanged; Metastasio's aria and recitative texts were manipulated in the ensembles and finales devised by Mazzolà, who for a short time occupied Da Ponte's former position as Imperial poet. Reduced by a third, the libretto gains clarity and the musical numbers pertinence, at some cost to dramatic weight.

Mozart probably composed all of *La clemenza* between late July and September 1791. He arrived in Prague on 28 August and finished work on the eve of the performance. The chief artistic drawback of the short time available was that Mozart sub-contracted the simple recitatives, probably to Franz Xaver Süssmayr. The choruses and ensembles were worked out with Mazzolà in Vienna and written there, as were some arias. The singer Mozart knew best was Baglioni, two of whose arias were written in Vienna; the only ensemble composed in Prague (the trio early in Act 2) probably replaced intended arias for Vitellia and Sextus. Problems in these roles are apparent from surviving sketch and autograph material. Mozart began by assuming that Sextus would be a tenor, and Vitellia's 'Non più di fiori', the Act 2 rondò, is distinctly lower in tessitura than the rest of the role.

The first-night reception before royalty and its hangers-on was modest, but the Prague audience enjoyed the work and a triumphant last night was reported to Mozart (who had left Prague on 15 September) on the day of the premiere of *Die Zauberflöte* (30 September). Concert performances of extracts and of the whole opera were arranged by Constanze Mozart for her own benefit after Mozart's death. In Vienna on 29 December 1791 and in later performances Aloysia Lange sang Sextus. After a further performance in Vienna in 1795 Constanze took the work to Graz, Leipzig, and Berlin, herself singing Vitellia. In 1796 a German translation by Rochlitz was performed in Dresden and used in most German centres (including Vienna) within the next 15 years. The first performance outside Germany and Austria was also the first of any Mozart opera in London, on 27 March 1806, for the benefit of Mrs Billington. Performances followed in all the main European centres, usually in Italian (1809, Naples; 1816, Paris and Milan; 1817, in Russian, St Petersburg). Although few productions adhered faithfully to Mozart's score, *La clemenza di Tito* was one of Mozart's most popular operas until about 1830, after which it went into eclipse. It has never fully entered the modern repertory and was often described as unworthy, hastily assembled for a commission Mozart could not refuse. Critical estimates have risen since World War II, and it is now seen as a positive step towards further reform of *opera seria*.

*   *   *

Despite its lack of overt thematic connection with the rest of the opera, the fine overture has been described as a dramatic argument according to Gluck's principles (Heartz, 1991). The form, with reversed recapitulation, is unusual in Mozart.

ACT I *Vitellia's apartments*   Titus is reportedly in love with the Jewish queen Berenice; Vitellia denies being jealous, but believes she, an emperor's daughter, should be his consort. Overtly motivated by the need to avenge her father, she induces Sextus to lead an assassination plot. Though a loyal friend of Titus, he adores her blindly and cannot resist her commands. He begs her to say how he can please her, for she is his destiny (duet, 'Come ti piace, imponi'). She asks why he is delaying; he requests only a tender glance. In the Allegro, both admit the confusion of their feelings. Annius reports that Titus has dismissed Berenice for reasons of state. Vitellia hopes she herself may be chosen, and tells Sextus to suspend the plot without giving a reason. In measured tones (a slow minuet) she declares that to win her he must not exhaust her with suspicions (Metastasio: 'Deh se piacer me vuoi'). The following Allegro returns to the opening words; its principal message, conveyed in a capricious mixture of sturdy rhythms and decorative flourishes, is that doubt merely encourages deception. Annius asks Sextus for his sister's hand, which he gladly grants in the duettino ('Deh prendi un dolce amplesso'), a winning expression of brotherly affection.

Before the Roman forum   Senators and delegates from the provinces gather at the heart of the Imperial city. Titus enters in state, with lictors, guards, and citizens. A march leads directly to a chorus in praise of the emperor (Metastasio: 'Serbate, o dei custodi'). After formal expressions of homage from Publius and Annius, Titus replies that his sole aim is to be a good father to his people. The chorus is repeated; Titus calls for Sextus, and the stage is cleared during a repeat of the march. Private conversation (with Annius present) reveals the close friendship of Sextus and Titus. The emperor must publicly deny his love for Berenice by taking a Roman wife; who better than his friend's sister? Annius bravely eulogizes the emperor's choice. In a mellow Andante (Metastasio: 'Del più sublime soglio') Titus declares that the only happiness afforded by supreme power is to reward virtue. Annius reveals the emperor's decision to Servilia; the exquisite melody of their farewell (duet, 'Ah perdona al primo affetto') touches a nerve of painful tenderness within this severely political opera.

A garden in the Imperial palace on the Palatine To Publius Titus expounds his philosophy of disarming enmity by forgiveness. Servilia dares to confess that she and Annius are in love; he thanks heaven for her frankness, and releases her (Metastasio: 'Ah, se fosse intorno al trono'). The sweep of the melody in this short Allegro conveys his open-hearted nature; if the throne were flanked by such honesty, the cares of office would turn to joy. Vitellia bitterly compliments Servilia who, piqued, does not reveal that she has refused the emperor. Deaf to reason, Vitellia upbraids Sextus for dilatoriness: Titus must die. Before embarking on his fatal mission he asks again for the loving glance which destroys his loyalty and assures his happiness (Metastasio: 'Parto, parto'). This aria with basset clarinet obbligato is in three sections, accelerating, as sentiment yields to determination, from a nobly extended Adagio through an impassioned Allegro ('Guardami, e tutto obblio') to a brilliant conclusion. Publius and Annius announce to Vitellia that she is after all the emperor's chosen consort (this moment of dramatic irony is the end of Metastasio's first act). In the trio ('Vengo! aspettate!'), the others mistake her confusion for excess of joy and comment sympathetically, but she is terrified that it is too late to stop the plot. This gripping movement is dominated by Vitellia's agitation, expressed in gasping phrases and, when the musical line is more sustained, cruelly high tessitura (touching d'''').

A portico before the Capitol Sextus has launched the conspiracy, but is wracked by guilt (*recitativo obbligato*); his weakness has made him a traitor. He cannot turn back; the Capitol is already in flames. The bulk of the finale is an action ensemble. Sextus, in words Metastasio intended as recitative, seems to launch an aria (a prayer for Titus's safety), but when Annius appears, he can only babble of his shame and rush away. Annius is prevented from following by the need to keep Servilia out of danger. Cries of horror are heard from the offstage chorus; Publius appears, fearing for Titus, then Vitellia, frantically searching for Sextus. He returns, looking for a place to hide; all believe Titus dead. Sextus is about to confess, but Vitellia silences him. In a concluding Andante all the characters and the distant chorus join in lamenting the murderous treachery.

ACT 2 *Palace gardens* Annius tells Sextus that Titus is alive. Sextus admits that he instigated the plot, refusing to give any reason. Annius gently urges him to throw himself on the emperor's mercy ('Torna di Tito a lato'), this sound advice emphasized by his repetition, to the end, of 'torna' ('return'). Vitellia warns Sextus that he will be arrested, but she comes too late; Publius enters with guards. In the trio ('Se a volto mai ti senti') the principal melodic ideas belong to Sextus, bidding Vitellia a lingering farewell; the music darkens suddenly as her admiration for his devotion conflicts with her fear that he will implicate her. In the Allegretto, Sextus asks Vitellia to remember his love; she is gripped with remorse; Publius, though touched, remains firm (Metastasio's second act ends here).

A large room in the palace, with a writing-table   The chorus (patricians, praetorian guards, and people) thank Fate for sparing Titus ('Ah grazie si rendano'). In the middle section of this serene Andante, Titus thanks them for their loyalty. He tries to understand the conspirators; Lentulus (who led the attack) is clearly guilty; perhaps he has accused Sextus to protect himself. In a short aria (Metastasio: 'Tardi, s'avvede') Publius comments that the good-natured find it hard to believe others capable of betrayal. A moment later he returns with Sextus's confession and news of his condemnation by the Senate. Annius pleads for mercy ('Tu fosti tradito'): Titus has been betrayed, but hope remains if he consults his heart (Mazzolà omits an episode in which Annius is himself accused). Bitterly hurt, Titus condemns his own hesitation in signing the death warrant, but the word 'death' stops him short (*recitativo obbligato*, 'Che orror! che tradimento!'). He sends for Sextus; incisive orchestral gestures yield to sustained harmonies as he persuades himself that he cannot refuse the hearing which justice offers the meanest citizen. Publius brings in Sextus. The first speeches are sung aside (trio, 'Quello di Tito è il volto'). Sextus's fear appears in string tremolandos, his desperation in wide intervals and an anguished turn to the minor: can this be the face of Titus? Titus can barely recognize his guilt-ridden friend; Publius witnesses the emperor's tangled emotions. Titus commands Sextus to approach, but he is rooted to the spot. The ensemble freezes in the Allegro, Sextus's angular line again dominating while the others comment on his evident terror. Titus reduces Sextus to tears of contrition by addressing him kindly. But Sextus, protecting Vitellia, cannot justify his treachery. Titus dismisses him coldly. Gathering his feelings into a nobly arching melody, Sextus asks Titus to remember their earlier friendship (rondò, 'Deh, per questo istante solo'). In the Allegro the boundaries of the tonic (A major) are twice burst by cries of despair (in C and F majors); its gentler principal melody ('Tanto affanno soffre un core') becomes hectic in the faster coda.

Left alone, Titus signs the fatal paper, then tears it up; he is no Brutus, and cannot begin a career of tyranny by executing a friend. He tells Publius only that Sextus's fate is settled. In his aria (Metastasio: 'Se all' impero, amici dei') he asserts that if the gods require an emperor to be cruel, they must deprive him of his empire, or give him another heart. This is the only aria in the modern equivalent of da capo form; its weight, balanced by considerable floridity, prepares fully for Titus's renunciation of revenge, while underlining his strength of purpose in a march-like coda.

Publius tells Vitellia he has heard nothing of the emperor's conversation with Sextus. Annius and Servilia ask the empress-designate to intercede. Servilia's lightly scored minuet (Metastasio: 'S'altro che lagrime') is a gentle but penetrating plea; weeping is not enough to save Sextus. Moved by Sextus's constancy, Vitellia is at the point of decision (*recitativo obbligato*, 'Ecco il punto, o Vitellia'); can she betray him to die alone? No chains of flowers will accompany the descent of Hymen (rondò, 'Non più di fiori'); the music, with basset-horn obbligato, paints the serene image which she must renounce. Her despair breaks out in the Allegro ('Infelice! qual orrore!'); she cannot live knowing the horror of what she has done. The aria merges into a transition with the character of a slow march.

A public place, before a temple The chorus acclaims the godlike emperor ('Che del ciel'). Annius and Servilia ask for mercy, but Titus addresses Sextus with severity. Before he can pronounce sentence (which all assume will be death) Vitellia intervenes, claiming sole responsibility for the conspiracy. Titus is bewildered; he was about to absolve one criminal, and another appears (*recitativo obbligato*, 'Ma, che giorno'). But he defies the stars to deter him; all must be forgiven. In the finale they praise him and he rewards them with his confidence, wishing to die when Rome's good is not his chief concern. Chorus and principals together ask the gods to grant him long life.

*   *   *

La clemenza di Tito, like several of its predecessors, ends in forgiveness, here predicated in the title. The goodness of Titus (in contrast to his counterparts in *Lucio Silla* and *Die Entführung*) is apparent throughout in his arias, and the outcome of his struggle in Act 2 is inevitable; his role remained close to Metastasio's conception and his music has a correspondingly old-fashioned cut (for which Baglioni may also be partly responsible). Vitellia is capricious in the opening scenes, selfish but perplexed about her own motivation in the Act 1 trio, yet capable of noble renunciation ('Non più di fiori'). Sextus is an equally rewarding role, with two large arias and the dominant part in several ensembles.

As in *Così*, several of the musical numbers are very brief, allowing the expansion of crucial arias and the first-act finale within a short opera. The use of accompanied recitative is traditional, but the arias range from *buffo* simplicity for Servilia and Publius, through the more developed but still direct style of Annius, to the fully elaborated arias of the three main characters: of these two are rondòs, and two were given obbligatos for the clarinettist and basset-horn player Anton Stadler. In the context of *opera seria*, however, the highest originality lies in the ensembles. There is a strong predilection for movements with two tempi (the usual slow-fast being reversed in the first finale). While the folk-like duets of the first act approach the style of *Die Zauberflöte*, the trios show that *buffo* textures are equally suited to tragic situations. The first finale is unique in Mozart's output, bridging the gap between Gluck and the 19th century in the realism of its opening, its stark modulation from E♭ to G♭ (by implied C and G minors and B♭, bars 17–24), and its offstage chorus and tremolando; compared to *Idomeneo*, the sparing use of such effects corresponds to the absence of a supernatural dimension to the plot.

Had he lived to prepare further performances, Mozart would surely have replaced the simple recitatives (which in Act 2 do not always end in an appropriate key). He might have increased the orchestrated recitative to a quantity approaching that in *Così* and, as he had planned for *Idomeneo*, rearranged the vocal forces, with a tenor Sextus. Now that performances and recordings, and a general revival of 18th-century repertory, encourage reassessment of its virtues, *La clemenza di Tito* appears a conception not fully realized, but still masterly and amply rewarding study and performance.

Die Zauberflöte

('The Magic Flute')

Singspiel in two acts, K620, to a libretto by Emanuel Schikaneder; first performed in the Theater auf der Wieden, Vienna, on 30 September 1791.

Schikaneder himself sang Papageno at the première; Benedikt Schack was Tamino; the Queen was Mozart's sister-in-law Josepha Hofer; Pamina was Anna Gottlieb (the first Barbarina, still only 17); Monostatos was Johann Joseph Nouseul; Sarastro, Franz Gerl.

Sarastro *Priest of the Sun*	bass
Tamino *a Javanese Prince*	tenor
An Elderly Priest ['Sprecher'; Orator, Speaker]	bass
Three priests	bass, tenor, spoken role
The Queen of Night	coloratura soprano
Pamina *her daughter*	soprano
Three Boys	2 sopranos, mezzo-soprano
Papagena	soprano
Papageno *a birdcatcher, employed by the Queen*	baritone
Monostatos *a Moor, overseer of the Temple*	tenor
Two Men in Armour	tenor, bass
Three Slaves	spoken roles

Priests, Attendants, Acolytes, Slaves

Die Zauberflöte is an allegory set in no real locality or historical period. Ancient Egypt is evoked by the mysteries, but early productions also showed Islamic influence on costumes and neo-classical architecture appropriate to the Enlightenment. The exotic costumes and setting (and Tamino's nationality) are a mask for what may be intended as a coded representation of Freemasonry.

Carl Ludwig Gieseke (who originally played the First Slave) claimed many years later that he had contributed as much as Schikaneder to the libretto. His claim was proved false by Komorzynski and more scientifically by Rommel (Branscombe, 1991) but still receives some credence. His contribution, if any, cannot be assessed, but in Schikaneder's company collaboration was normal procedure, even in musical composition. The sources of the libretto are diverse. Christoph Martin Wieland provided the title (*Lulu, oder Die Zauberflöte*, from *Dschinnistan*) and the source of Gieseke and Wranitzky's opera *Oberon* (both 1789). Egyptological sources include Gebler's *Thamos, König in Aegypten*, for which Mozart had written incidental music with choruses anticipating the style of *Die Zauberflöte*. But in the main the libretto is original and contemporary in its significance.

There is no external evidence to assist interpretation, and it is fortunate that different interpretations based on the internal evidence can coexist. One is that the Queen represents Maria Theresia, or Catholicism more generally, and Tamino her reforming son Joseph II, while Sarastro could be Ignaz von Born (formerly Master of a masonic lodge and representative of science and the Enlightenment). The masonic allegory (evident in the Egyptian/mystic devices which illustrate the printed libretto) is transparent except for the role of Pamina (see below), and in the unlikely speed of Tamino's rise from initiate to ruler-designate. Political interpretations require more special pleading, and on a level not to be despised as insignificant, the work is also a genial fairy-tale in the form of a quest, and open to the understanding of children; Mozart's delight in his son Carl's enjoyment has been shared by parents ever since.

Die Zauberflöte was mostly composed before *La clemenza di Tito* which, however, was performed first. Mozart entered the 'Introduction' [*sic*] in his catalogue in July, but the March of Priests and Overture are dated 28 September, two days before the premiere. Schikaneder had successfully presented popular 'machine-comedies' at the out-of-town Theater an der Wieden since 1789, including *Der Stein der Weisen* in 1790, to which Mozart probably contributed music (at least the duet K625/592a) along with Schack, Gerl, and the theatre's music director Johann Baptist Henneberg. Minor parts were taken by members of the theatre company including

Schikaneder's brother and the wives of Schack and Gerl. Although it was not a fashionable venue, audiences were good and drawn from all ranks of society. Salieri attended a performance with Cavalieri, and complimented Mozart warmly. On one occasion Mozart tested Schikaneder's nerve and improvisatory powers by fooling with the glockenspiel part in his Act 2 aria.

In Vienna, there were 20 performances in the first month, and publication of extracts began in November; Schikaneder had given over 200 performances by 1800. The first Burgtheater performance was in 1801. Soon after Mozart's death *Die Zauberflöte* was given in Prague and then in all principal centres of German opera (including Warsaw and St Petersburg) before 1798. Goethe projected a sequel; one by Schikaneder, *Das Labyrinth*, was set by Mozart's erstwhile foe Peter von Winter (1798). The first British performances were in Italian (1811), and it was frequently billed as *Il flauto magico*. English-language versions reached London and New York in 1833. No major operatic centre was without a production in the 19th century, and while understanding of it may alter, its popularity has never waned. Among later presentations Ingmar Bergman's sensitive film, sung in Swedish, reached an international audience.

*   *   *

Overture: three chords (a masonic number: five if the short upbeats are counted) establish and question the tonic E♭, before a deliberate but mysterious progression to the dominant. The Allegro is monothematic, its principal idea (taken from a piano sonata by Clementi) presented in fugue and (in the dominant) as a counterpoint to smoother wind phrases. The B♭ cadence is marked by three times three tutti chords, the 'dreimalige Akkord'. The development is a tour de force and the recapitulation miraculously transforms the material by new dynamics and counterpoint.

ACT 1 *Rocky country, with trees and mountains; in the foreground a temple*
Tamino is pursued by a monstrous serpent, his terror evoked by *Sturm und Drang* gestures (Introduction, 'Zu hilfe! sonst bin ich verloren'). Three Ladies arrive; they kill the monster and triumph in the first of many delectable multi-sectioned ensembles. They take stock of the unconscious Prince and quarrel over who will remain to guard him while the others tell the Queen. Spitefully (a skipping 6/8) they decide they must all go, and make a lingering farewell.

Papageno punctuates a folk-like song about his métier with high-pitched piping ('Der Vogelfänger bin ich ja', in three strophes). In the first extended dialogue Tamino asks who he is. His answer hints at one of the work's themes: 'a man, like you'. He lives by eating and drinking; he catches birds for the starry Queen. Papageno accepts Tamino's misdirected thanks for killing the serpent, whereupon the Ladies bring him water and a stone instead of wine and bread, and padlock his mouth. They give Tamino a portrait of Pamina, the Queen's daughter. He contemplates its beauty and falls in love (aria, 'Dies Bildnis ist bezaubernd schön'). The tender appoggiaturas and pulsations bespeak his wonder and his racing heart. He is told that Pamina has been kidnapped by the tyrant Sarastro. The mountains are sundered, revealing a sumptuous chamber; the Queen is discovered on a starry throne ('O zitt're nicht, mein lieber Sohn!'; 'Do not fear, dear son'). The first part of her aria is a melting G minor Larghetto, the first music in triple time ('Zum Leiden bin ich auserkoren': her daughter's loss torments her). The fiery Allegro ('Du wirst sie zu befreien gehen') ends in giddy coloratura ascending to f'''. The aria forms Tamino's commission to rescue Pamina, and its passion and brilliance leave him no room to suspect ulterior motives. The finale to the first scene is a quintet ('Hm hm hm hm'). Papageno can only grunt until the Ladies unlock his mouth. All sing the moral: if liars were gagged brotherly love would prevail. Tamino receives a magic flute, which protects him and can change sorrow to joy. Papageno is instructed to accompany Tamino, in whom he has no confidence; Sarastro will surely eat them. He is given a chime of silver bells for his protection. To a final Andante of transcendent simplicity, clarinets entering for the first time, they are told that three wise and lovely boys will guide them.

A fine Egyptian-style chamber in Sarastro's apartment Slaves discuss Pamina's escape from the lustful Monostatos. But he has caught her after all (trio, 'Du feines Täubchen, nur herein!'). In the *buffo* style that characterizes him throughout, the Moor has the protesting maiden bound. As she faints, Papageno appears; he and Monostatos terrify each other and run away. With unexpected courage, Papageno is the first to return (if birds are black, he reasons, why not a man?). He identifies and frees Pamina, and tells her of the Prince who loves her. He, for his part, has no mate. Princess and bird-catcher reflect on the mutual dependence of wife and man: united by love, they approach the divine (duet, 'Bei Männern, welche Liebe'). This duet epitomizes the opera's moral, as well as its musical directness. With the simplest accompaniment, it consists only of two almost identical 16-bar strophes (each lightly touching on the dominant) and a coda of the same length. The pastoral 6/8 is nevertheless in E♭, the opera's 'Masonic' tonic, also the key of love in Tamino's first aria. Only Pamina's serene ornamentation differentiates the voices: it is a vision of classless, as well as domestic and sexual, harmony.

A grove, with three beautiful temples: at the back, 'Wisdom'; on the right, 'Reason'; on the left, 'Nature' The holy place is evoked by the sturdy rhythms of the trombones, silent since the overture, at the opening of the finale. The Three Boys have led Tamino here, and urge him to be steadfast, patient, and silent—the first clear hint of masonic practice. Tamino, in a recitative, assimilates his surroundings: surely this is a home of virtue. His purpose is honest; let the tyrant tremble! But his approaches to the temples of reason and nature (to music reminiscent of the Priest's speech in *Idomeneo*) are rebuffed by unseen voices. The old Priest (Orator, sometimes rendered as 'Speaker') emerges from the temple of wisdom, and in an awe-inspiring dialogue finds Tamino's sentiments worthy but his mind clouded by prejudice; he should not trust a woman's tears. He can say nothing of Pamina 'Sobald dich führt der Freundschaft Hand/Ins Heiligtum zum ew'gen Band' ('Until sacred friendship leads you by the hand to join the eternal Order'). Tamino asks when light will come to him; the unseen chorus, while the cellos repeat the Orator's arioso cadence, replies: 'Soon, or never'. They tell him Pamina is alive. In an outburst of gratitude he plays the magic flute: wild animals come to listen, but not Pamina. Then he hears Papageno's pipe, answers it, and runs after the sound. Pamina and Papageno are caught by Monostatos as he sarcastically completes their cadences. As the slaves bring chains, Papageno remembers his bells, and sets them dancing. He and Pamina celebrate their escape with the folk-like 'Könnte jeder brave Mann'. Trumpets announce Sarastro, in a chariot drawn by lions, acclaimed in the first substantial chorus. Papageno trembles but Pamina tells him the truth: her flight was not from him but from Monostatos. Sarastro reassures her, but her mother's pride is beyond forgiveness, and Pamina must stay to learn the ways of virtue from men. Monostatos brings in Tamino; he and Pamina embrace, to the chorus's surprise and Monostatos's fury. Sarastro rewards the Moor with a beating (the chorus again sings Sarastro's praise, but *sotto voce*) and orders the strangers to be veiled and led to the temple for purification. The act ends with a masonic chorus ('Wenn Tugend und Gerechtigkeit') which anticipates the end of *Fidelio*: virtue and justice will make a paradise on earth.

ACT 2 *A palm grove, with 18 seats: on each, a pyramid and a horn* The priests enter bearing palm-fronds, to strains of a solemn march, coloured by flutes, basset horns, and trombones. Punctuated by the 'dreimalige Akkord', Sarastro tells the Priests that Tamino awaits their consent to undergo the ordeals. Pamina is his destined bride and their union a defence against the malice of Night. The Orator inquires whether Tamino will endure the trial: he is, after all, a prince. More, replies Sarastro: he is a man. The scene closes with a noble invocation by Sarastro of the Egyptian gods ('O Isis und Osiris, schenket der Weisheit Geist').

A small forecourt, in darkness: thunder   The Orator tells Tamino he can still withdraw, but he is determined to seek the light. Papageno, terrified of the dark, is told he will find no wife without undergoing the trials ('I'll stay single'). But he agrees to try when he learns that he will have his reward in Papagena, whom he has not yet seen. The piquant contrast of Tamino's quest through obedience to priestly instruction, and the popular-theatre gags of Schikaneder as Papageno, continues throughout the trials. They are warned by the two priests to mistrust women's arts, and meet them with silence ('Bewahret euch vor Weibertücken'). The Three Ladies ask why they are in this place of death; they are lost if they disobey the Queen, who is already within the sacred precinct (quintet, 'Wie? Ihr an diesem Schreckensort?'). Papageno believes everything, but Tamino silences him. The Ladies try a softer approach, but admit defeat and vanish (thunder and offstage chorus), leaving Papageno fainting to a minor-mode cadence. After the threefold chords they are led to new trials.

A garden   Monostatos prepares to rape the sleeping Pamina (aria, 'Alles fühlt der Liebe Freuden'). Mozart asked the orchestra to sound distant; the piccolo and fast tempo suggest Turkish music. Why cannot a black slave share the delights of love? the moon had better close its eyes. The Queen's arrival sees him off, but she now exposes her true motivation to her daughter. She wants the power conferred by the sevenfold circle of the Sun, which her dying husband confided to the initiates. Tamino and Pamina will both be cursed unless hell's fury is assuaged by Sarastro's blood (aria, 'Der Hölle Rache'). Surpassing her Act 1 aria in brilliance (though not in difficulty), this Allegro reaches f''' four times, and adds a flood of triplet figuration; yet in addition to agility it demands the passion of a Donna Anna, with similar chromatic harmony in a vengeful D minor. Monostatos has overheard, and offers Pamina death or submission; but Sarastro intervenes, banishing the Moor. Pamina begs mercy for her mother who, he says, is punished by her own actions. His aria ('In diesen heil'gen Hallen') expresses his humanistic creed; the two verses, in E major, have the purity of folksong, the authority of wisdom. In these sacred halls, they govern not by vengeance but by love, which alone can overcome tyranny.

A large hall   The candidates are left alone, bound to silence. Papageno grumbles; his desire for a drink is answered by a very old lady bringing water. She is 18 (not 80) and her boyfriend is . . . Papageno! A thunderclap covers the sound of her own name as she is spirited away. The Three Boys bring real refreshments ('Seid uns zum zweiten Mal willkommen'). Their exquisite E major trio is a warning of imminent crisis. Tamino plays the flute, leaving Papageno to eat. Pamina enters, joyful at finding them; Tamino, mindful of instructions, turns away in silence. Her hurt is palpable in Mozart's most haunting G minor aria ('Ach, ich fühl's'), its ornate melody arched over the simplest accompaniment so that every note bears its weight of pathos. The threefold chord summons them; Papageno remains behind to continue eating.

The vault of a pyramid. Two priests carry an illuminated pyramid; others hold pyramidal lamps The happy outcome of Tamino's trials is anticipated in a radiant D major chorus ('O Isis und Osiris, welche Wonne!'). Sarastro brings Pamina to him; they must say a last farewell before the greater trials (trio, 'Soll ich dich, Teurer, nicht mehr sehn?'). Sarastro is reassuring; Tamino expresses confidence, but Pamina is full of fears, for him rather than herself. Papageno comes running but the Orator tells him he will never reach enlightenment; he would settle for a drink, and is given wine. Ringing the bells (their part more elaborate with each of the three verses), he sings his second Volkslied: all he wants is a little wife ('Ein Mädchen oder Weibchen'). The power of the bells brings her dancing in, still looking 80. Somewhat reluctantly, he promises to be true, and she is revealed as the lovely Papagena and again whisked away.

A small garden The finale is preceded by an introduction for wind band. The Three Boys evoke sunrise, which banishes darkness and death; without change of tempo, the homophonic trio develops into a dramatic quartet. The boys watch the grief-stricken Pamina greet her mother's dagger as bridegroom. At the last moment they intervene (Allegro, 3/4), restoring E♭, and with affectionate assurances lead her to Tamino.

Rocky landscape with two mountains, one gushing forth water, the other fire. After a solemn introduction two Men in Armour sing a penitential chorale melody ('Ach Gott, vom Himmel sieh' darein') over nervous counterpoint, but the text foretells the triumph of the brave. Tamino, in ritual garb (unshod), declares himself ready. Pamina calls; they respond with rapture; even death cannot separate them now. The tonality having settled into A♭, F major has the luminosity of a sharper key, and it brings Pamina ('Tamino mein! o welch'ein Glück') with the rising major 6th which seems especially significant in Mozart (as at the Count's plea for forgiveness in *Figaro*). She takes Tamino's hand: he must play the flute, which her father carved in a magic hour of violent storm, deep in an ancient wood. The disarmingly simple C major of the slow march for flute, brass, and timpani forms a complement to what should be magnificent scenic effects, typical of Schikaneder's productions. Tamino plays as they pass through fire and water; the chorus acclaims their triumph.

The small garden   Papageno blows his pipe but cannot bring back Papagena. His sincere agitation, expressed in an obsessive rondo form, demands our sympathy despite the preceding sublimity and the certainty of a happy outcome. He is about to hang himself in pantomime style, enlisting the aid of the audience to delay the event, when the boys remind him of the bells; their magic brings back Papagena in feathered youthfulness, and the stammering duet develops into an excited hymn to domesticity with lots of children. Monostatos leads the Queen and Ladies beneath the temple ('Nur stille, stille', a sinister little march). The Queen, bereft of high notes, stoops to offering the defector her daughter. But the sun beams forth, and Sarastro appears on high with Tamino and Pamina in priestly robes. At this transfiguration the demons are exorcised. The Armed Men's introduction recurs, radiant in the E♭ major Andante 'Heil sei euch Geweihten!': 'Hail chosen ones, who have overcome Night . . . [Allegro] Steadfastness conquers and grants the crown to beauty and wisdom'.

*   *   *

For the usual allegorical interpretation, the end is strikingly unorthodox. Masons left their wives at home, whereas Pamina undergoes tests of constancy (the Queen's temptation; Tamino's rejection; her willingness to die) equal to Tamino's, before joining him in trials by fire and water. Like *Così*, *Die Zauberflöte* has been accused of hostility to women. This is to confuse the attitudes of characters, including the absurdly misogynist priests in their duet at the beginning of Act 2 (itself a stage in Tamino's trials rather than dogma), with the meaning of the drama. If the Queen is the source of evil, Pamina is the strongest force for good and a necessary complement to Tamino: their union is divinely ordained. However alien to freemasonry, the implication that women should become initiates is the opera's title to true Enlightenment.

There is no evidence to support the often-reiterated claim that the authors changed the plot, and that the Queen was originally good and Sarastro evil. If even Mozart's music cannot unequivocally distinguish hypocrisy from sincerity it is a condition (not really a deficiency) of the art. That the flute and bells come from the Queen is a problem more apparent than real. By the traditions of magic stories, such objects are neutral, or can only help the righteous; and the Queen surely believes in the justice of her own cause. She takes a greater risk in offering Tamino the guidance of the wise Boys, but it is the Orator who begins his process of enlightenment. Monostatos, the untrustworthy servant, represents ordinary nature going bad; as cowardly as Papageno, the other representative of Everyman, he chooses evil and seeks power (over Pamina, by misused sexuality, and by joining the Queen). He is punished, whereas Papageno, falling short of enlightenment, is good-hearted and achieves domestic contentment.

Die Zauberflöte possesses attributes of pantomime, but is not ramshackle. It unfolds in many short scenes, a pseudo-Shakespearian dramaturgy which effectively contrasts the grave with the comical, the austerely hieratic with the earthily improvisational. The only possible weakness is Tamino's second rejection of Pamina. This scene may be an addition to the original plan, and was perhaps misplaced from earlier in Act 2; even disguised as a formal trio of farewell ('Soll ich dich, Teurer') it appears redundant, coming between 'Ach, ich fühl's' and Pamina's attempted suicide.

The most satisfactory approach to performance is to accept the work's nature and retain all or most of the dialogue. Even the slaves' scene adds to our understanding, and the priestly debates are indispensable (Mozart snubbed a booby who seemed to find them funny). The musical numbers function by contrast, employing an unprecedented stylistic range. Yet interconnections exist (such as the echo of the Queen's 'O zitt're nicht' in Tamino's invocation 'O ew'ge Nacht' in the first finale). The musical architecture also appears in distinctive instrumentation (emblematic flute, bells, trombones) and tonalities (the E♭/C axis which gives unusual prominence to C minor). Diversity and discontinuity do not deprive the score of the right to be considered as an entity, and a masterpiece of Mozart's late style.

The Librettists

The Earliest Operas (to 1769)

The librettists of Mozart's earliest operas include the Salzburg worthies **Rufinus Widl** (*Apollo et Hyacinthus*) and **Johann Andreas Schachtner**. Widl (1731–98) was a Benedictine monk who taught syntax and philosophy at the Salzburg Gymnasium (high school) and university. Schachtner (1731–95) is known as a court trumpeter and violinist, and an intimate of the Mozart household who provided many of the known anecdotes about the prodigy's early childhood. Besides adapting the librettos for a possible Salzburg production of *Bastien und Bastienne*, he contributed new text for *Zaide* and additional text for Mozart's incidental music to Gebler's *Thamos, König in Aegypten*. He also translated *Idomeneo* for the bilingual published libretto. [J.R.] *Bastien und Bastienne* originated as a parody of Jean-Jacques Rousseau's *Le Devin du village* by, or by close associates of, Charles-Simon Favart (1710–92), perhaps the most important literary figure in the rapid development of Opéra Comique. Favart engaged in a long correspondence with Count Giacomo Durazzo, Empress Maria Theresia's theatre director, providing the librettos and traditional melodies that formed the basis of a considerable output in this genre for the Viennese court theatre (Burgtheater), arranged, and eventually composed, by Christoph Willibald Gluck. This libretto may have reached Vienna by this route, or been collected by the Mozarts in Paris. The other opera of 1768, *La finta semplice*, is still more distinguished in its antecedents, as it is based on work by Goldoni.

Carlo Goldoni was born in Venice on 25 February 1707; he died in Paris on 6 or 7 February 1793. His best comedies, distinguished by a seemingly effortless dramatic technique and an acute observation of character and manners, place him in the front rank of Italy's dramatic authors. In a career that began slowly but at its peak made uncommon demands on his creative energies (in 1750–51 he promised, and delivered, 16 new comedies), Goldoni also found time to write some 80 librettos, most of them comic, and he also wrote *opere serie*, cantatas, and oratorios.

Goldoni had studied law at Padua and was admitted to the bar in Venice in 1732. Meanwhile he had written some comic intermezzos (1729/30, 1732) and a *dramma per musica*, which he himself destroyed (1733). Finding his legal profession unprofitable, he attached himself to a *commedia dell'arte* troupe in 1734, furnishing them with spoken tragicomedies and sung intermezzos, the latter set to music by mostly unknown composers and performed between the acts of the spoken plays. At the same time he was hired to assist Domenico Lalli, the poet-in-residence at the chief opera house in Venice, San Giovanni Grisostomo; this involved helping to stage *opere serie* and adapting or rewriting their librettos. He appears to have aspired to the dignity of tragic poet, for the years 1736 to 1741 saw the modestly successful production of five or six serious operas at the same theatre.

In 1743 he left Venice, settling in Tuscany to practice law. When he returned in 1748 he was under contract to another *commedia dell'arte* troupe. Abandoning traditional scenarios [and improvisation] in favour of wholly written-out comedies, Goldoni at the age of 40 finally embarked on the career that gained him his place in Italian literature. At the same time, he launched his long series of *opera buffa* librettos, working at first with the composer Francesco Ciampi, but from 1749 with Baldassare Galuppi, in a collaboration that over the next seven years produced some of the century's most successful comic operas. Goldoni worked fast; a comic opera libretto took him four days, as he testified in a letter of 1762. He was then on his way to Paris, where he arrived that August. There he settled, never to return to Italy.

In his autobiographical writings, Goldoni studiously belittled his librettos; indeed, once he had become famous he signed them with his Arcadian sobriquet, Polisseno Fegejo, as if to distinguish them from the works on which he wished to rest his reputation. To him they were a lucrative sideline, but he permitted, and probably supervised, at least the first collection of his comic librettos, in four volumes (1753), and very probably approved the ten-volume set (Venice, 1794–5) published shortly after his death. At least three other collected editions appeared during his lifetime. Goldoni was no Metastasio: his librettos do not stand up as literature. Yet they worked remarkably well in the theatre and were repeatedly set to new music.

Goldoni's flair for the living stage prevented any of his productions from ever smacking of literature; they were meant to be seen rather than read. The same genius that produced vignettes of everyday life in the spoken plays provided talented composers with the most variegated materials, drawn mostly from fantasy and rich in spectacle and twists of plot. An opening ensemble (eventually termed 'introduzione'), providing a colourful tableau and some inkling of the action to follow, plentiful ensembles sprinkled throughout the rest of the three-act work, a duet between two principals just before the concluding scene of Act 3: these are some of the hallmarks of the typical Goldoni *opera buffa* libretto. His principal contribution, however, and one recognized as such by his contemporaries, was the lengthy, action-studded finale, designed for continuous musical setting, that invariably concluded each of the first two acts. It is here that composers learned to deal musically with one element in opera (action or incident) that had traditionally been relegated to recitative.

Before extensive comparisons have been made of the librettos of less eminent contemporary authors, it is not possible to state categorically that every single aspect of this new, mid-18th-century *opera buffa* type originated with Goldoni. There is no doubt, however, as to the sheer quantity and immense popularity of his librettos. His *Il filosofo di campagna*, set by Galuppi in 1754, and *La buona figliuola*, in the 1760 resetting by Piccinni, were possibly the most influential, certainly the most successful operas of the period. His was a pivotal role in the history of the genre; at the very least he helped to give *opera buffa* the shape in which, in the mid-18th century, it gained its ascendancy. [P.W.] In *Arcadia in Brenta* (1749) and *Il mondo della luna* (1750) Goldoni established the pattern of the sub-genre of *opera buffa* known as *dramma giocoso*. This requires the composer to respond creatively to the mixture of social classes among the dramatis personae. Like Metastasio's, Goldoni's librettos were subjected to adaptation and new settings, including some by Joseph Haydn. But his composers were not always so famous: *La finta semplice* was first set by one Perillo in 1764.

Neither Favart nor Goldoni actually collaborated with Mozart, but all Mozart's later Italian comedies built upon Goldoni's achievement. *La finta semplice* was adapted from a Goldoni libretto by **Marco Coltellini** (1719–77), who is usually remembered for the serious librettos written under the influence of the opera theorist Francesco Algarotti and Ranieri de' Calzabigi, the reforming librettist of Gluck's *Orfeo* (1762) and *Alceste* (1767). Coltellini was in Vienna from 1763, and had recently collaborated with Tommaso Traetta (*Ifigenia in Tauride*, 1763) and Gluck (*Telemaco*, 1765).

Along with Mattia Verazi, he is one of the librettists whose work surely lies behind the synthesis of French and Italian styles in *Idomeneo*, but he also wrote a number of comedies. [J.R.]

The Milan Operas: 1770–3

Mozart's connection with figures of exceptional literary distinction continued with his first Italian opera, *Mitridate, re di Ponto*. Its source lay in a drama by the greatest neo-classical French playwright, Jean Racine (1639–99). His *Alexandre le grand, Iphigénie,* and *Phèdre* also formed the basis of operas, the last two by Gluck and Rameau; the first was the source of Metastasio's *Alessandro nell'Indie*. The Italian translation of *Mithridate* (1673) by Giuseppe Parini formed the basis of the libretto first set for Turin by Quirino Gasparini in 1767.

The librettist **Vittorio Amedeo Cigna-Santi** was born in Poirino, near Turin, around 1730; he died sometime after 1795. Very little is known about his life and activities. He published only a few celebratory poems before being appointed principal librettist in the Teatro Regio, Turin, from 1754–5, a post he kept for nearly 30 years. A volume of poetry published in 1760 ascribes his education to the Accademia dei Trasformati of Milan. Most of the original librettos he wrote for Turin achieved at least modest success outside the city as well, including *Mitridate, re di Ponto*. His most successful libretto, *Montezuma*, is typical of his dramaturgical style and was adapted and set, after its premiere in a version by G. F. Majo for Turin in 1765, by Mysliveček, Paisiello, Galuppi, Sacchini, Anfossi, Insanguine, and Zingarelli over the next 16 years (the Zingarelli version was revised and restaged by Haydn at Eszterháza in 1785). Cigna-Santi's poetry is less polished and elegant than that of either Zeno or Metastasio, whom he imitates; but Metastasio found Cigna-Santi's poetry worthy of public praise. The choice of Montezuma as a subject is itself telling, influenced by the wave of exotic settings popular in the 1760s and 70s. The usual balance among five to seven roles is also strained, with the three main characters almost entirely dominant. Arias are sometimes overplayed in the drama for simple effects, and motivation for the characters' actions is not always clear. *Alcina e Ruggero*, his last *dramma per musica*, was staged primarily for visual display, with spectacular effects and intricate machines, a kind of production Cigna-Santi later defended. By his own account he spent much of his energy adapting other librettos for local performance. [D.E.M.]

The librettist of *Ascanio in Alba*, **Giuseppe Parini** (see also Milan, below), was the translator of Racine whose version was used by Cigna-Santi, and like the latter he belonged to the Milan Accademia dei Trasformati. He compiled reports for the *Gazzetta di Milano*, and wrote of *Mitridate* that the prima donna's arias 'vividly express the passions and touch the heart', and that Mozart 'studies the beauty of nature and exhibits it adorned with the rarest of musical graces'—praise indeed. A poet and commentator on contemporary mores, which he deplored, he was a natural choice for Count Firmian when a libretto was required for the wedding serenata, designed to demonstrate the virtues of constancy and dutifulness. [J.R.]

Mozart's only opera of this period not written for Milan was *Il sogno di Scipione*, the first of three librettos (the others being *Il re pastore* and *La clemenza di Tito*) adapted for Mozart from works by Metastasio. Mozart set many other verses by this poet, mainly as concert arias. **Pietro (Antonio Domenico Bonaventura) Metastasio [Trapassi]** was born in Rome on 3 January 1698; he died in Vienna on 12 April 1782. His fame rests chiefly with his 27 *opera seria* librettos written between 1723 and 1771. In settings by over 300 composers, adapted versions of these texts span a period of over a hundred years that stretches well into the 19th century.

Metastasio's family was poor, and his early education was arranged by his godfather, Cardinal Pietro Ottoboni. In 1708, it was taken over by Gian Vincenzo Gravina, a jurist and a man of letters who, impressed by the boy's intelligence and ability at verse improvisation, adopted him and directed his studies in the classics, projecting for him a career in law (the name change from 'Trapassi' to 'Metastasio', the hellenized equivalent, was engineered by Gravina in 1715). Gravina also encouraged him to recite at social gatherings and to participate in improvisation contests. At Scalea in Calabria he studied with Gravina's cousin, Gregorio Caloprese, a noted scholar of Cartesian philosophy. Upon his return to Rome, Metastasio studied jurisprudence while maintaining his interest in poetry. He took minor orders at the Lateran Basilica in 1714.

When Gravina died (January 1718), Metastasio was left well educated, well connected, and well provided for. Unprepared for financial independence, Metastasio squandered most of the 15,000 scudi left him by Gravina and had to find employment. In Naples he worked in a law office, but he also found recognition in aristocratic circles as a poet. Over the next two years he fulfilled various commissions with odes and *azioni*, two of which were performed in Naples as birthday celebrations to honour the Empress Elizabeth.

In 1723 he reworked a libretto, *Siface re di Numidia*, for setting by Feo. His first original libretto, *Didone abbandonata*, launched his career in Naples the following year in a setting by Sarro. While writing this work

Metastasio lived in the home of Giuseppe Bulgarelli and his wife, the singer-actress Maria Anna Benti, who probably influenced the shape of the work. In her salon he met the composers who set his early works, and began his lifelong friendship with the castrato Farinelli (Carlo Broschi). Metastasio's second original drama, *Siroe re di Persia* (1726), was given in Venice with music by Leonardo Vinci. When *Catone in Utica* opened in Rome two years later, again set by Vinci, Metastasio had the satisfaction of seeing his first three original texts given successively in the three major opera centres in Italy. Following the premiere of *Ezio* (1728, Venice), three more dramas opened in Rome during the period 1729–30, all set by Vinci: *Semiramide riconosciuta* in February and, for the following carnival season, the two librettos that were to gain the greatest popularity, *Alessandro nell'- Indie* and *Artaserse*.

In 1729 Metastasio received an invitation to take up the position of Caesarian court poet in Vienna, where he moved in April 1730. Over the next ten years he wrote, in addition to smaller works, another eleven dramas, including *L'olimpiade, Demofoonte,* and *La clemenza di Tito,* seven oratorios, and eleven occasional pieces to celebrate royal birthdays or namedays. Changes in Austrian affairs of state and theatre policy worked against Metastasio. Maria Theresia's reign (from 1740) was beset by wars with Prussia; this, together with internal politics and inherited debt, relegated new opera commissions to a low priority. From 1740 to c.1750 in Vienna his operas were mainly first productions there of works already written, followed by new settings of existing texts. From the early 1750s to the mid-1760s, Metastasian opera representations at the court theatres dwindled almost to nothing. Between 1740 and 1782 several of Metastasio's best works had premieres outside Vienna, while the imperial court's demands were for in-house entertainments and works to honour only the most special royal events. In addition to smaller works, he produced, during this 42-year period, texts for 16 occasional pieces and only eight designated dramas for the *opera seria,* of which the most successful had their premieres at Dresden and Madrid.

Half of Metastasio's dramas received over 30 different musical settings during the 18th and early 19th centuries: *Artaserse,* his most popular, close to 90. Only the first composer to set any given text did so as Metastasio wrote it, and a setting by any composer for a different location could also be subject to further changes. Metastasio's renown was chiefly proclaimed by the number of editions of his works, continued settings and imitations of his texts, and literary commentaries. [Extracts from his works were also used in the training of composers up to the time of Schubert.]

Each of Metastasio's librettos for the *opera seria* is labelled 'dramma' or 'dramma musicale', and together they exhibit certain fundamental characteristics. Generally, the plots concern six or seven characters of royal or noble birth, their interrelationships and their complex dilemmas, which are intensified as the action proceeds and finally resolved in a *lieto fine*. The dramas are in three acts, each with an average of 12 scenes, defined by a character's entry or exit. A series of scenes is often linked by a character common to all of them, and a change of location often follows the end of such a series. Apart from the occasional duet, almost always for the principal couple, the usual set musical piece is the aria which, if included in a scene, has its expected place at the end. Opening scenes usually begin with a situation already in progress; each of the first two acts generally concludes with a climactic scene for a principal character or a duet; and the third normally ends with a united 'coro' for all the *dramatis personae*.

Metastasio once stated that he had 'wasted his entire life in order to instruct mankind in a pleasing way'. He held that 'pleasures that do not succeed in making impressions on the mind and on the heart are of short duration'. Thus emerges his aim of instructing under the guise of giving pleasure, and reinforcing a moral issue by arousing emotions. The creation of pleasure in poetry for its own sake meant exercising care over the basic construction of a dramatic work as well as its poetic style. Aristotle and Horace had advice to offer on the first of these considerations, which included the choice of events and the interest created in them, the conduct of the characters and the probability of their actions, and the exploitation of the dramatic elements of conflict, contrast, and accumulated intensity. 'Arcadia' [the Arcadian Academy of Rome under the patronage of Cardinal Ottoboni, founded in 1690] had much to say about the manipulation of poetic elements. For example, such matters as choice of words, versification, figures of speech, and eloquence of style, discussed in several of Metastasio's letters, are discussed as items of 'external' beauty by Giovanni Crescimbeni, the first president of the Accademia degli Arcadi, and as elements of 'corporeal' beauty by Lodovico Muratori, a friend of Zeno and an associate of the Accademia degli Accesi in Bologna.

Metastasio's verses are concise, economical, and mellifluous, and, for all his claims towards literary drama, his musical education allowed him to hear his verses mentally as he wrote them as operatic vocal lines. He possessed an unmatched facility to express the subtle nuances of a vast range of human emotions while conveying the meaning vividly and in a few words which, in combination, could exploit the consonance, assonance, and rhythm appropriate to the emotion of the moment. In addition, in writing arias for da capo settings, he generally supplied two stanzas (mostly quatrains), mindful of the appropriate vowel placement for coloratura extensions.

Poetry as a means of instruction meant, to Metastasio, the process of 'inducing, by way of pleasure, the love of virtue so necessary for general happiness'. For Crescimbeni this was the area of 'internal' beauty, for Muratori that of 'incorporeal' beauty, and it included matters of profundity, hidden mysteries, philosophy, and theology. Metastasio's poetry, however, was to prove the best example of what Crescimbeni called 'mixed' beauty, the highest achievement of all, with its emphasis on internal matters without losing sight of 'external' considerations. His leanings towards 'internal' beauty established his texts as moral dramas that realized on stage the principles set out in René Descartes' treatise on moral philosophy, *Les passions de l'âme*. Further contacts with Cartesian philosophy came from Metastasio's studies and knowledge of French 17th-century drama. Burney acknowledged Metastasio a master at unfolding and displaying 'all the passions of the human heart'. Metastasio saw passions as 'the necessary winds by which one navigates through the sea of life', and was at one with Descartes in the belief that all the passions are 'good in themselves' and that 'we have nothing to avoid but their evil uses or excesses'. Indeed, morality was seen to exist, above all, in the power of the individual to gain control over the desires that arise from human passions and so prevent the actions to which these passion-incited desires may lead.

In demonstrating such a process, Metastasian drama became a drama of moral forces personified by specified characters who are differentiated by emotionally charged actions and reactions that drive them towards either personal moral victory or moral self-defeat. At the centre is a moral hero or heroine, like Scipio or Titus, who must not only triumph over his own spontaneous desires but also uphold a moral vision against the onslaughts of the morally weak who fall victim to their personal desires. For the sake of the veiled exhortation to moral endurance, the moral crusader must succeed in the *lieto fine*, and the power of the achievement will be marred if the antagonists are not brought to moral truth (along with the audience) by the example; and at court performances, the moral hero served to set before the monarch the ideal of the morally inspired ruler. [D.N.]

These principles apply equally to librettos written under Metastasio's influence, including *Mitridate* and Mozart's last Milan opera, *Lucio Silla*. This time the librettist was **Giovanni de Gamerra**, born in Livorno in 1743; he died in Vicenza on 29 August 1803. A cleric, he served in the Austrian army (1765–70) after studying law at Pisa and produced many plays and poems. After 1771, when he was appointed poet to the Regio Ducal Teatro in Milan, his literary output was dominated by opera texts. Some of his early serious librettos—*Lucio Silla*, *Erifile*, and *Medonte, re d'Epiro*—were set repeatedly by leading composers. De Gamerra's flirtation with revolutionary politics, during the period of the French Revolution, nearly cost him his career: in 1791 Emperor Leopold II urged his brother Ferdinand not to engage him as librettist for La Scala, describing him as 'fanatic to excess, hot-headed, imprudent concerning liberty, very dangerous'. In 1793, however [under Leopold's son Emperor Franz], he was appointed house librettist for the court theatres in Vienna, and during the next decade he collaborated with Salieri and Weigl as well as providing librettos for Winter, Paer, and Mayr. He is also said to have made the first Italian translation of *Die Zauberflöte*.

De Gamerra's librettos are typical of late 18th-century developments in Italian musical drama: the product of a poet steeped in the traditions of Metastasian opera but eager to incorporate ideas of the kind proposed by Calzabigi, Verazi, and other innovators [such as Coltellini]. In 'Osservazioni sull' opera in musica', published in 1771 in his *Armida* libretto (of which no setting is known), he argued in favour of more 'spectacle' in *dramma per musica* in the form of chorus, ballet, and elaborate scenery, and he put those ideas into practice with tableaux like the dimly lit *ombra* scene among the funeral urns in Act 1 of *Lucio Silla* and, in *Pirro*, with large-scale action ensembles including an assassination attempt on stage. In his late librettos De Gamerra adapted to Viennese taste by combining comic and serious elements. [J.A.R.] In this he may have been reacting to Mozart, though it is just as likely to have been the eternally popular *Die Zauberflöte* that influenced him as the more obvious Italian model, *Don Giovanni*.

Mozart's Middle Period: 1775–81

Following his Italian adventures, Mozart's next opera, and his first for Munich, was *La finta giardiniera*, of which the libretto remains a minor mystery. Although the opera had appeared in Rome the previous year, with music by Pasquale Anfossi, the published libretto of *La finta giardiniera* failed to mention the author. Various names have been offered including (improbably) Calzabigi; a little less improbably, the reviser of *La finta semplice*, Coltellini; and Giuseppe Petrosellini (1727–99), although this more plausible hypothesis remains unproven. Certainly Petrosellini was in the right place at the right time, and had previously collaborated with Anfossi. But there seems more evidence to attribute a later Mozart work (*Lo sposo deluso*) to him.

Il re pastore counts among Metastasio's lighter works; he had dealt with Alexander's invasion of India in another drama. He wrote *Il re pastore* in 1751 for performance by noble amateurs at the Habsburg court; the music was by Giuseppe Bonno, later promoted to Imperial Kapellmeister. Mozart may have seen a version in London in 1765, with English text; another was performed in Paris three years later. Mozart's setting was composed to a cut-down version of the libretto, and presented in Salzburg to entertain the youngest son of Maria Theresia who had commissioned the libretto in the first place.

Mozart's next operatic endeavour was the unfinished work now known as *Zaide*, which Mozart and Schachtner based on a Singspiel by Franz Josef Sebastiani, *Das Serail*, set earlier in 1779 by Joseph von Friebert. Sebastiani derived his story from Voltaire's *Zaïre* which, however, is a grisly tragedy; in line with operatic normality, Sebastiani contrived a happy ending. But the main work of this period was *Idomeneo*, composed again for Munich, with the same theatre intendant as in 1775 (Count Seeau) but with Carl Theodor, formerly Elector Palatinate with his court in Mannheim, as Elector of Bavaria. The chosen libretto was an adaptation of a French *tragédie lyrique*, *Idoménée*, written by Antoine Danchet and set by André Campra in 1712. The topic had already been made into a French play, having come to prominence in a work Mozart had read, the didactic novel *Télémaque* (1696) by the Abbé Fénelon. The task of the librettist Varesco was to convert this post-Racine, but also post-Quinault, French opera with a tragic ending into a Metastasian moral drama with a *lieto fine* (Neville, in Rushton 1993).

(Girolamo) Giovanni Battista [Gianbattista] Varesco was baptized in Trent, on 26 November 1735; he died in Salzburg, on 25 August 1805. A cleric, poet, and musician, he was educated at the Jesuit college in his home town from 1753 to 1756. In 1766 he became a chaplain to the Archbishop of Salzburg, serving also as a musician in the archbishop's orchestra. When Mozart received the commission for *Idomeneo*, he turned not to an established theatrical poet but to Varesco, who, as an Italian educated by the Jesuits in the liberal arts, was as capable as more prolific librettists. Furthermore, his presence in Salzburg allowed Mozart to work closely with him during the preparation of the libretto and the early stages of composition. Varesco translated and reworked Danchet's *tragédie lyrique* under Mozart's [and Leopold Mozart's] supervision, producing a libretto in which the grand choruses, spectacular effects, and supernatural elements reflect its French origins and probably the influence of Gluck's *Alceste*. Varesco's work is fluent and theatrical, with moments of great beauty, both poetic and dramatic.

Although Varesco was offended by Mozart's persistent attempts to alter the libretto of *Idomeneo*, that did not keep him from a second collaboration with Mozart. When Joseph II organized an *opera buffa* troupe in Vienna in 1783, Mozart, eager to display his abilities as a composer of Italian comic opera, set to work with Varesco on *L'oca del Cairo*. Varesco later collaborated with Michael Haydn on the *opera seria Andromeda e Perseo* (1787). Having survived Mozart by 14 years, Varesco died in poverty in his adopted city. **[J.A.R.]**

The Early Vienna Years

Once in Vienna, Mozart tried to interest Gottlieb Stephanie in *Zaide*, but was instead offered a slightly newer libretto with a strikingly similar theme. Its original author, **Christoph Friedrich Bretzner**, was born in Leipzig on 10 December 1748; he died there on 31 August 1807. He spent his entire life as a businessman in Leipzig, and began writing plays in 1771. A set of four comic opera texts printed in 1779 quickly established him as a fashionable librettist in Germany. Colourful and exotic, they offer great scope for music; Viennese as well as northern composers greeted them warmly. Bretzner is best remembered as the author of *Belmont und Constanze*, written for the Berlin composer Johann André in 1780 and subsequently adapted for Mozart as *Die Entführung aus dem Serail*. (The much-quoted 'protest' against Mozart of 1782 is a fabrication, although in 1783 Bretzner did publicly denigrate Stephanie's poetic additions.) A second set of librettos, issued in 1796, shows Bretzner's facility at imitating *opera buffa* in German. In addition to writing original opera texts and one melodrama, he translated several Italian texts for the German stage, including Mozart's *Così fan tutte* (as *Weibertreu, oder Die Mädchen sind von Flandern*) and Salieri's *La scuola de' gelosi* (*Die Schule der Eifersüchtigen*), both in 1794. **[T.B.]**

Gottlieb Stephanie was born in Breslau on 19 February 1741, and died in Vienna, on 23 January 1800. He was an actor, playwright, and librettist, and was mainly active in Vienna. Called Stephanie der Jüngere (the younger) to distinguish him from his elder brother, the actor Christian Gottlob, Stephanie was prevented from studying law by his conscription into the army of Frederick the Great. He was captured at Landshut and later joined the Austrian forces; after serving as a recruiter, he began a career in 1769 as an actor in Vienna but soon turned to writing plays (40 in all, 29 of them written before 1780). He involved himself actively in theatrical affairs, ingratiated himself at court, and was named one of the five inspectors of the Nationaltheater, established by Joseph II in 1776. He also participated in the National-Singspiel, created in 1778, as a translator and adapter of French and Italian comic operas. In 1781 its direction was placed in his hands.

Stephanie earned a dark reputation as an inveterate intriguer, but he remained a warm supporter and friend of Mozart, facilitating the commissioning of *Die Entführung* in 1781 as well as choosing and adapting the text. After the demise of the National-Singspiel in 1783, he continued to provide texts for the German companies at the Kärntnertortheater, including several of Dittersdorf's most successful operas.

As a playwright Stephanie enjoyed sustained popularity in Vienna but scant critical acclaim. His librettos vary considerably in tone, plot, and characterization, depending on the stage for which they were intended. Those for the National-Singspiel are more refined than his later texts for the Kärntnertor. As a translator of foreign operas for the National-Singspiel, he showed uncommon skill in placing new German texts beneath the original music. In his own operas his verses gained little esteem and he often resorted to pilfering from or adapting other poets for this purpose. He frequently adapted German texts for new settings by local composers, although the extent of his revisions of C. F. Bretzner's *Belmont und Constanze* for Mozart is unusual, and Bretzner publicly ridiculed the new musical numbers Stephanie wrote for *Die Entführung*. In 1792 Stephanie published his original librettos and included an informative preface on many of the conventions that governed German comic opera at Vienna during the 1780s. [T.B.] Stephanie was also responsible for the text of *Der Schauspieldirektor* (1786).

When the National-Singspiel was disbanded, and an Italian opera buffa company engaged, Mozart was determined to overcome any prejudice against German composers and take part in its repertoire. Despairing of finding a good libretto, he first fell back on Varesco for *L'oca del Cairo*, then found, or was given, an existing libretto. *Lo sposo deluso*, originally called *Le donne rivali*, is of uncertain authorship, but has been attributed to **Giuseppe Petrosellini**. The following lines are indebted to the article in *The New Grove* by Mary Hunter. As one of Goldoni's prolific and skilful successors, Petrosellini had already been set by several of the brightest lights in the *opera buffa* firmament, including, before Mozart took an interest in what may be his work, Galuppi, Piccinni, Anfossi, Salieri, Paisiello, and Cimarosa. Significantly, he was the librettist who adapted a play by Beaumarchais for Giovanni Paisiello (*Il barbiere di Siviglia*, 1782)—although some doubt has been cast on his authorship as the libretto was first published anonymously. This opera was first given in St Petersburg, but there was considerable cultural traffic between the courts there and in Vienna, and it is not surprising to find Paisiello's opera transferred to the repertory of the Burgtheater the following year, with some of the singers who later took part in the first production of *Figaro*. The first Vienna performance (13 August 1783) took place while Mozart was in Salzburg, but it was given a number of times after his return and certainly played a part not only in the selection of the sequel for Mozart's opera, but in the formation of the music (Heartz, 1990).

The Da Ponte Operas

Lorenzo da Ponte, whom Mozart first assumed would not collaborate with him as he would be in league with Salieri (letter of 7 May 1783), eventually became his finest librettist. Da Ponte has been unfairly criticized for lacking originality, but this was not especially necessary for a librettist in a culture happy to witness new settings of librettos, both serious and comic, and new treatments of old subjects, whether from Greek mythology or *commedia dell'arte*. Whichever of them decided on the subjects of their collaboration— Da Ponte, in his memoirs, is not a reliable witness, while Mozart tells us nothing—they chose well: behind them lies literary distinction in the works of Beaumarchais, Molière, other authors associated with Don Juan legends, and the various threads that were spun into *Così fan tutte*.

Pierre-Augustin (Caron de) Beaumarchais was born in Paris on 24 January 1732; he died there on 18 May 1799. He is remembered today as the author of two genial stage comedies, *Le Barbier de Séville, ou La Précaution inutile* and *La folle journée, ou Le Mariage de Figaro*, both destined for immortality as opera librettos. To his contemporaries his notoriety had many other sources. He began his career in 1753 as a watchmaker, the king, Mme de Pompadour and other nobility soon becoming his clients; then he served as harp teacher to Louis XV's four daughters (1757). He bought his way into the nobility (1761) and became a judge (1763), later an occasional diplomat and even a spy. He was an eternal litigant, and the popularity of his witty—if unscrupulous—pamphlets pillorying his legal opponents rivalled that of the *Provincial Letters* of Pascal. He was also a supplier, or would-be supplier, of arms to both the American and the French Revolutions. In 1794, while he was abroad, mishaps caused his name to be inscribed on the list of criminal émigrés and his family placed under arrest. Returning to Paris in 1796, his finances and his health in disarray, he spent the remaining three years of his life recuperating his losses.

Beaumarchais also emerged as the last great writer of comedy of the *ancien régime*. His first publicly staged plays were 'drames', inspired mainly by Diderot: *Eugénie* (first performed 1767) and *Les deux amis* (1770). Beaumarchais' own *Essai sur le genre dramatique sérieux* (published with *Eugénie* in 1767), owing much to Diderot, remains one of the clearest expositions of the 'drame' written during the century. *Le Barbier de Séville*, though belonging to the classical Molière tradition, was designed to be the first episode in a cycle that would finally include two more plays: *Le Mariage de Figaro* and *La Mère coupable* (the author had hoped to add still more). This was a daringly original conception; it was unheard of before Beaumarchais to invent stage characters who, play by play, would grow older and change, and who were to be imagined as leading lives outside the texts the author wrote for them.

The first two Figaro comedies lent themselves exceptionally well to musical setting. *Le Barbier* was turned into opera at least four times, by F. L. Benda, Paisiello, Isouard, and Rossini. The play in its original version (1772) had been intended as an *opéra comique* for the Comédie-Italienne. Even when it was revised as a stage play for the Comédie-Française, the plot featured various twists that were perfectly designed for the incidental music which Antoine-Laurent Baudron, principal violinist of the theatre orchestra, composed and orchestrated for it. Baudron's musical 'storm' between Acts 3 and 4 made a hit with the audience, a unique example of incidental music being remarked on at that theatre. 'Je suis Lindor' was used by Mozart for a theme and variations for piano (K354/299a).

Le Mariage, the longest stage comedy of the century, overflowed with incidental songs, dances, and musical ceremonies composed mainly by Baudron. It came closer to an *opéra comique* than any previous French play, a feature upon which Mozart and Da Ponte capitalized. The structure of Beaumarchais' comedy largely survived the transformation into an opera libretto, and one of the enduring elements was Beaumarchais' innovative strategy (part of his long-standing feminism) in giving the lead to women— the Countess and Suzanne—to devise the deceptions of the plot, rather than to males, as was the more usual theatrical practice. Conservative Vienna demanded certain *adoucissements*, mainly political but also sexual. Figaro's enormous monologue, with its daring thrusts against the nobility, disappeared almost entirely. The sexual overtones of the relationship between the Countess and the young page, Chérubin, considered almost shocking in the original comedy, were played down, as were Marceline's feminist outbursts. The trial scene, unsuitable for opera, was excised completely. Though in Beaumarchais' play the Countess's final gesture of forgiveness was touching enough, it could never have had the sublimity it achieved in the Mozart-Da Ponte opera: his Countess was not so innocent as theirs.

In 1793 a heavily revised version of the Mozart-Da Ponte opera was produced at the Paris Opéra, in French translation. As in an *opéra comique*, extensive parts of Beaumarchais' original spoken dialogue were reinserted in place of the recitatives. The production had no success.

The last instalment of the Figaro trilogy, a 'drame' whose full title is *L'autre Tartuffe, ou La Mère coupable*, was staged during the Revolution (1792), and in its painful emotions and dark-coloured settings it intensely reflected the new spirit of the times. The 'guilty mother' is the Countess, who has had an illegitimate son by Chérubin, following a moment of *égarement* in which he forced his will upon her. Later Chérubin was killed in a far-off land, and his death seems to have drained the life and gaiety from the remaining characters. Just as in Molière's *Tartuffe*, the entire family in the last act faces financial disaster, but this time there is a hair's breadth escape thanks to Figaro's wits, while the Count is called upon to make a dramatic gesture of forgiveness towards the guilty mother, even as the Countess had earlier done for him. Although praised by connoisseurs such as Victor Hugo and Charles Péguy, the play is all but forgotten today. Grétry apparently offered to provide music for parts of the text, but it became an opera only with Milhaud's setting (1966, Geneva).

In 1782 Beaumarchais submitted a revision of Voltaire's libretto *Samson* (music by Rameau, unperformed) to the Opéra. Five years later he produced an opera libretto of his own making, *Tarare*, with music by Salieri; sometimes considered this composer's masterpiece, it was performed at the Opéra in 1787 and frequently revived there until 1826. Much influenced by Gluck, Beaumarchais in his preface set forth a challenging conception of the relationships between plot, words, and music, a theory that seems to prefigure the reforms of Wagner. The moral lesson of the piece, that success depends on character rather than rank, looks back to Figaro and probably also to the materialism of Diderot. [**W.E.R.**] *Tarare* was adapted as an Italian opera (*Axur, re d'Ormus*) for Vienna by Lorenzo da Ponte for production in 1788, where it was a considerable success.

Lorenzo [Conegliano, Emmanuele] da Ponte was born in Ceneda [now Vittorio Veneto] on 10 March 1749; he died in New York on 17 August 1838. His involvement in the remarkable flowering of *opera buffa* in Vienna from 1783 to 1790 and his collaborations with Martín y Soler, Salieri, and above all Mozart make him arguably the most significant librettist of his generation: his three librettos for Mozart are justifiably regarded as peaks of the genre. Da Ponte's biographers rely largely on his *Memorie*. Written from the age of 60 onwards as an apologia for a life plagued by (often self-induced) misfortune, they present a carefully constructed image [or images] of the man and his work. Accounts of raffish adventures in the manner of his friend Casanova mix with vainglorious statements of achievement and accusations of treachery by friend and foe; sometimes fact can only with difficulty be separated from fiction.

Da Ponte adopted the name of the Bishop of Ceneda, Lorenzo da Ponte, when his father, a Jewish tanner, converted to Christianity in 1763. Da Ponte's early training in Ceneda and Portogruaro prepared him for the priesthood (he was ordained in 1773) and for teaching at seminaries. However, his penchant for liberal politics and married women led to a ban on his teaching in the Veneto and, on 17 December 1779, a 15-year exile from Venice. He went first to Gorizia and then to Dresden, believing that his friend, the poet and librettist Caterino Mazzolà, would secure him a court post. There he worked with Mazzolà translating and arranging plays and librettos. Mazzolà then provided Da Ponte with a recommendation to Salieri in Vienna: he arrived there in late 1781, meeting Metastasio just before his death. Da Ponte attracted the favour of Joseph II, and when Joseph abandoned his pursuit of German opera and revived the Italian company (in 1783), Da Ponte was appointed poet to the court theatre [at an annual salary of 600 florins, which may be compared to 4500 for the most expensive singers and the fee of 450 florins paid for composing an opera].

Da Ponte's facility for versifying, his ready wit, and his sound knowledge of languages made him an ideal theatre poet. His work included translating texts from French to Italian, reworking old librettos for revivals, and providing new works (themselves often adaptations) for Viennese composers. His first new libretto for Salieri as musical director of the company, *Il ricco d'un giorno*, was a failure (Da Ponte blamed the music [while Salieri blamed the poet (Rice, 1998)]). But in 1786 his position was assured by the success of *Il burbero di buon cuore* for Martín y Soler. That year saw a remarkable output of six operas to Da Ponte's librettos, including *Le nozze di Figaro* and the hugely popular *Una cosa rara* (again by Martín y Soler). [The others were by Giuseppe Gazzaniga (*Il finto cieco*), Vincenzo Righini (*Il demogorgone*), and the English composer Stephen Storace, brother of the leading singer (*Gli equivoci*).]

Da Ponte had an uneasy relationship with Count Rosenberg, director of the theatre, and his rivalry with the poet Giambattista Casti found expression in satirical poems (notably the *Epistola nell'Abate Casti*, Vienna, 1786) and even on the stage. Nor did Da Ponte's arrogance (see Michael Kelly's *Reminiscences*, 1826) help matters. He managed to regain Salieri's favour, providing *Axur, re d'Ormus* while writing *L'arbore di Diana* for Martín y Soler and *Don Giovanni* for Mozart; he later produced three other librettos for Salieri. He also published a volume of *Saggi poetici* (Vienna, 1788). In 1789 Da Ponte was involved in the revival of *Figaro*, probably providing the new texts for arias to be sung by his mistress, Adriana Ferrarese (the new Susanna), and he also wrote *Così fan tutte* in that year [for Salieri, although it was eventually set by Mozart]. In addition, he claims to have saved the Italian opera in Vienna from threatened closure. However, the death of his patron Joseph II on 20 February 1790 and court intrigue on the succession of Leopold II led to his dismissal (for which he blamed Salieri, among others) in 1791.

Da Ponte was denied permission to return to Venice, and although a reported meeting (in Trieste) with the short-lived Leopold II and the support of Leopold's successor Francis II went some way towards healing the rift, he never re-established himself in Vienna. Instead, having married an Englishwoman, Ann (Nancy) Grahl, on 12 August 1792, he set off for Paris and then, discouraged by the unstable political situation, headed for London. Doubtless he hoped to join forces with his former colleagues in Vienna, Kelly and Storace. After a futile year attempting to establish Italian opera in Brussels, Rotterdam, and The Hague, he was appointed to the King's Theatre, Haymarket, by the new manager, William Taylor. There Da Ponte arranged operas by Cimarosa and others, and collaborated on two operas with Martín y Soler during his stay in London from 1794 to 1796. He also provided librettos for Francesco Bianchi. A trip to Italy in 1798 to recruit singers reunited him with his family and his beloved Venice, although his old enemies forced a quick departure. His return to London saw his position blocked by intrigue—he was dismissed in 1799—and the King's Theatre in financial disarray: his unwise involvement in Taylor's dubious dealings led to Da Ponte declaring himself bankrupt in February 1800. He was reinstated at the theatre in 1801 and collaborated with Peter von Winter on three new operas, but, pursued by creditors, he followed Nancy to America in 1805.

Da Ponte became a grocer and general merchant in New York, then Sunbury (Pennsylvania) and Philadelphia, supplementing his income with private teaching and dealing in Italian books (an activity begun in London). He also produced an early version (1807) of his autobiography. Returning to New York in 1819, he determined to bring Italian culture to his newly adopted country (he took American citizenship) through teaching and book-dealing; he also occupied the (largely honorary) post of professor of Italian at Columbia College in 1825 and from 1827 until his death.

The publication both of a complete version of the *Memorie* (1823–7) and a volume of *Poesie varie* (New York, 1830) seems to have formed part of this endeavour; he also issued other translations, catalogues, and miscellaneous prose. He saw *Don Giovanni* performed by Manuel García's visiting company in 1826, and new editions of *Figaro*, *Don Giovanni*, *Axur*, and his tragedy *Il Mezenzio*, reportedly the only dramatic works from his European period that he had with him in America, was published that year. Notwithstanding his grief at Nancy's death (he issued a volume of commemorative verse in 1832), Da Ponte became financially involved in the ill-fated tour of the Montresor company in 1832–3 (he published an account in 1833) and acted briefly as manager of the newly built Italian Opera House. The initiative brought financial loss, and also a sense that his life's work had been for nothing—a projected final volume of the *Memorie* was never completed.

Accounts of Da Ponte's working methods rely heavily on the *Memorie*, and one need not set much store by his claim of writing *Axur*, *L'arbore di Diana*, and *Don Giovanni* concurrently, sustained by his snuff-box, a bottle of Tokay, and the ministrations of a 16-year-old Calliope ('whom I would have liked to love simply as a daughter, but . . .'). However, the *Memorie* offers intriguing insights into theatre life in Vienna, London, and New York, as well as into Da Ponte's own perception of his art: 'poetry is the door to music, which can be very handsome, and much admired for its exterior, but nobody else can see its internal beauties if the door is wanting'. He also made comments on contemporary librettists (whom he generally derided) and on the composers with whom he worked. Da Ponte was well aware of the different talents of his collaborators and carefully crafted his librettos to suit their needs. Although an obvious admirer of Mozart, he was less enthusiastic than one might expect, while he praised Salieri (with only a little irony) as an educated and worthy *maestro di cappella*. But his favourite composer seems to have been Martín y Soler: Da Ponte viewed *L'arbore di Diana* as his best libretto. Other composers such as Righini and Francesco Piticchio are roundly dismissed.

The prodigiousness of Da Ponte's output was doubtless due to his facility as a poet: significantly, he was a skilled improviser. But it also reflects his reliance on existing works: nearly all his librettos involve some adaptation, and he appears less happy when inventing original dramatic situations. However, adaptation was common in the period, and Da Ponte's skill lay in his precise knowledge of the dynamics of opera: he condensed situations, pinpointed characters, and focused the action in a manner allowing the composer freedom to create drama through music. Beaumarchais, Da

Ponte reported, admired the libretto of *Le nozze di Figaro* for 'contracting so many *colpi di scena* in so short a time, without the one destroying the other'. Even if the remark is apocryphal, it reflects Da Ponte's perception of his achievement.

Da Ponte had a profound sense of the literary and dramatic traditions within which he was working. He claimed to have admired Metastasio from childhood; echoes of and quotations from Metastasio abound in his librettos. But Da Ponte took his heritage further back still to the Renaissance. His linking of *Axur* with Tasso, *L'arbore di Diana* with Petrarch, and *Don Giovanni* with Dante is no coincidence: as his later teaching proved, he was intimately familiar with Italian Renaissance poetry. Again, references and quotations in his librettos emphasize the point: Dante, Petrarch, Boccaccio, Ariosto, Sannazaro, Tasso, and Guarini all make appearances (and Da Ponte arranged Guarini's celebrated *Il pastor fido* for Salieri in 1789). Moreover, Da Ponte made careful use of rhyme and metre as well as complex syntactical and rhetorical patterns. The rich resonances and subtle structures give his librettos a literary emphasis that sets them apart from the workaday efforts of his contemporaries. He was well aware of his skill: his texts often refer to, as they deliberately surpass, verse by Bertati, Casti, and Mazzolà.

Two dramatists rarely mentioned in the *Memorie* are Goldoni and Carlo Gozzi, perhaps because they were too close to home. Da Ponte's first success, *Il burbero di buon cuore*, was an adaptation of Goldoni, and from him Da Ponte learned the secret of comic pacing, of lexical manipulation (in particular, witty '-ino' and '-etto' diminutives), and of taut poetic structures. The debt is particularly apparent in *Don Giovanni*, notwithstanding its more immediate borrowings from Bertati's recent libretto (set by Gazzaniga; Da Ponte later reworked this version in London). Da Ponte's 'dramma giocoso' (the term itself derives from Goldoni) owes much to Goldoni's play *Don Giovanni Tenorio*, as well as to Molière, and Leporello's opening solo has clear echoes of *Il servitore di due padroni*. Da Ponte claimed [probably without foundation] that the mixture of comedy and seriousness in the opera was his idea, and it relates directly to Goldoni's notion of a new kind of drama for the 18th century. [Da Ponte's statement that Mozart had to be persuaded to include comic elements is not credible.]

As for Gozzi (whom he knew in Venice in the late 1770s), Da Ponte entered his fantasy world in *L'arbore di Diana*, while Gozzi's *Le droghe d'amore* (1777) may have influenced *Così fan tutte*. In *Così* (which the librettist always called *La scuola degli amanti*) Da Ponte's sense of literary play reaches its peak. It is perhaps best viewed as an opera about opera—failure to do this accounts for the oft-perceived 'problems' of the work—in the vein of Casti's *Prima la musica e poi le parole* [set by Salieri, 1786] (there are echoes in the text). Da Ponte ranked the libretto below *Figaro* and *Don Giovanni*, probably because of the opera's poor critical reception, but, as Dent [1913] realized, it contains his best work. Attempts to find a single source for the story have largely failed. However, Da Ponte clearly placed the drama in the time-honoured tradition of the pastoral (in Act 1 Don Alfonso quotes directly from Sannazaro: 'Nel mare solca e nell'arena semina'). He also revelled in the allegorical play of essentially abstract characters and situations. Whether or not Mozart fully grasped this aspect of the libretto is another matter; moreover, opera was soon to move in very different directions. But *Così* marks an eloquent testament both to Da Ponte's literary heritage and to opera in the Age of Enlightenment. **[T.C.]**

The Operas of 1791

One could not hope for a more marked contrast between Da Ponte, whom Mozart was no doubt sorry to see leaving Vienna, and the librettist of his next opera, *Die Zauberflöte*. From the utmost literary polish in *Così fan tutte*, Mozart both rose and descended to a religious sublimity and to the demotic, and brought them together. He was to work again with a sophisticated Italian poet and friend of Da Ponte in Caterino Mazzolà, but before tackling his version of Metastasio's *La clemenza di Tito*, he engaged with the work of an all-round and hands-on man of the theatre who acted and even sang on the stage.

Emanuel (Johann Joseph [Baptist]) Schikaneder [Schickaneder] was born in Straubing on 1 September 1751; he died in Vienna on 21 September 1812. He was a dramatist, theatre director, actor, singer, and composer. Educated at the Jesuit Gymnasium at Regensburg, where he was a cathedral chorister, Schikaneder may briefly have been a town musician before he became an actor with F. J. Moser's troupe in 1773 or 1774. In 1774 he danced in a court ballet at Innsbruck, where his Singspiel *Die Lyranten* (of which he wrote both words and music) was performed in 1775 or 1776. The Innsbruck company, then under Andreas Schopf and Theresia Schimann, moved in 1776 to Augsburg, where on 9 February 1777 he married an actress in the company, Maria Magdalena (known as Eleonore) Arth (born Hermannstadt, 1751; died Vienna, 22 June 1821). In 1777–8 they were in Nuremberg with Moser's company, and in December 1777 Schikaneder made a famous guest appearance as Hamlet at the Munich court theatre, where he was obliged to repeat the final scene. From January 1778 he was director of the troupe, travelling widely in German and Austrian centres before beginning a lengthy season at Salzburg in September, during which he became friendly with the Mozarts. Further travels through Austria included summer seasons at Graz in 1781 and 1782, the winter of 1782–3 in Pressburg (now Bratislava), and a guest appearance in summer 1783 at the Kärntnertortheater, Vienna.

After further visits to Pest and Pressburg, where Joseph II saw him perform in October 1784, Schikaneder was invited to play in Vienna. He and Hubert Kumpf began a three-month season of operas and Singspiels at the Kärntnertortheater on 5 November. Thereafter, Schikaneder was a member of the Nationaltheater, performing in plays and operas, from 1 March 1785 until 28 February 1786. During this time his own troupe was run by his wife and Johann Friedel; it toured in southern Austria until it moved into the Freihaus-Theater auf der Wieden, Vienna, in November 1788. Schikaneder himself had been granted an imperial licence to build a suburban theatre in February 1786, but made no use of it for 15 years. Instead he formed a new company specializing in Singspiels and operas, which he took to Salzburg, Augsburg, and Memmingen. In February 1787 he took over the Prince of Thurn and Taxis's court theatre at Regensburg. When Johann Friedel died at the end of March 1789 Schikaneder and his wife took over the Freihaus-Theater in Vienna, bringing from Regensburg the singer-composers Schack and Gerl. Schikaneder's reign at the Freihaus began on 12 July 1789 with the first performance of his 'Anton' opera *Der dumme Gärtner* [with music by Schack and Gerl: in 1791, Mozart wrote his last set of piano variations, K613, on a popular number from this opera]. From this time dates the beginning of the steady series of plays and operas and Singspiel librettos which were the backbone of the repertory of Schikaneder's theatre, but which were also performed elsewhere, sometimes with new music.

Schikaneder's years of travel had seen the production of more straight plays than operas; in Vienna he placed the emphasis firmly on opera, and commissioned settings of his own texts from Mozart (*Die Zauberflöte*), Süssmayr (*Der Spiegel von Arkadien*), Wölfl (*Der Höllenberg*), Mederitsch, and Winter (one act each of *Babylons Pyramiden*). Winter also set *Das Labyrinth*, a sequel to *Die Zauberflöte*. Of the 12 greatest successes at the Freihaus, which closed on 12 June 1801, eight—including the first five— were written by Schikaneder himself. He also received scores from his theatre Kapellmeister, Henneberg, Haibel, and Seyfried. As the 1790s advanced, Schikaneder began to suffer increasing financial difficulties as he strove to surpass the achievements of his rivals and his own greatest successes. In

1799 he handed over management of the theatre while continuing his artistic direction.

On 13 June 1801 Schikaneder opened the new Theater an der Wien, using the licence he had previously been granted; it was the most lavishly equipped and one of the largest theatres of its age, and has continued in almost unbroken use. It opened with Teyber's setting of Schikaneder's libretto *Alexander*, but a change in public taste and a decline in Schikaneder's standards and powers of judgment were influential in the decision to sell the licence after less than a year. Schikaneder continued to supply plays and librettos, and to act, but despite two further periods as artistic director his fortunes were waning. After the sale of the theatre in 1806 Schikaneder left Vienna and took over the Brno Theatre. At Easter 1809 he was back in Vienna, but financial ruin and failing mental health darkened his last years. On his way to Budapest to take up an appointment as director of a new German theatre company in 1812 he became mad, returned to Vienna, and died in penury shortly after.

Schikaneder was one of the most talented and influential theatre men of his age. Although it is fashionable to decry his plays (of which there are nearly 50) and librettos, they more than satisfied the demands of their day. Goethe praised his skill at creating strong dramatic situations, and though the verse is often trite the libretto of *Die Zauberflöte* is by no means unworthy of Mozart's music. Some of Schikaneder's comedies continued to be performed for many years and strongly influenced the later development of the Viennese *Lokalstück* ('local play'). Early in his career Schikaneder composed two, and perhaps several more, theatre scores: it has long been known that the music as well as the text of *Die Lyranten* was his work; and for the production of his Singspiel *Das Urianische Schloss* (1786, Salzburg) at the Theater in der Leopoldstadt in November 1787 a score by him is specifically mentioned by Wenzel Müller in his diary ('Opera by Em: Schikaneder, music, and book'). [A small amount of *Der Stein der Weisen* is attributed to him in the source that also names Mozart as composer of more than one section; Buch, 2000.]

Schikaneder's brother Urban (1746–1818) was an actor and singer; he sang First Priest in the premiere of *Die Zauberflöte* in 1791 and took a part in the administration of Emanuel's travelling company. Urban's daughter Anna (Nanny or Nanette, 1767–1862) sang First Boy in *Die Zauberflöte* and was later a member of the Theater in der Leopoldstadt company, singing the Queen of Night when it first gave *Die Zauberflöte* in 1811. **[P.B.]**

Caterino Mazzolà was born in Longarone on 18 January 1745; he died in Venice on 16 July 1806. About 1767–8 his family moved to Venice, where

Caterino's firm grounding in Latin and the classics began at a Jesuit school before he moved on to a Somaschi institution in Treviso. By the time he married, in 1780, his career as a librettist had already begun. He had also become a known figure in the houses of men of letters in Venice, where he met Casanova in 1774 and Lorenzo da Ponte in 1777. The following year the composer Joseph Schuster helped secure his appointment as court poet at Dresden, a position Mazzolà held from 1780 to 1796. For six months in 1780 Mazzolà was joined in Dresden by Da Ponte and gave him the letter of introduction to Salieri that led to his appointment in Vienna. That the inaugural performance (1783) was a production of the Salieri/Mazzolà opera *La scuola de' gelosi* was probably no mere coincidence. From 1790 Da Ponte began to fall from favour, but it is likely that both he and Salieri were instrumental in gaining the position of court poet for Mazzolà for a brief period early in 1791 through their influence with Count Rosenberg, the court theatre director. Rosenberg was replaced, however, and Giovanni Bertati was subsequently named to the position. Mazzolà is described as a generous and gracious man who seems to have been much appreciated by his employer in Saxony. When he left Dresden in 1796, Friedrich August III obtained diplomatic work in Venice for him and also requested that some of his writings be sent back to the Saxon court each year.

Most of Mazzolà's librettos are for *opera buffa*, and were set mainly by the Dresden composers Naumann, Schuster, and Seydelmann. Salieri's interest in his friend's texts was to be expected, but Mazzolà's librettos were also set by other important composers of the time. Da Ponte described him as 'possibly the first to know how to write a comic libretto', and *La scuola de' gelosi* bears a striking resemblance to *Le nozze di Figaro*, not only in its similarities of plot but also because of its rapid pace and clear delineation of characters. Mazzolà's masonic opera *Osiride* was known to Mozart, with whom he may have discussed *Die Zauberflöte* in Vienna from May to July 1791. His collaboration with Mozart in adapting Metastasio's *La clemenza di Tito* for Prague in 1791 produced a libretto that vividly reflects contemporary trends in the content and structure of Italian serious opera. These trends, often originating in *opera buffa*, include the two-act structure, opening duet, medial ensembles, rapid pace, and directness of emotional expression, characteristics to be found in Mazzolà's earlier librettos. *Il mostro*, a text that antedates the *Tito* revision by six years, provides a particularly clear example. [D.N.]

There were naturally other librettists in the ambience within which Mozart lived, and whose work he would have known, such as Verazi, Bertati, and Casti. We can only guess at the identity of the authors of the 100-odd *opera buffa* libretti he claimed to have read before commissioning Varesco to try his hand at an original text (for which the latter was clearly unsuited). But in setting work derived from Racine, Goldoni, and Beaumarchais, working on material derived from popular traditions (especially in *La finta semplice* and *Don Giovanni*), re-setting Metastasio, and collaborating with Coltellini, Da Ponte, and Mazzolà, Mozart by any measure was at the centre of the developing literary and theatrical culture of Italian opera in his time. That a number of his sources were also French is not surprising, despite his dislike of French music. His proximity to the centre of German literary culture, given the North German origins of his two harem operas (*Zaide* and *Die Entführung*) and Goethe's interest in him, is also clear. The only surprising omission from a composer who called himself a regular Englishman is of material from Britain such as appeared in Opéra Comique, Singspiel, and even *opera buffa*, for *Gli equivoci*, written by Da Ponte for Mozart's friend Stephen Storace, is closely based on Shakespeare's *A Comedy of Errors*. Mozart's inability or refusal to accept invitations from London in the mid to late 1780s is one of many factors that tempt speculation on an alternative music history; but that, and the enterprising works of fiction based on Mozart's work or alluding to it, is beyond the scope of this book.

{ *The Performers*

The performers of Mozart's operas were primarily singers, a class of musicians about whom the quantity of biographical information, despite major research undertaken in recent years, is highly variable. We may trace the entire career of Nancy Storace, but for other singers even dates of birth and death have not been established.

Mozart played little or no part in choosing singers for his operas. Nevertheless, his well-known concern to write effectively for them conditioned his working methods. Awaiting the arrival of a singer in Milan, his father wrote: 'Wolfgang refuses to do the work twice over and prefers to wait for his arrival so as to fit the costume to his figure' (letter of 24 November 1770). Writing home from Mannheim (28 February 1778), Mozart echoed this remark in connection with concert arias for Raaff, Dorothea Wendling, and Aloysia Weber: 'I like an aria to fit a singer as perfectly as a well-made suit of clothes'. Many operas of the time were only performed during one season, even if they were successful, like Mozart's Milan *opere serie*.

If operas were revived, or, like *La finta semplice*, were planned for one theatre but performed only in another, the modern assumption would be that the singers had to adapt to the existing score. But in the 18th century, it was just as likely that the existing score would be adapted for the singers. There may be a few exceptions to the rule that Mozart wrote arias only after acquainting himself with the singer, and revivals of *Idomeneo* and *Le nozze di Figaro* show that he was willing to write new arias to suit a new cast. With the same motive, he was adept at providing arias for insertion into other composers' operas in a revival where the composer was not present; this probably happened in Salzburg, and certainly in Vienna, resulting in beautiful pieces for singers such as Lange, Adamberger, Calvesi, and Villeneuve.

Modern practice in works of reference is to label singers by voice type: soprano, tenor, and so forth. In Mozart's time the importance of these categories was secondary to the individual characteristics of a singer, and the type of role being played; and contemporary comments often refer as much to their looks, and to their acting, as to their singing ability, at least in *opera buffa*. The *prima donna* was usually what we would call soprano. The female contralto was rare, the classification mezzo-soprano not used; if a soprano had exceptional high notes, like the Weber sisters (see Lange, Hofer), Mozart would use them but if not, not. In *opera seria* the *primo uomo* (hero, lover) could be a soprano or alto castrato, while in *opera buffa* and Singspiel he is usually a tenor. Lower male voices—in *opera seria*, tenor and less often bass, in *opera buffa* what we now call baritone or bass—played roles such as fathers, rulers, and priests, and in *opera buffa* comic roles are usually for low voices. In praising Benucci, Mozart did not call him 'the bass' but 'the buffo'; the nature of his talent was thus communicated to Leopold not by the range of his voice, but the type of role he played (in fact, judging by the music Mozart and others wrote for him, he could function as either baritone or bass; he had a range of two octaves or more). There are roles for both women and men of the type Mozart called 'middle character' (*mezzo carattere*: letter of 7 May 1783). Among women Donna Elvira (*Don Giovanni*), a lady of rank who loses her dignity and 'prudenza' in pursuit of justice, is one such; among men, Giovanni himself, in modern classification a baritone, is another. Generic classifications by range, therefore, can be anachronistic. Where Mozart is concerned this becomes important with respect to the only company for which he composed more than one opera, the *buffa* troupe at the Burgtheater, for which he planned *Lo sposo deluso* and wrote *Le nozze di Figaro*, *Così fan tutte*, and the revisions to *Don Giovanni*, as well as insertion pieces.

The other musicians involved in an opera production should not be forgotten, although there is usually even less information about them: the Kapellmeister himself might be paid less than the singers, and mere instrumentalists were of little concern to audiences. Mozart, however, offered favours to his friends in various orchestras in the form of obbligato parts in arias, as well as much other music that is a joy to play. It was the custom for the composer to direct the first three performances of an opera, after which it was taken over by the local maestro or director of music—for instance in Milan, Lampugnani; at the Burgtheater, Salieri or his deputy; and at Schikaneder's theatre, Henneberg.

Salzburg

Apart from isolated arias, Mozart's first dramatic work to reach performance was given by local singers in Salzburg: children and students (*Apollo et Hyacinthus*) and the members of the archbishop's Kapelle (which includes the female singers who were not normally permitted to perform in church and whose duties were thus secular) for the oratorio *Die Schuldigkeit des ersten Gebotes*, the cantata *Grabmusik*, both of 1767, and in 1769 the possible performance of *La finta semplice*. The main female singers included the Lipp sisters, Maria Magdalena, married to Michael Haydn, and Maria Josepha Judith, wife of Antonio Brunetti, the court violinist. Maria Magdalena sang 'Godly mercy' in *Die Schuldigkeit* and was cast as the leading role, Rosina, in the opera. Whether or not *Il sogno di Scipione* was performed in full, it was certainly planned for the available Salzburg singers and Mozart must have had confidence in their ability to tackle difficult music. Among the male singers in the oratorio and in *La finta semplice* were Franz de Paula Anton Spitzeder (1735–96) and Joseph Nikolaus Meissner (c. 1725–95), both friends of the Mozart family. Spitzeder was a tenor, and a well-equipped musician whose singing Leopold Mozart praised; Meissner seems to have encompassed roles attributable to tenor or bass, but it was as a tenor that Mozart compared him, in some respects to his advantage, with the far more distinguished Anton Raaff (letter of 12 June 1778).

In principle the Kapelle included one or more castratos, but for Mozart's next production there, *Il re pastore*, the title-role (Aminta) was taken by one imported for the occasion from Munich, **Tommaso Consoli** (c.1753– after 1811). He had almost certainly created the role of Ramiro in *La finta giardiniera* earlier in 1775, and while the role of Aminta rises a little higher, both concentrate in much the same tessitura, essentially that of a modern mezzo-soprano. Consoli was not retained when Carl Theodor moved to Munich in 1778, and returned to Italy, ending his career in the Sistine Chapel choir.

The influence of singers who did not pursue stage careers should not be discounted, for they too performed operatic music and helped Mozart hone his skills as a dramatic composer. In 1777, the castrato **Francesco Ceccarelli** (1752–1814) came to Salzburg and became friendly with the Mozarts. He presumably sang the soprano solos in Mozart's last masses and vespers in Salzburg. On arriving in Vienna in 1781, Mozart composed a scena for him (K374), to entertain guests of the archbishop. Working with Ceccarelli surely gave Mozart satisfaction in the absence of operatic commissions in his last years under the Archbishop. The Bohemian soprano **Josepha Dušek** (or Duschek, née Hambacher; 1754–1824) visited Salzburg with her husband in 1777 and they also became friends of the Mozarts. Mozart wrote the first of his two arias for her (K272) at that time. The other (K528) was written when Mozart was staying at her summer house in Prague, finishing *Don Giovanni*; both are long and demanding pieces. Dušek took part in some of Mozart's concerts on his North German tour of 1789 and included arias from Mozart's operas in her repertoire. **[J.R.]**

Milan, 1770–73

As a boy of fourteen, Mozart not surprisingly encountered some difficulties with his first opera for Milan, even though he had the support of Firmian, Lampugnani, and the prima donna. The soprano **Antonia Bernasconi** (1741–1803), who sang Aspasia in *Mitridate*, was German, despite her Italian name, taken from her stepfather. The Mozarts had met her in Vienna, where she had recently created the title-role in Gluck's *Alceste*. The troupe that performed this masterpiece of serious reform was mainly experienced in *opera buffa*, and Mozart had intended Bernasconi to sing Ninetta in *La finta semplice*. In Milan, she rejected any suggestion that she should sing arias not by Mozart, while making him work hard to suit her voice in the new arias. She subsequently sang in London, but returned to Vienna about 1780, again singing in operas by Gluck; but she was not engaged for the new *opera buffa* company. **[J.R.]** Little is known of the *seconda donna* and *secondo uomo*.

We do not know whether Mozart was perturbed by the restless wandering of the tribe of castratos, who operated in a sellers' market, thanks to the limited supply of musically gifted boys unfortunate enough to meet with the 'accident' that made them eunuchs. On his first visit to Milan he had composed arias, perhaps for Giuseppe Aprile, whose singing he admired (letters of 26 January and 5 June 1770). They heard that the *primo uomo* for *Mitridate* was to be Santorini; finally, it was Pietro Benedetti (Sifare), who arrived less than four weeks before the premiere. He was, perhaps, better behaved than the tenor who took the title-role. **Guglielmo Ettore [d'Ettore]** was born on Sicily, around 1740; he died in Ludwigsburg, in the winter of 1771–2. He appeared in several Italian centres in the 1760s, among them Turin, where in 1767 he sang in Quirino Gasparini's *Mitridate, re di Ponto*. He sang the title role in Bernasconi's *La clemenza di Tito* at Munich in 1768 and Admetus in Guglielmi's *Alceste* the next year in Milan. Burney heard him in Padua in 1770 and reported that he was reckoned 'the best singer of his kind on the serious opera stage'. Schubart wrote that he had 'never heard anyone sing with the feeling of a d'Ettore' (*Schubart's Leben und Gesinnungen*, Stuttgart, 1791–3, i, p. 94). Later that year he sang the title role in Mozart's *Mitridate*; the young composer had to rewrite one aria four times for him, and Ettore ultimately included an aria by Gasparini (displaying his splendid top *c″*) in place of another of Mozart's. Ettore was engaged at the Württemberg court on 28 January 1771 but died the next winter. **[H.J.-W.]** Years later Leopold Mozart, urging Mozart to keep up his courage and overcome obstacles, reminded Mozart of d'Ettore and the intrigues of De Amicis among the trials Mozart had had to overcome before triumphing in Milan (letter of 6 May 1778).

The personnel was different for each of Mozart's three Milan operas. In 1771 it must have been a relief to find an experienced singer—moreover, his old teacher—in the title role of *Ascanio in Alba*, even if his vocal range had gone down. **Giovanni Manzuoli** was born in Florence around 1720; he died there in 1782. He was first a soprano castrato and later a contralto. After appearances in operas in Florence (1731) and Verona (1735) he settled in Naples and by the mid-1740s he was singing leading parts at the San Carlo. After a season at Milan he performed in ten productions in Madrid (1749–52). He left after an incident occasioned by his arrogant temperament, sang in Parma in the 1754 Carnival, and was in Lisbon for the opening of the Teatro de los Paços Ribeira in 1755 and briefly back in Madrid. He returned to Italy and remained there until 1764 except for a trip to Vienna, where according to Metastasio his performance in Hasse's *Alcide al bivio* (1760) made him the idol of the city. In the 1764–5 season Manzuoli, a fine actor whose voice was 'the most powerful and voluminous soprano that had been heard . . . since the time of Farinelli' (Burney), drew 'a universal thunder' of applause at the King's Theatre, London; there he became acquainted with the Mozarts and sang in the premiere of J. C. Bach's *Adriano in Siria*. He retired to Florence in 1768 after three successful seasons in Italy (Verona, Turin, Venice, and Milan), but sang again in Rome in 1770 and in Milan the next year in Hasse's *Ruggiero* as well as *Ascanio in Alba*. **[K.K.H.]** He stalked off without taking his fee, because he considered what he was offered inadequate (Mozart's letter of 24 November 1771 castigates him for this stupidity).

In 1772, for *Lucio Silla*, Milan engaged a completely different group of singers. The minor ones, except the late substitute tenor Bassano Morgnoni in the title-role, may have arrived in good time, and no doubt performed adequately; the role of the *secondo uomo* Cinna (Felicità Suardi) is not by any means elementary. But the success of an opera would usually stand or fall by its two principals, the couple Junia and Cecilius, and for these Milan had engaged major performers in the Italian soprano De Amicis and the castrato Rauzzini.

Anna Lucia de Amicis [De Amicis-Buonsollazzi] was born in Naples c. 1733; she died there in 1816. She began performing in comic operas with her family in the 1750s in Italy, Paris, and Brussels, then in 1762 appeared in London at the King's Theatre. Following her debut as a serious singer in J. C. Bach's *Orione* (1763), she left comic opera. As prima donna in Milan (1764–5), Venice (1764), Innsbruck (1765), and Naples (1766), she became involved in theatrical disputes and wished to retire. But after marriage (1768) to a Florentine physician she resumed her career, singing in Venice (1768–9, 1770–71) and Naples (1769–70, 1771–2), in Jommelli's *Armida abbandonata* [in which Mozart admired her singing: letter of 5 June 1770], and *Ifigenia in Tauride*. In the role of Junia she ensured the success of *Lucio Silla* in Milan (1772). Engagements in Naples (1773–6), Turin (1776–9), and the Italian premiere of Gluck's *Alceste* (1778, Bologna) concluded her brilliant career, though she sang for at least another ten years in private Neapolitan productions.

De Amicis amazed listeners with her vocal agility. Burney described her as the first to sing staccato divisions, and the first to 'go up to E flat in altissimo, with true, clear, and powerful *real* voice'. She was equally impressive as an actress: Metastasio wrote that 'among the dramatic heroines . . . there was absolutely no one but the signora De Amicis suited to portray the character . . . with the fire, the boldness, the frankness, and the expression necessary'. **[K.K.H.]** As already mentioned, Leopold Mozart added her to d'Ettore as one who had proved trying to work with, but at the time of *Lucio Silla* he was full of praise and grateful for her friendliness; she was the victim of an unfortunate but hilarious incident on the first night (letter of 2 January 1773). According to a later anecdote, she offered to help the composer by writing her own arias. She reached Milan late on 4 December when Mozart still had 14 numbers to compose (letter of 5 December 1772). Happily the *primo uomo* had arrived two weeks earlier.

Venanzio Rauzzini was born in Camerino, near Rome, and was baptized on 19 December 1746; he died in Bath, on 8 April 1810. He was an Italian soprano castrato and composer. After early studies in Rome and possibly also in Naples with Porpora, he made his debut at the Teatro della Valle in Rome in Piccinni's *Il finto astrologo* (7 February 1765). His first major role was in Guglielmi's *Sesostri* at Venice during Ascension Fair 1766. In the same year he entered the service of the Elector Maximilian III Joseph at Munich, where he remained until 1772. He first appeared there in Traetta's

Siroe (Carnival 1767), and later that year was given leave to perform at Venice and at Vienna, where the Mozarts heard him in Hasse's *Partenope*. Burney, visiting Rauzzini in August 1772, praised his virtuosity and the quality of his voice, but was most impressed by his abilities as a composer and harpsichordist. His last known operatic performance in Munich was in Bernasconi's *Demetrio* (Carnival 1772). According to Michael Kelly he was forced to leave because of difficulties with noblewomen engendered by his good looks.

Rauzzini performed for two more years in Italy before moving permanently to England. Engaged for Carnival 1773 at Milan, he was *primo uomo* in Mozart's *Lucio Silla* and Paisiello's *Sismano nel Mogol* (30 January 1773). In January Mozart wrote for him the brilliant motet *Exsultate, jubilate* K165/158a. Later that year he sang at Venice and Padua, and in 1774 at Turin (Carnival) and Venice (Ascension Fair).

From November 1774 to July 1777 Rauzzini sang regularly at the King's Theatre in London, making his simultaneous debut as singer and composer in the pasticcio *Armida*. Bingley reported that his acting in Sacchini's *Montezuma* (7 February 1775) greatly impressed Garrick. Both Burney and Lord Mount Edgcumbe, however, deemed his voice sweet but too feeble, a defect Burney ascribed to Rauzzini's devoting too much time to composition. In the following years many of his works, both vocal and instrumental, were performed and published in London.

In autumn 1777 Rauzzini took up residence in Bath, where he managed concerts by many renowned performers, among them his pupils John Braham, Nancy Storace, Charles Incledon, Mrs Billington, and Mme Mara. At Dublin in 1778 he met and taught Michael Kelly and promoted his career with advice to study in Naples. He was intermittently in London during the next few seasons to stage his operas. The London premiere of his opera *La vestale* (1 May 1787) was unsuccessful, and thereafter he remained permanently at Bath. Near the end of his life Rauzzini [composed a Requiem and] published a set of 12 vocal exercises with an introduction summing up his ideas on the art of singing and reflecting his own tasteful execution. [K.K.H.]

Mannheim and Munich

Count Joseph Anton Seeau (1713–99), theatre intendant in Munich, remained in post after Carl Theodor became Elector of Bavaria in 1778. He was thus involved with both operas commissioned from Mozart for Munich. Leopold Mozart clearly regarded him as an ally, but Mozart came to distrust him, having heard that Seeau had put it about in Mannheim that *La finta giardiniera* had been a failure (letter of 12 November 1778). If Seeau opposed Mozart's selection to compose the Carnival opera for 1781, *Idomeneo*, he was overruled by Carl Theodor, and the support of the musicians translated from Mannheim made this period, when he escaped Salzburg to write the opera, one of the happiest of Mozart's life. Seeau made one contribution to the score by refusing to engage the trombones Mozart wanted for the oracle.

The Konzertmeister in Mannheim, and subsequently in Munich, was very friendly to Mozart. **Christian Cannabich** (1731–98), a violinist, conductor, and composer, first met Mozart as a child in 1763, and welcomed him cordially back to Mannheim in 1777. Mozart admired his musicianship ('the best conductor I have ever seen': letter of 9 July 1778), and taught piano to his daughter Rosina ('Rosa', b.1764). Cannabich helped preparations for *Idomeneo* and probably directed the premiere with Mozart himself. Mozart did not much admire his compositions, and the best part of Cannabich's commemorative ode to Mozart is a citation from *Don Giovanni*. But he was in charge of the finest orchestra in Europe, which Burney called 'an army of generals, each as fitted to plan a battle, as to fight it'. Among these were the outstanding woodwind players, Wendling (flute), Ramm (oboe), and Ritter (bassoon) for whom, with the travelling horn-player Punto, Mozart had composed a Sinfonia concertante in Paris. Their expressive playing, with the local horn-player, is enshrined in the aria for Ilia (Dorothea Wendling), 'Se il padre perdei'. [J.R.]

On his first visit to Mannheim, although he composed arias for Wendling and Raaff, the singer who impressed him most (for personal as well as musical reasons) was the second of the Weber sisters, his eventual sister-in-law **Aloysia Lange**. Born Maria Aloysia [Aloisia, Aloysia Louise] Antonia Weber in Zell or Mannheim, probably in 1761, she died in Salzburg on 8 June 1839. Her elder sister became Josepha Hofer (q.v.), her younger sisters Constanze Mozart (1762–1842) and Sophie Haibel (1763–1846). Aloysia studied in Mannheim with Vogler and Mozart, her association with whom produced seven concert arias and a role in *Der Schauspieldirektor* (as well as a letter by Mozart [30 July 1778] notable for elucidating his views on vocal performance and training). Their first encounter, during Mozart's stay in Mannheim in 1777–8 (when he fell in love with her) resulted in the concert arias K294 and 316/300b, and probably the beginning of K538 [completed in 1787]. She moved from Mannheim to Munich in 1778, where she made her debut as Parthenia in Schweitzer's *Alceste* (Carnival 1779); she was then engaged for the new National-Singspiel in Vienna [where she was the most highly paid female singer]. She made her debut there on 9 September 1779 as Hännchen in a German adaptation of Philidor's *La rosière de Salency*. She married the court actor and painter Joseph Lange on 31 October 1780. [She was pregnant in 1781 which may explain why Cavalieri was preferred for the role of Konstanze in *Die Entführung*, although Mozart was perhaps not yet entirely reconciled with Aloysia.]

When in 1782 Joseph II reinstated Italian comic opera at the Burgtheater, Aloysia Lange was retained as a leading singer of the troupe. For her debut, as Clorinda in Anfossi's *Il curioso indiscreto* (1783), Mozart composed two substitute arias, K418 and 419. Lange participated regularly in Italian opera for only eight months; probably she fell out of favour because of disagreements over salary and roles as well as missed performances. In 1785 she was among the German singers transferred to the less prestigious Kärntnertortheater, where she revived many roles of her early career with the important addition of Konstanze in *Die Entführung* (1785–8). Lange continued to appear occasionally at the Burgtheater, notably for a German revival in 1785 of Gluck's *La rencontre imprévue*, for the Vienna premiere of Mozart's *Don Giovanni* (as Donna Anna), and for Cimarosa's *Il fanatico burlato*, both in 1788. She was retained by Leopold II for his *opera seria* venture in Vienna in 1790, as a *seconda donna*. In 1795 Aloysia undertook a concert tour with her sister Constanze, continuing her successes as Mozart's Sextus, a role she had performed in Vienna.

A report in the *Deutsches Museum* (1781) states that she 'has a very pleasing voice, though it is too weak for the theatre', and Gerber pronounced her voice 'more suited for an ordinary room than the theatre'. Leopold Mozart corroborates this view in a letter to his daughter of 25 March 1785:

It can scarcely be denied that she sings with the greatest expression: only now I understand why some persons I frequently asked would say that she has a very weak voice, while others said she has a very loud voice. Both are true. The held notes and all expressive notes are astonishingly loud; the tender moments, the passage work and embellishments, and high notes are very delicate, so that for my taste the one contrasts too strongly with the other. In an ordinary room the loud notes assault the ear, while in the theatre the delicate passages demand a great attentiveness and stillness on the part of the audience.

Mozart's compositions give the clearest picture of her voice. His sensitivity to Lange's small instrument may be seen in the light orchestration and relatively high tessitura. Her music exploits expressive, cantabile delivery and gives ample opportunity for portamento and the addition of ornaments. Her *fioriture* consist primarily of scale work and *abbellimenti* spun out in varied, flexible rhythmic configurations, and there is an almost casual assaying of her remarkable upper range, extending to *g'''* (as Blanka in Umlauf's *Das Irrlicht*, 1782, she sang to *a'''*). Gebler regarded her as 'a splendid singer, [with] a tone and an expression that goes to the heart [and] an extraordinary upper range; she correctly performs the most difficult passages and blends them with the song as it should be done'. **[P.L.G.]**

When Mozart returned from Paris via Mannheim, many of his friends had gone ahead to Munich. Eventually he followed, receiving a cold shoulder from Aloysia and comforted at one of the lowest points of his life by friends including the flautist Becke, who had visited Salzburg with Consoli for *Il re pastore*. Leopold Mozart was dubious about the moral influence of the Wendling family on his son, but two of the three female singers gave rise to some of his finest vocal music in *Idomeneo*.

Dorothea Wendling, born Dorothea Spurni in Stuttgart on 21 March 1736, died in Munich on 20 August 1811. The daughter of a Stuttgart horn player, she was appointed a singer at the Mannheim court in 1752; on 9 January that year she married the flautist Johann Baptist Wendling. Her first role was Hermione in Galuppi's *Antigona* (17 January 1753). In 1758 she sang the prima donna role in Holzbauer's *Nitteti* and for the next 20 years was the most celebrated soprano at Mannheim. Her salary, 1200 florins in 1759, increased to 1500 in 1778. She appeared in serious operas by Jommelli, Holzbauer, Piccinni, and J. C. Bach, and took the title roles in Traetta's *Sofonisba* (1762) and Majo's *Ifigenia in Tauride* (1764). She also sang in the Italian comic operas performed at Mannheim in the 1770s, and appeared in more than 30 roles in 25 years. Mozart admired her voice and wrote the concert aria K486a/295a for her in 1778. Wieland, who heard her during rehearsals for Schweitzer's *Rosamunde*, wrote: 'Her style of singing surpasses everything I have ever heard, even the famous Mara' [a singer Mozart, incidentally, did not favour]. Heinse and Schubart praised her as one of the most expressive singers of the day, though the latter also mentioned an unfortunate 'warble'. She remained active in Mannheim after the court transferred to Munich in 1778, and created the title roles in Holzbauer's *La morte di Didone* (1779, Mannheim) and J. P. Verazi's *Laodamia* (1780, Oggersheim). She appeared as a guest in Munich, singing Calipso in Franz Paul Grua's *Telemaco* (1780) and Ilia in Mozart's *Idomeneo* (1781). After she left the stage, she continued to sing in concerts and taught singing in Mannheim and Munich. Her daughter, Elisabeth Augusta ('Gustl'), also occasionally performed in comic operas at Mannheim and Schwetzingen. **[P.C.]** Elisabeth Augusta also had a period as Carl Theodor's mistress. Mozart wrote some French songs for her; she should not be confused with the first Elektra, her aunt by marriage.

Elisabeth Wendling was born Elisabeth Augusta Sarselli in Mannheim on 20 February 1746; she died in Munich on 10 January 1786. Her parents, the tenor Pietro Sarselli and his wife Carolina, were singers at Mannheim. She accompanied her future husband to Italy in 1760 and after her return to Mannheim in 1761 was appointed a court musician. She married Franz Wendling, the violinist and brother of Johann Baptist, on 1 December 1764. Beginning with the role of Cirene in Traetta's *Sofonisba* (1762), she was cast in the seconda donna roles at the Hoftheater, singing opposite her sister-in-law, Dorothea. She accompanied the court to Munich in 1778, and there created her most famous role, Elektra in *Idomeneo* (1781). She also sang the title role in Salieri's *Semiramide* (1782); her last role was Zelmira in Prati's *Armida abbandonata* (1785). **[P.C.]**

Fortunate in his sopranos, Mozart had problems with the principal male singers in *Idomeneo*, especially the castrato. **Vincenzo dal Prato** [Del Prato] was the same age as Mozart; he was born in Imola on 5 May 1756, and died in Munich in 1828. He studied with Lorenzo Gibelli and made his debut at the opera house in Fano in 1772. After touring extensively in Germany and the Netherlands, he sang at Stuttgart in 1779 for the future Russian Tsar Paul I. In 1780 Dal Prato was appointed to the court in Munich, where he spent the rest of his career. His voice was apparently a high mezzo. His most famous role was Idamantes in *Idomeneo*, and he also sang in Salieri's *Semiramide* (1782), Holzbauer's *Tancredi* (1783), and Vogler's *Castore e Polluce* (1787). Mozart complained that the inexperienced singer's stage presence was poor, and that he had to teach him his music 'as if he were a child'. But Dal Prato was apparently eager to learn, and Mozart referred to him as his 'molto amato castrato Dal Prato'. His singing was admired more for its grace and polished execution than its power or dramatic qualities. **[P.C.]** His music in *Idomeneo* is considerably less demanding, however, than the women's, or that of the first two tenors.

As in *Mitridate* and *Lucio Silla*, the title-role in *Idomeneo* was the leading tenor; and his intervention may have helped gain the commission for Mozart. **Anton Raaff** [Raff] was born in Gelsdorf, near Bonn, and baptized on 6 May 1714; he died in Munich on 28 May 1797. After being appointed to the service of Clement Augustus, Elector of Cologne, Raaff was sent in 1736 to Munich, where he studied with Ferrandini and sang in one of his operas. The following year he studied with Bernacchi in

Bologna, remaining in Italy until 1741–2, when he returned to electoral service in Bonn. In 1749 he left for Vienna where he sang in several operas composed and directed by Jommelli. He was in Italy in 1751–2, when he was called to the court of Lisbon; from there he went in 1755 to Madrid and, in 1759, he travelled with Farinelli to Naples.

For the next decade Raaff was the principal tenor on the Neapolitan and Florentine stages, appearing in operas by Hasse, Majo, and J. C. Bach, as well as Sacchini, Piccinni, and Mysliveček. In August 1770 he arrived at Mannheim, where he sang the title roles in Piccinni's *Catone in Utica* (1770) and Bach's *Temistocle* (1772) and *Lucio Silla* (1775). Mozart was critical of his singing and acting in the title role of Holzbauer's *Günther von Schwarzburg* (1777), but was more sympathetic after hearing him sing Bach's 'Non so d'onde viene' from *Alessandro nell'Indie* at the Concert Spirituel in Paris during June 1778. Mozart won his favour by composing a setting of one of the tenor's favourite texts, 'Se al labbro mio' (K295). Idomeneus was Raaff's last role.

Though Raaff's voice was praised by Schubart as having an unusually large range from bass to alto, with flexible coloratura throughout, Mozart found it small in range and limited in technique. Yet Raaff sang well enough in 1787 to impress Michael Kelly, who wrote that 'he still retained his fine *voce di petto* and sostenuto notes, and pure style of singing'. He was one of the last and greatest representatives of the legato technique and portamento, brought to perfection by Bernacchi and his school. **[D.H. (with P.C.)]** It should be remembered that Mozart composed for Raaff only in the final stages of the tenor's long career—he was 66 at the time of *Idomeneo*—and that the composer expressed a personal dislike of 'the Bernacchi school' (letter of 12 June 1778).

Idomeneo in 1781 was already an opera for three tenors (in 1786 it was for four tenors). The second was **Domenico Panzacchi** [Pansacchi], born in Bologna around 1730; he died there in 1805. He too is said to have been a pupil of Bernacchi. He sang in *opera seria* from 1746, and in 1748–9 in Vienna where he first worked with Raaff, who was to overshadow him in parts of his later career. In 1751–7 he was at Madrid (Raaff arriving at a higher salary in 1755) and from 1760 until his pensioning in 1782 he was in the service of the Munich court (which Raaff joined after 1778), with occasional operatic engagements in Italy. He is remembered for creating Arbaces in *Idomeneo* (1781), Mozart finding his singing and acting still worthy of respect despite his age. **[D.L.]** Mozart contrasted his acting favourably with that of Raaff and Dal Prato: 'we must try to oblige this honest old chap. He would like his recitative ['Sventurata Sidon', in Act 3] lengthened by a couple of lines, which will be effective because of his *chiaro e oscuro* and his being a very good actor' (letter of 5 December 1780). The third tenor was Giovanni Valesi (1735–1816), a German whose name was Italianized from Walleshauser. He was a teacher of Adamberger; in *Idomeneo* he sang the small but important role of the High Priest.

Vienna (1): Singspiel

The personnel of Joseph II's National-Singspiel, when Mozart wrote for it, included at least two good sopranos in addition to Aloysia Lange: Caterina Cavalieri and Therese Teyber. The former, although she was close to Salieri, seems to have remained in friendly contact with Mozart; she was his guest at a performance of *Die Zauberflöte*. The most interesting observations Mozart makes about his dramatic music refer to the outstanding principal male singers, Adamberger and Fischer, and are quoted above. Adamberger in particular remained a close friend to Mozart; he too was a freemason.

Caterina [Kavalier, Franziska Helena Appolonia] Cavalieri [Cavallieri] was born in Vienna on 19 February 1760; she died there on 30 June 1801. During a career confined almost exclusively to Vienna, she appeared with equal success in comic and serious roles in both the Italian and German repertories. In her early career Cavalieri possessed an impressive upper range, to d''''. An extraordinary stamina and flexibility are reflected in consistently large-scale bravura arias. Of her debut in Vienna (19 June 1775 at the Kärntnertortheater), as Sandrina in Anfossi's *La finta giardiniera*, Count Khevenhüller wrote that she possessed a very strong chest voice and met with 'well-deserved approbation'. In 1776–7 she belonged to a troupe of Italian singers. In 1778 she sang Sophie in Umlauf's *Die Bergknappen*, the inaugural production of the National-Singspiel, and went on to sing 18 leading roles in the company including Nannette in Salieri's *Der Rauchfangkehrer* (1781) and Konstanze in Mozart's *Die Entführung* (1782). Of the challenging *fioriture* in 'Ach ich liebte', Mozart wrote to his father (26 September 1781): 'I have sacrificed Konstanze's aria a little to the flexible throat of Mlle Cavallieri'. When Joseph II inaugurated *opera buffa* at the Burgtheater, Cavalieri was put to use both as a serious and comic lead. Her hard-hitting bravura is evident in rewritten or new solo numbers in works by Salieri and Cimarosa.

Cavalieri is best known through Mozart's music for her. Her aria as Mme Silberklang in *Der Schauspieldirektor* (1786) has muscular tunes, with driving, vigorous two-note phrases and quaver scales. For her appearance as

Donna Elvira in the first Vienna production of *Don Giovanni* (1788), Mozart composed a large-scale aria ('Mi tradì'); she clearly no longer commanded her earlier high notes. For the revival of *Le nozze di Figaro* (1789), in which Cavalieri sang the Countess, Mozart rewrote 'Dove sono', eliminating the repeat of the intimate, restrained initial material and adding *fioriture* in the faster section.

Early in her career, Cavalieri was said to want 'animation and accuracy, and a firmer assurance', and was criticized for almost 'unintelligible' speech (M. A. Schmitt, *Meine Empfindungen im Theater*, 1781). The Viennese dramatist Gebler, writing in 1780–81, said she had 'a strong and pleasant voice, in both the high and the low notes, a combination which one seldom encounters; [she] sings equally well the most difficult passages'. Zinzendorf noted that in a duet in Sarti's *Giulio Sabino* 'Cavalieri drowned Marchesini's voice with her shouts' (4 August 1785), but two days later recorded that 'she screamed less'. **[P.L.G.]** Despite these conflicting reports of her ability, and the fact that she was paid less than Lange and remained subordinate to such new arrivals in the *opera buffa* troupe as Storace and Ferrarese, Cavalieri must have been a good singer to wring such music out of Mozart.

Therese Teyber was born in Vienna, and baptized on 15 October 1760; she died in Vienna on 15 April 1830. She was the sister of Elisabeth Teyber, herself a soprano. A pupil of Bonno and Tesi, she made her debut at the Vienna court theatre as Fiametta in Ulbrich's *Frühling und Liebe* (1778). Teyber was a popular portrayer of young lovers and artless girls and created the role of Blonde in *Die Entführung aus dem Serail* (1782); she also appeared with success in many other operas and Singspiels. The charm of her acting and singing was praised in contemporary reports. She and her husband, the tenor Ferdinand Arnold, are reported to have performed together with much success at Hamburg, Berlin, Warsaw, and Riga, though the chronology of these appearances is confused. She appeared as Zerlina in some Viennese performances of *Don Giovanni* (1788) and is certainly the 'Mad.selle Täuber' referred to in Mozart's letter of 29 March 1783 [after she sang an aria from *Lucio Silla*]. **[P.B.]**

Valentin Josef Adamberger was born in Munich on 6 July 1743; he died in Vienna on 24 August 1804. In 1755 he studied singing with Valesi while at the Domus Gregoriana, a Jesuit institution in Munich. In 1760 he joined the Kapelle of Duke Clemens and on Clemens's death in 1770 was taken into the elector's Hofkapelle. He sang leading tenor roles in *opere serie* at Modena, Venice, Florence, Pisa, and Rome from 1775 to 1777, then at the King's Theatre in London until 1779, and again in Italy until he joined the

National Singspiel at Vienna, where he made his debut on 21 August 1780. In 1781 he married the Viennese actress Marie Anne Jacquet (1753–1804). On the demise of the National Singspiel in 1783 Adamberger joined the Italian company, then in 1785 the new German troupe under imperial subvention at the Kärntnertortheater, and on its dissolution in 1789 the Italian company at the Burgtheater once again. He retired from the stage in 1793 but continued as a member of the imperial Hofkapelle and as an eminent singing teacher.

Adamberger's voice was universally admired for its pliancy, agility, and precision, although Schubart and Mount Edgcumbe also remarked on its nasal quality. Mozart wrote the parts of Belmonte in *Die Entführung* (1782) and Vogelsang in *Der Schauspieldirektor* (1786) for him, as well as several fine arias (K420, K431, and solos in the oratorio *Davidde penitente* K469, and the cantata *Die Maurerfreude* K471). Before coming to Vienna, Adamberger created leading tenor parts in serious operas by J. C. Bach, Sarti, Pietro Guglielmi, Sacchini, Bertoni, and others. The arias they wrote for his voice reveal a fondness for moderate tempos, B♭ major, obbligato clarinets, and expressive chromatic inflections. At Vienna Mozart (*Die Entführung*), Umlauf (*Das Irrlicht*), and Dittersdorf (*Doktor und Apotheker*) perpetuated these features, which made Adamberger 'the favourite singer of softer hearts', according to a local journalist. [T.B.]

The second tenor in *Die Entführung*, **Johann [Joseph] Ernst Dauer**, was born in Hildburghausen in 1746; he died in Vienna on 12 September 1812. He began his career in 1768, and in 1771 was engaged in Hamburg, where he sang in Singspiels. In 1775 he went to Gotha and in 1777 to Frankfurt and Mannheim. In 1779 he was engaged at the Vienna Burgtheater, initially in the Singspiel company (making his debut as Alexis in Monsigny's *Le déserteur*) and, the following year, also acting in the spoken theatre company. He created Pedrillo in *Die Entführung* and Sturmwald in Dittersdorf's *Der Apotheker und der Doktor* (1786). He was a useful though uninspired performer: according to the actor F. L. Schröder, 'He touched the heart in neither serious nor comic roles. His manner was a little cold and remote; his movement somewhat wooden'. He played secondary lovers, character roles, and sturdy, unpolished lads. [C.R., D.L.]

Johann Ignaz [Karl] Ludwig Fischer was born in Mainz on 18 August 1745; he died in Berlin on 10 July 1825. He studied violin and cello, then singing with Anton Raaff from about 1769 in Mannheim, where he became *virtuoso da camera* in 1772. He moved with the court to Munich (1778), where he married the singer Barbara Strasser (born 1758; died after 1825). From 1780 to 1783 the couple worked in Vienna, where Fischer sang Osmin in *Die Entführung*, much to the satisfaction of Mozart, who frequently wrote about him in letters and gave him an introduction for Paris. He then secured his reputation with a tour of Italy and visited Vienna, Prague, and Dresden. After serving in Regensburg from 1785 he received a lifelong appointment in Berlin in 1789. Guest appearances in London (1794, 1798), Leipzig (1798), Hamburg (1801–2), and elsewhere added to his fame. He gave up public performance in 1812.

Fischer was regarded as Germany's leading serious bass. His voice, said to range from *D* to *a'*, was praised by Reichardt as having 'the depth of a cello and the natural height of a tenor'. He also composed. His autobiography, covering up to 1790, is in manuscript in the Berlin Staatsbibliothek. His son (?Anton) Joseph Fischer (born Berlin, 1780; died Mannheim, 1862) was a bass and composer and his daughters Josepha Fischer-Vernier (born 1782) and Wilhelmine (born 1785) were also distinguished singers. [R.W.] Mozart's high opinion is confirmed by two demanding concert arias (κ432 in 1783 and κ 512 in 1787), of which the first was probably and the latter certainly for Fischer.

Vienna (2): *Opera Buffa*

Mozart's debut with the Italian troupe at the Burgtheater was preceded by *Der Schauspieldirektor*, which employed singers with whom Mozart was thoroughly familiar (Lange, Cavalieri, Adamberger), and the *Idomeneo* revival. Earlier, Mozart had wanted to alter the part of Idamantes for a tenor (Adamberger), and that of Idomeneus for bass (Fischer). In the event only the former change was made. The single performance took place at the private theatre of the Auersperg palace and its importance should not be underrated just because the singers were amateurs, for some of them were influential people; they were probably rather good. Count August Clemens von Hatzfeld (1754–87), a friend of Mozart, played the obbligato in a new aria for the tenor Idamantes (κ490), to be sung by Baron Antonio Pulini. The latter was long known to Mozart; Leopold mentions him as a suitable tenor for *opera buffa* in a letter of 30 January 1768 (with *La finta semplice* in mind). Baroness Anna von Pufendorf (c.1757–1843), a singer and promoter of concerts, sang Ilia, and Hatzfeld's sister-in-law, Countess Hortensia (1750–1813) Elektra. The Countess was a generous patron and a pianist as well as a singer, and later supported Beethoven. Although her most demanding aria, in Act 3, was not included, she apparently held the performance together and 'almost excels our Mme Storaze [sic]', as was reported in the Salzburg journal *Pfeffer und Salz*. Giuseppe Antonio Bridi sang Idomeneus, requiring a simplified—albeit still demanding—version of his Act 2 aria. The role of Arbaces was virtually eliminated.

The Mozarts had met the Burgtheater manager Count Rosenberg-Orsini in Florence in 1770, when he assisted them in obtaining an interview with the Grand Duke. He had approved the commission for *Die Entführung* and encouraged Mozart's ambition to write *opera buffa*. The music director of the theatres was none other than Antonio Salieri, who had recently had considerable success in Paris with *Les Danaïdes* and was to continue his career in Vienna with *La grotta di Trofonio* (1785) and *Prima la musica*, performed with *Der Schauspieldirektor*. He returned to Paris for *Les Horaces* and *Tarare* (1786 and 1787) and surely did not direct every performance even when in Vienna. From 1785, his pupil Joseph Weigl (the younger 1766–1846), Joseph Haydn's godson and an admirer of Mozart, took over the duties of repetiteur and worked on *Le nozze di Figaro*, no doubt learning much that contributed to his later success as a composer (notably with *Die Schweizerfamilie*, 1809).

Operatic history is shot through with stories of rival *prime donne*, and the Vienna troupe was no exception; *Der Schauspieldirektor* was hardly the first indication that such stimulating conflict had Imperial sanction. Mozart himself reported a certain coolness between Lange and Storace (letter of 2 July 1783). That year, doubtless eager to demonstrate his abilities in the genre, Mozart contributed two arias for Lange in Anfossi's *Il curioso indiscreto* (K418 and 419), because the originals were unsuited to her. She performed them despite a certain amount of opposition from the Italian party (according to Mozart, Adamberger was tricked into not performing his aria for the same opera, K 420). The ambitions of Joseph II were not confined to switching languages; he wanted singers trained in Italy, and by Italians. His agents abroad included the Austrian ambassador to Venice, Gluck's former supporter Count Giacomo Durazzo, but Joseph himself travelled to Italy in 1783 on diplomatic and theatre business. In Naples he recruited the *buffa* soprano Celeste Coltellini (1760–1829), daughter of the librettist Marco Coltellini and a student of Manzuoli, to set up a rivalry to Storace. Coltellini took no part in the Mozart-Da Ponte premieres, but she sang Mandina in Bianchi's *La villanella rapita* in 1785, and thus in the trio and quartet (K479, 480) supplied by Mozart. Another soprano, **Maria Mandini**, was daughter of a Versailles court official and wife of the singer Stefano Mandini. They were engaged together between 1783 and 1787. She made her Burgtheater debut in 1783 as Madama Brillante in Cimarosa's *L'italiana in Londra* and then sang Countess Belfiore in Sarti's *Fra i due litiganti*. She is known to have created three small roles: Marina in Martín y

Soler's *Il burbero di buon cuore* (1786), Marcellina in *Le noẓẓe di Figaro*, and Britomarte in Martín y Soler's *L'arbore di Diana*. In 1787 she appeared in Cimarosa's *Le trame deluse* and sang Livietta in Paisiello's *Le due contesse*. Nothing is known of her later career. She was apparently attractive but a poor singer. Count Zinzendorf wrote of her performance as Marina: 'La Mandini let us see her beautiful hair'. As Britomarte she was said to sound 'like an enraged cat' and the performing score contains a pencilled comment at the head of her only aria: 'canta male'. **[C.R.]** All of which shows that, much as one would like to have been there, the standards of the company were perhaps not always of the highest, and the brilliance of its reputation today derives from the outstanding quality of its repertory. As now appears, there were even reservations concerning the singing of one of its most famous stars.

Nancy [Ann Selina; Anna] Storace was born in London on 27 October 1765; she died in Dulwich on 24 August 1817. She was the daughter of Stefano Storace, an Italian double bass player, and adapter of Italian opera into English, and sister of the composer Stephen Storace. A vocal prodigy, she appeared in Southampton in 1773 as 'a Child not eight Years old'; her first London concert was at the Haymarket Theatre in April the following year. On 29 February 1776 she appeared with the celebrated Caterina Gabrielli in the premiere of Venanzio Rauzzini's *Le ali d'amore*. Her teachers in London were Rauzzini and the composer Antonio Sacchini.

In 1778 she followed her brother to Italy where she began her career in *opera seria*, singing *seconda donna* roles; this was followed by appearances in revivals of comic opera (1780–81) in which she took both *prima seria* and *prima buffa* roles. In 1782 she sang in Milan, Turin, Parma, Rome, and Venice. The first opera specifically composed for her was one of the most acclaimed of its time, Sarti's *Fra i due litiganti* (1782, Milan); Kelly, who sang with her in Venice at the Teatro San Samuele in 1783, recalled that she 'drew overflowing houses' and was 'quite the rage' and when 'she announced a benefit, the first ever given to any performer at Venice . . . the kind-hearted and liberal Venetians not only paid the usual entrance money, but left all kinds of trinkets, watch chains, rings, etc., to be given her'. [This opera was equally popular in Vienna, and is one of those quoted in the supper scene in Mozart's *Don Giovanni*]. This celebrity caused Durazzo to engage her for the newly organized Italian opera in Vienna the same year. For her debut she sang a role created for her at the San Samuele, the Countess in Salieri's *La scuola dei gelosi*. During her first season at the Burgtheater, Storace sang in half of the 14 productions; her contract provided for a salary achieved by only the most sought-after singers of the day. In late 1783 she married the composer J. A. Fisher, but he apparently treated her cruelly and they soon parted; in 1786–7 she had a close relationship with Lord Barrard.

Her years in Vienna (1783–7) are important for the roles that major composers (Paisiello, Martín y Soler, Mozart) created for her. Her early vocal training and her experience in serious opera in Italy had helped her acquire vocal and dramatic resources that she could integrate into her comic performances; composers responded with roles of stylistic richness and variety. [Mozart planned Eugenia, in *Lo sposo deluso*, for her, under the name 'Signora Fisher'.] Her vocal qualities can be inferred from her music in the greatest operas written for her, Mozart's *Le nozze di Figaro* and Martín y Soler's *Una cosa rara* (this latter the greatest popular triumph of Viennese music theatre). Both Susanna and Lilla exploit her formidable dramatic talents, her precise declamation, and her preference for melodies within a limited vocal range and in *nota e parola* style. Mozart's sensitivity to Storace's low tessitura caused him to begin composing the role of Susanna below that of the Countess (subsequently reversed). Although Storace's music on occasion contained bravura elements, it is rarely ambitious in range or difficulty. Similar vocal writing is found in Mozart's other compositions for Storace, which include a single aria from the aborted *Lo sposo deluso* and the concert scena with piano obbligato, 'Chi'io mi scordi di te . . . Non temer amato bene' (K505), written for her farewell concert in Vienna.

In February 1787 Storace, her mother, Mozart's composition student Attwood, and Michael Kelly left for London where on 24 April she appeared in Paisiello's *Gli schiavi per amore* at the King's Theatre, with additional arias by her brother, Corri, and Mazzinghi. Stephen wrote that his sister 'has had great opposition from the Italians—who consider it as an infringement on their rights—that any person should be able to sing that was not born in Italy'. In 1789 she moved to Drury Lane to join her brother for the 1789–90 season, making her debut as Adelia in her brother's *The Haunted Tower*, for which she received top billing (unusual for a woman on London playbills); its success was in large measure due to its prima donna and her large-scale Italianate piece, 'Be mine tender passion'. Other leading roles in operas by her brother included Margaretta in *No Song, no Supper*, Lilla in *The Siege of Belgrade*, and Fabulina in *The Pirates*. There is reason to think she had a close relationship with the Prince of Wales in the early 1790s, when he, the Duke of Bedford, and the Marquis of Salisbury attempted to hire her for their secret court theatre at the Pantheon concert hall in Oxford Street. She sang at the King's Theatre for a season in 1793.

After her brother's death in 1796 she left Drury Lane and in 1797 she and her lover, the tenor John Braham, left for a tour of the Continent. Her farewell performance, and that of her friend Kelly, was at Drury Lane in *No Song, no Supper* in 1808.

After her death in 1817 Storace was under-praised by English writers. Burney called her 'a lively and intelligent actress' but said her voice had 'a certain crack and roughness' and 'a deficiency of natural sweetness'. Lord Mount Edgcumbe wrote that she was unfitted for serious opera and was undoubtedly most successful in comic parts: 'In her own particular line . . . she was unrivalled, being an excellent actress, as well as a masterly singer'. These evaluations suggest that it could not have been her virtuosity or purity of tone that made her voice so compelling to composers but rather that her intelligence, wit, and charm inspired some of the most vocally and dramatically incisive music of its time. **[P.L.G., B.M.]**

Luisa Laschi [Mombelli] was born in Florence in the 1760s. [Her father, Filippo Laschi, was a tenor who would have sung *La finta semplice* in Vienna in 1768.] When Luisa made her Viennese debut in 1784 in Cimarosa's *Giannina e Bernardone*, the *Wiener Kronik* said: 'she has a beautiful clear voice, which in time will become rounder and fuller; she is very musical, sings with more expression than the usual opera singers and has a beautiful figure'. In 1785 she sang [replacing Storace] Rosina in Paisiello's *Il barbiere di Siviglia* 'very well, and was much applauded' (Zinzendorf). Joseph II grudgingly released her for the 1785 season in Naples, but she returned in 1786 and created Countess Almaviva in *Le nozze di Figaro*. She had a further success on 15 May as Barbarina in Anfossi's *Il trionfo delle donne*, and in August appeared with her future husband, the tenor Domenico Mombelli, in Sarti's *I finti eredi*. In November she created the role of Queen Isabella in Martín y Soler's *Una cosa rara*, and in 1787 Cupid in his *L'arbore di Diana*, a role that required her to appear alternately as a shepherdess and as Cupid. A contemporary reviewer described her as 'Grace personified . . . ; ah, who is not enchanted by it, what painter could better depict the arch smile, what sculptor the grace in all her gestures, what singer could match the singing, so melting and sighing, with the same naturalness and true, warm expression?'

In January 1788 Mombelli appeared in the premiere of Salieri's *Axur, re d'Ormus* and in May she sang Zerlina in the first Vienna performance of Mozart's *Don Giovanni*; Mozart composed a new duet for her and Benucci. She was already seven months pregnant but continued singing until the day before her confinement and reappeared four weeks later. But there were difficulties between the Italian company and the management and the emperor gave the Mombellis notice. In September Luisa created the role of Carolina in Salieri's *Il talismano* and in February 1789 she made her farewell appearance as Donna Farinella in *L'ape musicale*; nothing further seems to be known about her, but in 1791 Domenico, by now apparently a widower, married the ballerina Vincenza Vigano, by whom he had 12 children. [C.R.]

Dorotea Bussani, who alone among the *buffa* sopranos created two Mozart roles, was born Dorothea Sardi in Vienna in 1763, and died sometime after 1810. On 20 March 1786 she married the Italian *buffo* Francesco Bussani. She specialized in *opera buffa* and made her debut creating Cherubino in *Le nozze di Figaro* (1786); she also created Ghita in Martín y Soler's *Una cosa rara* (1786), Despina in *Così fan tutte* (1790), and Fidalma in Cimarosa's *Il matrimonio segreto* (1792). She always pleased the public, and a contemporary wrote that he had never heard such a beautiful and charming chest voice nor one used with such humour and so mischievously (*Grundsätze zur Theaterkritik*, 1790). Lorenzo da Ponte, on the other hand, wrote: 'though awkward and of little merit, by dint of grimaces and clowning and perhaps by means even more theatrical, she built up a large following among cooks, grooms, servants, lackeys and wigmakers, and in consequence was considered a gem' (*Memorie*, 1823–7). [There was, however, some animosity between the Bussanis and the librettist. Dorotea Bussani was considerably less well paid than the other sopranos.] In 1795 Bussani went to Florence and she sang in Italy during the next decade. She appeared in Lisbon, 1807–9, and at the King's Theatre, London; Parke later described her as one having 'plenty of voice, but whose person and age were not calculated to fascinate an English audience' (*Musical Memoirs*, 1830). [C.R.]

Three different singers created the tenor roles in the Da Ponte operas, and a fourth sang in the Vienna *Don Giovanni*. The one with whom Mozart was probably most friendly and most delighted was the Irish Michael Kelly (sometimes known as O'Kelly). Before Kelly's arrival, the tenor Vincenzo Calvesi took the lead in a number of operas; they were probably very different types of singers, but had to appear as twins in Storace's *Gli equivoci*.

Vincenzo Calvesi [Caldesi] was an Italian, probably born in Faenza, whose career flourished between 1780 and 1794. After successful appearances in Verona (as Count Bandiera in Salieri's *La scuola de' gelosi*, 1780) and Venice, he made his Vienna debut in 1785 as Sandrino in Paisiello's *Il re Teodoro* and remained there until 1788. He went to Naples but returned to Vienna in 1789 and stayed until 1794 with occasional absences (he sang in Moscow in 1790). As the leading Italian lyric tenor in Vienna, he created

Prince Giovanni in Martín's *Una cosa rara* (1786) and Endymion in *L'arbore di Diana* (1787), as well as roles in operas by Storace (*Gli sposi malcontenti* and *Gli equivoci*) and Salieri (*La grotta di Trofonio* and *Axur, re d'Ormus*). In 1785 he sang the Count in the quartet 'Dite almeno, in che mancai' (K479) and the trio 'Mandina amabile' (K480) written by Mozart for Bianchi's *La villanella rapita*. He created Eufemio of Syracuse in *Gli equivoci* (1786), and Ferrando in *Così fan tutte* (1790). He was described in *Grundsätze zur Theaterkritik* (1790) as 'one of the best tenors from Italy . . . with a voice naturally sweet, pleasant and sonorous'. Calvesi also acted as impresario, at Faenza in 1788, and later in Rome (c. 1800–4). [C.R., D.L.] His wife, Teresa, a soprano, was part of the Burgtheater company but had little success.

Michael Kelly was born in Dublin on 25 December 1762; he died in Margate on 9 October 1826. He was a tenor, composer, theatre manager, and music publisher. The eldest of the 14 children of Thomas Kelly (Master of the Ceremonies at Dublin Castle, and a wine merchant), Michael Kelly grew up amid the rich musical life of Dublin, and received singing lessons from various immigrant Italians, notably Passerini and Rauzzini. His piano teachers included Michael Arne. Having made his earliest operatic appearances in Piccinni's *La buona figliuola*, Dibdin's *Lionel and Clarissa*, and Michael Arne's *Cymon*, Kelly left Dublin in 1779, on Rauzzini's advice, to study in Naples.

His most influential teachers there were Finaroli and Aprile. Equally important, perhaps, was the patronage of Sir William Hamilton. Kelly made his way northwards, obtaining engagements in many opera houses. In Venice his fortunes took a decisive turn when Count Durazzo offered him an engagement along with Storace, Benucci, and Mandini. The four years that Kelly spent in Vienna were to prove the climax of his musical career. Not only did he create the parts of Don Curzio and Don Basilio in *Le nozze di Figaro* [and Eufemio of Ephesus in *Gli equivoci*], but he also met most of the great composers and singers of the day.

In his *Reminiscences* Kelly left a vivid picture of his acquaintance with Mozart, both socially and in the opera house. Although Kelly's comments on musical life in Vienna are often superficial, he saw humanity in the round with keen observation and humorous detachment. It is these qualities which make the book so attractive: its first volume, particularly, is a valuable source of information about the music and manners of the time. [Besides describing Mozart rehearsing Benucci in 'Non più andrai', Kelly claims to have adopted a stammer for the role of Don Curzio, as in Beaumarchais' play, and not only in recitative, but in the sextet as well. He also said that Mozart had praised his modest compositions.]

In February 1787, with the Storaces and Attwood, Kelly left Vienna, visiting Mozart's father en route. Kelly quickly established himself in London, and his services as a singer were in continual demand throughout the British Isles during the next 30 years. He won greater approval for his technique than for the quality of his voice. In his *Memoirs of the Life of John Philip Kemble* (1825), James Boaden wrote: 'His voice had amazing power and steadiness, his compass was extraordinary. In vigorous passages he never cheated the ear with the feeble wailings of falsetto, but sprung upon the ascending fifth with a sustaining energy that often electrified an audience '. Mount Edgcumbe, however, no mean judge, expressed a less favourable view in his *Musical Reminiscences* (1825): 'Though he was a good musician and not a bad singer, having been long in Italy, yet he had retained, or regained, so much of the English vulgarity of manner that he was never greatly liked at this theatre [Drury Lane]'.

As a composer, Kelly claimed to have written over 60 theatre pieces between 1797 and 1821. But for many of these he contributed just a few songs; at other times he wrote in collaboration. He commanded a limited but prolific vein of melodic invention and seems to have relied on others for harmony and orchestration. In 1801, Thomas Moore wrote: 'Poor Mick is rather an imposer than a composer. He cannot mark the time in writing three bars of music: his understrappers, however, do all that for him'. He caught the current taste so well that his music became widely popular: it was extensively pirated in America, resulting in some 200 separate issues. *Blue Beard* remained in the repertory for 26 years. In 1801 Kelly set up as a publisher, in premises so close to the King's Theatre that he could offer patrons a private entrance through the shop, directly on to the stage. His publications included operas in vocal score and a considerable number of single songs. But the business seems to have needed more time than he could spare and was declared bankrupt in 1811. Kelly also engaged in the wine trade which, added to the suspicion that some of his compositions came from abroad, induced Sheridan to suggest that his shop-sign should read 'Michael Kelly, composer of wines and importer of music'.

Much of Kelly's time and energy was devoted to the King's Theatre; he became its stage manager in 1793 and served it with little intermission for nearly 31 years. Thus as singer, publisher, and manager, he lived in the heart of London's musical life. The Garrick Club possesses two portraits, one by De Wild showing him in costume as Cymon, the other a half-length by James Lonsdale. [A.H.K.]

The modern classification of range and voice type can be particularly misleading when we consider lower male voices. A youthful quality of sound is suited to a 'young and extremely licentious gentleman'—whether Count Almaviva or Don Giovanni—and this we usually call 'baritone'. A weightier, darker sound is equally suited to the elderly—such as the Commendatore—and to the buffoon—Bartolo. This quality which involves more exploration of the lower notes is also used for servants—Figaro, Leporello.

Although Mozart composed *Don Giovanni* for the Prague company, the production in Vienna, and thus the original cast of *Le nozze di Figaro*, must have been in his mind. Unfortunately the baritone population changed, if not quite as rapidly as the tenor, and he may have been sorry to lose the chance to write again for Stefano Mandini, the first Count Almaviva. He had previously planned for him the role of Don Asdrubale in *Lo sposo deluso*, noting by it 'Primo mezzo carattere'—a perfect prescription for a Don Giovanni.

Stefano Mandini was born in 1750; he died c. 1810. He appeared at Venice in 1775–6 and at Parma in 1776, described as 'primo buffo mezzo carattere'. In 1783 he and his wife were engaged by Joseph II for Vienna; Stefano was a leading member during its finest period. There is some confusion between Stefano and his younger brother Paolo. Stefano made his Vienna debut on 5 May 1783 in Cimarosa's *L'italiana in Londra*. That season he appeared as several roles including Mingone in *Fra i due litiganti*, and Count Almaviva in Paisiello's *Il barbiere di Siviglia*; in the last, Zinzendorf noted, he excelled in all four disguises in Almaviva's role. The following season among other roles he created the title role in Paisiello's *Il re Teodoro in Venezia*. In 1785 he created Artidoro in Storace's *Gli sposi malcontenti* and Plistene in *La grotta di Trofonio* [and sang Pippo in Bianchi's *La villanella rapita*, including Mozart's two ensembles, K479 and 480].

Mandini created three roles in 1786: the Poet in Salieri's *Prima la musica*, Count Almaviva in *Le nozze di Figaro*, and Lubino in *Una cosa rara*. He also sang in Sarti's *I finti eredi* and Paisiello's *Le gare generose*. In 1787–8 he appeared as Leandro in Paisiello's *Le due contesse* and created Doristo in Martín's *L'arbore di Diana* and Biscroma in Salieri's *Axur, re d'Ormus*. He was then released to go to Naples. Later he sang at the Théâtre de Monsieur in Paris, having considerable success in *Il barbiere di Siviglia*, *Una cosa rara*, and *La villanella rapita*. In 1794–5 he returned to Vienna for Piccinni's *La Griselda* and Paisiello's *La molinara*; he then went to St Petersburg, where the painter Elisabeth Vigée Le Brun remarked that he was an excellent performer and sang wonderfully. Nothing is known for certain of his later career, though it was probably he rather than Paolo who appeared in Berlin in 1804. An extremely versatile singer, he acquitted himself well both as the comic servant (e.g. Doristo) and as the serious lover (e.g. Lubino). **[C.R.]** He is sometimes said to have switched from tenor to baritone, because the role of Count Almaviva in *Il barbiere* is written in the tenor clef, and in *Figaro* in a bass clef. The Paisiello role was not written for Mandini but for a singer in St Petersburg; it is a role of striking character, but remarkably narrow range, eschewing high notes and well within the scope of a baritone. Mozart used a tenor clef for Mandini in *Lo sposo deluso* but, requiring a few lower notes, chose bass clef in *Figaro*. There was no switch of voice-type.

The versatile singers with lower tessitura exchanged roles between the two operas based on Beaumarchais, since Bartolo, in *Il barbiere*, is the role for a *primo buffo*, whereas in *Figaro* the title-role is far more important.

Francesco Benucci was born around 1745; he died in Florence on 5 April 1824. He sang at Pistoia in 1769, then more widely in Italy, appearing as the leading character *buffo* in Venice (1778–9), and singing with great success in Milan (1779–82) and Rome (1783–4). He first appeared in Vienna in 1783 and became the leading member of the company there, creating Tita in Martín y Soler's *Una cosa rara* and four Salieri roles including Trofonio and Axur. Mozart described him as 'particularly good' (letter of 7 May 1783) [and planned the role of Bocconio in *Lo sposo deluso* for him]; he created the role of Figaro, sang Leporello in the first Vienna performance of *Don Giovanni* (1788), when Mozart composed an extra duet for him, and Guglielmo in the premiere of *Così fan tutte* (1790). In 1789 he went to London where he sang Bartolo in Paisiello's *Il barbiere di Siviglia* and appeared in Gazzaniga's *La vendemmia* opposite Nancy Storace. They introduced the first piece from any Mozart opera to be heard on the London stage, the duet 'Crudel! perchè finora' from *Figaro*. Benucci returned to Vienna later in 1789, remaining until 1795. His last great triumph was to create Count Robinson in Cimarosa's *Il matrimonio segreto* in 1792. He had a round, beautifully full voice, more bass than baritone; probably he was the finest artist for whom Mozart wrote, and as a *buffo* outshone his contemporaries as a singer and actor. **[C.R., D.L.]** Benucci's roles included one that extended to g'', while Count Robinson descends to E. That role, and Guglielmo in *Così*, show that Benucci was able to adapt to upper-class as well as servant roles, and represent older and younger men. Although Guglielmo takes the bass line in ensembles, his solos are of substantially higher tessitura than Figaro's, though not as high as the long aria (K584) cut from the role but nevertheless entered in Mozart's personal catalogue as 'for Benucci'.

The second buffo of lower range throughout this time in Vienna was **Francesco Bussani**, born in Rome in 1743; he died after 1807. He started as a tenor, appearing in Rome in 1763 in Guglielmi's *Le contadine bizzare*. He sang in Venice, Milan, and Rome for the next 15 years and first appeared in Vienna in 1771. In 1777 he was described in Florence as singing *primo buffo* and *mezzo carattere* roles; by this time his voice was bass-baritone. He appeared in Venice from 1779 and in 1783 was invited to Vienna where he remained until 1794. With 20 years' experience of the theatre, he was engaged not only as a singer but also as manager of scenery and costumes. He appeared regularly in the Italian repertory. [Mozart used a tenor clef for Pulcherio, the role he hope Bussani would take in *Lo sposo deluso*, but bass clef for Biaggio in the quartet (K479) added to *La villanella rapita* (1785) and in *Figaro*.] Bussani doubled the roles of Bartolo and Antonio in the premiere of *Le nozze di Figaro*. He was an active member of the Italian faction in Vienna during the 1780s and according to Da Ponte (*Memorie*, 1823–7) intrigued against him and Mozart when *Figaro* was in rehearsal. Da Ponte described Bussani as knowing something of every profession except that of a gentleman.

Bussani sang the Commendatore and Masetto in the first Vienna performance of *Don Giovanni* (1788) and created Don Alfonso in *Così fan tutte* (1790) [a role which, though dramatically complex, has no full-length aria]. Again according to Da Ponte, Bussani found little favour with the new emperor, Leopold II. He was always in the shadow of Benucci, who had the stronger stage personality and was the public's favourite. In 1795 Bussani sang in Florence, in 1799 in Rome, and in 1800–1 in Naples and Palermo. He remained active in Italy and went with his wife to Lisbon in 1807. [C.R.]

Prague, 1787

Mozart was happy working in Prague and, we may infer, felt less troubled by theatre politics than in Vienna. The personnel, whom he thought generally slower to learn than the Viennese (letter of 15 October 1787), functioned as a team rather than a group of stars, and was supported by a fine orchestra. But the individuals within the team are more obscure, or certainly less researched, than those in Vienna.

The impresario **Pasquale Bondini** was probably born in Bonn around 1737; he died in Bruneck, in the Tyrol, on 30 or 31 October 1789. He is first mentioned as a *buffo* bass in Cajetan Molinari's opera company at Prague in the 1762–3 season. He was later a prominent member of Bustelli's company in Prague and Dresden. In 1777 he became director of the Elector of Saxony's new company at Dresden; he also assumed responsibility for

Leipzig. The company's repertory included plays by Shakespeare, Lessing, and Schiller, and operas by virtually all the leading Italian composers of the day. In 1781 Bondini took over direction of the theatre at Count Thun's palace in Prague and shortly afterwards Count Nostitz's theatre. His company performed at Leipzig mainly in the summer and gave *Die Entführung* there at Michaelmas 1783 and at Dresden in January 1785. Because he and his personnel were so heavily extended by his many activities Bondini was obliged to engage other troupes and managers. His most important assistant was Domenico Guardasoni, who in 1787 became his co-director and in 1788 or 1789 his successor as impresario of the operatic side of his companies. Johann Joseph Strobach became musical director in 1785, and though the opera ensemble was small, it was highly regarded and very popular.

In December 1786 Bondini mounted *Figaro*, and in January he invited Mozart and his wife to Prague to share in its triumph; during his stay Mozart conducted a performance. Before returning to Vienna in February he had been commissioned by Bondini to write *Don Giovanni*; after delays due to illness in the company, the work was first performed on 29 October 1787 with Mozart conducting. His letter to Gottfried von Jacquin of 15–25 October contains valuable but tantalizingly brief comments on Bondini's ensemble and on the preparations for the work. Within a year of the premiere Bondini's fortunes had waned; ill-health led him to make Franz Seconda responsible for the drama company, and in the summer of 1789 he handed over his remaining assets before setting off for a visit to Italy. He died at Bruneck on the way. **[P.B.]**

Teresa Saporiti [Codecasa] was born in 1763; she died in Milan, on 17 March 1869. As a member of Bondini's company she sang, with her elder sister Antonia (who died in 1787), in Leipzig, Dresden, and Prague. A report in the *Litteratur und Theater Zeitung* (summer 1782) refers to 'both Demoiselles Saporiti' being engaged for Bondini's company: 'The . . . younger sister is half a beginner as an actress and singer, and is acclaimed only because of her figure . . . the younger Demoiselle Saporiti often appears in man's costume and takes over the role of a castrato, which she does poorly and with a bad grace'.

Mozart thought well enough of Saporiti, however, to write elaborate and demanding music for her as Donna Anna. She appeared in Venice in P. A. Guglielmi's *Arsace* (1788) and *Rinaldo* (1789), and in Bianchi's *Nitteti* at La Scala (1789), and she sang in Bologna, Parma, and Modena. In 1795 she was designated *prima buffa assoluta* in a company at St Petersburg, where she achieved a personal success in Cimarosa's *L'italiana in Londra* and

Paisiello's *Il barbiere di Siviglia* (1796). [C.R.] Little is known of her later life, other than its extraordinary length.

Donna Elvira is the *mezzo carattere* role (equivalent to Mandini among the men) and Zerlina the *buffa*. We know little of the first Elvira, Caterina Micelli, and this role was generally relegated below the others in later productions, and in the 19th century, her arias being redistributed or omitted. The Zerlina, **Caterina Bondini**, wife of the impresario, was a popular soprano in her husband's company in the mid-1780s. She sang Susanna in the first Prague production of *Figaro*, and on 14 December a performance was given for her benefit; her praises were sung in poems distributed in the theatre. From the rehearsals of *Don Giovanni* date the anecdote that Mozart taught her to scream effectively during the abduction scene in the finale of Act 1 by grabbing her unexpectedly round the waist. Her daughter Marianna Bondini (1780–1813) sang Susanna in the French premiere of *Figaro* and often appeared with her husband, the bass Luigi Barilli, later manager of the Théâtre de l'Odéon in Paris. [P.B.]

The Italian tenor **Antonio Baglioni** flourished in the 1780s and 90s. He sang in productions of comic opera, particularly in Venice during the late 1780s and early 1790s, and of serious opera. [He sang Giovanni in Gazzaniga's *Don Giovanni* in 1787.] Two of his most important roles were Don Ottavio in the first production of *Don Giovanni* and Titus in *La clemenza di Tito* (1791). His range encompassed e to b". He was said to have had a well-trained, pure, and expressive voice. As a singing teacher, he taught, among others, Giulietta da Ponte, the niece of Mozart's librettist, Lorenzo da Ponte, who claimed that Baglioni was 'a man of perfect taste and great musical knowledge who had trained the most celebrated singers in Italy'. [B.D.M.] There is, exceptionally, some doubt about whether Mozart knew Baglioni well before composing *Don Giovanni*, as he was not in the earlier *Figaro* cast. The title-role of the opera, on the other hand, was written for a young singer who had played Count Almaviva. We know little of the other male roles—even Leporello—but since Giovanni himself has been sung by, in modern terms, tenors and basses as well as baritones, it is fortunate that we know something of the singer for whom Mozart wrote it.

Luigi Bassi was born in Pesaro on 4 September 1766; he probably died in Dresden in 1825. He studied in Senigallia with Pietro Morandi and appeared on the stage at the age of 13. He completed his studies with Laschi in Florence, where he appeared at the Pergola Theatre. In 1784 he joined Bondini's company and having sung Count Almaviva, he created the title-role in *Don Giovanni*. He is said to have asked Mozart to write him another aria in place of 'Fin ch'han dal vino', and to have induced Mozart to rewrite

'Là ci darem' five times [though this is doubtful]. In later years he stressed that no two performances were the same and that Mozart had specifically wished that he should improvise as long as he paid attention to the orchestra. Bassi was praised in the *Gothaer Taschenkalendar* (1793): 'This rewarding singer was from the start the ornament of the company and he still is. His voice is as melodious as his acting is masterly. Immediately he comes on, joy and cheerfulness pervade the whole audience and he never leaves the theatre without unequivocal and loud applause'.

In 1793 Bassi sang Papageno in Italian at Leipzig. But by 1800 his voice had deteriorated, although his histrionic ability remained unimpaired. According to the *Allgemeine musikalische Zeitung* (1800): 'Bassi was an excellent singer before he lost his voice, and he still knows very well how to use what remains. It lies between tenor and bass, and though it sounds somewhat hollow, it is still very flexible, full and pleasant. Herr Bassi is furthermore a very skilled actor in tragedy with no trace of burlesque, and with no vulgarity or tastelessness in comedy. In his truly artful and droll way he can parody the faults of the other singers so subtly that only the audience notices and they themselves are unaware of it. His best roles are Axur, Don Giovanni, Teodoro, the Notary in *La molinara*, the Count in *Figaro* and others'.

In 1806 Bassi left Prague because of the war and relied on the patronage of Prince Lobkowitz, making occasional appearances in Vienna. In 1814 he returned to Prague, where Weber consulted him about *Don Giovanni*. In the autumn he was engaged for the Italian company in Dresden; and in 1815 he was made director. He still appeared in Mozart's operas; in 1816 he sang Count Almaviva, although he could no longer encompass the role vocally, but in 1817 he was well received as Guglielmo. He no longer performed Don Giovanni but sang Masetto, for which he was criticized because his figure was unsuited to the part. His contract with the Dresden company continued until his death. **[C.R.]**

Vienna (3): 1788–90

The cast of *Don Giovanni* in 1788 would ideally have been as nearly identical to that of *Le nozze di Figaro* as it was in Prague; but Storace was back in England. In fact, however, it might have been awkward determining which role was best for her. She would still have had to be the prima donna, and so either Zerlina would have had to sing the last aria or Storace would have sung Anna, for whom her talents were less suited. In the event Anna was taken without alteration by Lange; it may be significant that Mozart had recently finished a concert aria for her (K538). Elvira was Cavalieri, richly rewarded with a new scena, and Zerlina was at first Mombelli, then Teyber; the farcical new duet was mainly intended to enlarge Benucci's role, and thus appease the Viennese for whom this opera might otherwise appear too serious.

While the casting of Benucci as Leporello and Bussani as Masetto and the Commendatore followed naturally, the higher male voices were new. Kelly had departed and Calvesi was on leave. The new tenor, Francesco Morella, lacked Baglioni's virtuoso, *opera seria* technique, exploited by Mozart in 'Il mio tesoro'. The new aria, 'Dalla sua pace', was better placed dramatically, in Act 1, and is a masterpiece of delicate sentiment; but it is almost the only imprint Morella seems to have left in Vienna.

The Giovanni was **Francesco Albertarelli**, a member of the company from 1788 until 1790. He made his debut as Biscroma in Salieri's *Axur, re d'Ormus*, appeared in Paisiello's *La modista raggiratrice*, sang the title role in *Don Giovanni*, and created the role of the Marchese in Weigl's *Il pazzo per forza*. Albertarelli sang Brunetto in Da Ponte's 1789 pasticcio *L'ape musicale*. In 1790 he sang Rusticone in Salieri's *La cifra* in Milan, and in 1791 he appeared at the King's Theatre in London. [D.L.] Perhaps because his role, like Lange's, was unchanged, Mozart wrote him a delightful *buffa* aria, 'Un bacio di mano' (K541), for insertion in his role as Don Pompeo in Anfossi's *Le gelosio fortunate*. The melody turns up again in the first movement of his last symphony, the 'Jupiter' (K551).

The male singers for *Così fan tutte* in January 1790, Calvesi and Benucci as the officers and Bussani as Alfonso, were already familiar to Mozart, as was Dorothea Bussani, the Despina. The two sisters 'from Ferrara' were relative newcomers, their fictional origin presumably a tribute to the Fiordiligi, Adriana Ferrarese. Contrary to rumour, they were not sisters.

Adriana [Andreanna, Andriana] Ferrarese [Ferraresi, Ferrarese del Bene] was born in 1759; she died sometime after 1800. She studied at the Mendicanti in Venice from 1780 to 1782, and was once mistakenly identified with a Francesca Gabrielli, 'detta la Ferrarese', whom Burney heard in Venice in 1770. She eloped with Luigi del Bene in 1783 and appeared at the Teatro Pergola, Florence, on 8 May 1784.

In 1785–6 Ferrarese sang in London, at first in serious opera and then comic (though her roles were in *seria* style), and was generally well received. She returned to Florence, where her roles included Tarchi's Iphigenia and Gluck's Alkestis. In 1788 she settled in Vienna. Her background in *opera seria* made her particularly effective in heroic roles, such as Diana in Martín y Soler's *L'arbore di Diana* (her debut role there), Eurilla in

Salieri's *La cifra* (1789), and her most famous role, Mozart's Fiordiligi. Her tenure of 30 months coincided with the peak of Da Ponte's influence; she was romantically involved with him and they were dismissed together early in 1791. She continued her career throughout Italy until the late 1790s, after which there are no further records.

Music written for Ferrarese tends to emphasize *fioriture*, *cantar di sbalzo* (large leaps), and the low end of her range. She appears to have been unsuited for the comic style; every adaptation of existing music for revivals and new music written for her tends to enhance the serious style at the expense of the comic. Weigl (*Il pazzo per forza*) and Salieri (*La cifra*) met her vocal requirements successfully within roles that made limited demands on her modest acting ability. Her singing won much praise, notably from Zinzendorf, who wrote that 'La Ferrarese chanta à merveille' (27 February 1789). The casting of Ferrarese as Susanna for the 1789 *Figaro* met with only qualified enthusiasm from Mozart, who wrote that 'the little aria [K577] I have made for Ferrarese I believe will please, if she is capable of singing it in an artless manner, which I very much doubt' (19 August 1789); he also composed a large-scale rondò in *opera seria* style (K579) to replace 'Deh, vieni, non tardar'. As Fiordiligi in *Così fan tutte* her vain temperament and formidable vocal resources were exploited to perfection by Mozart, creating a rigid *seria* character who is the object of comic intrigue. [J.A.R.]

In 1787–8 the soprano **Luisa [Louise, Luigia] Villeneuve** sang in Venice in operas by Guglielmi and Martín y Soler; in Milan in 1788 her roles included Amore (Cupid) in Martín's *L'arbore di Diana*. She spent 1789–90 and 1790–91 in Vienna, making her debut on 27 June 1789 as Amore, when she was admired for 'her charming appearance, her sensitive and expressive acting and her artful, beautiful singing' (*Wiener Zeitung*, lii (1789), 1673). Mozart supplied arias for her in Cimarosa's *I due baroni* (K578) and Martín's *Il burbero di buon cuore* (K582–3), and wrote for her Dorabella in *Così fan tutte*, alluding in her Act 2 aria to her role as Amore. Zinzendorf noted in his diary (11 February 1791) that she caught the fancy of Leopold II. She appeared in Livorno in 1794. [D.L.]

Vienna, 1791: Schikaneder's Troupe

The musical director of Schikaneder's company was himself a talented composer. Johann Baptist Henneberg (1768–1822) was Kapellmeister at the Theater auf der Wieden from 1790, and at this young age he contributed some good music for the collaborative venture *Der Stein der*

Weisen. Henneberg directed rehearsals for *Die Zauberflöte*, conducting it after the third performance. Mozart knew the personnel well before composing for the company. Among the large cast, including trios of ladies and 'boys' (originally sung by women), the contribution of the principals to the shaping of roles was considerable. Schikaneder, Schack, and Gerl must be accounted among his friends, Gottlieb had sung in *Figaro*, and Hofer was his sister-in-law. Some performers were more actors than singers, though clearly musically competent; Schikaneder was one of these, as was Johann Joseph Nouseul, who played Monostatos.

Josepha Hofer was born Maria Josepha Weber in Zell in 1758, and died as Josepha Mayer in Vienna on 29 December 1819. She was the eldest daughter of Fridolin Weber (1733–79), and thus Mozart's sister-in-law. After her father's death she moved to Vienna, and was then engaged at Graz, 1785–7. On 21 July 1788 she married the court musician Franz de Paula Hofer (1755–96), and began performing at the suburban Theater auf der Wieden the next January. According to contemporary reports, she commanded a very high tessitura but had a rough edge to her voice and lacked stage presence. In September 1789 Mozart wrote for her the bravura insertion aria 'Schon lacht der holde Frühling' (K580, for a German version of Paisiello's *Il barbiere di Siviglia*). Two years later he composed the Queen of Night for her; she finally ceded the role to Antonia Campi in 1801. Josepha's second husband, from 1797, was (Friedrich) Sebastian Mayer (1773–1835), who created Pizarro in Beethoven's *Fidelio* (*Leonore*) in 1805. In that year Josepha retired from the stage, to be replaced by her daughter Josefa Hofer. [T.B.]

Maria Anna Josepha Francisca [Nanette] Gottlieb, was born in Vienna on 29 April 1774; she died there on 1 February 1856. She was a daughter of two members of the German drama company at the Nationaltheater. At the age of five she started appearing there in small acting and singing roles. When she was 12 she created Barbarina in *Le nozze di Figaro*. In 1789 she was engaged by Emanuel Schikaneder for the Freihaustheater, where Mozart wrote Pamina for her in *Die Zauberflöte*. That role represented the artistic peak of her career, although she was not yet 18.

In 1792 she was engaged at the Leopoldstädter Theater, at that time under the direction of Marinelli. During her 36 years there she gradually moved from a youthful singer to a character actress playing comic old women. Her best years saw her singing in Gluck's *Die Pilgrime von Mekka* (*La rencontre imprévue*) and works by Dalayrac. Her greatest successes were in the roles she created in Singspiels and travesties, including Hulda in *Das Donauweibchen* (1798, Hensler and Kauer), a role she performed over a thousand times. She was absent from the stage in 1808–11 and returned with diminishing success, finally singing mainly secondary roles. She was dismissed without a pension in 1828 and sank into poverty. In 1842 she introduced herself to L. V. Frankl, editor of the *Sonntagsblätter*, as 'the first Pamina' and the last living friend of Mozart; his emotional appeal on her behalf raised enough money to send her to Salzburg for the unveiling of the Mozart monument. She died in the year of Mozart's centenary and, like Mozart, was buried in St Mark's cemetery. [C.H.]

Benedikt Emanuel Schack [Cziak, Schak, Žák, Ziak], Austrian composer and tenor of Bohemian origin, was born in Mirotice on 7 February 1758; he died in Munich on 10 December 1826. After early musical training from his father, he became a pupil and singer at a Jesuit monastery at the age of 11, and later studied in Prague, where he was also a chorister at St Vitus's Cathedral. In 1775 he moved to Vienna to study medicine and took singing lessons with Karl Frieberth. After several years as Kapellmeister to Prince Heinrich von Schönaich-Carolath in Silesia (from 1780), he joined Emanuel Schikaneder's travelling troupe in 1786 as a tenor and composer. The company made visits to Augsburg and Regensburg and shorter stops in other southern cities, including Salzburg. Leopold Mozart commented in a letter to his daughter (26 May 1786) that Schack 'sings excellently, has a beautiful voice, an effortlessly smooth throat and a beautiful method'.

During the first four years the troupe spent in Vienna, from 1789, Schack composed numerous operas for the Theater auf der Wieden and sang principal tenor roles in many of its productions. He became well acquainted with Mozart, who composed the role of Tamino for him (although it is doubtful that, as often stated, Schack played the flute parts himself). In 1793 Schack secured an appointment in Graz. In 1796, he moved to Munich to become a member of the ensemble of the Hoftheater, and seems to have composed no operas there. Around 1813 he was pensioned off because of his declining voice.

Schack composed almost all his operas for suburban theatres and travelling troupes. He was best known for the series of 'Anton' Singspiels that he composed with F. X. Gerl to librettos by Schikaneder. Anton, like the character Kasperl at the rival Theater in der Leopoldstadt, was a descendant of Hanswurst and Bernardon from Viennese comedies of the early and mid-18th century. In the 'Anton' Singspiels and others like them—in contrast to the scenically and musically elaborate heroic-comic operas like *Die Zauberflöte*—the serious portions of the plot were played down, the central comic character became the focus of the story, and the music consisted most often of short numbers based on a popular folk style. *Der dumme Gärtner*, the first and most successful of the 'Anton' works, serves as a representative example. Several of the solos are strophic lieder with square-cut phrasing and simple melodies, while others depend on two- and three-part forms, and a few have a two-tempo (slow-fast) format. The ensembles are the most extended numbers of the work; several changes of tempo, conversational interaction between characters and *buffo*-style patter set them apart from the solos and choruses. There is little or no use in the work of recitative, coloratura, or complex orchestral writing.

Der dumme Gärtner, along with numerous other Viennese suburban Singspiels, found favour on stages throughout Germany. In some northern cities the texts of many of these works were revised while the music was retained. This type of treatment contrasted with the frequent practice in southern theatres (both national and suburban) of adopting librettos from the north but setting them to new music. Schack's regular collaboration with Gerl in composing operas was of a sort not unusual for the Theater auf der Wieden in the 1790s. Schikaneder regularly commissioned compositional 'teams' (another prominent duo was Ignaz von Seyfried and Matthäus Stegmayr) to set librettos written by himself or others: the most likely reason for this was the heavy production schedule, which demanded new Singspiels every month. Schack's recognition as an opera composer, resting mostly on the 'Anton' Singspiels and *Der Stein der Weisen*, declined rapidly after the 1790s, with the number of performances of his works steadily decreasing. [L.T.]

Franz Xaver Gerl [Görl], Austrian bass and composer, was born in Andorf, Upper Austria, on 30 November 1764; he died in Mannheim on 9 March 1827. The son of a village schoolmaster and organist, by 1777 he was an alto chorister at Salzburg, where he may have been a pupil of Leopold Mozart. He was at the Salzburg Gymnasium, 1778–82, then studied logic and physics at the university. In autumn 1785 he went to Erlangen as a bass, joining the theatrical company of Ludwig Schmidt, who had earlier been at Salzburg. In 1786 he joined G. F. W. Grossmann's company, performing in the Rhineland, and specialized in 'comic roles in comedies and Singspiels'. By 1787 he was a member of Schikaneder's company at Regensburg, making his debut in *Wenn zwei sich streiten* (Sarti's *Fra i due litiganti*) and appearing as Osmin in *Die Entführung*. On 2 September 1789 he married the soprano Barbara Reisinger [who sang Papagena; having played Lubanara in *Der Stein der Weisen*, she was the cat in the duet contributed by Mozart]. Gerl's name first appears as one of the composers of *Der dumme Gärtner aus dem Gebirge* (*Der dumme Anton*), Schikaneder's first new production at his new theatre, on 12 July 1789; it is unlikely that this was Gerl's first theatre score since Schikaneder would hardly have entrusted such an important task to a novice. *Der dumme Gärtner* proved so successful that it had no fewer than six sequels; Gerl certainly performed in two of these, though he and Schack may not have written all the scores. Between 1789 and 1793 Gerl wrote music for several more plays and Singspiels.

Gerl played a wide variety of parts in plays and operas during his Vienna years (including Don Giovanni and Figaro in German), but is most often associated with the role of Sarastro in *Die Zauberflöte*, which he created and continued to sing at least until November 1792 (the 83rd performance, announced by Schikaneder as the 100th). The Gerls appear to have left the Freihaus-Theater in 1793; they were at Brünn (Brno), 1794–1801, and from 1802 Gerl was a member of the Mannheim Hoftheater. Apart from operatic roles he also appeared frequently in plays; he retired in 1826. That year he married Magdalena Dengler (née Reisinger—his first wife's elder sister), the widow of Georg Dengler, director of the Mainz theatre.

Although the paucity of the surviving material and the difficulty of identifying Gerl's contribution to collaborative scores make it impossible to evaluate him as a composer, the works he wrote were popular in their day. His career as a singer is better documented. When Schröder, the greatest actor-manager of his age, went to Vienna in 1791 he was told not to miss hearing Schack and Gerl at Schikaneder's theatre. At the end of May he heard Wranitzky's *Oberon*, in which both were singing, and thought Gerl's singing of the Oracle 'very good'. Mozart's high regard for his qualities is evident in the aria 'Per questa bella mano' (K612), written for Gerl in March 1791, and above all in Sarastro's music. Mozart's friendly relationship with Gerl is attested by the fact that Gerl was one of the singers who is said, on Mozart's last afternoon, to have joined the dying composer in an impromptu sing-through of the Requiem (the others were Schack and Mozart's brother-in-law Franz Hofer). [P.B.]

Prague, 1791

With the departure of Bondini, Domenico Guardasoni assumed control of the Prague theatre and it was he who offered the commission for *La clemenza di Tito* to Mozart after Salieri turned it down. Mozart was surely glad to write another opera for Prague, but since the occasion was the coronation of the Emperor as King of Bohemia, Guardasoni had to shop around for principal singers better than those locally available. Although the remaining roles were cast locally, only Antonio Baglioni, the 1787 Don

Ottavio, was previously familiar to Mozart; this cannot have helped him, given the short time available to compose the opera. In this he may have been assisted by Franz Xaver Süssmayr (1766–1803), who had studied with Salieri but became attached to Mozart during his last year, and may have assisted him by composing the simple recitatives. Besides completing Mozart's Requiem and part of a horn concerto, Süssmayr had a career as a composer of sacred and theatre music, including one of the most successful follow-ups to *Die Zauberflöte* at the Theater auf der Wieden, *Der Spiegel von Arkadien*. Mozart also brought Anton Stadler (1753–1812) with him, to play the clarinet and basset-horn solos in first aria for the primo uomo and the final rondò for the prima donna, both singers specially imported for the occasion. On returning to Vienna, Mozart completed his last concerto for Stadler.

Maria (?Vincenza) Marchetti Fantozzi [née Marchetti], was born c. 1760; she died probably sometime after 1800. She was one of the leading singers of *opera seria* during the 1780s and 90s. Around 1783 she married the tenor Angelo Fantozzi and thereafter usually identified herself as Maria Marchetti Fantozzi. She was praised throughout Italy for her acting as well as her singing, particularly in Naples, where she performed in at least seven different operas in 1785–6. Marchetti was a specialist in the portrayal of passionate, tragic heroines like Semiramide and Cleopatra; she was thus ideally suited to create the role of Vitellia. The music that she sang in that opera shows her to have been an extraordinary virtuoso, with a large range and a capacity for difficult coloratura. [J.A.R.] According to Zinzendorf, her performance attracted the Emperor (perhaps contributing to the Empress's known dislike of the opera). Marchetti subsequently became prima donna in the court opera in Berlin. The composer Johann Friedrich Reichardt wrote that her 'strong, full' voice had 'great effect in the theatre . . . she filled the whole opera house, without shouting at all'. He also admired her acting. However another report of this time considered her range narrow and her low notes to be 'rough and dull' (Rice, 1991). The latter effect may mean that the noticeably lower tessitura of the final rondò, 'Non più di fiori', which descends to g, was designed by Mozart to exploit precisely that quality, since Vitellia is now defeated and must acknowledge her crime to Titus. The trio in Act 1 ascends briefly to d'''.

The primo uomo, **Domenico Bedini**, was a castrato soprano, probably born in Fossombrone, c. 1745; he died sometime after 1795. His career began intermittently in comic opera at Pesaro (1762) and Rome (1764), and as secondo uomo in *opera seria* at Venice (1768). In 1770–71 he was secondo uomo in five Italian houses and then entered the service of the Munich court, resuming his career in Italy in 1776 and soon becoming primo uomo in leading houses. He is mostly remembered as the first Sextus. He retired after singing at Florence in Carnival 1792 and by 1795 was in the *cappella* of the San Casa of Loreto in his native region. [D.L.] Unlike Mozart's most recent castrato, Dal Prato, Bedini, if not one of the greatest, was at least among the most experienced castrati available and his repertory generally suggests that his Sextus was probably an excellent match for the prima donna and the tenor roles. He was in Florence in 1780, where the English connoisseur William Beckford compared him to a porpoise: 'If these animals were to sing, I should conjecture it would be in this style'. But this view was clearly not shared by the Grand Duke of Tuscany, in whose honour, as Leopold II, *La clemenza di Tito* was composed.

{ *The Cities*

The principal cities in which Mozart lived and worked as a composer of opera, or one intent on composing opera, naturally start with his birthplace, Salzburg, where some of his work can be related to long-standing local traditions. He was clearly influenced by his visit to London, and by both his visits to Paris. By the time of his second visit to the French capital he was already a seasoned opera composer and complained that he was taken for a beginner (letter of 31 July 1778); his only theatre music was part of a ballet score whose name (*Les petits riens*—the little nothings) speaks volumes. Another city whose music influenced him profoundly but for which he composed no operas was Mannheim, visited on the journey to and from Paris (1777–79). In Italy, only Milan, under Austrian rule, commissioned operas from him, the latest performed at the end of 1772 when he was not quite 17. The principal centres of his later activity were confined to the triangle of cities in Bavaria and territories of the Austrian Empire: Munich, Vienna, and Prague. Productions of his operas elsewhere in his lifetime were mainly of *Die Entführung* and the Singspiel versions of *La finta giardiniera* and *Don Giovanni*. Usually he was not present, although he heard *Die Entführung* in Berlin (1789) and helped prepare *Le nozze di Figaro* in Mannheim the following year on his return journey from the coronation of Leopold II as Holy Roman Emperor in Frankfurt.

Salzburg

From the eighth century until 1806 the city of **Salzburg** was the seat of a series of prince-archbishops, whose court became the centre of the city's musical life. Archbishop Marcus Sitticus von Hohenems (reigned 1612–19),

was half-Italian and cultivated economic and cultural links with Italy, especially with the court at Mantua. During his reign Salzburg enjoyed the first
flowering of the Baroque: monody and opera were introduced, their earliest appearance north of the Alps. In 1614 a stage was erected in the archbishop's residence and inaugurated with an Italian 'Hoftragicomedia', the
first opera performance outside Italy. On 10 February the pastoral *Orfeo*
was given, probably with music by Monteverdi. Guest performers from
Italy probably joined local artists for Salzburg opera performances. In 1617
the Benedictine Gymnasium was founded; with the university (founded in
1622) it formed an important centre for drama and music. The Benedictine
drama performed there developed during the 17th century and increasingly came to resemble opera.

    Under succeeding prince-archbishops, music in Salzburg prospered.
Among composers active in the city were the Alsatian Georg Muffat
(1678–90), the Bohemian H. I. F. von Biber (1670–1704), and the local
composer Andreas Hofer (from 1653). All three composed dramatic music,
which enjoyed new prominence, principally during the rule of Johann
Ernst von Thun. Hofer, Muffat, and particularly Biber also set to music a
large number of Benedictine school dramas (*Schuldramen*). At the beginning of the 18th century the most prolific composer of Benedictine drama
was Matthias Sigismund Biechteler von Greiffenthal, in court service from
1688. The Viennese deputy Hofkapellmeister Antonio Caldara came to
Salzburg to compose operas and between 1716 and 1728 at least 16 of his
operas and staged oratorios were performed there.

    The transition to the Rococo took place under J. E. Eberlin, who became
court organist (1726) and Kapellmeister (1749); his compositions influenced a series of Salzburg court musicians, among them Leopold Mozart
(court violinist from 1743 and deputy Hofkapellmeister from 1763), Michael
Haydn (from 1763), Anton Cajetan Adlgasser (court organist from 1750)
and Joseph Meissner (a court bass from 1747). [In 1772 Archbishop Hi-
eronymus Colloredo succeeded Sigismond Schrattenbach, who had already appointed the younger Mozart to the rank of Konzertmeister (at first
unpaid). Mozart held that position from 1769 to 1777, and was paid a modest salary from 1773; on returning from Paris he was court organist from
1779 to 1781.] Mozart's dramatic works given in Salzburg include the Latin
intermezzo *Apollo et Hyacinthus* (1767, at the university), *La finta semplice*
(1769), *Il sogno di Scipione* (1772), and *Il re pastore* (1775), the last three at
the archbishop's palace. [Possibly also *Bastien und Bastienne* (a revival in
1774); later works were included in the repertoire of touring companies,

including possibly *La finta giardiniera*, but in German, c.1780, and *Die Entführung aus dem Serail* in 1784.]

In 1775, on the initiative of Colloredo but at the city's expense, the Ballhaus was converted into the prince-archbishops' Hoftheater, where for the most part travelling companies played, including those of Wahr, Schikaneder, Böhm, and [Franz Anton] Weber [father of the composer Carl Maria von Weber, uncle of Mozart's wife, Constanze]. In 1803 the spiritual princedoms of Passau and Eichstädt had come under Salzburg's rule and their court musicians swelled the ranks of the musical establishment. [Colloredo fled from advancing French troops in 1800 and in 1806 the independence of Salzburg ended: always necessarily close to the Habsburg dynasty in Vienna, the prince-archbishopric now became a provincial town, resulting in some cultural stagnation at the time when Mozart's sister, sister-in-law, and widow were living out their final years there.] The former Hoftheater survived as the Nationaltheater, thanks to the public's love of the theatre. Singspiels by Weigl, Dittersdorf, and Wenzel Müller and operas by Rossini, Cherubini, Mozart, and Weber offered a varied musical fare, but with the departure from Salzburg of Michael Haydn's most gifted pupils—Weber, Neukomm, and Wölfl—the city and its theatre lost an important source of musical impulse.

The Dommusikverein und Mozarteum was founded in 1841, for 'the promotion of all branches of music, but especially church music', and in 1870 the Internationale Mozart-Stiftung was established, with a broad programme for encouraging musical activity. The Nationaltheater was replaced in 1893 by the larger Stadttheater, inaugurated with Mozart's *La clemenza di Tito* and renamed the Landestheater in 1938. Operas and operettas are given there during the winter months. A much-loved local institution is the Marionetten-Theater, founded in 1913, which with its accomplished performances to recordings (mainly of Mozart) has toured abroad many times. In the 20th century, however, Salzburg is chiefly known for the annual summer festival, held from the end of July to the end of August. [G.C.]

Mozart's earliest journeys took him to Munich, where he was eventually to create two operas, and on to France and England. In Paris he shared his father's dislike of the long-established Opéra (Académie Royale de Musique), whose repertory, even on his third visit in 1778, still included works by Lully and Rameau. Even in the 1760s, however, modern or Italian influence, apparently dismissed from the Opéra by the Querelle des bouffons of 1752–3, was re-entering by way of a revivified popular form:

the fair theatres staging Opéra Comique had abandoned their dependence on traditional melodies and were commissioning new scores from Egidio Duni, François-André Danican Philidor, Pierre-Alexandre Monsigny, and from 1768 André Ernest Modeste Grétry, in which even Leopold Mozart was constrained to find some merit. In London, the chief resident opera composer was Johann Christian Bach, whose influence on Mozart was certainly more profound. Indeed, it is not too much to say that the foundation of the Mozartian manner was laid down by Bach, 'the first composer', as Dr Burney remarked, 'who observed the law of *contrast*, as a *principle*'. This influence is possibly clearest in instrumental music, but Bach together with Manzuoli may have been the trigger that fired Mozart's ambition to excel in Italian operatic music, while Bach and Hasse, whom Mozart soon met in Vienna, were role models—German composers training in Italy and excelling in this field. It was natural, after the encounter with Hasse in 1768, for Leopold Mozart to make his next move across the Alps. The Mozarts witnessed a number of operas during their travels in Italy, but the focus of activity was Austrian-ruled Milan, where three Mozart operas were given their premieres and, during his lifetime, their only performances.

Milan

Milan is still the home of the most famous Italian opera house, the Teatro alla Scala, and has been a principal centre of Italian opera since the late 18th century, when it was the main city from which northern Italy was governed. Religious processions with music and dialogue are known there from the 14th century, and stage entertainments with music, song, and dancing became popular at court during the 15th and 16th centuries. At the beginning of the 17th century Milan could offer few original theatrical productions, but welcomed those from other cities, in particular Venice.

At the start of the 18th century, Austrian government replaced Spanish rule in Milan. This was the beginning of a new age of prosperity and peace that lasted until 1796 and saw a flowering of culture and the arts and an increasing addiction to spectacles and entertainments. Relations between Milan and Vienna were close and continuous, with exchanges of operas, musicians, and singers. On 26 December 1717 [the first day of Carnival], the new Regio Ducal theatre was inaugurated.

The city was still not a creative or dynamic force in opera, but rather an eclectic and receptive centre open to widely varying tendencies. Comic opera was popular and from 1745 Milan had its own spring season. Later the *opera buffa* season was fixed in the autumn, and three different operas were produced, so that comic opera acquired the same importance as *opera seria*, two of which were performed between 26 December and the last day of the Ambrosian carnival, the Saturday after Ash Wednesday. Maria Theresia, who acceded to the imperial throne in 1740, realized that the theatre was a social necessity in Italy. The arrival of Francesco III d'Este, Duke of Modena, as governor in 1754, and even more the active presence of his minister plenipotentiary Count Firmian and the supreme chancellor Wenzel von Kaunitz, ensured a central role in city life for the Regio Ducal Teatro.

In the second half of the 18th century Milan was one of the most enlightened of Italian cultural centres, with thinkers and men of letters such as the Verri, Cesare Beccaria, and Giuseppe Parini; in instrumental music the innovations of Giovanni Battista Sammartini heralded Viennese Classicism. In opera, however, Milanese taste was still narrowly traditional, with little room for the innovatory ideas of Gluck and Calzabigi. When the Cavalieri Direttori decided to produce *Alceste*, Gluck's music was rejected and a new score composed by P. A. Guglielmi. Parini had the task of revising Calzabigi's libretto, adding irrelevant arias to please the singers and trivializing the plot. Calzabigi was indignant, and Parini defended himself by saying that he had done the work 'to suit the unavoidable present circumstances of our theatre', which according to Calzabigi meant 'to draw out the performance to the ridiculous length of five hours and to be able to have supper during the performance'. Moreover, the insertion of ballets between acts of serious and even comic operas had become custom since about 1738. This then was the atmosphere in Milan when the young Mozart visited the city for the first time early in 1770.

At the palace of Count Firmian Mozart met many musicians, and was commissioned to write an opera. He returned to Milan to compose *Mitridate* (premiere 26 December 1770), and direct the first three performances, with an orchestra of 60. Mozart's next visit to Milan (21 August–5 December 1771) was in connection with the important commission he had received for a *festa teatrale*, *Ascanio in Alba* to a text by Parini. Mozart was in Milan for the last time in 1772–3, when the third opera he wrote for the theatre, *Lucio Silla* to a libretto by Giovanni de Gamerra (who had been appointed the theatre's poet in 1771), was performed on 26 December 1772.

At the turn of the 19th century Milan began to develop into a modern city based on the activity of a prosperous middle class, which eventually turned it into the most important industrial centre of Italy. Ruled for some time by the French, Lombardy was returned to Austrian control in 1815;

renewed Viennese connections resulted in a large patrician and upper class supporting cultural life. A new operatic era began with the success of Rossini, who quickly came to dominate Italian opera along with Donizetti and Bellini; from then on, Milan's musical history became virtually identified with that of Italian opera, of which La Scala was perhaps the most notable centre (it was also at that time that cycles of Mozart operas began to be mounted there). By the 1830s La Scala was one of the leading opera houses in Europe; 40 premieres were given in that decade and in 1839 Verdi's first opera, *Oberto, conte di San Bonifacio*, was performed there. [M.D.] Although the theatre covered the great 19th- and 20th-century repertoire, and its size may seem excessive in an age when revival of original performing conditions is so much of an issue as at present, Mozart is not neglected there. The first British conductor to open a season at La Scala, Daniel Harding, did so with *Idomeneo* (autumn 2005).

Munich

Apart from the production of *Il sogno di Scipione* and *Il re pastore*, and the composition of the unfinished *Zaide*, Mozart's next operas were written for the city that lies between Salzburg and his father's birthplace, Augsburg (both Mozarts referred to themselves as German composers, the antithesis of Italian, rather than as Austrians). In Munich, capital of Bavaria, opera as now understood began with courtly musical spectacles on mythological subjects and featuring allegorical characters, performed as acts of homage from about the mid-17th century. Until the later 18th century Italian court opera reigned supreme, but German Singspiel gained an increasingly firm foothold thereafter.

From 1253 onwards Munich was the seat of the Wittelsbach dukes of Bavaria. Duke Albrecht III (1435–60), whose first wife, Agnes Bernauer, took an interest in music and literature, laid the foundations for theatrical development by encouraging the humanist *Schuldrama*. Munich reached a cultural peak on the occasion of the famous royal wedding of Duke Wilhelm to Renée of Lorraine in 1568. Contemporary accounts record that an Italian *commedia dell'arte* was presented for the first time with the cooperation of Orlando de Lassus, who also performed the musical interludes with instrumentalists and singers of the Hofkapelle. After a period of stagnation, artistic pursuits at court began to revive; Bavaria was raised to the status of an electorate in 1623, and Ferdinand Maria (1651–79) and his highly gifted wife Adelaide of Savoy were responsible for the introduction of Italian opera, which flourished during the first decade of rule by the artistically inclined Elector Maximilian II Emanuel (1679–1726). Even at this early date, German operas were occasionally performed, though Singspiel could not have offered Italian opera any serious competition. When Maximilian Emanuel became governor of the Spanish Netherlands in 1691 the court moved to Brussels with him. Only church and chamber music continued to be regularly performed at the ducal residence in Munich. The period between Maximilian Emanuel's return in 1715 and his death in 1726 restored the musical life of Munich to its former glory; despite French influences, Italian opera still predominated.

Although the Habsburg Elector Carl Albert (1726–45, Emperor Carl VII from 1742) also liked magnificence, unpropitious political developments (the reoccupation of Bavaria as a result of the War of the Austrian Succession) eventually made it impossible for him to maintain the high cultural standards previously established. Maximilian III Joseph (1745–77), however, raised a new monument to opera when he commissioned the Residenztheater, built by François Cuvilliés (hence also known as the Cuvilliéstheater). It was ceremonially opened in 1753.

Count Joseph Anton von Seeau contributed to the development of musical drama in the city when in 1756 he became Intendant of all the theatres. While the Residenztheater was reserved for *opera seria* and ballet, middle-class audiences in particular were catered for in the old Opernhaus am Salvatorplatz. Mozart's *La finta giardiniera* had its premiere there in 1775, while *Idomeneo*, composed for Carnival 1781, was performed in the Residenztheater. [In 1778, Maximilian III had been succeeded by Carl Theodor, Elector Palatinate at Mannheim, whom Mozart had cultivated assiduously the previous year. This meant that many of the personnel of the Mannheim opera, personally well known to Mozart, were available to perform in Munich.]

Seeau's long term of office saw a quantitative increase in productions. During Carnival, German Singspiels, usually translations of *opéra comique* and *opera buffa*, were performed on Sundays in the Salvatorplatz, and court society then attended a ball in the Redoutensaal. Now that *opera buffa* in German translation had become well established, from the 1770s onwards Singspiel finally made a breakthrough [thanks to Carl Theodor's arrival, bringing with him Theobald Hilarius Marchand, director of the German theatre in Mannheim, where the repertory included works of French origin; Marchand knew the Mozarts and entrusted the musical education of his gifted daughter Margarethe and son Heinrich to Leopold Mozart in Salzburg.] Marchand introduced *opéra comique* to Munich, and for the first time French influence really made itself felt, although it could not displace Italian opera. Not until the end of the 1780s can a decline in the popularity of *opera seria* be traced. The genre had one of its last successes with Vogler's carnival opera *Castore e Polluce* (1787); in the same year Carl Theodor issued a decree prohibiting Italian opera. The Hof-National-Schaubühne, which opened that year with Anton Schweitzer's *Alceste*, set the tone. After 45 years in his post, Seeau left the Munich theatres in a state of remarkable mismanagement (the reasons are obscure because the records have disappeared), and after his death in 1799 it was hard for much progress in theatrical affairs to be made. The ban on Italian opera was not lifted until 1805, a year before Bavaria became a kingdom.

The records indicate that Weber's Singspiel *Abu Hassan*, given its premiere in 1811 at the Residenztheater, met with a friendly reception. In the same year King Max I laid the foundation stone of a new and larger Königliches Hof- und Nationaltheater. In 1836 Franz Paul Lachner was appointed chief conductor and principal musical director. Lachner established Munich's reputation as an operatic centre. Initially he produced the works of Beethoven and Mozart, but soon concentrated on the work of his contemporaries, and extended the repertory to include French and Italian opera. Lachner conducted the first Munich performances of *Tannhäuser* and *Lohengrin*, but he retired when Wagner's connections with Munich became closer after 1864 through his friendship with King Ludwig II, and the city prepared to become a Wagnerian centre, as it were by royal decree. In 1858, the court musical director Karl von Perfall took over the direction of the court opera, remaining in the post until 1893. In 1875 Perfall founded the Munich Opera Festival; the first summer festival included operas by Mozart and Wagner. Two keystones of the continuing Munich operatic tradition were thus in place (another—Richard Strauss—was added later). [J.L., K.J.S.] It was Strauss who conducted *Così fan tutte* in the Residenztheater in 1897, with a translation by Hofmannsthal, later Strauss's own librettist, and Hermann Levi; this is considered the first revival properly to explore the psychological subtleties of the libretto (Brown, 1995). It was also Strauss who revived Mozart's greater Munich opera, *Idomeneo*, for its 150th anniversary, but in an altered form and in Vienna.

Vienna

Now the capital of Austria, **Vienna** was formerly the capital of the Austro-Hungarian monarchy and before that the centre of the Habsburg Empire. It has been a great European centre of opera (Italian and French as well as German) since Cesti's *Il pomo d'oro* was given at the Court in 1668, through the Viennese 'Classical' period when several of Gluck's and Mozart's mature operas and Beethoven's *Fidelio*, among many other works, had their premieres there, and throughout the 19th and early 20th centuries, though eventually less as a centre for new music than as one where performances of high prestige were given. Vienna has also been a famous centre of more popular operatic entertainments, from the Singspiels of Mozart and his contemporaries to the operettas of Johann Strauss and his followers.

For most of the first decade of her reign Maria Theresia (reigned 1740–80) was preoccupied with maintaining her throne in the face of invasion, and consequently gave little attention to local spectacle. *Opera seria* productions at court became rare despite the presence of Metastasio, ceasing altogether after his and Hasse's *Ipermestra* of 1744. Italian opera continued in the Burgtheater in the Michaelerplatz (managed by impresarios; originally a tennis court, it was refurbished as a theatre in 1741). Works by court composers such as Bonno and Wagenseil alternated with pieces by foreign composers, notably Jommelli, Hasse, and Galuppi. In 1747 the Galli-Bibiena opera house in the Hofburg was converted into two (still extant) Redoutensäle for balls [Mozart composed many dances for them in his capacity, from 1788, as Imperial Kammermusikus].

The Burgtheater was renovated to designs by Nicolas Jadot, and reopened with Gluck's first work for Vienna, *Semiramide riconosciuta* (1748), in whose title character the victorious empress could easily be recognized. Despite several remodellings, the Burgtheater was to retain its small dimensions and intimate acoustics up to its demolition in 1888. The first performances in a new theatre in the Schönbrunn palace (the Schlosstheater) took place in 1747, and in 1753 a small theatre was constructed in the garden of the Laxenburg palace. In the Kärntnertortheater during this period a German-language troupe performed heroic-comic dramas and farces, often improvised and featuring local versions of *commedia dell'arte* characters. Some of these works included music (commissioned at a florin an aria) by the young Joseph Haydn.

In 1752, the empress reconstituted the Viennese theatres under court control. She banned improvised pieces (though only temporarily) and, in a reflection of Austria's political rapprochement with France, substituted a company of French actors for the planned Italian opera company at the Burgtheater. This troupe's repertory soon came to include *opéras comiques* from Paris, arranged by Gluck. A resident of Vienna since 1750, he was made musical director of the Burgtheater in about 1754 by the theatre Intendant, Giacomo Durazzo. Gluck's own *opéras comiques*, as well as French imports (procured after 1759 through Favart), supplanted the expensive Italian opera during much of the Seven Years War (1756–63).

Italian opera returned with the itinerant Mingotti troupe in 1759, but far more significant were the works celebrating the marriage in 1760 of Archduke Joseph to Isabella of Parma, in both Parma (an *opéra-ballet* by Traetta) and Vienna (operas by Hasse and Gluck). There was much interchange of personnel between the two courts' theatrical forces, both headed by persons sympathetic to French spectacle. Isabella's birthday in 1761 was celebrated in Vienna with Traetta's *Armida*, based on Durazzo's prose adaptation of Quinault's libretto for Lully, and the next year the reform continued with Calzabigi and Gluck's *Orfeo ed Euridice*. Calzabigi was the focal point of the anti-Metastasian 'sect' described by Burney, which valued dramatic truth, theatrical illusion, and continuity, over poetic niceties and purely musical display. The abundant use of both chorus and ballet in *Orfeo* [its genre being *azione teatrale*, not *opera seria*] was a result of Durazzo's ability to combine the resources of the Burgtheater and the Kärntnertortheater, for which he was also responsible. Metastasio's principal ally was Hasse, a special favourite of the empress, but there is also considerable evidence of support for Gluck from the imperial family. The German theatre, though benefiting from the example of the French actors, suffered financial neglect during this period. Musical plays were few, and translations of *opéras comiques* began only about 1764.

Durazzo was dismissed in 1764, and with Emperor Francis's death in 1765 the French troupe had to leave as well. The theatres were closed during the empress's protracted mourning, and when they reopened it was again under a series of luckless impresarios. The bankruptcy of Giuseppe d'Affligio in 1770 seriously affected the finances of Gluck, one of his associates. [It might, however, have pleased Leopold Mozart, who held d'Affligio responsible for Vienna's failure to perform *La finta semplice*.] Opera reform continued with Calzabigi and Gluck's *Alceste* of 1767, which paid tribute to Maria Theresia as a loving widow. But circumstances generally favoured neither *opera seria* nor experimentation. Musical theatre was dominated by large-scale pantomime ballets, presented by Jean-Georges Noverre between 1767 and 1773, and by *opere buffe*, directed by Gluck's successor Florian Gassmann and after 1774 by Gassmann's pupil Antonio Salieri. Local librettists included both Calzabigi and his protégé Coltellini, but by 1773 Calzabigi had left Vienna in frustration and long-term subscribers such as Prince Khevenhüller were relinquishing their boxes on account of the shabbiness of theatrical offerings under the management of Count Koháry.

Characteristically taking quick and drastic action, in 1776 Emperor Joseph II suspended the agreement with the bankrupt Koháry's trustee, dismissed the Italian singers and their orchestra, and installed the German actors in the Burgtheater, henceforth called a 'Nationaltheater'. At the same time, he declared a 'Schauspielfreiheit' (an end to the court's monopoly on spectacles), allowing other companies or individuals to use the Kärntnertortheater and (on free evenings) the Burgtheater, as well as other venues. Joseph and his new *Musikgraf*, Count Orsini-Rosenberg, managed the theatres directly, without an impresario. At first Joseph's main concern was the spoken repertory, but audiences soon clamoured for opera, and Joseph accordingly sent his troupe's director, J. H. F. Müller, on a long recruiting trip for German singers capable of performing in *opéra comique* and *opera buffa*, not mere 'Liedsänger' as in much north German opera [the young Aloysia Weber was among those selected, in 1779]. The first Singspiel presented (in 1778) was *Die Bergknappen* by Ignaz Umlauf. Subsequent repertory consisted largely of translations from the French or Italian, but other local composers such as Franz Asplmayr and Salieri contributed as well. Dancers were lacking until a 1779 production of the pointedly chosen *Zémire et Azor* by Grétry showed the need for them. Also in 1779 the talented Gottlieb Stephanie replaced Müller as house poet and director of the Singspiel.

For the 1781–2 visit of the Russian Archduke Paul and his wife, the emperor and Chancellor Kaunitz decided on revivals of three major operas by Gluck [*Orfeo* and *Alceste* in their original Italian, and *Iphigenia auf Tauris* in German, translated from the French] as representing the best in Viennese musical theatre. Around the same time performances of a German translation of Gluck's *opéra comique La Rencontre imprévue* as *Die Pilgrimme von Mekka* delayed and also influenced the closely related Singspiel *Die Entführung aus dem Serail* by Mozart. Despite the phenomenal success of the latter and nationalist sentiment against foreign spectacles, Joseph and the Viennese critics found that the Nationaltheater offered too few Singspiels of too meagre a quality (musical and literary), especially when compared to the French or Italian originals they remembered, and in 1783 Joseph ended the experiment and engaged an *opera buffa* company. The once-disgraced Count Durazzo, now imperial ambassador in Venice, was instrumental in recruiting these singers, who included Michael Kelly, *prima buffa* Nancy Storace, and *primo buffo* Francesco Benucci, around whose comic talents the repertory was chosen or created. The singers quickly brought their acting into line with the recently raised standards of the German players, and were remembered by Caroline Pichler as the finest *buffo* company in Europe.

As his theatre poet Joseph engaged Lorenzo da Ponte, who at first collaborated with Salieri. The failure of *Il ricco d'un giorno* and rivalry with

Count Rosenberg's protégé Giambattista Casti led to a falling-out, and Da Ponte next worked with Martín y Soler, while Casti collaborated with the visiting Paisiello in 1784 on *Il re Teodoro in Venezia* [and with Salieri on *La grotta di Trofonio* (1785) and *Prima la musica* (1786)]. Influences from Paisiello's work, and his *Il barbiere di Siviglia* (performed in 1783), are to be found in Mozart and Da Ponte's operas. Mozart's three great comedies (including *Don Giovanni*, written for Prague) won the approval of Viennese audiences, though performances of *Così fan tutte* (1790) were cut short by the emperor's death.

The *opera buffa* ensemble did not enjoy the undivided support of Viennese high society, or even of the emperor. In 1785 Joseph installed a 'Deutsche Opéra Comique' in the Kärntnertortheater as healthy competition for the Italians. Their performances, which included operas by Dittersdorf, quickly dwindled, ending in February 1788 with *Die Entführung*, after which the theatre closed down. That same year, preoccupied by the Turkish war and irritated by singers' misbehaviour and greed, Joseph for a while contemplated dismissing the Italian company. Advocates of German culture urged such action, but were disappointed.

Joseph's successor, Leopold II, was initially aloof from theatrical affairs and concentrated on ending the war and restoring order to his realms. But in 1791 [the year of his coronation in Prague, for which Mozart composed *La clemenza di Tito*] he turned to opera in earnest, drawing on his experience as regent in Tuscany and in several ways returning to practices and genres of his mother Maria Theresia's reign. Leopold and his new *Musikgraf*, Johann Wenzel Ugarte, removed control of the theatres from the bureaucracy and made a fresh start on personnel, dismissing Da Ponte and his mistress, Adriana Ferrarese; Joseph Weigl replaced Salieri as director of the opera. Although plans to build a larger theatre were not realized, Leopold did reopen the Kärntnertortheater. He re-established both ballet and *opera seria* among the offerings, the latter in alternation with comic operas mostly less complex than those of Mozart and Da Ponte. Leopold first hired Caterino Mazzolà as theatre poet, and then Giovanni Bertati, whose first libretto for Vienna was *Il matrimonio segreto* (set by Cimarosa, 1792 [and one of the most resounding triumphs of Viennese *opera buffa*]).

Mozart, having received no preferment from the new emperor, in 1791 accepted an opera commission at Emanuel Schikaneder's suburban Freihaus-Theater auf der Wieden (built 1787). *Die Zauberflöte* displays both Masonic ideals and features typical of the popular musical and machine comedies dominating the fare at that theatre, which, like Karl Marinelli's Theater in der Leopoldstadt (founded 1781), owed its existence to Joseph's 'Schauspiel-freiheit'.

Of later 18th-century operas that have survived into the modern reper-tory, a disproportionate number were created in Vienna, despite widely varying tastes and forms of theatrical management. An explanation is sug-gested by Calzabigi, who in 1790 described the city's audiences as 'the dis-tillation of all nations' and on the whole far more cultivated than their Italian counterparts. As the capital of a large and polyglot empire, Vienna was perhaps uniquely capable of producing such a golden age of opera.

Absent from the repertory after his death, except in Schikaneder's the-atre, Mozart's operas began to reappear in the late 1790s. *Le nozze di Figaro* and *Don Giovanni* (as *Don Juan*) were given in 1798 (the former received four performances in Italian in 1807 and a few more in 1824–5, but German was the normal language for Mozart's Italian operas in Vienna in the 19th century, as it was for Gluck's works). *Die Entführung* was revived in 1801, and in the same year *Die Zauberflöte* was staged at the court opera for the first time, in a production so inept that Schikaneder parodied its deficien-cies in his own performances; with a new production in 1812 it became an established cornerstone of the repertory. *La clemenza di Tito* (as *Titus der Gütige*) and *Così fan tutte* (as *Mädchentreue*) shared about a hundred per-formances between 1804 and 1830, but *Idomeneo* (*Idomeneus, König von Creta*) disappeared after five performances in 1806 and was no more suc-cessful when put on again in 1819–20.

Between 1897 and 1907 Gustav Mahler held the directorship of the Hof-oper. Mahler made Vienna's opera once more the finest in Europe. In par-ticular he conducted the five great Mozart operas in a stylistically more faithful manner, accompanying the recitatives on the piano and, later, the harpsichord. In the period after World War II, the Viennese Mozart style be-came famous throughout the world, represented by the conductors Josef Krips and Karl Böhm, the director Oscar Fritz Schuh, and singers such as Sena Jurinac, Hilde Konetzni, Wilma Lipp, Emmy Loose, Irmgard Seefried, Elisabeth Schwarzkopf, Ljuba Welitsch, Anton Dermota, Hans Hotter, Erich Kunz, Julius Patzak, Paul Schöffler, and Ludwig Weber. Mozart's Italian operas, as well as most foreign works, continued to be sung in Ger-man. [H.S., B.A.B., P.B., M.C., R.K, H.G.]

This practice of translating Italian to German worked both ways, with London, for instance, staging *Il seraglio* and *Il flauto magico*. Fortunate in-deed are cities that, like post–World War II London, can have opera both in the original tongue and in that of most of the audience. Prague in

Mozart's time was another city which could claim to be polyglot, and one in which he found himself particularly at home.

Prague

Capital city of Czechoslovakia from 1918 and from 1992 of the Czech Republic, and formerly capital of Bohemia, **Prague** has been an important operatic centre since the 18th century, first as an outpost of the Habsburg empire, and later as the focal point of Czech nationalism. The first operatic performance in Prague took place on 27 November 1627 at the castle, on the occasion of the coronation of Ferdinand III. This new art form was unconnected with any native tradition in Bohemia, but its history was naturally influenced by the political situation in the Czech lands in the 17th century. Following the resignation of Rudolf II in 1611 the imperial court had moved from Prague to Vienna; [then came the 30 Years' War (1618–48)]. After defeat in the Battle of White Mountain (1620), the greater part of the non-Catholic nobility had to leave Bohemia. Courtly entertainment therefore found little room in Prague; the aristocratic culture that arrived from Vienna developed slowly, at the country seats of the nobility as much as in Prague itself. The imperial court was twice more situated in Prague during the 17th century, when operas were staged. Of great importance were the court festivities marking the coronation of Charles VI (August 1723), which included the premiere of Fux's *Costanza e Fortezza*.

The first opera impresario to work in Prague was apparently G. F. Sartorio, between 1701 and 1705. In 1724 Count Sporck invited Antonio Denzio's Italian company to his summer palace, and from 1725 to 1734 the same company also performed at his theatre in Prague. Denzio presented 57 operas by Vivaldi (several of them premieres), Albinoni, Porta, and others. During 1737–40 a company directed by the composer Santo Lapis performed in Prague, first at Sporck's theatre and later in the new theatre at Kotce known as the Comoedia-Haus or the Kotzen Opera (sometimes called simply the 'Nuovo Teatro'—new theatre). This opened in 1738 or 1739 in a former commercial building and became the main venue for performances (mostly of *opera buffa*) by Italian companies. The most important impresarios at Kotce were Angelo and Pietro Mingotti (1743–6), who put on operas by Pergolesi, Pinazzi, Galuppi, Vinci, and Gluck; G. B. Locatelli (1748–57), who mounted the premieres of Gluck's *Ezio* (1750) and *Issipile* (1752), as well as operas by Galuppi and others; J. F. von Kurz (1758–64) and his lessee Molinari, with operas by Galuppi, Auletta, and Fischietti; and Giuseppe Bustelli (1764–81), who put on works by Galuppi,

Piccinni, Guglielmi, Mysliveček, and Kozeluch, while his lessees J. J. Brunian (1769–78) and Karl Wahr presented Singspiels, including *Die Entführung aus dem Serail* in 1782. The theatre at Kotce closed in 1783.

On 21 April 1783 the Nostitzsches Nationaltheater, built by Count F. A. Nostitz (1725–94) with a capacity of over 1000, was opened; until 1862 it was Prague's main opera house. Among its early lessees were Pasquale Bondini (1784–8), who had been invited to the Thun theatre in Prague by the nobility in 1781, and Domenico Guardasoni (1788–1806). They each presented two operas by Mozart: *Le nozze di Figaro* in 1786 and subsequent years, the premieres of *Don Giovanni* (1787, commissioned by Bondini for royal wedding celebrations) and *La clemenza di Tito* (1791, commissioned by Guardasoni for the festivities surrounding the coronation of Leopold II), and a revival of *Die Zauberflöte* (1792). Guardasoni was the last impresario in Prague to maintain Italian as the language of performance. [Although *Die Zauberflöte* was in German, it was translated into Italian in 1794.] His productions included works by Cimarosa and Paisiello, as well as Singspiels. In 1798 the theatre was purchased by the Bohemian Estates; as the Stavovské Divadlo or Ständetheater (Estates Theatre) it became a centre for German opera. C. M. von Weber [first cousin of Constanze Mozart] worked there as conductor from 1813 to 1816, presenting, among other works, Beethoven's *Fidelio* (1814), the premiere of Spohr's *Faust* (1816), and a number of French operas. His *Der Freischütz* was performed in Prague 50 times between 1821 and 1823.

Most of the aristocratic theatres had ceased to exist by 1800, but the nobility continued to support performances by the Prague Conservatory, which presented operas by Mozart between 1828 and 1831 at the theatre of Count Vrtba (*La clemenza di Tito*, 1828; *Die Entführung*, 1829) and later at the Dominican monastery (*Così fan tutte*, 1839) and at the Estates Theatre (*Don Giovanni*, 1842; *Figaro*, 1843).

The first serious attempts to stage opera in Czech occurred only in the late 18th century. Czech theatre had for a long time lacked the support of the nobility and the wealthy, and was starved of good professional forces. At Kotce Czech arrangements of Singspiels and, later, translations of Italian operas were presented, and after 1770 Bustelli and Wahr put on original operas in Czech. In 1786 Bondini's Vlastenské Divadlo (Patriotic Theatre) company began to perform in Czech and German at a new wooden theatre, and from 1789 to 1802 the same company presented about 50 works in Czech at the U Hybernů monastery, including *Die Zauberflöte* in 1794 and operas by Süssmayr, Dittersdorf, Müller, Kauer, and Tuček.

For a time from 1862, opera in German was given only at the Estates Theatre. From 1885 to 1910 its director was Angelo Neumann, and in 1885–6 Mahler was conductor. Mozart operas continued to be performed there, but in 1888 the Deutscher Theaterverein opened the Neues Deutsches Theater as the chief German theatre in Prague. After 1945 the Estates Theatre became a second stage for the National Theatre under the name Tylovo Divadlo (Tyl Theatre; now again the Estates Theatre) and continued to present only operas by Mozart and plays. In 1977–83 the National Theatre was reconstructed and the Nová Scéna (New Stage) built to present plays and, occasionally, chamber operas. [J.L.]

Glossary

Act The main subdivision of an opera, completing a part of the action and with its own climax. The classical and Shakespearian five-act division was adopted in early operas, but in Italian opera a three-act scheme became standard, as in Mozart's full-length operas up to *Die Entführung*. A two-act design became accepted for *opera buffa* and *Singspiel*, sometimes subdivided into four (*Il barbiere di Siviglia*; *Le nozze di Figaro*), and applied to *opera seria* with *Il re pastore* and *La clemenza di Tito*.

Alto *See* Castrato and Contralto

Appoggiatura (It.) A 'leaning note', normally one step above the note it precedes. If not notated, appoggiaturas may be introduced in recitatives and arias in 18th-century opera, to make the musical line conform to the natural inflection of the words and enhance expression.

Aria (It.), **Air** A closed number for solo voice, the standard vehicle for individual expression—lyrical, brilliant, sentimental, infuriated. Small arias appeared in the earliest operas. By the early 18th century they were usually longer, and followed a da capo pattern (*ABA*), the third section repeating the first, sometimes a little shortened but otherwise unaltered unless by improvised embellishment. Typically *opera seria* consisted almost entirely of such arias separated by *recitativo semplice*; *opera buffa* was also dominated by arias until late in the century.

In Mozart's time arias took various forms. The principal form in his early years was a 'modified da capo', in which the third section ran the same course (in words and musical themes) as the first, but with a different key-scheme: the first section ended in the dominant key, the third in the tonic (see Key: hence 'sonata-form aria' is sometimes used). Mozart's resourcefulness in rearranging material in the tonic, so that it still lies in the singer's best register, is apparent as early as *La finta semplice*; a particularly good example is Ilia's first aria 'Se il padre perdei' in *Idomeneo*.

Some arias are simple rondos in one tempo, the main theme recurring at least twice. The aria in two (or more) speeds gained favour late in the century. A type of slow-fast aria popular in Mozart's Vienna is called rondò (note the spelling), in which each section returns to its opening key and theme, creating a rondo-like key scheme that governs both sections.

The 18th-century slow-fast aria is not the direct ancestor of the double 'cantabile-cabaletta' aria popular in 19th-century Italian opera, which consists of two self-contained arias, dramatically linked. The aria ceased to be a detachable unit later in the 19th century; some 20th-century composers (e.g., Stravinsky, in the neo-classical *The Rake's Progress*) have revived the aria, which is favoured where a formal or artificial element is required. Other numbers called 'aria' ('air' in French or English) are shorter and some bear such designations as cavatina, canzonetta, or romance. 'Air' is also used in ballet; a movement may be called 'Air de dance'.

Arioso (It.) 'Like an aria': a singing (as opposed to a declamatory) style of performance for a short passage in a regular tempo in the middle or at the end of a recitative; a short aria.

Azione teatrale (It.) A short opera or 'serenata' cultivated for festive occasions, particularly at Habsburg courts. Gluck's *Orfeo ed Euridice* was originally so described. It is virtually interchangeable with *festa teatrale*, and is appropriate to three Mozart works (*Ascanio in Alba, Il sogno di Scipione, Il re pastore*).

Baritone A voice of medium pitch, normally in the range A–f', centred on the range most natural to male voices, without the lowest bass notes. This range was important in the late 18th century, although the word 'baritone' was not normally used ('bass' served for both types, or singers were simply called '*buffo*').

Bass The lowest male voice, normally in the range F–e'. It is used in operas for gods, figures of authority (king, priest, father), and for villains and sinister characters, but was rarely used in Italian serious opera. Subclasses include *basso buffo* (in Italian comic opera), *basso cantante* or French *basse-chantante* (for a more lyrical role), and *basso profundo* (a heavy, deep, voice).

Breeches part [trouser role] Term for a man or boy's part sung by a woman in men's clothing ('travesty'), such as Cherubino in *Le nozze di Figaro* and Annio in *La clemenza di Tito*, a tradition extending to Oktavian in Strauss's *Der Rosenkavalier*. In Baroque opera male roles were often sung by women but, with the issue confused by the existence of castrati, casting was unspecific, as it is not with Cherubino and Oktavian.

Cadenza (It.) Literally 'cadence'. A virtuoso passage inserted in an aria or concerto movement, marked by a fermata near the end. In 18th-century opera, improvised by the singer; in 19th-century opera, frequently written out by the composer (and included in duets).

Canzone (It.) Term used for items presented as diegetic songs: music sung within the dramatic action. An example is Cherubino's 'Voi che sapete' in *Le* *no̧ze di Figaro* (Mozart called it 'Arietta'), as this was already a song in the Beaumarchais play.

Canzonetta (It.)   A diminutive of Canzone, used in the same sense; used for Don Giovanni's serenade 'Deh vieni alla finestra'.

Castrato (It.)   A male singer, castrated before puberty to preserve the unbroken voice. Castrati divide loosely into soprano or contralto ranges, although the sopranos could not range as high as women singers, and would nowadays be called mezzo-soprano.

Castratos figured in opera from its inception. In the papal states, where women were banned on stage, castratos sang all female roles. Everywhere they performed heroic male roles and lovers, and few outside France took exception to this characterization. They dominated the stage during the era of Metastasian *opera seria*, but were seldom employed in naturalistic *opera buffa*.

Castratos originated entirely in Italy, but Burney was unable to discover in which city the deed was done; it was attributed to an 'accident', but was undoubtedly performed in many cases because parents of large families saw a way of making a musical son economically productive (whereas after puberty he might not become a good tenor or bass). Castratos achieved international reputations, and often behaved with the capriciousness of prima donnas. Mozart was taught by a castrato (Manzuoli) and composed arias and roles for castratos in his earlier operas and in *La finta giardiniera*, *Il re pastore*, *Idomeneo*, and *La clemenza di Tito*. In the 19th century castrato roles appeared in a few operas (e.g., by Rossini and Meyerbeer), but the supply ran out and romantic art did not favour the artificial voice. The last known was Alessandro Moreschi (1858–1922) who in 1902–3 made recordings in which the distinctive, passionate, yet curiously disembodied quality of his voice is apparent.

Cavatina (It.)   In 18th-century opera a short aria, without da capo, often an entrance aria. Mozart used the term three times in *Le nozze di Figaro*, most typically for the Countess's entrance. In the 19th century, although still often an entrance aria, the term was applied to the double aria (cantabile-cabaletta); this usage has no 18th-century application.

Chaconne (Fr.)   A Baroque dance in triple metre and moderate tempo, used in opera or French-influenced opera, particularly as the final dance of a group (or of the entire work). Examples appear in some of Gluck's operas and *Idomeneo*. They do not use the ground bass typical of chaconnes by Lully and Purcell.

Coloratura, fioreture (It.)   Florid figuration, ornamentation, embellishment. The term is usually applied to high-pitched florid writing. The provision of coloratura was a requirement of baroque opera and its successors, *opera seria* and *azione teatrale*. There is accordingly profuse coloratura in most of Mozart's works, but it is increasingly used as a means of specific characterization, notably in the roles of Fiordiligi (*Così fan tutte*) and the Queen of Night (*Die Zauber-flöte*). The term 'coloratura soprano' signifies a singer of high pitch, lightness, and agility, appropriate to such roles.

Commedia dell'arte (It.)   A comic stage presentation, developed in 16th-century Italy, characterised by the use of masks (or fixed parts), earthy buffoonery, and improvisation. Its stock characters (Harlequin, Scaramouche, etc.; the buffoon Pantaleone, Columbine, the sly servant), or characters developed from them, were often introduced into comic operas such as Pergolesi's *La serva padrona*, the Beaumarchais operas (Bartolo), and *Don Giovanni* (Leporello); later incarnations appear in Busoni's *Arlecchino*, Strauss's *Ariadne auf Naxos*, and Stravinsky's ballet *Pulcinella* based on 18th-century music (mostly not by Pergolesi to whom it was attributed).

Continuo   The bass line, usually played on a sustaining instrument (cello, double bass, viola da gamba, bassoon), served to support the harmony provided by a keyboard—harpsichord, organ, eventually the early pianoforte—or a plucked instrument. Figures above the notes define the chords that should be played, but were omitted when the chord was simple and obviously deducible from the bass and melody. Continuo usage persisted to the end of the 18th century, but there remain differences of opinion as to how it should be applied, especially in *recitativo semplice*: should a cello be used, and if so, does it sustain while the harpsichord's harmony fades away? Should the keyboard player reiterate chords to maintain the sound, or improvise above the bass? Should the player risk distracting attention from the stage, in *opera buffa*, by witty interventions? In Mozart's time the composer or music director would usually supervise the performance from the harpsichord and the scope for improvisation was certainly there, but there is strong evidence in favour of reticent, supportive, realisation.

Contralto (It.) A voice normally written for the range *g–g″*. In modern English the term denotes the lowest female voice, but the term could in theory also denote a male falsetto singer ('male alto' or 'counter-tenor') or a castrato of low tessitura. In opera, true contralto roles are comparatively rare, although they occurred in the 17th century for old women, usually comic. In the 18th century some composers came to appreciate the dramatic qualities of the contralto, but singers were seldom available and there are no such roles in Mozart.

Da capo (It.)   An instruction (usually abbreviated D.C.) to return to the beginning and repeat the first section of music (until 'fine': 'end'). The 'da capo aria' was standard in the late Baroque (see Aria). It was partially superseded by the 'dal segno' aria (repeat 'from the sign'—placed usually after the orchestral introduction or ritornello), or the abbreviated da capo aria, in which a sign partway through the first section marks the point of reprise.

Dominant.   The chord or key a fifth above the tonic; *see* Key.

Dramma giocoso (It.)   Term used in Italian librettos from the mid-18th century for a comic opera, particularly the type favoured by Goldoni and his followers, in which character-types closer to serious opera appeared alongside those traditional in comedy. The *dramma giocoso* was not a distinct genre and the designation was used interchangeably with others; Mozart's *Don Giovanni* and *Così fan tutte* are described on the librettos as *dramma giocoso* and on the scores and in the composer's catalogue as *opera buffa*.

Duet (It., duetto, diminutive duettino)   An ensemble for two singers, not unlike an aria but used far more rarely than the solo aria. Most baroque operas have only one or two duets, ending an act when the principal lovers are united or about to be parted, a usage that survives in Mozart's serious operas. The love duet became characterized by singing in 3rds or 6ths, a mellifluous sound appropriate to shared emotion. Often—increasingly in the 19th century—the voices are used singly at first and join together later, symbolizing some dramatic development: a Mozart example is 'Fra gli amplessi' in *Così fan tutte*, which begins as if the singer were launching an aria. Its potential for comedy is fully realised in *Figaro*, which opens with two duets; several more follow.

Falsetto (It.)   The unbroken voice of an adult male singer, achieved through a technique whereby the vocal chords vibrate in a length shorter than usual. It was rarely used in opera until the later 20th century, except for occasional comic effect. Nowadays falsetto singers (male altos, counter-tenors) are appropriating castrato roles which modern revivals formerly, perforce, offered to women. It should be noted, therefore, that Beaumarchais expressly stated that, in the interests of decency, Chérubin (Cherubino) should not be acted by a boy or young man.

Festa teatrale (It.)   A short opera or serenata (see *azione teatrale*); typically the subject matter was allegorical and the production part of a celebration of a court event such as a wedding.

Finale (It.)   The concluding section of an opera act, continuously in measured music except for occasional brief interruptions by recitative. The ensemble finale developed in the middle of the 18th century, largely through the changes wrought in comic opera by Goldoni, who made act finales longer, bringing in more singers and increasing the density of the plot; responding to this, composers changed tempo and key frequently ('chain finale'), usually getting steadily faster—in Mozart, the field of some of his most audacious musical architecture.

Key   The key of a composition, major or minor, is selected by the composer in advance of composition. The keynote or tonic is like the music's centre of gravity: wherever it goes, the music must eventually fall (hence 'cadence') to end in the main key. The choice of keys in the 18th century was limited, at least in orchestral music; certain instruments (notably clarinets, brass, and timpani) could only negotiate a limited number of keys, and few relished keys with more than four sharps or flats; even these were rarely used by Mozart.

Libretto (It.) The poetic or prose text of an opera. The word derives from the literal meaning 'small book', the printed booklet containing the words of an opera and traditionally on sale at performances. When opera houses were candle-lit and lights were not dimmed, librettos could be consulted during the performance; when an opera was given in a language other than that of the audience, librettos sometimes offered parallel texts. 'Librettist' is now the standard term for the author of the words of an opera, who in Mozart's time was the 'poet'.

Lieto fine (It.) 'Happy ending', almost obligatory in serious operas of the 18th century. In operas based on myth, such as *Idomeneo*, the *lieto fine* may require the appearance of a benevolent deity (*deus ex machina*) to resolve a potentially tragic situation. Most *opera seria*, however, was historical rather than mythological and the *lieto fine* is obtained by an act of magnanimity, as in *Lucio Silla* and as foreshadowed in the title *La clemenza di Tito*.

Melisma A passage of florid writing in which several notes are sung in the same syllable. See *coloratura*, *fioreture*.

Melodrama A kind of drama, or a technique used within a drama, in which the action is carried forward by the protagonist speaking, with pauses filled by expressive music (orchestral, at least in opera). More rarely the words are spoken through the music. The technique resembles operatic accompanied recitative (*recitativo obbligato*), reserved for situations of strong emotion. Its invention is usually ascribed to J.-J. Rousseau (*Pygmalion*, c.1762). Georg Benda was its chief exponent in Germany; Mozart admired Benda and wrote melodrama sections in *Thamos* and *Zaide*. Beethoven used melodrama in the dungeon scene of *Fidelio*, and Weber in the Wolf's Glen scene in *Der Freischütz*.

Mezzo-soprano Term for a female (or a castrato) voice, normally written within the range a–$g^{1\prime\prime\prime}$, and perhaps weightier than a soprano. The term was not much used in the 18th century, but the castrato Senesino, for whom Handel composed several roles, was described as having a 'penetrating, clear, even, and pleasant deep soprano voice (mezzo soprano)'. The distinction was more keenly sensed in the 19th century, although the mezzo-soprano range was often extended to $b^{b\,\prime\prime}$. The mezzo-soprano is more suited than the full soprano to breeches parts, including adolescent roles such as Cherubino (*Figaro*), Ascanio (*Benvenuto Cellini*), and Oktavian (*Der Rosenkavalier*).

Modulation Key-change; the process of moving from one key to another. In Mozart's time virtually all musical numbers modulated to a closely related key and back again (perhaps with excursions on the way). Within a chain finale, key-change may mark a dramatic change such as the entrance of a new character (in which case the tempo may change with the modulation). Modulation is also a useful resource to suggest changes of mood, even within a continuous movement.

Motif or motive. A short musical idea, melodic, rhythmic, or harmonic (or any combination of these).

Music drama, Musical drama Equivalent to dramma per musica. The term was used by Handel for *Hercules* (1745), to distinguish it from opera and Sacred Drama. In more recent usage, the meaning attached to 'music drama' derives from Wagner, where it is applied to operas in which the musical, verbal, and scenic elements cohere to serve one dramatic end. Wagner deliberately underrated the extent to which this was already true in the multi-authored operas of earlier periods; the term fits such works as *Orfeo ed Euridice*, *Idomeneo*, and *Die Zauberflöte*, in which scenic elements were a vital component as well as (and inevitably) words and music. Premiere productions of 18th-century opera were usually directed by the poet, with the composer in charge of the music. Current theatrical practice qualifies this creative unity by performing operas with the original music and words but freshly invented scenic elements; authorial stage directions are not accorded the same status as the rest of the librettist's work.

Number opera Term for an opera consisting of individual sections or 'numbers' which can be detached from the whole, as distinct from an opera consisting of continuous music which can only be interrupted by emending the score. Nearly all 18th-century opera is 'number opera' as is much in the 19th century. Arias would normally be applauded (or the opposite), and could be encored before the performance continued. Mozart, mainly in *Idomeneo*, sometimes composed transitions from the end of an aria to the next number, but applause probably broke out nevertheless. Wagner made number opera appear old-fashioned (Richard Strauss's version turns *Idomeneo* into continuous opera). Number opera revived in the 20th century under the impact of neoclassicism and music theatre (e.g., Brecht and Weill). The modern practice of withholding applause until the end of an act means Mozart operas are sometimes played as if they were continuous in the Wagnerian sense.

Ombra (It., 'shadow') A style, formed of a combination of musical elements, harmonic, rhythmic, and orchestral, used in opera to evoke darkness, mystery, and menace.

Opera buffa (It.) Italian comic opera. Unlike comic opera in English, French, and German, *opera buffa* is sung throughout, with recitative rather than spoken dialogue. Though now applied generically, *opera buffa* was one of the several terms used in the 18th century, such as *dramma giocoso*. It developed from possible origins in *commedia dell'arte*, and, partly through cross-fertilization with serious opera, it reached a level of musical sophistication which eventually put it on an equivalent artistic plane to *opera seria*. This process involved the development of action ensembles and finales, which in turn came to influence *opera seria* (as in *La clemenza di Tito*).

Opera seria (It.)   Italian serious opera, sung throughout, on a heroic or tragic subject, of the 18th century and the early 19th; the more usual contemporary designation is 'dramma per musica'. *Opera seria* is usually in three acts, has five to seven characters, and consists primarily of arias in Da Capo form or its derivatives, in which characters express their emotional states, then leave the stage, ending a scene. The action takes place in recitative, with an occasional *recitativo obbligato* to mark a dramatic high point, and one or two duets; there are also occasionally trios and quartets (those in *Idomeneo* were far from being isolated examples in that period). Metastasian *opera seria* typically involves a moral dilemma, such as 'love or duty', and the plot is usually resolved in a *lieto fine*.

Overture   An orchestral piece that precedes a dramatic work. The form is usually classified as French (two sections, slow and majestic, fast and often fugal) or Italian (three movements: fast-slow-fast). The Italian is called Sinfonia and is indistinguishable from the independent symphony without minuet. In *Ascanio in Alba* Mozart linked the sinfonia to the opera by making the third movement the opening chorus; for concert use he added a new finale. Another three-part design consists of a single fast movement in which a slow section is enclosed (e.g., *Die Entführung*). Mozart's later works have single-movement overtures, resembling the first movements of a late 18th-century symphony but without repeats; this became normal in the 19th century.

The overture was sometimes intended to set the mood of the coming drama; the dedication to Gluck's *Alceste* emphasizes this point. In *Don Giovanni, Così fan tutte*, and *Die Zauberflöte* the overture uses music from the opera, and in common with most overtures between 1790 and 1820, these have a slow introduction. The notion of tying the overture to the opera in mood and theme, first developed in France, appealed to later German composers such as Beethoven, Weber, and Wagner.

Pasticcio (It.)   Term for an opera normally cooked up by a 'house' librettist and composer (even a distinguished one, such as Handel), the ingredients, at least in part, taken from existing works by a variety of composers; term derived from pastry-making. The practice persisted through most of the 18th century and was essentially commercial: success was better assured if singers were allowed to recycle favourite arias from other operas.

Pastorale   A literary, dramatic, or musical genre that depicts the characters and scenes of rural life or is expressive of its atmosphere, usually in idealized form.

The pastoral tradition was important in early opera, and continued to resonate, sometimes quite subtly, during the 18th century, mingled with heroic themes, as in *Il re pastore*, or comedies like Martín's *Una cosa rara* and, according to Goehring (2004), *Così fan tutte*.

Prima donna (It.)   'First lady': the principal female singer on the roster of an opera company, almost always a soprano. The expression came into use around the mid-17th century, with the opening of public opera houses in Venice, where the singers' ability to attract audiences became important. Singers insisted on using the title; when conflicts arose, managerial ingenuity devised such expressions as 'altra prima donna', 'prima donna assoluta' and even 'prima donna assoluta e sola' (see *Der Schauspieldirektor*). The 'seconda donna'—second lady—was nevertheless an important member of the company.

Some prima donnas made it a point of status to be difficult. Leopold Mozart referred darkly to the intrigues of de Amicis. The cult grew stronger in the next century: Adelina Patti (1843–1919), at the height of her career, stipulated that her name appear on posters in letters at least one-third larger than those used for other singers, and that she be excused from rehearsals. The need to meet prima donnas' demands shaped many librettos and scores, particularly because their status was reflected in the number and character of their arias—for instance, in Mozart's time, the late placement of the prima donna's rondò (*Don Giovanni*, the 1789 *Figaro*, *La clemenza di Tito*).

Primo uomo (It.)   'First man': the principal male singer on the roster of an opera company; in *opera seria*, usually a castrato. His importance was evident from his roles, generally on a par with the prima donna's (e.g., in Handel's *Giulio Cesare* Cleopatra and Caesar each have eight arias). During the later 18th century 'primo uomo' could also be applied to tenors.

Quartet   An ensemble for four singers. Quartets appear in opera as early as the 17th century, in serious and comic operas. Mozart sometimes used ensembles to further the dramatic action; quartet examples are the act 2 finale of *Die Entführung*, where the sequence of sections shows the consolidation of the relationships between the two pairs of lovers, and in act 1 of *Don Giovanni*, where 'Non ti fidar' draws together the dramatic threads. The quartet in the last act of *Idomeneo* is more an exploration by separate characters of their emotional positions (thus an 'aria a quattro').

Quintet   An ensemble for five singers. Quintets, except within ensemble finales, are comparatively rare, but there are two in *Così fan tutte*.

Recitative (*recitativo*)   Vocal writing developed with Italian texts and more or less successfully imitated by other languages. Recitative is closely based on the natural rhythms and accentuation of speech, not governed by a regular tempo or formal organization. It derived from the late 16th-century invention of a declamation with the flexible support of a continuo player or—less flexibly—a group, permitting emotionally charged treatment of the words. Recitative became a vehicle for dialogue, connecting arias. The instrumental cadence became a convention, as did the addition of vocal appoggiaturas at cadences.

Recitativo semplice or secco ('simple' or 'dry' recitative).   A more rapid, even delivery developed with the simplest accompaniment, to promote a conversational speed and manner, used in *opera seria* and perhaps most effectively in the cut and thrust of *opera buffa* dialogue. Simple recitative fell out of use early in the 19th century (more slowly in Italian comedy: comedy in other languages did not use it). Stravinsky and Britten revived the practice of accompanying recitative with a keyboard instrument (*The Rake's Progress, Death in Venice*).

Recitativo obbligato, stromentato, or accompagnato   Recitative with fully notated instrumental accompaniment (see also Melodrama), usually orchestral. Orchestrated recitative cannot be performed with equivalent freedom to simple recitative, because the orchestral ensemble must be conducted. For practical reasons the orchestra is usually confined to strings, but Mozart began introducing wind instruments, to excellent effect, for instance for Cecilio in *Lucio Silla* and the Count in *La finta giardiniera*. The voice itself is often left unaccompanied to enable the singer to put across the sense of the text; the orchestra 'paints' the requisite feeling. This type of recitative grew in importance during the 18th century to mark dramatic high points, and when combined with an aria forms a 'scena' (Mozart wrote several, on operatic texts, for concert performance).

Ritornello (It.)   A recurring instrumental passage, introducing an aria or concerto (two forms with much in common) and returning in modified (often shorter) form between solo sections.

Romance   In 18th- and 19th-century opera, a ballad-like or strophic song, sung diegetically like the Canzona (q.v.). It was an important element in *opéra comique*, and thus in Singspiel—for example, Pedrillo's 'Im Mohrenland' in *Die Entführung*, which also had a dramatic function.

Scena (It.), **Scène** (Fr.)   Term used to mean (1) the stage (e.g., 'sulla scena', on the stage; 'derrière la scène', behind the stage), (2) the scene represented on the stage, (3) a division of an act (*see* Scene). In Italian opera it also means an episode or defined unit within the structure of an opera, made up of diverse elements, such as a *recitativo obbligato* and aria.

Scene   (1) The location of a drama, or an act or part of an act; by extension, any part of a drama in one location. (2) In earlier usage, a scene was a section of an act culminating in an aria (or occasionally an ensemble); any substantial (in some operas, any at all) change in the personnel on stage was numbered as a new scene, even without any change in location.

Serenata (It.)   A dramatic cantata, akin to a short opera, usually on a pastoral, allegorical, or mythological topic and given in honour of a person or an occasion; not necessarily fully staged. From *sereno* (It.), 'a clear night sky', referring to the usual performance circumstances, the term was used in the 17th and 18th centuries for works performed in courtly or aristocratic surroundings, lavishly set and in a quasi-dramatic manner. The serenata was popular in Venice and Rome, and in Vienna; see *Azione teatrale*, *Festa teatrale*. The derived term 'serenade' may be employed for a wooing song (Don Giovanni's Canzonetta) or for instrumental music (the wind ensemble in Act II of *Così fan tutte*); in Act I Ferrando promises 'una bella serenata'.

Sextet   An ensemble for six singers. Sextets are rare, except within act finales, but each of Mozart's Da Ponte operas includes a notable example.

Singspiel (Ger.)   Literally, a play with songs. Although the term was used in 18th-century Germany for almost any kind of dramatic entertainment with music, including serious opera, Singspiel has come to mean a German comic opera with spoken dialogue. The genre was particularly popular during the late 18th century in Vienna and North Germany. It was influenced by the English ballad opera, then by French Opéra comique, which was often performed in German translation: Gluck's finest opéra comique, *La rencontre imprévue*, was composed in French for Vienna, and reappeared under more than one German title. Italian works translated into German, with dialogue replacing recitatives, include *La finta giardiniera* (under various titles) and *Don Giovanni* (as *Don Juan*). Other important original Singspiels were by Dittersdorf, Weigl, Beethoven (*Fidelio*), and Weber (*Der Freischütz*).

Soprano (It.)   The highest female voice, normally written within the range $c'–a''$ but often ranging higher to exploit the resources of a particular singer. The word is also applied to a boy treble and to a high castrato. The soprano was used for expressive roles in the earliest operas, but was soon found suitable to brilliant vocal display. When a singer became famous it was usually because of an ability to perform elaborate music with precision as well as beauty of tone. The heroine's role was sung by the best soprano, the prima donna; to her were assigned more, and more difficult and expressive, arias. The development of the different categories of soprano belongs to the 19th century, but is foreshadowed in the variety of roles and styles found in Mozart's operas; but in his time type-casting was not rigid and more emphasis is placed on the individual singer than on the voice-type.

Stretta, Stretto (It.)   Term used to indicate a faster tempo at the climactic ending of pieces such as an *opera buffa* finale.

Strophic A song or aria in which all stanzas of the text are set to the same music. 'Strophic variations' imply a melody or accompaniment varied in successive stanzas while remaining unchanged in structure. Although used in serious opera in early 17th-century Italy ('Possente spirito' in Monteverdi's *Orfeo*), strophic forms in Mozart's time are lighter pieces, sometimes ballads or romances (Pedrillo's 'Im Mohrenland', which is also diegetic; *see* 'Canzone').

Tenor The highest natural male voice, normally within the range *c–a'*. Although the tenor voice was valued in early opera, heroic roles in late Baroque *opera seria* were mainly assigned to the castrato, with tenors taking older characters and usually the second or third male role. In comedy, however, the tenor could play the lover, or take a *buffo* role such as the Mayor in *La finta giardiniera*. By the late 18th century, tenors were regularly given central roles in all types of opera; Mozart's—Belmonte, Basilio, Ottavio, Ferrando, Titus: heroic lover, comic, docile lover, more virile lover, benevolent monarch—define their scope at this period. Pitch in Mozart's time was somewhat lower, but his tenor parts seldom reach as high as those of the next century and some singers apparently operated as both tenor and baritone (e.g., Mandini, Bussani).

Terzet *See* Trio.

Tessitura (It.) Literally 'Texture': the part of a vocal compass in which a piece of music lies—whether high or low, etc; it is not measured by the extremes of range but by which part of the range is most used.

Tonal Term used for music in a particular key (see Key), or a pitch centre to which the music naturally gravitates. The use of tonalities, or the interplay of keys, can be an important dramatic weapon in the opera composer's armoury.

Tonic *See* Key.

Trio An ensemble for three singers. Terzets or trios have been used throughout the history of opera. Mozart wrote particularly fine action trios in *Le nozze di Figaro* Act 1, and *Don Giovanni*, Act 2. Other examples (two in *La clemenza di Tito*) are akin to arias with comments from the other characters.

Vaudeville (Fr.) A French poem or song of satirical or epigrammatic character common in the 17th and 18th centuries; vaudevilles made up much of the repertory at the Paris fair theatres. As the *opéra comique* developed from these ventures, more original music was added. The French *comédie en vaudeville* had an international influence. Placed at the end of an act or play, the *vaudeville final* reassembled the important characters and required each to sing one or more verses of a strophic song, usually with a choral refrain. This transferred naturally to *opéra comique* and thence to Singspiel, and its influence may be seen in surprising places, such in Gluck's *Orfeo*. It is more at home at the end of *Die Entführung* and Rossini's *Il barbiere di Siviglia*.

Versification   The organisation of poetry into lines with fixed numbers of syllables and accents (see Verso). The counting of syllables in Italian poetry is partly governed by elisions, whereby adjacent vowels count as one syllable, and can be set to one note in the music. The elision may override weak punctuation; in 'Porgi, amor, qualche ristoro' (*Figaro*, Act II) the first comma (which is perhaps optional) does not stop Mozart correctly setting the first two words to three, not four, notes, as Por—gia—mor. In recitative, syllables which are considered to be elided within the structure of the poetry are sometimes set to two notes in the interest of intelligibility.

Verso (It.)   A line of poetry. Italian verse consists of lines of a number of syllables, calculated on the basis of 'soft' lines (*versi piani*), ending with an unaccented syllable (examples from *Figaro*, his first aria: 'Se vuol ballare', five syllables). 'Hard' lines (*versi tronchi*) in the same metrical structure end with an accented syllable, and thus have one fewer syllable ('Le suonerò'). Soft lines are much the most common, with hard lines usually ending a stanza (in the above example, a four-line stanza or quatrain). 'Slippery' lines (*versi sdruccioli*) are rarer; they end with two unaccented syllables and in five-syllable stanzas they require six notes (from the same aria, 'Tutte le macchine').

Index of Role Names

*signifies originally castrato

Aceste (tenor)	*Ascanio in Alba*
Agenor/Agenore (tenor)	*Il re pastore*
Alexander (the Great)/Alessandro (tenor)	*Il re pastore*
Alfonso (baritone/bass)	*Così fan tutte*
Allazim (bass)	*Zaide*
Almaviva, Count (baritone)	*Le nozze di Figaro*
Almaviva, Countess (Rosina) (soprano)	*Le nozze di Figaro*
Amyntas/Aminta (*soprano)	*Il re pastore*
Anna (soprano)	*Don Giovanni*
Annius/Annio (soprano: breeches role)	*La clemenza di Tito*
Antonio (bass)	*Le nozze di Figaro*
Apollo (treble)	*Apollo et Hyacinthus*
Arbaces/Arbace (tenor)	*Idomeneo*
Arbates/Arbate (*soprano)	*Mitridate*
Arminda (soprano)	*La finta giardiniera*
Ascanio (*soprano)	*Ascanio in Alba*
Asdrubale (tenor/baritone)	*Lo sposo deluso*
Aspasia (soprano)	*Mitridate*
Aufidius/Aufidio (tenor)	*Lucio Silla*
Aurelia (soprano)	*L'oca del Cairo*
Barbarina (soprano)	*Le nozze di Figaro*
Bartolo (bass)	*Le nozze di Figaro*
Basilio (tenor)	*Le nozze di Figaro*
Bastien (tenor)	*Bastien und Bastienne*
Bastienne (soprano)	*Bastien und Bastienne*
Belfiore, Count/contino (tenor)	*La finta giardiniera*
Belmonte (tenor)	*Die Entführung aus dem Serail*
Bettina (soprano)	*Lo sposo deluso*
Biondello (tenor)	*L'oca del Cairo*
Blonde (soprano)	*Die Entführung aus dem Serail*
Bocconio (bass)	*Lo sposo deluso*
Calandrino (tenor)	*L'oca del Cairo*
Cassandro (bass)	*La finta semplice*
Cecilius/Cecilio (*soprano)	*Lucio Silla*
Celia (soprano)	*Lucio Silla*

Oracle (bass)	*Idomeneo*
Osmin (bass)	*Die Entführung aus dem Serail*
Osmin (bass)	*Zaide*
Ottavio (tenor)	*Don Giovanni*
Pamina (soprano)	*Die Zauberflöte*
Papagena (soprano)	*Die Zauberflöte*
Papageno (bass/baritone)	*Die Zauberflöte*
Pedrillo (tenor)	*Die Entführung aus dem Serail*
Pharnaces/Farnace (*alto)	*Mitridate*
Podestà (Don Anchise) (tenor)	*La finta giardiniera*
Polidoro (tenor)	*La finta semplice*
Publius/Publio (bass)	*La clemenza di Tito*
Publius/Publio (tenor)	*Il sogno di Scipione*
Pulcherio (tenor/baritone)	*Lo sposo deluso*
Queen of Night (soprano)	*Die Zauberflöte*
Ramiro (*soprano)	*La finta giardiniera*
Roberto/Nardo (baritone)	*La finta giardiniera*
Rosina (soprano)	*La finta semplice*
Sandrina, see Violante	
Sarastro (bass)	*Die Zauberflöte*
Scipio/Scipione (tenor)	*Il sogno di Scipione*
Selim, Pasha (spoken role)	*Die Entführung aus dem Serail*
Serpetta (soprano)	*La finta giardiniera*
Servilia (soprano)	*La clemenza di Tito*
Sextus/Sesto (*soprano)	*La clemenza di Tito*
Silberklang, Mlle (soprano)	*Der Schauspieldirektor*
Silvia/Sylvia (soprano)	*Ascanio in Alba*
Simone (bass)	*La finta semplice*
Soliman, Sultan (tenor)	*Zaide*
Speaker/Orator (bass)	*Die Zauberflöte*
Sulla, Lucius/Silla, Lucio (tenor)	*Lucio Silla*
Susanna (soprano)	*Le nozze di Figaro*
Tamino (tenor)	*Die Zauberflöte*
Tamyris/Tamiri (soprano)	*Il re pastore*
Titus/Tito (tenor)	*La clemenza di Tito*
Venus/Venere (soprano)	*Ascanio in Alba*
Violante Onesti, Marchioness (Sandrina) (soprano)	*La finta giardiniera*
Vitellia (soprano)	*La clemenza di Tito*
Vogelsang (tenor)	*Der Schauspieldirektor*
Xiphares/Sifare (*soprano)	*Mitridate*
Zaide (soprano)	*Zaide*
Zephyrus (treble)	*Apollo et Hyacinthus*
Zerlina (soprano)	*Don Giovanni*

Suggested Listening Guide

Recordings of the later Mozart operas are plentiful, and more constantly become available. What follows can only be a personal tribute to those the author has enjoyed, and is almost inevitably out of date. Apologies are offered to those—and there will be many—whose favourite conductors and singers are not represented; but with over 50 performances of *Don Giovanni* in the catalogue, and substantial numbers for the other most popular operas (*Figaro, Così fan tutte, Die Entführung, Die Zauberflöte*), no comprehensive or scientific classification is possible.

Recent transfers to CD are often at tempting prices, but often come with no libretto and only a synopsis of the plot. This is a handicap for those unacquainted with the drama, and for those who wish to listen intently and have no copy of the words from another source and no score. The lack of historical, biographical, and interpretative commentary may cause less anguish (except to those of us sometimes commissioned to write it). Listeners who like opera in their own language will be grateful to Chandos for a series of excellent performances in English that by now includes all the major operas, but I am only considering original-language recordings here.

The imbalance between works with multiple recordings, and those for which there are only one or two, is very great, and only the more popular exist so far on DVD. With Mozart there are also divisions between performances reflecting early to mid-20th-century performance traditions, and those that reflect a more modern tradition based on historical information, and in some cases using historical instruments. The latter are not necessarily characterised by faster tempi, but there is usually a cleaner—some might say clinical—quality to the sound; the pitch may be lower; and the singing may be affected by additional ornamentation (recitative appoggiaturas, cadenzas, decorated repeats). Those who hear such interventions in the notated texts with distaste, despite their evident historical justification, will do well to stick to older recordings.

Understanding and enjoyment of Mozart's operas can only be enhanced by some knowledge of his predecessors and contemporaries. Besides numerous recordings of operas by Gluck, and a few of influential predecessors like Hasse, Jommelli, Piccinni, and Bach, there are now recordings of operas from the repertoire of Vienna in the 1780s such as Paisiello's *Il barbiere di Siviglia*, Salieri's *La grotta di Trofonio* and *Axur, re d'Ormus*, and Martín y Soler's *Una cosa rara*. Complete recordings of Mozart operas are supplemented by innumerable anthologies of arias—arias for the stage and concert arias—going back to the earliest artists captured on recordings, such as Adelina Patti.

First, a cordial recommendation for the **Philips Complete Edition**, compiled from recordings made over some 15 years to commemorate the bicentenary of Mozart's death in 1991. The operas have at times been made available separately or in small groups. The standard of performance is inevitably a little uneven but is never less than competent, and the edition includes the only, or almost the only, versions of early and unfinished works. The style is not 'historically informed' in any dogmatic sense, and the performances are lively and musical.

The Complete Edition is thus a safe recommendation for *Apollo et Hyacinthus*, *Bastien und Bastienne*, *La finta semplice*, *Mitridate, re di Ponto*, *Ascanio in Alba*, *Il sogno di Scipione*, and *Lucio Silla*. Most of these works were played by the orchestra of the Salzburg Mozarteum, conducted by Leopold Hager.

MITRIDATE, RE DI PONTO

A recent version by Les Talens lyriques under Christophe Rousset on Decca (1998) is a serious rival, with Giuseppe Sabbatini (Mithridates), Cecilia Bartoli (Xiphares), Natalie Dessay (Aspasia), and a counter-tenor (Brian Asawa) taking the lower castrato role of Pharnaces.

ASCANIO IN ALBA

An excellent alternative is at bargain price (Naxos, 1995) from the Budapest Concerto Armonico under Jacques Grimbert. Michael Chance as Amyntas is another counter-tenor to appropriate a castrato role, a bold move amply justified by results. Jill Feldman sings Silvia, and Rosa Mannion the more vertiginous castrato role, Fauno.

LUCIO SILLA

A typically vital performance directed by Nikolaus Harnoncourt on TelDec has Peter Schreier in the title-role, with Edita Gruberovà, Cecilia Bartoli, and Dawn Upshaw; but it is not quite complete. The Philips Complete Edition under Hager also has Schreier in the title-role: no substitute tenor, as at the original performance, but one of best and most intelligent of his generation. The strong female contingent includes Julia Varady, Arleen Augér, and Edith Mathis.

LA FINTA GIARDINIERA

At a time (1972) when the only complete version of *La finta giardiniera* was in German, it was recorded by the orchestra of North German Radio under Hans Schmidt-Isserstedt, with Helga Donath (Sandrina/Violante), Jessye Norman (Arminda), and other roles taken by Ileana Cotrubas, Tatiana Troyanos, Werner Hollweg, Hermann Prey, and Gerhard Unger (Philips). The full Italian text was recovered in time to be recorded by Hager for the Philips Complete Edition (1980).

IL RE PASTORE

The Philips Complete Edition, this time employed the Academy of St Martin in the Fields under Neville Marriner, with Jerry Hadley (Alexander), Angela Maria

Blasi (Amyntas), and Sylvia McNair (Elisa). This enjoyable all-round performance was one of the more recent in the edition (1989); there is an alternative directed by Harnoncourt.

ZAIDE

The Philips recording with Peter Schreier, Edith Mathis, and Werner Hollweg is strongly rivalled by Harmonia Mundi's 1998 issue on period instruments, by the Academy of Ancient Music under Paul Goodwin, with Lynne Dawson (Zaide), Hans Peter Blochwitz (Gomatz), Olaf Bär (Allazim), and Herbert Lippert (Sultan).

IDOMENEO, RE DI CRETA

Abbreviated cast lists in parentheses are in the order Idomeneus, Idamantes, Ilia, Elektra. Most earlier recordings of this difficult opera were severely curtailed or otherwise unsatisfactory. Schmidt Isserstedt with the Dresden Staatskapelle in 1971 (Philips) presented a full text, but with a tenor Idamantes singing the castrato line an octave too low, even in the ensembles that Mozart recomposed. The best of the four tenors, Peter Schreier, sang the least interesting role, Arbaces. More dramatic performances of somewhat reduced versions appeared under Colin Davis (Philips Complete Edition) and two under John Pritchard (one from Glyndebourne with Richard Lewis in the title-role; one with the Vienna Philharmonic and Luciano Pavarotti who, however, sings the simpler version of 'Fuor del mar'). More than with the later works, these versions are superseded by more recent performances.

Nikolaus Harnoncourt's many Mozart performances are clearly affected by his prior work with period instruments. His *Idomeneo* with Zürich Opera (TelDec, with Werner Hollweg, Trudeliese Schimdt, Rachel Yakar, Felicity Palmer) packs tremendous dramatic punch, and while it is sometimes eccentric in interpreting Mozart's notation, it distances *Idomeneo* from any notion that it is cold or classical.

Something like a definitive performance came on period instruments (DGG Archiv: Monteverdi Choir and English Baroque Soloists under John Eliot Gardiner). The very full musical text includes variants and a lengthy ballet sequence, and the cast is excellent (Anthony Rolfe Johnson, Anne Sofie von Otter, Sylvia McNair, Hillevi Martinpelto). Also worth noting are

> Metropolitan Opera (DGG) under James Levine, with a starry cast including Placido Domingo, Cecilia Bartoli, Heidi Grant-Murphy, and Carol Vaness.
>
> Scottish Chamber Orchestra (EMI) under Charles Mackerras (Ian Bostridge, Lorraine Hunt Lieberson, Lisa Milne, Barbara Frittoli).
>
> 1786 version: Dresden Staatskapelle (DGG) under Karl Böhm: the only recording of Mozart's version with a tenor Idamantes (Peter Schrier promoted to this role), including the new aria and duet (Wieslaw Ochman, Schreier, Edith Mathis, Julia Varady).

Perhaps Böhm's main contribution is to reinforce what appears to be the consensus: that in the absence of castrati, it is better to retain the pitch and texture of the music as first conceived, and have Idamantes sung by a woman (a procedure compatible with 18th-century practice). With a singer like von Otter (for Gardiner) questions of realism simply disappear.

DIE ENTFÜHRUNG AUS DEM SERAIL

Abbreviated cast lists are in the order Konstanze, Belmonte, Osmin. Lively and stylish performances under Thomas Beecham and Karl Böhm (with Arleen Augér and Kurt Moll) will satisfy those who prefer an earlier style of performance. *Die Entführung aus dem Serail* is also excellently served by period instrument recordings.

Les Arts Florissants under William Christie (Erato, 1999): this strips the dialogue to its bare essentials, but the singers themselves speak, rather than a separate group of actors (Christine Schäfer, Ian Bostridge, Alan Ewing, with Patricia Petibon as Blonde, Iain Paton as Pedrillo). John Eliot Gardiner (DGG Archiv, 1991) has Luba Orgonasova as a fine Konstanze, with Stanford Olsen and Cornelius Hauptmann. Christopher Hogwood with the Academy of Ancient Music (Oiseau-Lyre) has Lynne Dawson as Konstanze and Uwe Heilmann as Belmonte. A version under Charles Mackerras (Decca) serves as the soundtrack of the film *Mozart in Turkey*.

L'OCA DEL CAIRO and LO SPOSO DELUSO

The Philips edition treats us to the music of the two unfinished comedies. For *L'oca del Cairo* the numbers sketched by Mozart are stylishly completed by Erik Smith. The cast includes Dietrich Fischer-Dieskau (Pippo) and Peter Schreier (Biondello), who also directs the Chamber Orchestra 'Philip Emanuel Bach'. *Lo sposo deluso* has a starry cast for an unfinished work: Clifford Grant (Bocconio), Anthony Rolfe Johnson (Don Asdrubale), Robert Tear (Pulcherio), Ileana Cotrubas (Bettina), and Felicity Palmer (Eugenia), with the London Symphony Orchestra under Colin Davis.

THE DA PONTE OPERAS

With the Da Ponte operas, classic recordings date back to the early years of Glyndebourne opera in the 1930s, and include versions made during, and in the years immediately after, the Second World War, originally issued on 78s. The singers are not necessarily those best remembered today, and recordings are often from live performances, with the attendant vitality, but often poor sound. Many are fine examples of Mozart performance for that period. Glyndebourne's commitment to teamwork comes through in the recordings, which have been reissued on CD (bargain versions including those on Naxos Historical). Other historic recordings, naturally in mono, include some conducted by Wilhelm Furtwängler towards the end of his career.

Conductors nowadays tend to build sets of the late operas (the Da Ponte operas and *Die Zauberflöte*, but not always *La clemenza di Tito*). A generally reliable set emerges from the preserved and revived 18th-century Drottningholm Court Theatre near Stockholm, under Arnold Östman; other sets may have more glittering casts, but these have ensemble qualities recalling those of Glyndebourne, and several of the singers are very good indeed.

Le nozze di Figaro

Abbreviated cast in the order Figaro, Susanna, Count, Countess. If the list extends further, Cherubino, Marcellina, Bartolo, Basilio.

Opera conductors will all want their *Figaro* on record, and admirers of particular *maestri* will require no further recommendation. A modern gold standard was set by the Vienna Philharmonic Orchestra under Carlo Maria Giulini (EMI, 1959), the cast including Giuseppe Taddei, Anna Moffo, Eberhard Waechter, and Elizabeth Schwarzkopf. Other versions exist by Karl Böhm, Bernard Haitink (Warner DVD), and George Solti, whose cast includes Kiri te Kanawa and Thomas Allen. Any of these can be recommended, as can, with the added infusion of his more modern style, the performance under Harnoncourt (TelDec, 1994, with Anton Scharinger, Barbara Bonney, Thomas Hampson, Charlotte Margiono). Thoroughly recommended:

Arnold Östman (Decca, 1988) with Petteri Salomaa, Barbara Bonney, Håken Hagegård, Arleen Augér, Alicia Nafé, Della Jones, Carlos Feller, and Edoardo Gimenez.

John Eliot Gardiner (DGG Archiv, 1994: Bryn Terfel, Alison Hagley, Rodney Gilfry, Hillevi Martinpelto, Pamela Helen Stephen, Susan McCulloch, Carlos Feller, Francis Egerton) is also on DVD. Purists should note Gardiner's adoption of a modern 'tradition' (historically unfounded) of an altered scene-order in Act III, and his own eccentric reordering of elements in Act IV.

Don Giovanni

Casts are in the order Giovanni, Anna, Elvira, Zerlina, Ottavio, Leporello, Masetto and Commendatore. *Don Giovanni* is normally given in a combination of the versions for Prague and Vienna.

Furtwängler's various recordings include versions with singers of the vintage of Tito Gobbi, Elisabeth Schwarzkopf, and Irmgard Seefried. A classic version under Bruno Walter with Ezio Pinza in the title-role is reissued on Naxos Historical. The next generation of conductors associated with Austro-German repertoire set its stamp on this 'opera of operas': Otto Klemperer, Herbert von Karajan, Böhm, Solti and—more recently—Daniel Barenboim, usually with the opera orchestras of Berlin or Vienna, and distinguished casts. Böhm (RCA, 1955), for example, with Vienna forces, has George London, Lisa della Casa, Sena Jurinac, and Irmgard Seefried. Solti with the London Philharmonic Orchestra (Decca, 1996) has

Bryn Terfel in the title-role. Among earlier classics is one by Giulini in 1959 with the New Philharmonia (EMI), while the Philips Complete Edition reissued an admirable performance (1973) with forces from the Royal Opera House, Covent Garden, under Colin Davis (Ingvar Wixell, Martina Arroyo, Kiri te Kanawa, Mirella Freni).

Among period instrument performances, Roger Norrington's (EMI, 1993) stands out, as it makes both versions available; this required recording several sections twice over in the interests of continuity. The orchestra is the London Classical Players, with Andreas Schmidt, Amanda Halgrimson, Lynne Dawson, Nancy Argenta, John Mark Ainsley, Gregory Yurisich, Gerald Finley, Alastair Miles. Norrington's tempi really are faster than usual; John Eliot Gardiner (DGG Archiv, 1994) might for that reason be the preferred choice for period-instrument performance, the cast including Rodney Gilfry, Luba Orgonasova, and Charlotte Margiono.

Così fan tutte

Casts are in the order Fiordiligi, Dorabella, Despina, Ferrando, Guglielmo, Alfonso. *Così* is no longer the Cinderella among the Da Ponte operas. A vintage recording is that of Böhm with the Philharmonia Orchestra (EMI, 1962), the cast including Elisabeth Schwarzkopf and Christa Ludwig. Philips here used the Academy of St Martin in the Fields under Marriner, with Karita Mattila, Anne Sofie von Otter, Francisco Ariaza, Thomas Allen, Elzbieta Szmytka, and José van Dam. Arnold Östman's Drottningholm *Così* is cordially recommended for teamwork and some committed individual performances (L'Oiseau-Lyre, 1985; Rachel Yakar, Alicia Nafé, Gösta Winbergh, Tom Krause, Georgine Resick, Carlos Feller).

Period instrument performances include La Petite Bande under Sigiswald Kuijken (ACC, 1992: Soile Isokoski, Monica Groop, Markus Schäfer, Per Vollestad, Nancy Argenta, Huub Claessens) and, also available on DVD, Gardiner (DGG Archiv, 1993: Amanda Roocroft, Rosa Mannion, Rainer Trost, Rodney Gilfry, Eirian James, Carlos Feller).

DIE ZAUBERFLÖTE

Casts in the order Tamino, Pamina, Papageno, Sarastro, Queen of Night

Before turning to Mozart for a fairy opera all his own, Schikaneder may have co-opted him—or he may have co-opted himself—into a contribution to *Der Stein der Weisen*. This was decently recorded, with the period-instrument Boston Baroque orchestra under Martin Pearlman, on Telarc. Among well over thirty versions of *Die Zauberflöte*, classics include a lively one under Thomas Beecham. A Furtwängler recording was made with Ernst Haeflinger (Tamino), Irmgard Seefried (Pamina), Josef Greindl (Sarastro), and Wilma Lipp (Queen of Night). A particularly fine vintage recording is that under Ferenc Fricsay (DGG, 1954), with Haeflinger again, Maria Stader as Pamina, Dietrich Fischer-Dieskau as Papageno, Greindl again, and Rita Streich a remarkable Queen.

Die Zauberflöte was always intended as a visual as well as a musical entertainment, and it offers plenty of scope to an imaginative designer. The marvellous sets by David Hockney are available on DVD (DGG, 1991). This was a Metropolitan Opera production conducted by James Levine, with Katharine Battle and Francesco Ariaza as Pamina and Tamino, and Kurt Moll as Sarastro.

On CD, the Drottningholm version is again beguiling (Decca, 1993), under Östman, with Kurt Streit, Barbara Bonney, Gilles Cachemaille, Kristinn Sigmundsson, Sumi Jo. Roger Norrington with the London Classical Players (EMI, 1991) produced a characteristically brisk and no-nonsense rendering that lets the music speak for itself, while including more of the dialogue than usual, plus special effects including a genuine lion (Anthony Rolfe Johnson, Dawn Upshaw, Andreas Schmidt, Cornelius Hauptmann, Beverly Hoch). William Christie and Les Arts Florissants is a strong rival (Hans Peter Blochwitz, Rosa Mannion, Anton Scharinger, Reinhard Hagen, Natalie Dessay).

LA CLEMENZA DI TITO

Casts in the order Tito, Sesto, Vitellia, Servilia, Annio, Publio

The exception among Mozart's late operas, entirely serious in genre and arguably incomplete, *La clemenza di Tito* with committed artists can rise to heights fully worthy of the composer's prime. Two performances using period instruments are noteworthy: John Eliot Gardiner with the English Baroque Soloists and the Monteverdi Choir (DGG Archiv, 1991) has a cast similar to his excellent *Idomeneo* (Anthony Rolfe Johnson, Anne Sofie von Otter, Sylvia McNair, Julia Varady, Catherine Robbin, Cornelius Hauptmann). Christopher Hogwood with the orchestra and chorus of the Academy of Ancient Music (Decca, 1995) leads another excellent cast (Uwe Heilmann, Cecilia Bartoli, Della Jones, Barbara Bonney, Diana Montague, Gilles Cachemaille).

How to choose among such a wealth of committed talent? The only advice is to listen, follow your taste where singing and playing styles are concerned, and do not assume that one conductor, singer, or record company is necessarily going to deliver the best version of everything.

Select Bibliography

Complete forms of the articles on librettists, performers, and cities are found in *The New Grove Dictionary of Opera*, edited by Stanley Sadie (London and New York, 1992; also available online).

CONTEMPORARY AUTHORS REFERRED TO IN THE TEXT

C. Burney: *The Present State of Music in France and Italy* (London, 1771); *The Present State of Music in Germany and the Netherlands* (London, 1773); modern edition, P. A. Scholes, ed., *Dr Burney's Musical Tours in Europe* (2 vols., London, 1959).

C. Burney: *A General History of Music*, vol. iv (London, 1789); modern edition, F. Mercer, ed. (New York, 1935)

Da Ponte, Lorenzo: *Memorie* (New York, 1823–7)

M. Kelly: *Reminiscences* (London, 1826) modern edition, R. Fiske, ed. (London, 1975)

Zinzendorf: diaries of Count Karl Zinzendorf und Pottendorf, written in French. The parts relevant to opera are transcribed in D. Link, *The National Court Theatre in Mozart's Vienna*

C. D. F. Schubart: *Ideen zu einer Ästhetik der Tonkunst* (Vienna, 1806)

CATALOGUES, BIBLIOGRAPHIES, LETTERS, DOCUMENTS, ICONOGRAPHY

E. Anderson, ed.: *The Letters of Mozart and his Family* (London, 1938, 1985)

O. E. Deutsch: *Mozart: die Dokumente seines Lebens, gesammelt und erläutert* (Kassel, 1961; English translation as *Mozart: a Documentary Biography*, London, 1965; supplement 1978)

O. E. Deutsch: *Mozart und seine Welt in zeitgenössischen Bildern* (Kassel, 1961) [*Mozart and his World in Contemporary Pictures*: text in German and English]

W. A. Bauer, O. E. Deutsch and J. H. Eibl, eds.: *Mozart: Briefe und Aufzeichnungen* (Kassel, 1962–75) (the letters of the Mozart family in the original language, including many passages omitted by Anderson)

H. C. R. Landon, ed.: *The Mozart Compendium* (London, 1990)

C. Eisen: *New Mozart Documents. A Supplement to O. E. Deutsch's Documentary Biography* (London, 1991)

R. Spaethling: *Mozart's Letters, Mozart's Life* (New York and London, 2000)

C. Eisen and S. P. Keefe, ed.: *The Cambridge Mozart Encyclopedia* (Cambridge, 2005)

BIOGRAPHIES, STUDIES OF LIFE AND WORKS

A. Einstein: *Mozart: his Character, his Work* (English translation, New York, 1945: German original, 1947, 1960)

W. Hildesheimer: *Mozart* (Frankfurt, 1977; English translation, 1982)

S. Sadie: *The New Grove Mozart* (London, 1982)

P. Clive: *Mozart and his Circle: a Biographical Dictionary* (London, 1993)

M. Solomon: *Mozart, a Life* (London, 1995)

S. Sadie, ed.: *Wolfgang Amadè Mozart. Essays on his Life and Music* (Oxford, 1996)

J. Rosselli: *The Life of Mozart* (Cambridge, 1998)

R. Gutman: *Mozart. A Cultural Biography* (New York, 1999)

S. Sadie: *Mozart. The Early Years 1756–1781* (Oxford, 2006)

J. Rushton: *Mozart. An Extraordinary Life* (London, 2005)

J. Rushton: *Mozart. The Master Musicians* (New York, 2006)

LIFE AND WORKS, PARTICULAR PERIODS AND ASPECTS

C. Rosen: *The Classical Style: Haydn, Mozart, Beethoven* (London, 1971; rev. 1997)

A. Tyson: *Mozart: Studies of the Autograph Scores* (Cambridge, Mass., 1987)

H. C. R. Landon: *1791: Mozart's Last Year* (London, 1988)

H. C. R. Landon: *Mozart: the Golden Years, 1781–1791* (London, 1989)

J. Webster: 'The analysis of Mozart's Arias', in C. Eisen: *Mozart Studies* (Oxford, 1991), 101–211

D. Heartz: *Haydn, Mozart, and the Viennese School. 1740-1780* (New York, 1995)

D. Link, ed., with J. Nagley: *Words about Mozart: Essays in Honour of Stanley Sadie* (Woodbridge, 2005)

OPERAS

E. J. Dent: *Mozart's Operas: a Critical Study* (London, 1913, rev. 1947)

B. Brophy: *Mozart the Dramatist: a New View of Mozart, his Operas and His Age* (London, 1964, 1988)

C. Gianturco: *Le opere del giovane Mozart* (Pisa, 1976, enlarged 1978, English translation, *Mozart's Early Operas*, London, 1981)

W. Mann: *The Operas of Mozart* (London, 1977)

F. Noske: *The Signifier and the Signified: Studies in the Operas of Mozart and Verdi* (The Hague, 1977)

S. Kunze: *Mozarts Opern* (Stuttgart, 1984)

R. Angermüller: *Mozart: die Opern von der Uraufführung bis heute* (Fribourg, 1988; English translation, 1988, as *Mozart's Operas*)

D. Heartz, with T. Bauman: *Mozart's Operas* (Berkeley, 1990)

N. Till: *Mozart and the Enlightenment: Truth, Virtue and Beauty in Mozart's Operas* (London, 1992)

M. Hunter and J. Webster, eds: *Opera buffa in Mozart's Vienna* (Cambridge, 1997)

J. Rice: *Antonio Salieri and Viennese Opera* (Chicago, 1998)
D. Link: *The National Court Theatre in Mozart's Vienna* (Oxford, 1998)
M. Hunter: *The Culture of Opera Buffa in Mozart's Vienna* (Princeton, 1999)
D. Cairns: *Mozart and His Operas* (Harmondsworth, 2006)

INDIVIDUAL OPERAS

J. Rushton: *W. A. Mozart:* Idomeneo (Cambridge, 1993)
T. Bauman: *W. A. Mozart:* Die Entführung aus dem Serail (Cambridge, 1987)
M. Head: *Orientalism, Masquerade and Mozart's Turkish Music* (London, 2000)
A. Campana: 'Il libretto de "Lo sposo deluso" ', *Mozart-Jahrbuch* 1988–9, 573–88.
W. J. Allanbrook: *Rhythmic Gesture in Mozart:* Le nozze di Figaro *and* Don Giovanni (Chicago, 1983)
A. Steptoe: *The Mozart-Da Ponte Operas: the Cultural and Musical Background to* Le nozze di Figaro, Don Giovanni *and* Così fan tutte (Oxford, 1988)
T. Carter: *W. A. Mozart:* Le nozze di Figaro (Cambridge, 1987)
D. Link, ed.: *Arias for Nancy Storace, Mozart's First Susanna* (Middleton, Wis., 2002); *Arias for Francesco Benucci, Mozart's First Figaro* (Middleton, Wis., 2004)
J. Rushton: *W. A. Mozart:* Don Giovanni (Cambridge, 1981)
J. Miller, ed.: *The Don Giovanni Book. Myths of Seduction and Betrayal* (London, 1990)
C. Ford: *Così? Sexual Politics in Mozart's Operas* (Manchester, 1991)
B. A. Brown: *W. A. Mozart:* Così fan tutte (Cambridge, 1995)
E. J. Goehring, *Three Modes of Perception in Mozart. The Philosophical, Pastoral, and Comic in* Così fan tutte (Cambridge, 2004)
D. J. Buch: '*Der Stein der Weisen*. Mozart and collaborative Singspiels at Emanuel Schikaneder's Theater auf der Wieden', and Faye Ferguson, 'Interpreting the source tradition of *Der Stein der Weisen*', *Mozart Jahrbuch* 2000, 91–126 and 127–44
J. Chailley: '*La flûte enchantée*', *opéra maçonnique: essai d'explication du livret et de la musique* (Paris, 1968; English translation, 1972)
P. Branscombe: *W. A. Mozart:* Die Zauberflöte (Cambridge, 1991)
J. Rice: *W. A. Mozart:* La clemenza di Tito (Cambridge, 1991)

Printed in the United States
135353LV00002B/154/P

9858292R0

Made in the USA
Lexington, KY
03 June 2011

GOD'S
PLANS FOR
YOU

GOD'S
PLANS FOR
YOU

ANDREW MURRAY

w

WHITAKER
HOUSE

All Scripture quotations are taken from the King James Version (KJV) of the Bible.

Editor's note: This book has been edited for the modern reader. Words, expressions, and sentence structure have been updated for clarity and readability.

GOD'S PLANS FOR YOU
(previously published by Whitaker House under the title *How to Work for God*)

ISBN:0-88368-512-4
Printed in the United States of America
© 1983 by Whitaker House

Whitaker House
30 Hunt Valley Circle
New Kensington, PA 15068

Library of Congress Cataloging-in-Publication Data

Murray, Andrew, 1828–1917.
   [How to work for God]
   God's plans for you / Andrew Murray.
      p.   cm.
   Originally published: How to work for God. Springdale, Pa.:
Whitaker House, © 1983.
   ISBN 0-88368-512-4
   1. Vocation—Christianity. 2. Good works (Theology). I. Title.
BV4740.M87 1997
248.4—dc21   97-47202

CONTENTS

1
WAITING AND WORKING

But they that wait upon the LORD
shall renew their strength.
—Isaiah 40:31

Neither hath the eye seen, O God, beside thee,
what he hath prepared for him that
waiteth for him.
—Isaiah 64:4

The relationship between waiting and work-ing is made clear in the above verses. We see that waiting brings the needed strength for working—preparing us for joyful and unwea-ried work. *"They that wait upon the LORD shall renew their strength; they shall mount up with wings as eagles; they shall run, and not be weary; and they shall walk, and not faint"* (Isa. 40:31). Waiting on God has its value in this: it makes us strong to do His work. The second verse reveals the secret of this strength. *"Neither hath the eye seen...what he hath prepared for him that waiteth for him."* The waiting on God secures the working of God for us and in us, out of which our work must spring. The two passages teach the great

7

lesson that waiting on God lies at the root of all true working for God. Our great need is to hold the two sides of this truth in perfect harmony.

There are some who say they wait upon God, but they do not work for Him. There may be various reasons for this. They confuse true waiting on God (living in direct communication with Him) with the lazy, helpless waiting that excuses itself from all work. Some wait on God as one of the highest exercises of the Christian life. Yet they have never understood that the root of all true waiting must be surrender and readiness to be completely equipped for God's use in serving men. Others are ready to work as well as wait, but are looking for some great inflow of the Spirit's power to enable them to do mighty works, while they forget that as believers they already have the Spirit of Christ dwelling in them. They forget that more grace is given only to those who are faithful in the little (Luke 16:10), and that it is only in working that we can be taught by the Spirit how to do the greater works.

All Christians need to learn that waiting has working for its objective. It is only in working that waiting can attain its full perfection and blessedness. It is as we elevate working for God to its true place, as the highest exercise of spiritual privilege and power, that the absolute need and the divine blessing of waiting on God can be fully known.

On the other hand, there are many who work for God but know little of what it is to wait on Him. They have been led to take up Christian work under the impulse of natural or spiritual feeling or the urging of a pastor. However, they do so with very little sense of what a holy thing it is to work for God. They do not know that God's work can be done only in God's strength, by God Himself working in us.

The Son of God could do nothing of Himself (John 8:28). The Father in Him did the work as He lived in continual dependence before Him. Many have never learned that the believer can do nothing unless God works in him. They do not understand that it is only in utter weakness that we depend upon Him, so that His power can rest on us. They have no conception of a continual waiting on God as being one of the first and essential conditions of successful work. Christ's church and the world are sufferers today, not only because so many of its members are not working for God, but also because so much working for God is done without waiting on God.

Among the members of the body of Christ, there is a great diversity of gifts and operations. Some who are confined to their homes because of sickness or other duties may have more time for waiting on God. Others, who are overworked, find it very difficult to make time and be quiet before the Lord. These may mutually supply each other's lack.

Let those who have time for waiting on God definitely link themselves to some who are working. Let those who are working seek the help of those to whom the special ministry of waiting on God has been entrusted. Thus will the unity and health of the church be maintained. Those who wait will know that the outcome will be power for work. Those who work will realize their only strength is the grace obtained by waiting. Thus will God work for His church that waits on Him.

Let us pray as we proceed in these meditations on working for God that the Holy Spirit will show us how sacred and urgent our calling is to work, and how absolute our dependence is upon God's strength to work in us. May we also learn how sure it is that those who wait on Him will renew their strength. Then we will find waiting on God and working for God to be inseparably one.

1. It is only as God works for me, and in me, that I can work for Him.

2. All His work for me is through His life in me.

3. He will most surely work, if I wait on Him.

4. All His working for me, and my waiting on Him, has but one aim: to equip me for His work of saving men.

2
GOOD WORKS:
THE LIGHT OF THE WORLD

Ye are the light of the world....Let your light so shine before men, that they may see your good works, and glorify your Father which is in heaven.
—Matthew 5:14, 16

A light is meant for those in darkness to see. The sun lights up the darkness of this world. A lamp is hung in a room to give it light. The church of Christ is the light of men. The god of this world has blinded their eyes. (See 2 Corinthians 4:4.) Christ's disciples are to shine into the darkness and give light. Just as the rays of light stream forth from the sun and scatter that light all about, the light of the good works of believers streams out to conquer the surrounding darkness with its ignorance of God and alienation from Him.

What a high and holy place is thus given to our good works! What power is attributed to them! How much depends upon them! They are not only the light and health and joy of our own lives, but also the means of bringing lost souls "out of darkness into His marvellous light" (1 Pet. 2:9). They not only bless men, but they also glorify God in leading men to know Him as the Author of the grace seen in His children. Study the teaching of Scripture in regard to good works, especially all work done directly for God and His kingdom. Listen to what these words of the Master have to teach us.

The aim of good works is that God may be glorified. You remember how our Lord said to the Father: *"I have glorified thee on the earth: I have finished the work which thou gavest me to do"* (John 17:4). More than once we read of how the people glorified God because of His miracles. It was because what He had done was manifested by a divine power. Thus it is when our good works are something more than the ordinary virtues of refined men, and bear the imprint of God upon them, that men will glorify God. They must be the good works of which the Sermon on the Mount (see Matthew 5:1–7:29) is the embodiment—a life of God's children, doing more than others, seeking to be perfect as their Father in heaven is perfect. When Christians glorify God and reflect His love, they help prepare the unsaved for conversion. The works prepare the way for the testimony and demonstrate the reality of the divine truth that is taught.

The whole world was made for the glory of God. Christ came to redeem us from sin and bring us back to serve and glorify Him. Believers are placed in the world with this one purpose, that they may win others to God by the light of their good works. As truly as the light of the sun is meant to light up the world, the good works of God's children are meant to be the light of those who do not know or love God. We must clearly understand that good works bear the mark of something heavenly and divine and have the power of God in them.

The power is in good works. Of Christ it is written, *"In him was life; and the life was the light of men"* (John 1:4). The divine life gave out a divine light. Of His disciples Christ said, *"He that followeth me shall not walk in darkness, but shall have the light of life"* (John 8:12). Christ is our life and light. The deepest meaning of *"Let your light so shine"* is, let Christ, who dwells in you, be seen by everyone you meet. And because Christ in you is your light, your humble works can carry with them a power of divine conviction. The divine power working in you will be the same power working in those who see your works. Give way to the life and light of Christ dwelling in you, and men will glorify your Father who is in heaven for what they see in your good works.

There is an urgent need for good works in believers. As it is necessary that the sun shines every day, it is even more necessary that every believer lets his light shine before men. We have been created anew in Christ for this—to hold forth the Word of Life as lights in the world. Christ needs you urgently to let His light shine through you. The unsaved around you need your light if they are to find their way to God. God needs you to let His glory be seen through you. Just as a lamp functions to light up a room, every believer should function to light up the world.

Let us study what working for God is, and what good works are as part of this. We will then desire to follow Christ fully and have the light of life shine into our hearts and lives and, from us, shine out to the world.

1. *"Ye are the light of the world."* These words express the calling of the church as a whole. The fulfillment of her duty will depend upon the faithfulness with which each individual member loves and lives for those around him.

2. In all our efforts to awaken the church to evangelize the world, our first aim must be to raise the standard of life for the individual believer concerning the teaching: as truly as a candle exists with the objective of giving light in the darkness, *the one objective of your existence is to be a light to men.*

3. Pray that God by His Holy Spirit will reveal to you that you have nothing to live for but to let the light and love of God shine upon souls.

3
SON, GO WORK

Son, go work to day in my vineyard.
—Matthew 21:28

The father had two sons. To each he gave the command to go and work in his vineyard. The one went; the other did not. God has given the command and the power to every child of His to work in His vineyard, with the world as the field. The majority of God's children are not working for Him, and the world is perishing.

Of all the mysteries that surround us in the world, one of the strangest and most incomprehensible is that, after hundreds of years, the very name of Jesus is still unknown to so many.

Consider what this means. To restore the ruin sin had caused, God, the almighty Creator, actually sent His own Son to the world to tell men of His love and to bring them His life and salvation. When Christ made His disciples partakers of that salvation, and the unspeakable joy it brings, He emphasized that they should make it known to others and be the lights of the world. He spoke of all who would come to Him through their witness. He left the world with the specific instruction to carry the Gospel to all men and teach all nations to practice all that He had commanded. He also gave the definite assurance that all power for this work was in Him. By the power of His Holy Spirit, He would enable His people to be witnesses to the ends of the earth. And what do we see now? Many have yet to hear the name of Jesus, and many act as though they had never heard of Him!

Consider again what this means. All these dying millions have a right to come to the knowledge of Christ. Their salvation depends on their knowing Him. He could change their lives from sin and unhappiness to holy obedience and heavenly joy. Christ has a right to them. It would make His heart glad to have them come and be blessed in Him. Service to God is the connecting link. And yet, what His people do is nothing compared to what needs to be done, to what could be done, to what ought to be done.

What a revelation of the state of the church! The great majority of those who are counted as believers are doing nothing toward making Christ known to their fellowmen. There are those who are entirely in Christ's service, but they are not free to conquer the world because they are occupied with teaching and helping weak Christians! And so, with a finished salvation, a loving Redeemer, and a church set apart to spread the Gospel, many are still perishing!

There can be nothing of greater importance to the church than to consider what can be done to awaken believers to a sense of their holy calling and to make them see that *to work for God,* they must offer themselves as instruments *through whom God can do His work.* Two complaints that are continually heard are a lack of enthusiasm for God's kingdom in the majority of Christians and the vain attempts to awaken an interest in missions. Nothing less is needed than a revival that would raise the average Christian to an entirely new type of devotion. No true change can come until the truth is preached and accepted. The law of the kingdom is this: *every believer is to live wholly for God's service and work.*

The father who called his sons to go work in his vineyard did not leave it to their choice to do as much or as little as they chose. They lived in his home. They were his children; he counted on what they would give him—their time and strength. God expects this of His children. Until it is understood that each child of God is to give His whole heart to his Father's interest and work as a worker for God, the evangelization of the world cannot be accomplished. Listen carefully and the Father will say to you, *"Go work to day in my vineyard."*

1. Why is it that stirring appeals on behalf of missions often have so little permanent result? Because the command is brought to men who have not learned that absolute devotion and immediate obedience to the Lord are the essence of true salvation.

2. Once Christians see and confess their lack of interest in missions, they will be taking the first step to renewing their desire to live completely for God. Every missionary meeting will be a

consecration meeting to seek and surrender to the Holy Spirit's power.

3. The average standard of holiness and devotion can be no higher at home or in the church than it is in individual believers.

4. Not everyone can go abroad or give his whole time to direct work; but everyone, whatever his calling or circumstances, can give his whole heart to live for the winning of souls and the spreading of the kingdom.

4

TO EACH ONE HIS WORK

*For the Son of man is as a man taking a far
journey, who left his house, and gave authority to
his servants, and to every man his work,
and commanded the porter to watch.*
—Mark 13:34

What I have said about the failure of the church to do the Master's work has often led me to ask, "What must be done to arouse the church to a right sense of her calling?" This book attempts to give the answer. Working for God must take a very different and much more definite place in our teaching and training of Christ's disciples than it has before.

In studying the question, I have been helped very much by the life and writings of a great educator, Edward Thring. The opening sentence of the preface to his biography states, "Edward Thring was unquestionably the most original and striking figure in the schoolmaster world of his time in England." Thring attributed his own power and success to the prominence he gave to a few simple principles, and the faithfulness with which he carried them out at any sacrifice. I have found them helpful regarding the work of preaching as well as teaching, and to present them will help to clarify some of the chief lessons this book is meant to teach.

The basic principle that distinguished Thring's teaching from what was current at the time was this: every boy in school, regardless of ability, must have the same attention. At Eton, where he was educated and was first in his class, he saw the evil of the opposite system. Leaving the majority neglected, the school kept its prestige by training a number of men for the highest awards. He maintained that this was dishonest. There could be no truth in a school that did not care for all alike. Every boy had some gift. Every boy needed special attention. Every boy could, with care and patience, be equipped to know and fulfill his mission in life.

Apply this to the church. Every believer has the calling to live and work for the kingdom of his Lord. Every believer has an equal claim on the grace and power of the Holy Spirit, according to his gifts, to equip him for his work. And every believer has a right to be taught and helped by the church for the service our Lord expects of him. When every believer, even the weakest, is trained as a worker for God, the church can fulfill its mission. No one can be left out, because the Master entrusted His work to all believers.

Another of Thring's principles was this: it is a law of nature that work is pleasure. Make it voluntary and not compulsory. Do not lead people blindly. Show them why they have to work, what its value will be, what interest can be awakened in it, and what pleasure may be found in it.

What a field is opened for the preacher of the Gospel taking charge of Christ's disciples! The preacher must clarify the greatness, the glory, the divine blessedness of the work to be done. The preacher must show the value in carrying out God's will and gaining His approval. The preacher must lead us in introducing the Savior to the unsaved. The preacher must lead us in developing the spiritual vigor, the nobility of character, the spirit of self-sacrifice that leads to the true bearing of Christ's image.

A third truth on which Thring particularly insisted was the need for inspiring the belief in the assurance of attaining the goal. That goal is not to gain extensive knowledge, but rather, to cultivate the power to learn—this alone is true education. As a learner's powers of observation grow under guidance and teaching, he finds within himself a source of power and pleasure he never knew before. He feels a new self beginning to live, and the world around him acquires a new meaning. As Thring stated, "He becomes conscious of an infinity of unsuspected glory in the midst of which we go about our daily tasks, and becomes lord of an endless kingdom full of light and pleasure and power."

If this is the law and blessing of a true education, what light is shed on the calling of all teachers and leaders in Christ's church! The *know ye not*s of Scripture—that you are the temple of God (1 Cor. 3:16), that Christ is in you (2 Cor. 13:5), that the Holy Spirit dwells in you (1 Cor. 6:19)—acquire a new meaning. It tells us that the one thing that needs to be awakened in the hearts of Christians is the faith in *"the power that* *worketh in us"* (Eph. 3:20). As one comes to see the worth and the glory of the work to be done—as one believes in the possibility of his, too, being able to do that work well—as one learns to trust the very power and very Spirit of God working in him, "he will, in the fullest sense, become conscious of a new life, with an infinity of unsuspected glory in the midst of which we go about our daily task, and become lord of an endless kingdom full of light and pleasure and power." This is the royal life to which God has called all His people. The true Christian is one who knows God's power working in himself, and finds it his true joy to have the very life of God flowing into him, through him, and out from him to those around.

1. We must learn to believe in the value of every individual believer. As men are saved one by one, they must be trained one by one for work.

2. We must believe that work for Christ can become as natural, as much an attraction and a pleasure, in the spiritual as in the natural world.

3. We must believe and teach that every believer can become an effective worker in his area of work. Are you seeking to be filled with love for souls?

5
To Each according to His Ability

For the kingdom of heaven is as a man travelling into a far country, who called his own servants, and delivered unto them his goods. And unto one he gave five talents, to another two, and to another one; to every man according to his several ability; and straightway took his journey.
—Matthew 25:14–15

In the parable of the talents, we have an instructive summary of our Lord's teaching in regard to the work He has given to His servants to do. He tells us He is going to heaven and leaving His work on earth to the care of His church. He tells us He is giving everyone something to do, however different the gifts might be. He tells us He is expecting to get back His money with interest. He tells us of the failure of him who received least and what it was that led to that terrible neglect.

"[He] *called his own servants, and delivered unto them his goods...and straightway took his journey.*" This is literally what our Lord did. He went to heaven, leaving His work with all His goods to the care of His church. His goods were the riches of His grace, spiritual blessings in heavenly places, and His Word and Spirit. He gave these to His servants to be used in carrying out His work on earth. They were to continue the work he had begun. Our Lord took His people into partnership with Himself and entrusted His work on earth entirely to their care. Their neglect would cause it to suffer. Their diligence would be His enrichment. Here we have the true basic principle of Christian service—Christ has made Himself dependent on the faithfulness of His people for the extension of His kingdom.

"Unto one he gave five talents, to another two, and to another one; to every man according to his several ability." Though there was a difference in the measure, everyone received a portion of the master's goods. It is in connection with the service we are to provide each other that we read, *"Unto every one of us is given grace according to the measure of the gift of Christ"* (Eph. 4:7). This truth, that every believer without exception has been set apart to take an active part in the work of winning the world for Christ, has almost been lost. Christ was first a son, then a servant. Every believer is first a child of God, then a servant. It is the highest honor of a son to be a servant, to have the father's work entrusted to him. Neither the home nor the foreign missionary work of the church will ever be done right until every believer feels that the one purpose of his being in the world is to work for the kingdom. The first duty of the servants in the parable was to spend their lives in caring for their master's interests.

"After a long time the lord of those servants cometh, and reckoneth with them" (Matt. 25:19). Christ keeps watch over the work He has left to be done on earth. His kingdom and glory depend upon it. Not only will He hold us accountable when He comes again to judge, but He also comes unceasingly to ask His servants about their welfare and work. He comes to approve and encourage, to correct and warn. By His Word and Spirit, He questions whether we are using our talents diligently and whether we, as His devoted servants, are living only and entirely for His work. He finds some laboring diligently, and to them He frequently says, *"Enter thou into the joy of thy lord"* (v. 21). He sees that others are discouraged, and He inspires them with new hope. He finds some working in their own strength. These He reprimands. Still others He finds sleeping or hiding their talents. To such His voice speaks in solemn warning: *"From him that hath not shall be taken away even that which he hath"* (v. 29). Christ's heart is in His work. Every day He watches over it with the keenest interest. Let us not disappoint Him or deceive ourselves.

"I was afraid, and went and hid thy talent in the earth" (v. 25). It is a deeply solemn lesson that the man with the one talent was the one to fail and be so severely punished. It calls the church to beware. By neglecting to teach the weaker ones that their service is needed also, she lets their gifts lie unused. In teaching the great truth that every branch is to bear fruit, the church must lay special emphasis on the danger of thinking this is expected only of the strong and advanced Christian. When truth reigns in a school, the most

backward pupils receive the same attention as the more clever pupils. Care must be taken that the weakest Christians receive special training, so that they, too, may joyfully have their share in the service of their Lord and all the blessedness it brings. If Christ's work is to be done, not one can be missed.

"Lord, I knew thee that thou art an hard man... and I was afraid" (Matt. 25:24–25). Failure in service is caused chiefly by wrong thoughts of God and looking upon His service as that of a hard master. If the church is to care for the weak ones who are apt to be discouraged, we must teach them what God says of the sufficiency of grace and the certainty of success. They must learn to believe that the power of the Holy Spirit within them equips them for the work to which God has called them. They must learn to understand that God Himself will strengthen the inner man with might by His Spirit (Eph. 3:16). They must be taught that work is joy, health, and strength. Unbelief lies at the root of laziness. Faith opens the eyes to see the blessedness of God's service, the sufficiency of His strength, and His rich rewards. The church must awake to her calling to train the weakest of her members to know that Christ counts upon every redeemed individual to live entirely for His work. This alone is true Christianity. This alone is full salvation.

6
LIFE AND WORK

My meat is to do the will of him that sent me,
and to finish his work.
—John 4:34

I must work the works of him that sent me.
—John 9:4

I have glorified thee on the earth: I have finished
the work which thou gavest me to do. And now,
O Father, glorify thou me with thine own self.
—John 17:4–5

Carefully read these words of our Lord again, and see what divine glory there is in His work. In His work, Christ showed His own glory and the Father's glory. It was because of the work He had done, and because He had glorified the Father in it, that He claimed to share the glory of the Father in heaven. He performed the great works so that the Father might be glorified. Work is indeed the highest form of existence, the highest manifestation of the divine glory in the Father and in His Son.

What is true of God is true of men. Life is action and reveals itself in what it accomplishes. The bodily life, the intellectual, the moral, the spiritual life—individual, social, national life—each of these is judged by its work. The character and quality of the work depend on the life—as the life, so the work. And, on the other hand, the life depends on the work. Without this there can be no full development and manifestation and perfecting of the life—as the work, so the life.

This is especially true of the spiritual life—the life of the Spirit in us. There may be a great deal of religious work that is the result of human will and effort. But there is little true worth and power, because the divine life is weak. When the believer does not know that Christ is living in him and does not know the Spirit and power of God working in him, there may be much sincerity and diligence, with little that lasts for eternity. On the contrary, there may be much external weakness and apparent failure, yet results prove that the life is indeed of God.

The work depends upon the life, and the life depends on the work for its growth and perfection. All life has a destiny. It cannot accomplish its purpose without work. Life is perfected by work. The highest manifestation of its hidden nature and power comes out in its work. And so work is the great factor by which the hidden beauty and the divine possibilities of the Christian life are revealed. Work must not only be performed by the child of God for the result of being used as God's instrument, but also be given the same place it has in God Himself. As in the Father and the Son, and with the Holy Spirit dwelling in us, work is the highest manifestation of life.

Work must be restored to its right place in God's scheme of the Christian life as the highest form of existence. As God never ceases to perform His work of love and blessing in and through us, so our performing what He works in us is our highest proof of being created anew in His likeness.

Working for God must have much greater prominence given to it if God's purposes are to be carried out. Every believer must be taught that work is to be our highest glory as it is the only perfect manifestation and, therefore, the perfection of life in God throughout the world. We must ask if it is to be so in our own lives.

If our work is to be our highest glory, we must remember two things: first, it can come only by beginning to work. Those who have not had their attention directed to it cannot realize how great the temptation is to make work a matter of thought, prayer, and purpose, without its really being done. It is easier to hear than to think, easier to think than to speak, easier to speak than to act. We may listen and accept and admire God's will, and in our prayer profess our willingness to do, and yet not actually do it. Let us take up our calling as God's workers, and work hard for Him. Doing is the best teacher. If you want to know how to do a thing, begin and do it.

Then you will be able to understand the second aspect: there is sufficient grace in Christ for all the work you have to do. You will see with ever-increasing gladness how He, the Head, works all in you, the member. You will see how work for God may become your closest and fullest fellowship with Christ—your highest participation in the power of His risen and glorified life.

1. Beware of separating life and work. The more work you have, the more your work appears to be a failure. The more unfit you feel for work, the more time and care you should take to have your inner life renewed in close fellowship with God.

2. "Christ lives in me" is the secret of joy and hope, and also of power for work. Care for the life, and the life will care for the work. *Be filled with the Holy Ghost"* (Acts 9:17).

7
THE FATHER ABIDING IN ME DOES THE WORK

But Jesus answered them, My Father worketh hitherto, and I work.
—John 5:17

Believest thou not that I am in the Father, and the Father in me? the words that I speak unto you I speak not of myself: but the Father that dwelleth in me, he doeth the works.
—John 14:10

Jesus Christ became man so that He might show us what a true man is. He became man to show us how God meant to live and work in man. And He became man to show us how we can find purpose in our lives and do our work in God. In words like those above, our Lord opens up the inner mystery of His life and reveals to us the nature and the deepest secret of His working. He did not come to the world to work instead of the Father. Christ's work was the fruit, the earthly reflection, of the Father working. It was not as if Christ merely saw and copied what the Father willed or did—*"the Father that dwelleth in me, he doeth the works."* Christ did all His work in the power of the Father who was living and working in Him. So complete and real was His dependence on the Father that, in explaining it to the Jews, He used such strong expressions as *"The Son can do nothing of himself, but what he seeth the Father do"* (John 5:19) and *"I can of mine own self do nothing"* (v. 30). What He said—*"For without me ye can do nothing"* (John 15:5)—is as true of us as it is true of Him. *"The Father that dwelleth in me, he doeth the works."*

Jesus Christ became man so that He might show us what true man is, what the true relationship between man and God is, and what the true way of serving God and doing His work is. When we are made new creatures in Christ Jesus (2 Cor. 5:17), the life we receive is the very life that was and is in Christ. It is only by studying His life on earth that we know how we are to live. *"As the living Father hath sent me, and I live by the Father: so he that eateth me, even he shall live by me"* (John 6:57).

Christ did not consider it a humiliation to be able to do nothing of Himself—to be always and absolutely dependent on the Father. He counted it His highest glory because all His works were the works of the all-glorious God in Him. When will we understand that to wait on God, to bow before Him in perfect helplessness and let Him work everything in us, is our true nobility and the secret of the highest activity? This alone is the true Christ-life, the true life of every child of God. As this life is understood and maintained, the power for work will grow because the soul is in the attitude in which God can work in us, as the God who *"is good unto them that wait for him"* (Lam. 3:25).

By ignoring or neglecting the great truths, there can be no true work for God. The explanation of the extensive complaint of so much Christian activity with so little genuine result is that God works in us, yes, but He cannot work fully in us unless we live in absolute dependence on Him. The revival that many are longing and praying for must begin with this: the return of Christian ministers and workers to their true place before God—in Christ. And, like Christ, we must completely depend and continually wait on God to work in us.

I invite all workers, young and old, successful or disappointed, full of hope or full of fear, to come and learn from our Lord Jesus the secret of true work for God. *"My Father worketh hitherto, and I work." "The Father that dwelleth in me, he doeth the works."* Divine Fatherhood means that God is all, gives all, and works all. Continually depend on the Father, and receive, moment by moment, all the strength needed for His work. Try to grasp the great truth that because *"it is the same God which worketh all in all"* (1 Cor. 12:6), your one need is, in deep humility and weakness, to wait for and to trust in His working. From this, learn that God can work in us only as He dwells in us. *"The Father that dwelleth in me, he doeth the works."* Cultivate the holy sense of God's continual nearness and presence, of your being His temple, and of His dwelling in you. Offer yourself for Him to work in you all His good pleasure. You will find that work, instead of being a hindrance, can become your greatest incentive to a life of fellowship and childlike dependence.

At first it may appear as if the waiting for God to work will keep you back from your work. It may indeed—but only to bring the greater blessing, when you have learned the lesson of faith that believes on His working even when you do not feel it. You may have to do your work in weakness and fear and much trembling. You will know the merit of the power is of God and not of yourself. As you know yourself better and God better, you will be content that it should always be His strength made perfect in our weakness (2 Cor. 12:9).

1. *"The Father that dwelleth in me, he doeth the works."* There is the same law for the Head and the member, for Christ and the believer. *"It is the same God which worketh all in all"* (1 Cor. 12:6).

2. The Father worked in the Son while He was on earth, and now works through Him in heaven. It is as we believe in the Father's working in Christ that we will do the greater works. (See John 14:10–12.)

3. The indwelling and abiding God works in us. Allow God to live in you, and He will establish your good work.

4. Pray much for grace to say, in the name of Jesus, *"The Father that dwelleth in me, he doeth the works."*

8
GREATER WORKS

*Verily, verily, I say unto you, He that believeth on
me, the works that I do shall he do also;
and greater works than these shall he do;
because I go unto my Father. And whatsoever
ye shall ask in my name, that will I do,
that the Father may be glorified in the Son.
If ye shall ask any thing in my name, I will do it.*
—John 14:12–14

I n John 14:10, which says, *"The Father that
dwelleth in me, he doeth the works,"* Christ
reveals the secret of all divine service—man
yielding himself for God to dwell and to work in
him. The law of God working in man remains
unchanged when Christ promises, *"He that
believeth on me, the works that I do shall he do
also."* If Christ says, *"The Father that dwelleth in
me, he doeth the works,"* how much more must *we*
say it? With Christ and with us, it is *"the same
God which worketh all in all"* (1 Cor. 12:6).

We are taught how this is to be in the words,
"He that believeth on me." That does not only mean
that we must believe Christ for salvation, as a

Savior from sin. There is much more. In John 14:10–11 Christ said, *"The Father that dwelleth in me, he doeth the works. Believe me that I am in the Father, and the Father in me."* We need to believe in Christ as the One in and through whom the Father unceasingly works. To believe in Christ is to receive Him into the heart. When we see the Father working jointly with Christ, we know that to believe in Christ, and receive Him into our hearts, is to receive the Father dwelling in Him and working through Him. The works His disciples are to do cannot possibly be done in any other way than His own are done.

This becomes still clearer from what our Lord adds: *"And greater works than these shall he do; because I go unto my Father."* It is clear what the greater works are. Three thousand were baptized by the disciples at Pentecost, and multitudes were added to the Lord afterward. Philip at Samaria, the men of Cyprus and Cyrene, Barnabas at Antioch, Paul in his travels—always many people were added to the Lord. Countless servants down to our day have, in the ingathering of souls, done these greater works in, for, with, and through Christ.

When the Lord says, *"Because I go unto my Father,"* He clearly reveals the reason that we are enabled to do these greater works. When He entered the glory of the Father, all power in heaven and on earth was given to Him as our Redeemer. The Father was to work through Him in a way more glorious than ever. He was then to work through His disciples. His own work on earth received power from the Father in heaven. So His people, in their weakness, would do works like

His, and greater works in the same way, through power received from heaven. The law of the divine working is unchangeable—*God's work can be done only by God Himself.* It is as we see this in Christ and receive Him in this way, as the One in and through whom God works all, and yield ourselves completely to the Father working in Him and in us, that we will do greater works than He did.

The words that follow bring out still more strongly the great truths we have been learning, that it is our Lord Himself who will work all in us, even as the Father did in Him, and that our attitude is to be exactly what His was—one of entire receptivity and dependence. *"Greater works than these shall he do; because I go unto my Father. And whatsoever ye shall ask in my name, that will I do."* Christ connects the greater works the believer is to do with the promise that He will do whatever the believer asks. Prayer in the name of Jesus will be the expression of depending and waiting on Him for His working. He gives the promise: *"Whatsoever ye shall ask...that will I do,"* in you and through you. And when He adds, *"that the Father may be glorified in the Son,"* He reminds us how He had glorified the Father by yielding to Him as Father, to perform all His work in Himself as Son. In heaven Christ would still glorify the Father by receiving the power from the Father and by working in His disciples what the Father would. The believer, as Christ Himself, can give the Father no higher glory than yielding to Him to work all.

The believer can glorify the Father in no other way than by an absolute and unceasing dependence on the Son, in whom the Father works, to communicate and work in us all the Father's work. *"If ye shall ask any thing in my name, I will do it,"* and so, *"greater works than these shall he do."*

Let every believer strive to learn the blessed lesson—"I am to do the works I have seen Christ doing. I may even do greater works as I yield myself to Christ exalted on the throne in awesome power. I may count on Him working in me according to that power. I need the spirit of dependence and waiting, and prayer and faith, so that Christ abiding in me will do the works, even whatever I ask."

1. How was Christ able to work the works of God? By God abiding in Him! How can I do the works of Christ? By Christ abiding in me!

2. How can I do greater works than Christ? By believing not only in Christ, the Incarnate and Crucified, but also in Christ triumphant on the throne.

3. In work everything depends, dear believer, on the life, the inner life, the divine life. Pray to realize that work is vain except when it is done in the power of the Holy Spirit dwelling in you.

9
CREATED IN CHRIST JESUS FOR GOOD WORKS

*For by grace are ye saved through faith; and that
not of yourselves: it is the gift of God: not of works,
lest any man should boast. For we are
his workmanship, created in Christ Jesus
unto good works, which God hath before
ordained that we should walk in them.*
—Ephesians 2:8–10

We have been saved, not *by* works, but *for* good works. The difference is so great! The understanding of that difference is essential to the health of the Christian life. We are not saved *by* works that we have done. Yet we are saved *for* good works—the fruit and outcome of salvation, part of God's work in us, the one thing for which we have been created anew. Though our works are worthless in achieving salvation, their worth is infinite for which God has created and prepared us. We must seek to hold these two truths in the fullness of their spiritual meaning. The deeper our conviction that we have been saved, not by works, but by grace, the stronger the proof that we have been saved for good works.

"Not of works...for we are his workmanship." If works could have saved us, there was no need for our redemption. Because our works were all sinful and vain, God undertook to make us anew. We are now His workmanship, and all the good works we do are His workmanship, too. *"His workmanship, created in Jesus Christ."* So complete had been the ruin of sin, that God had to do the work of creation over again in Jesus Christ. In Him, and particularly in His resurrection from the dead, He created us anew, after His own image, into the likeness of the life that Christ had lived. In the power of that life and resurrection, we are able, we are perfectly equipped, for doing good works. The eye, because it was created for the light, is most perfectly adapted for its work. The branch of the vine, because it was created to bear grapes, does its work so naturally. We, who have been created in Jesus Christ for good works, may be assured that a divine capacity for good works is the very law of our being. If we simply know and believe in this our destiny, if we simply live our lives in Jesus Christ, as we were newly created in Him, we can and will be fruitful unto every good work.

"Created...unto good works, which God hath before ordained that we should walk in them." We have been prepared for the works, and the works prepared for us. To understand this, think of how God pre-appointed His servants of old—Moses and Joshua, Samuel and David, Peter and Paul—for the work He had for them, and pre-appointed equally the works He would have them do. The

Father has prepared works for the humblest of His children as much as for those who are counted chief. God has a life-plan for each of His children, with work distributed according to the power and grace provided for the work. And so, just as the teaching "salvation is not of works" is clear, so is its blessed counterpart, "salvation is for good works"—because God created us for them, and even prepared them for us.

The Scripture, therefore, confirms the double lesson this book desires to bring you: good works are God's design in the new life He has given you and ought to be your aim. As every human being was created for work and endowed with the necessary energy, man can live a true and healthy life only by working. Every believer, then, exists to do good works. In them his life will be perfected, his fellowmen will be blessed, and his Father in heaven will be glorified. We educate all our children with the thought that they must go out and work in the world. When will the church learn that its great work is to train every believer to take his share in *God's* great work and to abound in the good works for which he was created? We must each seek to take in the deep spiritual truth of the message, *"Created in Christ Jesus unto good works, which God hath before ordained,"* and joyfully take up the work awaiting us and do it eagerly.

Waiting on God is the one great thing needed on our part if we desire to do the good works God has prepared for us. We must take into our hearts the holy meaning of these words: we are God's workmanship, not by one act in the past, but in a continuous operation. We are created for good works, as the great means for glorifying God. The good works are prepared for each of us so that we might walk in them. Surrender to and dependence upon God's working is our one need. We must consider how our new creation for good works will become the habit of our souls and is all *in Christ Jesus,* and abiding *in Him,* believing *on Him,* and looking *for His strength alone. Created for good works* will reveal to us at once the divine command and the sufficient power to live a life in good works.

Let us pray for the Holy Spirit to work the Word into the very depths of our consciousness: *Created in Christ Jesus for good works!* In the light of this revelation, we will learn what a glorious destiny, what an infinite obligation, what a perfect capacity is ours.

1. Our creation in Adam was for good works. It resulted in entire failure. Our new creation in Christ is for good works again, but with this difference: perfect provision has been made for securing them.

2. God has created us for good works—let us pray for the Holy Spirit to show us and impart to us all that this means.

3. If life in fellowship with God is true, the power for the work will be perfected. As the life, so the work.

10
WORK, FOR IT IS GOD WHO WORKS IN YOU

Work out your own salvation with fear and trembling. For it is God which worketh in you both to will and to do of his good pleasure.
—Philippians 2:12–13

In the last chapter we saw what salvation is. It is our being God's workmanship, created in Jesus Christ for good works. The chapter concluded with one of its most important points: there is a treasury of good works that God has prepared for us to do. In the light of this thought, we get the true and full meaning of the leading Scripture for this chapter. To work out your own salvation, such as God meant it to be, is to walk in all the good works that God has prepared for you. Study to know exactly what the salvation is that God has prepared for you (all that He has meant and made possible for you to be), and work it out *"with fear and trembling."* Let the greatness of this divine and most holy life hidden in Christ, your own weakness, and the terrible dangers and temptations confronting you, make you work in fear and trembling.

And yet, that fear never needs to become unbelief; that trembling never needs to become discouragement, for it is God who works in you. Here is the secret of a power that is absolutely sufficient for everything we have to do, the perfect assurance that we can do all that God really means us to do. God works in us both to will and to work. First, to will—He gives the insight into what is to be done, the desire that makes the work pleasure, the firm purpose of the will that masters the whole being and makes it ready and eager for action. And then, to work—He does not give us the will and then leave us unaided to work it out ourselves. The will may see and accept the work, yet lack the power to perform it. In the seventh chapter of Romans, we see that the new man delights in God's law, yet he is ill-equipped to do because of the war between the flesh and the Spirit. However, by *"the law of the Spirit of life in Christ Jesus,"* man was set *"free from the law of sin and death"* (Rom. 8:2). Thus, the righteousness of the law could be fulfilled in Him as one who did not *"walk...after the flesh, but after the Spirit"* (v. 4).

One great reason why believers fail in their work is that they think since God has given them the will to do it, they will automatically work in the strength of that will. They have never learned the lesson that because God has created us in Christ Jesus for good works and has prepared the good works in which we are to walk, He must work them all in us Himself. They have never listened very long to the voice speaking, *"It is God which worketh in you."*

Here is one of the deepest, most spiritual, and most precious truths of Scripture—the unceasing operation of almighty God in our hearts and lives. In light of the very nature of God, as a spiritual being not confined to any place, but present everywhere, there can be no spiritual life unless it is supported by His personal indwelling.

Scripture states the deepest reason—He *"worketh all in all"* (1 Cor. 12:6). Not only *of* Him are all things as their first beginning, and *to* Him as their end, but also *through* Him, who alone maintains them.

The Father was the source of all that Christ did. In the new man, created in Jesus Christ, the unceasing dependence on the Father is our highest privilege, our truest nobility. This is indeed fellowship with God—God Himself working in us to will and to do.

We must seek to learn the true secret of working for God. It is not, as many think, that we do our best, then leave God to do the rest. By no means. Rather, it is this: we know that God's working His salvation in us is the secret of our working it out—that salvation includes *every* work we have to do. The faith of God working in us is the measure of our fitness to work effectively. The promises, *"According to your faith be it unto you"* (Matt. 9:29) and *"All things are possible to him that believeth"* (Mark 9:23), have their full application here. The deeper our faith in God's working in us, the more freely the power of God will work in us, and the truer and more fruitful our work will be.

Perhaps some Sunday school worker is reading this. Have you really believed that your only power to do God's work is as one who has been created in Jesus Christ for good works, as one in whom God Himself works to will and to work? Have you yielded yourself to wait for that working? Do you work because you know that God works in you? Do not say that these thoughts are too high. The work of leading young souls to Christ is too high for us, but if we live as little children in believing that God will work all in us, we will do His work in His strength. Pray much to learn and practice the lesson in all you do. Work, for God works in you.

1. I think we begin to feel that the spiritual understanding of this great truth, "God works in you," is what all workers greatly need.

2. The Holy Spirit is the mighty power of God, dwelling in believers for life and for work. Ask God to show you that in all our service our first care must be the daily renewing of the Holy Spirit.

3. Obey the command to be filled with the Holy Spirit. Believe in His indwelling. Wait for His teaching. Yield to His leading. Pray for His mighty working. Live in the Spirit.

4. What the mighty power of God works in us, we are surely able to do. Only give way to the power working in you.

11
FAITH WORKING BY LOVE

For in Jesus Christ neither circumcision availeth
any thing, nor uncircumcision; but faith which
worketh by love....But by love serve one another.
For all the law is fulfilled in one word, even in this;
Thou shalt love thy neighbour as thyself.
—Galatians 5:6, 13–14

I n Jesus Christ no external privilege is an
advantage. The Jew might boast of his circumcision, the token of God's covenant. The
Gentile might boast of his uncircumcision, with
an entrance into the kingdom free from the
Jewish laws. Neither was of use in the kingdom
of heaven—nothing but, as in Galatians 6:15, *"a*
new creature," in which *"old things are passed*
away...[and] *all things are become new"* (2 Cor.
5:17). Or, as our text describes it, nothing but
faith working by love, causing us to serve one
another in love.

What a perfect description of the new life!
First, you have faith, as the root, planted and
rooted in Jesus Christ. Then, as its aim, you have
works as the fruit. And then, between the two, as
the tree, growing down into the root and bearing
the fruit upward, you have love, with the life-sap

flowing through it by which the root brings forth the fruit. We do not need to speak of faith here. We have seen how believing in Jesus does the greater works, and we have seen how faith in the new creation and in God working in us is the secret of all work. Nor do we need to speak here of works. This whole book aims at securing them in place in every heart and life just as they are in God's heart and in His Word.

We must especially study the great truth that all work is to be done in love. Faith cannot do its work except through love. No works can have any worth unless they come from love. Love alone is the sufficient strength for all the work we have to do.

The power for work is love. It was love that moved God to all His work in creation and redemption. It was love that enabled Christ as man to work and to suffer as He did. It is love that can inspire us with the power of a self-sacrifice that does not seek its own, but is ready to live and die for others. It is love that gives us the patience that refuses to give up on those who are unthankful or hardened. It is love that reaches and overcomes the most hopeless. Love is the power for work in ourselves and in those for whom we labor. Let us love as Christ loved us.

The power for love is faith. Faith roots its life in the life of Jesus Christ, which is all love. Faith knows, even when we cannot fully realize the wonderful gift that has been given into our hearts in the Holy Spirit's outpouring of God's love. A spring in the earth may often be hidden or stopped up. Until it is opened, the fountain cannot flow out. Faith knows that there is a fountain of love within that can spring up into eternal life and can flow out as *"rivers of living water"* (John 7:38). It assures us that we can love, that we have a divine power to love within us, as an inherent gift of our new nature.

The power to exercise and show love is work. There is no such thing as power apart from concrete realities. It acts only as it is exercised. Power at rest cannot be found or felt. This is particularly true of the Christian graces, hidden as they are amid the weakness of our human nature. It is only by *doing* that you know that you *have.* A grace must be performed before we can rejoice in its possession. This is the unspeakable blessedness of work. Working is so essential to a healthy Christian life because it wakes up and strengthens love, and it makes us partakers of its joy.

Faith works by love. In Jesus Christ few things are of as much value as this. Workers for God, believe this! Practice it. Thank God much for the fountain of eternal love opened within you. Pray fervently and frequently that God may strengthen you with might by the power of His Spirit in your inner man, so that, with Christ dwelling in you, you may be *"rooted and grounded in love"* (Eph. 3:17). Live your daily life, then, in your own home, in all your dealings with men, in all your work, as a life of divine love. The ways of love are so gentle and heavenly, you may not learn them all at once. But be of good courage; believe in the power that works in you, and yield yourself to the work of love. It will surely gain the victory.

Faith works by love. Let me press home this message, too, on those who have never thought of working for God. Come and listen.

You owe everything to God's love. The salvation you have received is all love. God's one desire is to fill you with His love for His own satisfaction, for your own happiness, for the saving of men. Now, I ask you, will you not accept God's wonderful offer to be filled with His love? Oh, come and give your heart and life to the joy and the service of His love! Believe that the fountain of love is within you. It will begin to flow as you make a channel for it by deeds of love. Whatever work for God you try to do, seek to put love into it. Pray for the spirit of love. Give yourself to live a life of love. Think how you can love those around you by praying for them, by serving them, by laboring for their temporal and spiritual welfare. Faith working by love in Jesus Christ is of great value.

1. *"And now abideth faith, hope,* [love], *these three; but the greatest of these is* [love]*"* (1 Cor. 13:13). There is no faith or hope in God. *"God is love"* (1 John 4:8). The most Godlike thing is love.

2. Love is the nature of God. When it is *"shed abroad in our hearts by the Holy Ghost"* (Rom. 5:5), love becomes our new nature. Believe this, give yourself over to it, and act it out.

3. Love is God's power to do His work. Love was Christ's power. To work for God, pray earnestly to be filled with love for souls!

12
BEARING FRUIT IN EVERY GOOD WORK

That ye might walk worthy of the Lord unto all pleasing, being fruitful in every good work, and increasing in the knowledge of God; strengthened with all might, according to his glorious power, unto all patience and longsuffering with joyfulness.
—Colossians 1:10–11

There is a difference between fruit and work. Fruit is that which comes spontaneously, without thought or will—the natural and necessary outcome of a healthy life. Work, on the contrary, is the product of effort guided by intelligent thought and will. In the Christian life, we have the two elements combined. All true work must be fruit, the growth and product of our inner lives, the operation of God's Spirit within us. And yet all fruit must be work, the result of our deliberate purpose and effort. In the words *"being fruitful in every good work,"* we have the practical summing up of the truth taught in some previous chapters. Because God works by His life in us, the work we do is fruit. In having faith in His working, we desire to be used by Him and to bear fruit—work. The secret of all true work lies in the harmony between the perfect spontaneity that comes from God's life and Spirit animating us and our cooperation with Him as His intelligent fellow laborers.

In the words *"filled with the knowledge of his will in all wisdom and spiritual understanding"* (Col. 1:9), we have the human side, our need of knowledge and wisdom. In the words *"strengthened with all might, according to his glorious power,"* we have the divine side. God teaches and strengthens, and man learns to understand and patiently do His will. Such is the double life that will be fruitful in every good work.

It has been said of the Christian life that the natural man must first become spiritual, and then again the spiritual man must become natural. As the whole natural life becomes truly spiritual, all our work will partake of the nature of fruit, the outgrowth of the life of God within us. And as the spiritual again becomes perfectly natural to us, a second nature in which we are completely at home, all the fruit will bear the mark of true work, calling into full exercise every faculty of our being.

"Being fruitful in every good work" suggests again the great thought that, as an apple tree or a vine is planted solely for its fruit, so the great purpose of our redemption is that God may have us for His work and service. It has been well said, "The end of man is an action and not a thought, though it were of the noblest." It is in his work that the nobility of man's nature as ruler of the

world is proved. It is for good works that we have been created anew in Christ Jesus. It is when men see our good works that our Father in heaven will be glorified and have the honor that is His due His workmanship. In the parable of the vine, our Lord insisted on this. *"He that abideth in me, and I in him, the same bringeth forth much fruit"* (John 15:5). *"Herein is my Father glorified, that ye bear much fruit"* (v. 8). Few things give more honor to a farmer than to succeed in raising an abundant crop—much fruit is glory to God.

The great need is that every believer be encouraged, helped, and even trained to aim at producing much fruit. A little strawberry plant may, in its measure, bear a more abundant crop than a large apple tree. The call to be fruitful in every good work is for every Christian without exception. The grace that is needed to do this is available to everyone. Every branch fruitful in every good work—this is an essential part of God's Gospel.

We must get a true impression of the two sides of the divine truth *"being fruitful in every good work."* God's first creation of life was in the vegetable kingdom. It was a life without anything of will or self-effort. All growth and fruit was simply His own direct work, the spontaneous outcome of His hidden working. There was progress in the creation of the animal kingdom. New elements were introduced—thought and will and work. In man these elements were united in perfect harmony. The absolute dependence of the grass and the lily on the God who clothes them with their beauty was to be the groundwork of our relationship. Nature has nothing but what it receives from God. Our works are to be fruit, the product of a God-given power. But to this was added the true mark of our Godlikeness, the power of will and independent action—all fruit is to be our own work. As we grasp this concept, we will see how the most complete understanding of our having nothing in ourselves is consistent with the deepest sense of obligation and the strongest desire to exert our powers to the very utmost. We must study the lessons of the text as those who seek all their wisdom and strength from God alone. And we will boldly give ourselves, as those who are responsible for the use of that wisdom and strength, to the diligence, sacrifice, and effort needed for a life bearing fruit in every good work.

1. Much depends, for quality and quantity, on the healthy life of the tree. The life of God, of Jesus Christ, of His Spirit—the divine life in you—must be strong and sure.

2. That life is love. Believe in it. Act it out. Have it replenished day by day out of the fullness that is in Christ.

3. Let all your work be fruit. Let all your willing and working be inspired by the life of God. In this way you will *"walk worthy of the Lord unto all pleasing"* (Col. 1:10).

13

Always Abounding in the Work of the Lord

*Therefore, my beloved brethren, be ye stedfast,
unmoveable, always abounding in the work of the
Lord, forasmuch as ye know that your labour
is not in vain in the Lord.*
—1 Corinthians 15:58

The fifteenth chapter of 1 Corinthians presents the divine revelation of the meaning of Christ's resurrection, with all its blessings. It gives us a living Savior who revealed Himself from heaven to His disciples on earth and to Paul. It assures us of the complete deliverance from all sin. It is the pledge of His final victory over every enemy, when He gives up the kingdom to the Father, and God is all in all. It assures us of the resurrection of the body and our entrance to heavenly life. Paul had closed his argument with his triumphant appeal to death and sin and the law:

> *O death, where is thy sting? O grave, where
> is thy victory? The sting of death is sin; and*

> *the strength of sin is the law. But thanks be to God, which giveth us the victory through our Lord Jesus Christ.* (1 Cor. 15:55–57)

Then, after fifty-seven verses of exultant teaching concerning the mystery and the glory of the resurrection life in our Lord and His people, there is one verse of practical application. *"Therefore, my beloved brethren, be ye stedfast, unmoveable, always abounding in the work of the Lord."* The faith in a risen, living Christ, and in all that His resurrection is to us in time and eternity, is to equip us for, and to prove itself in, abounding work for our Lord!

It cannot be otherwise. Christ's resurrection was His final victory over sin, death, and Satan. It was His entry to His work of giving the Spirit from heaven and extending His kingdom throughout the earth. Those who shared the resurrection joy at once received the direction to make known the joyful news. It was so with Mary and the women. It was so with the disciples the evening of the resurrection day. *"As my Father hath sent me, even so send I you"* (John 20:21). It was so with all to whom the charge was given, *"Go ye into all the world, and preach the gospel to every creature"* (Mark 16:15). The Resurrection is the beginning and the pledge of Christ's victory over all the earth. That victory is to be carried out to its complete manifestation through His people. The faith and joy of the resurrection life are the inspiration and the power for the work of doing it. And so the call comes to all believers without exception: *"Therefore, my beloved brethren, be ye...always abounding in the work of the Lord."*

"In the work of the Lord." The connection tells us at once what that work is. It is nothing less than telling others of the risen Lord and proving to them what new life Christ has brought to us. As we indeed know and acknowledge Him as Lord over all we are, and live in the joy of His service, we will see that the work of the Lord is but one work—that of winning men to know Christ and to bow before Him. Amid all the forms of service, the one aim in the power of the life of the risen Lord is to make Him Lord of all.

This work of the Lord is no easy one. It cost Christ His life to conquer sin and Satan and gain the risen life. It will cost us our lives, too—the sacrifice of the life of nature. It needs the surrender of all on earth to live in the full power of resurrection newness of life. The power of sin and the world in those around us is strong. Satan does not easily give up his servants to our efforts. It needs a heart in close touch with the risen Lord, truly living the resurrection life, to be *"stedfast, unmoveable, always abounding in the work of the Lord."* But that is a life that can be lived because Jesus lives.

Paul added, *"Forasmuch as ye know that your labour is not in vain in the Lord."* I have spoken more than once of the mighty influence that the certainty of reward for work, in the shape of wages or riches, exerts on the millions of earth's workers. Christ's workers can, with assurance, believe that with such a Lord their reward is sure and great! The work is often difficult and slow, and apparently fruitless. We are apt to lose heart, because we are working in our strength and judging by our expectations. Listen to the message:

"Be ye...always abounding in the work of the Lord, forasmuch as ye know your labour is not in vain in the Lord." "Let not your hands be weak: for your work shall be rewarded" (2 Chron. 15:7). *"Ye know that your labour is not in vain in the Lord."*

"In the Lord." This expression is a significant one. Study it in Romans 16, where it occurs ten times, where Paul used the expressions: *"Receive her in the Lord"* (v. 2); *"my helpers in Christ Jesus"* (v. 3); *"who also were in Christ before me"* (v. 7); *"beloved in the Lord"* (v. 8); *"approved in Christ"* (v. 10); *"who labour in the Lord"* (v. 12); and *"chosen in the Lord"* (v. 13). The entire life and fellowship and service of these saints had one mark—they were, their labors were, in the Lord. Here is the secret of effective service. *"Your labour is not in vain in the Lord."* As a sense of His presence and the power of His life is maintained, and as all works are produced in Him, His strength works in our weakness. Our labor cannot be in vain in the Lord. Christ said, *"He that abideth in me, and I in him, the same bringeth forth much fruit"* (John 15:5). Do not let the children of this world, with their confidence that the masters whose work they are doing will certainly give them their due reward, put the children of light to shame. Let us rejoice and labor in the confident faith of the word: *"Therefore, beloved brethren, be ye...always abounding in the work of the Lord...your labour is not in vain in the Lord."*

14

ABOUNDING GRACE FOR ABOUNDING WORK

And God is able to make all grace abound toward you; that ye, always having all sufficiency in all things, may abound to every good work.
—2 Corinthians 9:8

In the previous chapter we were motivated to abounding work—the spirit of triumphant joy that Christ's resurrection inspires as it covers the past and the future. This chapter assures us that for this abounding work we have the ability provided. *"God is able to make all grace abound,"* so that we may abound to all good works. Every thought of abounding grace is to be connected with the abounding in good works for which it is given. And every thought of abounding work is to be connected with the abounding grace that equips us for it.

Abounding grace has abounding work for its aim. It is often thought that grace and good works are in disagreement with each other. This is not so. What Scripture calls the works of the law are our own works, the works of righteousness that we have done. They are dead works—works by which we seek to merit or to be made fit for God's favor. These are the very opposite of grace. But they are also the very opposite of the good works that spring from grace, for which grace is given. As incompatible as the works of the law are with the freedom of grace, the works of faith, good works, are essential and indispensable to the true Christian life. God makes grace abound, so that good works may abound. The measure of true grace is tested and proved by the measure of good works. God's grace abounds in us so that we may abound in good works. We need to have the truth deeply rooted in us. Remember, abounding grace has abounding work for its aim.

Abounding work needs abounding grace as its source and strength. There often is abounding work without abounding grace. Just as any man may be very diligent in an earthly pursuit, or a heathen in his religious service of an idol, so men may be very diligent in doing religious work in their own strength, with very little thought of the grace that alone can do true, spiritual, effective work. For all work that is to be really acceptable to God, and truly fruitful, not only for some visible result here on earth, but also for eternity, the grace of God is indispensable. Paul continually gave complete credit for his own work to the grace of God working in him. *"I laboured more abundantly than they all: yet not I, but the grace of God which was with me"* (1 Cor. 15:10). *"According to the gift of the grace of God given unto me by the effectual working of his power"* (Eph. 3:7). And he frequently called upon Christians to exercise their gifts *"according to the grace that is given to us"* (Rom. 12:6). *"But unto every one of us is given grace according to the measure of the gift of Christ"* (Eph. 4:7). It is only by the grace of God working in us that we can do what are truly good works. It is only as we seek and receive abounding grace that we can abound in every good work.

"God is able to make all grace abound toward you; that ye...may abound to every good work." Every Christian ought to praise God with great thanksgiving for the abounding grace that is thus provided for him. With great humiliation he ought to confess that his experience of, and his surrender to, that abounding grace has been so defective. And with great confidence he ought to believe that a life abounding in good works is indeed possible, because the abounding grace for it is so sure and so divinely sufficient. Then, with simple, childlike dependence, he should wait upon God day by day to receive more grace that He gives to the humble (James 4:6).

Child of God, take time to study and truly understand God's purpose for you, that you may abound in every good work! He means it! He has provided for it! Make the measure of your consecration to Him nothing less than His purpose for you. And claim, then, nothing less than the abounding grace He is able to bestow. Make His omnipotence and His faithfulness your confidence. And live ever in the practice of continual prayer and dependence upon His power working in you. This will make you abound in every good work. *"According to your faith be it unto you"* (Matt. 9:29).

Christian worker, learn here the secret of all failure and all success. Working in our own strength, with little prayer and waiting on God for His Spirit, is the cause of failure. The cultivation of the spirit of absolute weakness and unceasing dependence will open the heart for the workings of abounding grace. We will learn to credit all we do to God's grace. We will learn to measure all we have to do by God's grace. And our lives will increasingly be in the joy of God's making His grace abound in us, and our abounding in every good work.

1. *"That ye...may abound to every good work."* Pray over this now until you feel that this is what God has prepared for you.

2. If your ignorance and weakness appear to make it impossible, present yourself to God and say you are willing, if He will enable you to abound in good works, to be a branch that brings forth much fruit.

3. Take into your heart, as a living seed, these precious truths: *"He staggered not at the promise of God through unbelief; but was strong in faith, giving glory to God; and being fully persuaded that, what he had promised, he was able also to perform"* (Rom. 4:20–21), and *"Faithful is he that calleth you, who also will do it"* (1 Thess. 5:24).

4. Begin at once by doing lowly deeds of love. As a little child in kindergarten, *learn by doing.*

15

IN THE WORK OF MINISTERING

*And he gave some, apostles; and some, prophets;
and some, evangelists; and some, pastors and
teachers; for the perfecting of the saints,
for the work of the ministry,
for the edifying of the body of Christ.*
—Ephesians 4:11–12

Christ's objective, when He ascended to heaven and bestowed on His servants the various gifts that are mentioned, is three-fold. The first aim of the gifts is *"for the perfecting of the saints."* Believers, as saints, are to be led on in the pursuit of holiness until they *"stand perfect and complete in all the will of God"* (Col. 4:12). It was for this that Epaphras labored in prayer. Paul wrote of this: *"Whom we preach,...teaching every man in all wisdom; that we may present every man perfect in Christ Jesus"* (Col. 1:28).

This perfecting of the saints is, however, only a means to a higher end—*"for the work of the ministry,"* to equip all the saints to take part in the service to which every believer is called. The same word is used in texts such as, *"which ministered unto him of their substance"* (Luke 8:3) and *"ye have ministered to the saints, and do minister"* (Heb. 6:10). Two other examples of the use of this word are found in 1 Corinthians 16:15 and 1 Peter 4:11.

And this, again, is also a means to a still higher end—*"for the edifying of the body of Christ."* As every member of our body takes its part in working for the health and growth and maintenance of the whole, so every member of the body of Christ is to consider it his first great duty to take part in all that can help to build up the body of Christ—whether by the helping and strengthening of those who are already members, or the ingathering of those who are to belong to it.

And the great work of the church is, through its pastors and teachers, to labor for the perfecting of the saints in holiness and love and fitness for service, so that each one may take his part in the work of ministering, so that the body of Christ may be built up and perfected.

Of the three great objectives with which Christ has given His church apostles and teachers, the work of ministering stands thus in the middle. On the one hand, it is preceded by that on which it absolutely depends—the perfecting of the saints. On the other hand, it is followed by that which it is meant to accomplish—the building up of the body of Christ. Every believer without exception, every member of Christ's body, is called to take part in the work of ministering. Every reader must try to realize the sacredness of his holy calling.

We must learn what the qualifications are for our work. *"The perfecting of the saints"* prepares them for *"the work of the ministry."* It is the lack of true sainthood, the lack of true holiness, that causes such scarce and weak service. As Christ's saints are taught and truly learn what conformity to Christ means, a life like His will become the one thing for which we live. His life was given up in self-sacrifice for the service and salvation of men. His humility and love, His separation from the world and devotion to the fallen, are seen to be the very essence and blessedness of the life He gives—the work of ministering, the ministry of love. Humility and love—these are the two great virtues of the saint—they are the two great powers for the work of ministering. Humility makes us willing to serve. Love makes us wise to know how to do it. Love is inventive. It seeks patiently, and suffers long, until it finds a way to reach its purpose. Humility and love are equally turned away from self and its claims. Let us pray, let the church labor for *"the perfecting of the saints"* in humility and love, and the Holy Spirit will teach us how to minister.

We must look at what the great work is that the members of Christ have to do. It is to minister to each other. Place yourself at Christ's disposal for service to your fellow Christians. Count yourself their servant. Study their interests. Set yourself actively to promote the welfare of the Christians around you. Selfishness may cause us to hesitate, the feeling of weakness may discourage us, laziness and comfort may raise difficulties for us. But ask your Lord to reveal to you His will, and give yourself up to it. All around you there are Christians who are cold and worldly and wandering from their Lord. Begin to think what you can do for them. Accept as the will of the Head that you as a member should care for them. Pray for the Spirit of love. Begin somewhere—only begin, and do not continue hearing and thinking while you do nothing. Begin the work of ministering *"according to the measure of the gift of Christ"* (Eph. 4:7). He will give more grace.

We must believe in the power that works in us as sufficient for all we have to do. As I think of the thumb and finger holding the pen with which I write this, I ask, "How is it that during all these seventy years of my life they have always known just to do my will?" It was because the life of the head passed into and worked itself out in them. *"He that believeth on me,"* as his Head working in him, *"the works that I do shall he do also"* (John 14:12). Faith in Christ, whose strength is made perfect in our weakness, will give the power for all we are called to do.

Let us cry to God that all believers may wake up to the power of this great truth: every member of the body is to live completely for the building up of the body.

1. To be a true worker, the first thing is close, humble fellowship with Christ the Head, to be guided and empowered by Him.

2. The next is humble, loving fellowship with Christ's members serving one another in love.

3. This prepares and equips us for service in the world.

16
ACCORDING TO THE WORKING
OF EACH INDIVIDUAL PART

[That we] may grow up into him in all things, which is the head, even Christ: from whom the whole body fitly joined together and compacted by that which every joint supplieth, according to the effectual working in the measure of every part, maketh increase of the body unto the edifying of itself in love.
—Ephesians 4:15–16

Paul was speaking here of the growth, the increase, the building up of the body. This growth and increase has, as we have seen, a double reference. It includes both the spiritual uniting and strengthening of those who are already members in order to secure the health of the whole body, as well as the increase of the body by the addition of all who are as yet outside of it and are to be gathered into it. We spoke of the former in the previous chapter—of the mutual interdependence of all believers and the calling to care for each other's welfare. In this chapter we look at the growth from the other side—the calling of every member of Christ's body to labor for its increase by the labor of love that seeks to bring in those who are not yet a part of it. This increase of the body and building up of itself in love can be only by the working in due measure of each individual part.

Think of the body of a child. How does it reach the stature of a full-grown man? In no other way but by the working in due measure of every part. As each member takes its part, by the work it does in seeking and taking and assimilating food, the increase is made by its building up itself. The work that assures the growth comes from within, not without. Similarly, in no other way can Christ's body attain the stature of the fullness of Christ. As it is unto Christ the Head that we grow up, and as from Christ the Head the body increases itself, so it is through the contribution of every joint according to the working in due measure of each individual part. Let us see what this implies.

The body of Christ is to consist of all who believe in Him throughout the world. There is no possible way in which these members of the body can be gathered in except by the body building itself up in love. Our Lord has made Himself, as Head, absolutely dependent on His members to do this work. What nature teaches us of our own bodies, Scripture teaches us of Christ's body. The head of a child may have thoughts and plans of growth, but they will all be vain unless the members all do their parts in securing that growth. Jesus Christ has committed to His church the growth and increase of His body. He asks and expects that as He the Head lives for the growth and welfare of the body, every member of His body, even the very weakest, must do the same, to build up the body in love. Every believer is to count it his one duty and blessedness to live and labor for the increase of the body, the ingathering of all who are to be its members.

What is needed to bring the church to accept this calling, and to train and help the members of the body to know and fulfill it? One thing. We must see that the new birth and faith and all insight into truth, with all resolve and surrender and effort to live according to it, is only a preparation for our true work. What is needed is that in every believer Jesus Christ be so formed, and so dwells in the heart, that His life in us will be the impulse and inspiration of our love toward the whole body and our life for it. It is because self occupies the heart that it is so easy and natural and pleasing to care for ourselves. When Jesus Christ lives in us, it will be as easy and natural and pleasing to live completely for the body of Christ. As readily and naturally as the thumb and fingers respond to the will and movement of the head will the members of Christ's body respond to the Head as the body grows up into Him, and from Him makes itself increase.

Let us sum this up. For the great work the Head is doing in gathering new members from throughout the world and building up His body, *He is entirely dependent on the service of the existing members.* Not only our Lord, but also a perishing world is waiting and calling for the church to awake and give herself completely to this work— the perfecting of the number of Christ's members.

Every believer, even the very weakest, must learn to know his calling—to live with this as the main purpose of his existence. This great truth will be revealed to us in power and obtain precedence as we give ourselves to the work of ministering according to the grace we already have. We may confidently wait for the full revelation of Christ in us—the power to do all that He asks of us.

17
WOMEN ADORNED WITH GOOD WORKS

Women adorn themselves in modest apparel, with shamefacedness and sobriety; not with broided hair, or gold, or pearls, or costly array; but (which becometh women professing godliness) with good works.
—1 Timothy 2:9–10

Let not a widow be taken into the number under threescore years old, having been the wife of one man, well reported of for good works...if she have diligently followed every good work.
—1 Timothy 5:9–10

In the three Pastoral Epistles written to two young pastors to instruct them in regard to their duties, "good works" are more frequently mentioned than in Paul's other epistles.* In

---

*In 1 Timothy six times: 2:10; 3:1; 5:10; 5:25; 6:18. In 2 Timothy twice: 2:21; 3:17. In Titus six times: 1:16; 2:7, 14; 3:1, 8, 14.

writing to the churches, as in a chapter like Romans 12, Paul mentioned the individual good works by name. In writing to the pastors, he had to use this expression as a summary of their aim both in their own lives and their teaching of others. A minister was to be prepared and completely equipped to accomplish every good work—an example of good works. They were to teach Christians—the women to adorn themselves with good works, to follow diligently every good work, and to be well reported of for good works. The men were to be rich in good works, to be zealous of good works, to be ready for every good work, and to learn to maintain good works. No portion of God's work emphasizes more definitely the absolute necessity of good works as an essential, vital element in the Christian life.

Our two texts speak of the good works of Christian women. In the first, they are taught that their adorning is to be not with fancy hair and gold or pearls or costly clothing but, as becomes women preferring godliness, with good works. We know what adornment is. A leafless tree in winter has life. When spring comes it puts on its beautiful garments and rejoices in the adornment of foliage and blossom. The adorning of Christian women is not to be in hair or pearls or clothing, but in good works. Whether it is the good works that have reference to personal duty and conduct, or those works of charity that aim at the pleasing and helping of our neighbors, or those that more definitely seek the salvation of souls—the adorning that pleases God, that gives true heavenly beauty, that will truly attract others to come and serve God, too, is what

Christian women ought to seek. John saw the holy city descend from heaven, *"prepared as a bride adorned for her husband"* (Rev. 21:2). *"The fine linen is the righteousness of saints"* (Rev. 19:8). If only every Christian woman might seek to adorn herself to please the Lord!

In the second passage, we read of widows who were placed upon an honor roll in the early church, and to whom a certain charge was given over the younger women. No one was to be enrolled who was not *"well reported of for good works."* Some of these are mentioned: if she had been known for the careful upbringing of her children, for her hospitality to strangers, for her washing the saints' feet, for her relieving the afflicted. And then there is added, *"If she have diligently followed every good work."* If her life has been devoted to good works in her home and out of it, in caring for her own children, for strangers, and for fellow believers, she might indeed be considered fit to be an example and guide to others. The standard was a high one. It shows us the place good works took in the early church. It shows how a woman's blessed ministry of love was counted on and encouraged. It shows how, in the development of the Christian life, nothing so fits for rule and influence as a life given to good works.

Good works are part and parcel of the Christian life, equally indispensable to the health and growth of the individual, and to the welfare and extension of the church. And yet, what multitudes of Christian women there are whose active share in the good work of blessing their fellow creatures is little more than playing at good works. They are waiting for the preaching of a full Gospel, which will encourage and help and compel them to give their lives to work for their Lord, so that they, too, may be well reported of as diligently following every good work.

The time and money, the thought and feeling given to jewels or costly clothing, will be exchanged for the true goal. Christianity will no longer be a selfish desire for personal safety, but the joy of being like Christ, the Helper and Savior of the needy. Work for Christ will take its true place as the highest form of existence, the true adornment of the Christian life. And as diligence in the pursuits of earth is honored as one of the true elements of character and worth, following good works diligently in Christ's service will be found to give access to the highest reward and the fullest joy of the Lord.

1. We are beginning to awaken to the wonderful place women can take in church and school mission. This truth needs to be brought home to every one of the King's daughters, that the adorning in which they are to attract the world, to please their Lord, and enter His presence is only this: good works.

2. Women, as *"the meekness and gentleness of Christ"* (2 Cor. 10:1), are to teach men the beauty and the power of the long-suffering, self-sacrificing ministry of love.

3. The training for the service of love begins in the home. It is strengthened in the inner chamber. It reaches out to the needy around and finds its full scope in the world for which Christ died.

18
RICH IN GOOD WORKS

Charge them that are rich in this world…that they
do good, that they be rich in good works,
ready to distribute, willing to communicate;
laying up in store for themselves a good
foundation against the time to come,
that they may lay hold on eternal life.
—1 Timothy 6:17–19

If women are to regard good works as their adornment, men are to count them as their riches. As good works satisfy woman's eye and taste for beauty, they meet man's craving for possession and power. In the present world, riches have a wonderful significance. They are often God's reward for diligence, industry, and enterprise. They represent and embody the life-power that has been spent in procuring them. As such, they exercise power in the honor or service they secure from others. Their danger consists in their being of this world, in their misdirecting the heart from the living God and heavenly treasures. They may become a man's deadliest enemy. How difficult it is for those who have riches to enter the kingdom of heaven! (See Matthew 19:24.)

The Gospel never takes away anything from us without giving us something better in its place. It meets the desire for riches by the command to be rich in good works. The coin that is current in God's kingdom is good works. The reward in the world to come will be determined according to these. By abounding in good works, we lay up for ourselves treasures in heaven (Matt. 6:20). Even here on earth they constitute a treasure, in the testimony of a good conscience, in the consciousness of being well-pleasing to God (1 John 3), in the power of blessing others.

There is more. Wealth of gold is not only a symbol of the heavenly riches. It is actually, though so opposite in its nature, a means to it.

> *Charge them that are rich...that they do good, that they be rich in good works, ready to distribute, willing to communicate; laying up in store for themselves a good foundation.*

> *Make to yourselves friends of the mammon of unrighteousness; that, when ye fail, they may receive you into everlasting habitations.*
> (Luke 16:9)

Like the widow's mite, the gifts of the rich, when given in the same spirit, may be an offering with which God is well pleased (Heb. 13:16).

The man who is rich in money may become rich in good works if he follows the instructions in Scripture. The money must not be given to be seen of men, but as unto the Lord. Nor must it be given as from an owner, but as from a steward who administers the Lord's money with prayer for His guidance. Nor must it be given with any confidence in its power or influence, but in deep dependence on Him who alone can make it a blessing. Nor must it be given as a substitute for the personal work and witness that each believer is to give. As all Christian work, so our monetary giving has its value alone from the spirit in which it is done, even the spirit of Christ Jesus.

What a field there is in the world for accumulating these riches, these heavenly treasures! In relieving the poor; in educating the neglected; in helping the lost; in taking the Gospel to Christians, and to heathens in darkness, what investment might be made if Christians sought to be rich in good works—rich toward God! We may well ask the question, "What can be done to awaken a desire for these true riches among believers?" Men have made a science of the wealth of nations and carefully studied all the laws by which its increase and universal distribution can be promoted. How can the order to be rich in good works convict hearts that its pursuit will be as much a pleasure and a passion as the desire for the riches of the present world?

All depends upon the nature, the spirit, of man. To the earthly nature, earthly riches have a natural affinity and irresistible attraction. To foster the desire for the acquisition of what constitutes wealth in the heavenly kingdom, we must appeal to the spiritual nature. That spiritual nature needs to be taught and educated and trained into all the business habits that go into making a man rich.

There must be the ambition to rise above the level of a bare existence, the deadly contentment with just being saved. There must be some insight into the beauty and worth of good works as the expression of the divine life—God's working in us and our working in Him, as the means of bringing glory to God, as the source of life and blessing to men, as the laying up of a treasure in heaven for eternity. There must be a faith that these riches are actually within our reach, because the grace and Spirit of God are working in us. And there must be an outlook of doing the work of God to those around us at every opportunity, in the footsteps of Him who said, *"It is more blessed to give than to receive"* (Acts 20:35). Study and apply these principles. They will open the sure road to your becoming a rich man. A man who wants to be rich often begins on a small scale, but never loses an opportunity. Begin at once with some work of love, and ask Christ, who *"became poor, that ye through his poverty might be rich"* (2 Cor. 8:9), to help you.

1. Why does the appeal for money for missions meet with such insufficient response? It is because of the low spiritual state of the church. Christians have no proper idea of their calling to live completely for God and His kingdom.

2. How can the evil be remedied? Only when believers see and accept their divine calling to make God's kingdom their first care, and with humble confession of their sins yield themselves to God, will they truly seek the heavenly riches to be found in working for God.

3. Never cease to plead and labor for a true spiritual awakening throughout the church.

19
PREPARED UNTO EVERY GOOD WORK

If a man therefore purge himself from these, he shall be a vessel unto honour, sanctified, and meet for the master's use, and prepared unto every good work.
—2 Timothy 2:21

Paul spoke of the foundation of God standing sure, of the church as the great house built upon that foundation of vessels, not only of gold and silver, costly and lasting, but also of wood and of earth, common and perishable (2 Tim. 2:19–20). He distinguished between those who gave themselves to striving for words of praise, and those who truly sought to depart from all iniquity. Paul gave us the four steps of the path in which a man can become a vessel unto honor in the great household of God: (1) the cleansing from sin; (2) being sanctified; (3) the suitability for the Master to use as He will; and (4) the spirit of preparedness for every good work. It is not enough that we desire or attempt to do good works. As we need training and care to prepare us for every work we are to do on earth, we need to be prepared unto every *good* work that much more. It is this that constitutes the chief mark of vessels unto honor. *"If a man therefore purge himself from these."* A man must cleanse himself from that which characterizes the vessels of dishonor—the empty profession leading to ungodliness, against which Paul had warned. We insist that every dish and cup we use be clean. In God's house the vessels must be clean that much more. And everyone who would be truly prepared unto every good work must first see that he cleanses himself from all that is sin. Christ Himself could not enter upon His saving work in heaven until He had accomplished the cleansing of our sins. How can we become partners in His work unless we first have the same cleansing? Before Isaiah could say, *"Here am I; send me"* (Isa. 6:8), the fire of heaven had touched his lips, and he heard the voice say, *"Thy sin* [is] *purged"* (v. 7). An intense desire to be cleansed from every sin lies at the root of fitness for true service.

"He shall be a vessel unto honour, sanctified." Cleansing is the negative side, the emptying out and removal of all that is impure. Sanctification is the positive side, the refilling and being possessed of the spirit of holiness, through whom the soul becomes God-possessed, and so partakes of His holiness. *"Let us cleanse ourselves from all filthiness of the flesh and spirit, perfecting holiness in the fear of God"* (2 Cor. 7:1). In the temple the vessels were to be not only clean, but also holy, devoted to God's service alone. He who truly desires to work for God must follow after holiness—*"To the end he may stablish your hearts unblameable in*

holiness before God" (1 Thess. 3:13), a holy habit of mind and disposition, yielded up to God and marked by a sense of His presence, fit for God's work. The cleansing from sin secures the filling with the Spirit.

"Meet for the master's use." We are vessels for our Lord to use. In every work we do, it is to be Christ using us and working through us. The sense of being a servant, dependent on the Master's guidance, working under the Master's eye, instruments used by Him and His mighty power, lies at the root of effective service. It maintains that unbroken dependence, that quiet faith, through which the Lord can do His work. It keeps up that blessed consciousness of the work being all His, which leads the worker to become humbler the more he is used. His one desire is to be *"meet for the master's use."*

"Prepared unto every good work." "Prepared." The word not only refers to equipment and fitness, but also to disposition, the cheerful readiness that keeps a man on the outlook and makes him earnestly desire and joyfully avail himself of every opportunity of doing his Master's work. As he lives in touch with his Lord Jesus and holds himself as a cleansed and sanctified vessel, ready for Him to use, and he sees that he was redeemed for good works, they become the one thing for which he lives and proves his fellowship with his Lord. He is *"prepared unto every good work."*

1. *"Meet for the master's use"*—that is the central thought. A personal relationship to Christ, an entire surrender to His disposal, a dependent waiting to

be used by Him, a joyful confidence that He will use us—such is the secret of true work.

2. Let the beginning of your work be a giving of yourself into the hands of the Master, as your living, loving Lord.

20
FURNISHED COMPLETELY UNTO EVERY GOOD WORK

Study to show thyself approved unto God, a workman that needeth not to be ashamed, rightly dividing the word of truth.
—2 Timothy 2:15

All scripture is given by inspiration of God, and is profitable for doctrine, for reproof, for correction, for instruction in righteousness: that the man of God may be perfect, thoroughly furnished unto all good works.
—2 Timothy 3:16–17

A workman that does not need to be ashamed is one who is not afraid to have the master come and inspect his work. In hearty devotion to it, in thoroughness and skill, he presents himself approved to him who employs him. God's workers are to present themselves approved to Him to have their work worthy and well-pleasing unto Him. They are to be as workmen who do not need to be ashamed. A workman is one who knows his work, who gives himself completely to it, who is known as a working man, who takes delight in doing his work well. Thus, every Christian minister, every Christian worker, is to be a workman who concentrates on inviting and expecting the Master's approval.

"Rightly dividing the word of truth." The Word is a seed, a fire, a hammer, a sword, bread, and light. Workmen in any of these areas can be our example. In work for God, everything depends upon handling the Word correctly. Therefore, the one means of our being completely equipped for every good work is given in the Scripture that begins this paragraph—personal subjection to the Word and the experience of its power. God's workers must know that Scripture is inspired by God and has life-giving power in it. Inspiration is Spirit-breathed—as the life is in a seed, God's Holy Spirit is in the Word. The Spirit in the Word and the Spirit in our hearts is one. By the power of the Spirit within us, we take the Spirit-filled Word. Thus, we become spiritual. This Word is given for teaching—the revelation of the thoughts of God; for reproof—the discovery of our sins and mistakes; for correction—to remove what is defective and replace it by what is good; also for instruction—the communication of all the knowledge needed to walk before God righteously.

As one yields himself heartily to all this, and the true Spirit-filled Word gets mastery of his whole being, he becomes a man of God, furnished completely to every good work. He becomes a workman approved by God who does not need to be ashamed, rightly handling the Word of God. And so the man of God has the double mark—

his own life is completely molded and his work is directed by applying the Word.

"That the man of God may be perfect, thoroughly furnished unto all good works." In the previous chapter we learned how the cleansing and sanctification of the personal life changes the worker into a vessel *"meet for the master's use, and prepared unto every good work"* (2 Tim. 2:21). Here we learn the same lesson—it is the man of God who allows God's Word to do its work of reprimanding and correcting and instructing. Every worker for God must aim to be equipped for every good work.

A worker, aware of how defective his preparation is, might ask how this furnishing for every good work is to be attained. The analogy of an earthly workman, not needing to be ashamed, suggests the answer. The earthly worker would tell us that he owes his success, first of all, to devotion to his work. He gave it his close attention. He left other things to concentrate his efforts on mastering one thing. He made it a life-study to do his work perfectly. Those who wish to do Christ's work as a second thing, not as the first, and who are not willing to sacrifice all for it, will never be fully equipped to every good work.

The second thing he will speak of will be patient training and exercise. Proficiency comes only through painstaking effort. You may feel as if you do not know how to work correctly. Have no fear. All learning begins with ignorance and mistakes. Be of good courage. He who has endowed human nature with the wonderful power that has filled the world with such skilled and cunning workmen will give His children the grace they need to be His fellow workers even more, will He not? Let the necessity that is laid upon you—the necessity that you should glorify God; that you should bless the world; that you should, through work, advance and perfect your life and blessedness—urge you to give immediate and continual diligence to be a workman equipped unto every good work.

It is only in *doing* that we learn to do correctly. Begin working under Christ's training. He will perfect His work in you and make you fit for your work for Him.

1. The work God is doing, and seeking to have done in the world, is to win it back to Himself.

2. Every believer is expected to take part in this work.

3. God wants us to be skilled workmen who give our whole hearts to His work and delight in it.

4. God does His work by working in us, inspiring and strengthening us to do His work.

5. What God asks for is a heart and life devoted to Him in surrender and faith.

6. And God's work is all love; love is the power that works in us, inspiring our efforts and conquering its object.

21
ZEALOUS OF GOOD WORKS

Who gave himself for us, that he might redeem us
from all iniquity, and purify unto himself a peculiar
people, zealous of good works.
—Titus 2:14

In these words we have two truths: what Christ has done to make us His own and what He expects of us. In the first part we have a rich and beautiful summary of Christ's work for us. He gave Himself for us, He redeemed us from all iniquity, He cleansed us for Himself, He took us for a people, for His own possession. And all with the one objective that we should be a people *"zealous of good works."* The doctrinal half of this wonderful passage has had much attention given to it. Let us devote our attention to its practical part—we are to be a people *"zealous of good works."* Christ expects us to be zealots for good works.

This cannot be said to be the feeling with which most Christians regard good works. What can be done to cultivate this disposition? One of the first things that awakens zeal in work is a great and urgent sense of need. A great need awakens strong desire, stirs the heart and the will, and rouses all the energies of our being. It was this sense of need that roused many to be zealous of the law. They hoped their works would save them. The Gospel has robbed this motive of its power. Has it entirely taken away the need for good works? No. Indeed, it has given that urgent need a higher place than before.

Christ needs our good works urgently. We are His servants, the members of His body, without whom He cannot possibly carry on His work on earth. The work is so great (with millions still unsaved) that not one worker can be spared. Thousands of Christians today feel that their own business is urgent and must be attended to; they have no conception of the urgency of Christ's work entrusted to them. The church must wake up to teach each believer his responsibility.

The world needs our good works as urgently as Christ needs them. Men, women, and children around you need to be saved. To see men swept past us in a river stirs us to try to save them. Christ has placed His people in a perishing world with the expectation that they will give themselves, hearts and souls, to carry on His work of love. Let us sound forth the blessed gospel message: He gave Himself for us so that He might redeem us for Himself, a people of His own, to serve Him and carry on His work—zealous of good works.

A second great element of zeal in work is delight in it. An apprentice or a student mostly begins his work under a sense of duty. As he learns to understand and enjoy it, he does it with pleasure and becomes zealous in its performance. The church must train Christians to believe that when we give our hearts to the work of sharing in Christ's work of mercy and love, and seek the training that makes us in some degree skilled workmen, there is no greater joy. As physical and mental activity give pleasure and call for the devotion and zeal of thousands, the spiritual service of Christ can awaken our highest enthusiasm.

Then comes the highest motive, the personal one of attachment to Christ our Redeemer. *"For the love of Christ constraineth us"* (2 Cor. 5:14). Christ's love for us is the source and measure of our love for Him. Our love for Him becomes the power and the measure of our love for souls. This love, poured forth widely in our hearts by the Holy Spirit, becomes a zeal for Christ that shows itself as a zeal for good works. It becomes the link that unites the two parts of our text, the doctrinal and the practical, into one. Christ's love redeemed us, cleansed us, and made us a people of His own. When that love is believed in, known, and received into the heart, it makes the redeemed soul zealous in good works.

"Zealous of good works!" Let no believer look upon this grace as too high. It is divine, provided for and assured in the love of our Lord. Let us accept it as our calling. Let us be sure it is the very nature of the new life within us. Let us, in opposition to all that nature or feeling may say, in faith claim it as an integral part of our redemption—Christ Himself will make it true in us.

22
READY TO EVERY GOOD WORK

Put them in mind…to be ready
to every good work.
—Titus 3:1

"*ut them in mind.*" The words suggest the need for believers to have the truths of their calling to good works set before them again and again. A healthy tree spontaneously bears its fruit. Even where the life of the believer is in perfect health, Scripture teaches us how its growth and fruitfulness can come only through teaching and the influence that exerts on mind and will and heart. For all who have charge of others, the need of divine wisdom and faithfulness is great in order to teach and train all Christians. Let us consider some of the chief points of such training.

Teach them clearly what good works are. Lay the foundation in the will of God, as revealed in the law, and show them how integrity and righteousness and obedience are the groundwork of Christian character. Teach them how, in all the duties and relationships of daily life, true religion is to be carried out. Lead them on to the virtues that Jesus especially came to exhibit and teach—humility, meekness, gentleness, and love. Explain to them the meaning of a life of love, self-sacrifice, and charity—entirely dedicated to thinking of and caring for others. Then carry them on to what is the highest, the true life of good works—the winning of men to know and love God.

Teach them what an essential part of the Christian life good works are. They are not, as many think, a secondary element in the salvation that God gives. They are not merely to be done in token of our gratitude, or as a proof of the sincerity of our faith, or as a preparation for heaven. They are all this, but they are a great deal more. They are the very purpose for which we have been redeemed. We have been created anew unto good works. They alone are the evidence that man has been restored to his original destiny of working with, through, and in God. God has no higher glory than His works, particularly His work of saving love. In becoming imitators of God and walking and working in love, even as Christ loved us and gave Himself for us (Gal. 2:20), we have the very image and likeness of God restored in us. The works of a man not only reveal his life, but also develop, exercise, strengthen, and perfect it. Good works are the very essence of the divine life in us.

Teach them, too, what a rich reward they bring. All labor has its market value. From the poor man who can scarcely earn a little money, to the man who has made his millions, the thought of the reward for labor has been one of the great incentives to undertake it. Christ appeals to this feeling when He says, *"Your reward shall be great"*

(Luke 6:35). Let Christians understand that there is no service where the reward is so rich as that of God. Work is bracing; work is strength, and it cultivates the sense of mastery and conquest. Work awakens enthusiasm and brings out a man's noblest qualities. In a life of good works, the Christian becomes conscious of his divine ministry of dispensing the life and grace of God to others. Good works bring us into closer union with God. There is no higher fellowship with God than fellowship in His saving work of love. Work brings us into sympathy with Him and His purposes. It fills us with His love. It secures His approval. And great is the reward, too, for those around us. When others are won to Christ, when the weary and the erring and the despondent are helped and made partakers of the grace and life in Christ Jesus for them, God's servants share in the very joy in which our blessed Lord found His reward.

And now the chief thing. Teach them to believe that it is possible for each of us to abound in good works. Nothing is so fatal to successful effort as discouragement or despondency. Nothing is more a frequent cause of neglect of good works than the fear that we do not have the power to perform them. Put them in mind of the power of the Holy Spirit dwelling in them. Show them that God's promise and provision of strength is always equal to what He demands. Show them that sufficient grace is always available for all the good works to which we are called. Strive to awaken in them a faith in *"the power that worketh in us"* (Eph. 3:20) and in the fullness of the life that can flow out as *"rivers of living water"* (John 7:38). Train them to begin their service of love at once. Lead them to see how it is all God working in them and to offer themselves as empty vessels to be filled with His love and grace. And teach them that as they are faithful in a little, even in the midst of mistakes and shortcomings, the acting out of the life will strengthen the life itself, and work for God will become in full truth a second nature.

God grant that the teachers of the church may be faithful to its commission in regard to all her members—*"Put them in mind...to be ready for every good work."* Not only teach them, but also train them. Show them the work there is to be done by them. See that they do it. Encourage and help them to do it hopefully. There is no part of the office of a pastor more important, more sacred, or fuller of richer blessing. Let the aim be nothing less than to lead every believer to live entirely devoted to the work of God in winning men to Him. What a change it would make in the church and the world!

1. Get a firm hold of the great basic principle: every believer, every member of Christ's body, has his place in the body solely for the welfare of the whole body.

2. Pastors have been given for the perfecting of the saints with the work of ministering, of serving in love.

3. In ministers and members of the churches, Christ will work mightily if they will wait upon Him.

23
CAREFUL TO MAINTAIN GOOD WORKS

I will that thou affirm constantly, that they which have believed in God might be careful to maintain good works....And let ours also learn to maintain good works for necessary uses, that they be not unfruitful.
—Titus 3:8, 14

In the first part of this passage, Paul charged Titus to state confidently the truths of the blessed Gospel to the end, with the express purpose that all who had believed should be careful, should make a study of it, to maintain good works. Faith and good works were to be inseparable. The diligence of every believer in good works was to be a main aim of a pastor's work. Then Paul repeated the instruction, with the expression *let them learn.* As all work on earth has to be learned, so in the good works of the Christian life there is an equal need of thought and application and teachableness to learn how to do them correctly and abundantly.

There may be more than one reader of this book who has felt how little he has lived in accordance with all the teaching of God's Word—prepared for, thoroughly equipped for, ready unto, and zealous of good works. It appears so difficult to get rid of old habits, to break through the conventions of society, and to know how to begin and really enter into a life that can be full of good works to the glory of God. Let me try to give some suggestions that may be helpful. They may also aid those who have the training of Christian workers, in showing in what way the teaching and learning of good works may best succeed.

1. A learner must begin by beginning to work at once. There is no way of learning an art like swimming or music, a new language or a trade, but by practice. Let neither the fear that you cannot do it, nor the hope that something will happen that will make it easier for you, keep you back. Learn to do good works, the works of love, by beginning to do them. However insignificant they appear, do them. A kind word, a little help to someone in trouble, an act of loving attention to a stranger or a poor man, the sacrifice of a seat or a place to someone who longs for it—practice these things. All plants we cultivate are small at first. Cherish the consciousness that, for Jesus' sake, you are seeking to do what would please Him. It is only in doing that you can learn to do.

2. The learner must give his heart to the work and must take interest and pleasure in it. Delight in work ensures success. Let the tens of thousands around you in the world who throw their whole souls into their daily businesses teach you how to serve your blessed Master. Think sometimes

of the honor and privilege of doing good works, of serving others in love. It is God's own work, to love and save and bless men. He works it in you and through you. It makes you share the spirit and likeness of Christ. It strengthens your Christian character. Without actions, a man's intentions lower and condemn him instead of raising him. You really live only as much as you act. Think of the blessedness of doing good, of communicating life, of making others happy. Think of the exquisite joy of growing up into a life of charity and being a blessing to all you meet. Set your heart upon being a vessel fit for the Master's use, ready to do every good work.

3. Be of good courage, and fear not. The learner who says "I cannot" will surely fail. There is a divine power working in you. Study and believe what God's Word says about it. Let the holy self-reliance of Paul, grounded in his reliance on Christ, be your example—*"I can do all things through Christ which strengtheneth me"* (Phil. 4:13). Study and take to heart the wonderful promises about the power of the Holy Spirit, the abundance of grace, and Christ's strength made perfect in weakness, and see how all this can be made true to you only in *working*. Cultivate the noble consciousness that as you have been created to good works by God, He Himself will equip you for them. Believe, then, that just as it is natural to any workman to delight and succeed in his profession, it can be natural to the new nature in you to abound in every good work. Having this confidence, you never need to faint.

4. Above all, cling to your Lord Jesus as your Teacher and Master. He said, *"Learn of me; for I*

am meek and lowly in heart: and ye shall find rest unto your souls" (Matt. 11:29). Work as one who is a learner in His school, who is sure that none teaches like Him. Cling to Him, and let a sense of His presence and His power working in you make you meek and lowly, yet bold and strong. He who came to do the Father's work on earth and found it the path to the Father's glory will teach you what it is to work for God.

To sum up again, for the sake of any who want to learn how to work, or how to work better:

1. Yield yourself to Christ. Lay yourself on the altar and say you wish to give yourself completely for God's work.

2. Believe quietly that Christ accepts and takes charge of you for His work and will equip you for it.

3. Pray much that God would open to you the great truth of His own working in you. Nothing else can give true strength.

4. Seek to cultivate a spirit of humble, patient, trustful dependence upon God. Live in loving fellowship and obedience to Christ. You can count upon His strength being made perfect in your weakness.

24
As His Fellow Workers

For we are labourers together with God: ye are
God's husbandry, ye are God's building.
—1 Corinthians 3:9

We then, as workers together with him,
beseech you also that ye receive not
the grace of God in vain.
—2 Corinthians 6:1

We have discussed Paul's teaching on good works (chapters nine and twenty-two). Let us turn now to his personal experience and see if we can learn some of the secrets of effective service from him.

He spoke here of the church as God's building. As the Great Architect, God is building up the church into a holy temple and dwelling for Himself. Of his own work, Paul spoke as a master builder, to whom a part of the great building had been given to his charge. He had laid a foundation in Corinth. To all who were working there he said, *"For we are labourers together with God.... Let every man take heed how he buildeth there-upon"* (1 Cor. 3:9–10). The word is applicable not only to Paul, but also to all of God's servants who take part in His work. And because every believer has been called to give his life to God's service and to win others to His knowledge, every Christian needs to have the Word brought to him and taken home: we are God's fellow workers. How much it suggests in regard to our working for God!

As to the work we have to do, the eternal God is building for Himself a temple. Jesus Christ, God's Son, is the foundation. Believers are the living stones. The Holy Spirit is the mighty power of God through which believers are gathered out of the world, made fit for their places in the temple, and built up into it. As living stones, believers are at the same time the living workmen, whom God uses to carry out His work. They are equally God's workmanship and God's fellow workers. The work God is doing He does through them. The work they have to do is the very work God is doing. God's own work, in which He delights, on which His heart is set, is saving men and building them into His temple. This is the one work on which the heart of everyone who desires to be a fellow worker with God must be set. Only as we know how great this work of God is—giving life to dead souls, imparting His own life to them, and living in them—will we enter into the glory of our work. We will receive the very life of God and pass it on to men.

As to the strength for the work, Paul said of his work, as a mere master builder, that it was *"according to the grace of God which is given unto me"* (1 Cor. 3:10). For divine work, nothing but divine power suffices. The power by which God works must work in us. That power is His Holy Spirit. Study 1 Corinthians 2 and 2 Corinthians 3. You will see how absolute Paul's acknowledgment of his own powerlessness and his dependence on the teaching and power of the Holy Spirit was. The truth is that God's work can be done only by God's power in us. Our first need every day is to have the presence of God's Spirit renewed within us.

The power of the Holy Spirit is the power of love. God is love. All He works for the salvation of men is love. It is love alone that truly conquers and wins the heart. In all God's fellow workers, love is the power that reaches the hearts of men. Christ conquered and conquers still by the love of the cross. *"Let this mind be in you, which was also in Christ Jesus"* (Phil. 2:5)—the spirit of a love that sacrifices itself to the death, of a humble, patient, gentle love—and you will be made fit to be God's fellow worker.

As to the relationship we are to hold to God, let me say this. In executing the plans of a great building, the master builder has but one care: to carry out to the minutest detail the thoughts of the architect who designed it. He acts in constant consultation with him and is guided in everything by his will. His instructions to those under him all refer to one thing—the embodiment, in visible shape, of what the master mind has conceived. The great characteristics of fellow workers with God ought to be that of absolute surrender to His will, unceasing dependence on His teaching, and exact obedience to His wishes. God has revealed His plan in His Word. He has told us that His Spirit alone can enable us to enter into His plans, and fully master His purpose with the way He desires to have it carried out.

We must have clear insight into the divine glory of God's work of saving souls. We must see the utter insufficiency of our natural powers to do the work. We must know that He has made provision to strengthen and guide us in performance. We will then come to a greater understanding that a childlike teachableness (a continual looking upward and waiting on God) is always to be the chief mark of one who is His fellow laborer.

Out of a sense of humility, helplessness, and nothingness, there will grow a holy confidence and courage. We will know that our weaknesses do not need to hinder us, that Christ's strength is made perfect in weakness, and that God Himself is working out His purpose through us. Of all the blessings of the Christian life, the most wonderful will be that we are allowed to be God's fellow workers!

1. God's fellow worker! How easy to use the words, and even to understand some of the great truths they contain! How little we live in the power and the glory of what they actually involve!

2. Fellow workers with God! Everything depends upon knowing, in His holiness and love, the God with whom we are associated as partners.

3. He who has chosen us will equip us for His use, so that in and through us He might do His great work.

4. Let our posture be adoring worship, deep dependence, great waiting, and full obedience.

25
ACCORDING TO THE WORKING OF HIS POWER

Whom we preach, warning every man, and teaching every man in all wisdom; that we may present every man perfect in Christ Jesus: whereunto I also labour, striving according to his working, which worketh in me mightily.
—Colossians 1:28–29

The mystery of Christ...whereof I was made a minister, according to the gift of the grace of God given unto me by the effectual working of his power.
—Ephesians 3:4, 7

I n the words of Paul to the Philippians, which we have already considered in chapter nine, he called upon them and encouraged them to work because it was God who worked in them. This is one of the most momentous and comprehensive statements of the great truth that it is only by God's working in us that we can do true work. In our Scripture texts for this chapter, we have Paul's testimony about his own experience. His whole ministry was to be according to the grace that was given him according to the working of God's power. He said that his labor was a striving according to the power of Him who worked mightily in him.

We find here the same principle we found in our Lord—the Father doing the works in Him. Let every worker who reads this pause and say, "If the ever blessed Son and Paul could do their work only according to the working of His power who worked mightily in them, how much more do I need this working of God in me!" This is one of the deepest spiritual truths of God's Word. Let us look to the Holy Spirit within us to give it such a hold of our inmost life that it may become the deepest inspiration of all our work. We can do true work only as we yield ourselves to God to work in us.

We know the ground on which this truth rests. *"There is none good but one, that is, God"* (Matt. 19:17). *"There is none holy as the LORD"* (1 Sam. 2:2). *"Power belongeth unto God"* (Ps. 62:11). All goodness and holiness and power are to be found only in God and where He gives them. Only He can give them to man, not as something He parts with, but by His own actual presence and dwelling and working. God can work in His people only as He is allowed to have complete possession of their hearts and lives. As the will and life and love are yielded up in dependence and faith, and we wait on God as Christ waited on Him, God can work in us.

This is true of all spiritual life, but especially of our work for God. The work of saving souls is God's own work. None but He can do it. The gift of

His Son is the proof of how great and precious He considers the work, and how His heart is set upon it. His love never for one moment ceases working for the salvation of men. And when He calls His children to be partners in His work, He shares with them the joy and the glory of the work of saving and blessing men. He promises to work His work through them, inspiring and energizing them by His power working in them. To the individual who can say with Paul, *"I also labour, striving according to his working, which worketh in me mightily,"* his whole relationship to God becomes the counterpart and the continuation of Christ's—a blessed, unceasing, momentary, and most absolute dependence on the Father for every word He spoke and every work He did.

Christ is our pattern. Christ's life is our law, and it works in us. Paul lived his life of dependence on God as Christ did. Why should any of us hesitate to believe that the grace given to Paul of laboring and striving *"according to the...working of his power"* will also be given to us. Let every worker learn to say, "As the power that worked in Christ worked in Paul, too, that power works no less in me." There is no possible way of doing God's work correctly but by God working it in us.

How I wish that I could take every worker who reads this by the hand, and say, "Come. Let us quiet our minds and hush every thought in God's presence, as I whisper in your ears the wonderful secret that God is working in you. All the work you have to do for Him, God will work in you." Take time and think it over. It is a deep spiritual truth that the mind cannot grasp nor the heart realize. Accept it as a divine truth from heaven.

Believe that this word is a seed from which the very spiritual blessing of which it speaks can grow. And in the faith of the Holy Spirit's making it live within you, always consider: *God works in me.* All the work I have to work for Him, God will work in me.

The faith of this truth, and the desire to have it made true in you, will compel you to live very humbly and closely with God. You will see how work for God must be the most spiritual thing in a spiritual life. And you will again and again bow in holy stillness and acknowledge that God is working in you and will continue to work in you. Like Paul you can say, "I will work for Him according to the power that works in me mightily."

1. The gift of the grace of God (Eph. 2:7, 3:7), the power that works in us (Eph. 3:20), the strengthening with might by the Spirit (v. 16)—the three expressions all contain the same thought of God's working all in us.

2. The Holy Spirit is the power of God. Seek to be filled with the Spirit, to have your whole life led by Him, and you will become fit for God's working mightily in you.

3. *"Ye shall receive power, after that the Holy Ghost is come upon you"* (Acts 1:8). Through the Spirit dwelling in us, God can work in us mightily.

4. What holy fear, what humble watchfulness and dependence, what entire surrender and obedience becomes us if we believe in God's working in us!

26
LABORING MORE ABUNDANTLY

*By the grace of God I am what I am: and his grace
which was bestowed upon me was not in vain; but
I laboured more abundantly than they all: yet not I,
but the grace of God which was with me.*
—1 Corinthians 15:10

*And he said unto me, My grace is sufficient for
thee: for my strength is made perfect in weakness....For in nothing am I behind the very
chiefest apostles, though I be nothing.*
—2 Corinthians 12:9, 11

In both of these passages, Paul spoke of how he
had abounded in the work of the Lord. *"In nothing am I behind the very chiefest apostles."* *"I
laboured more abundantly than they all."* In both
he told how entirely it was God who worked in
him and not himself. In the first passage he said,
"Not I, but the grace of God which was with me."
Then, in the second, he showed how this grace
is Christ's strength working in us. While we are
nothing, we are told, *"He said unto me: My grace is
sufficient for thee: for my strength is made perfect in*

weakness." May God give us *"the spirit of wisdom and revelation"* (Eph. 1:17) and the enlightened eyes of the heart (see verse 18) to see this wonderful vision of a man who knew himself to be nothing. He was a man who gloried in his weakness so that the power of Christ would rest on him and work through him, and who labored more abundantly than all. What this teaches us as workers for God!

God's work can be done only in God's strength. It is only by God's power, that is, by God Himself working in us, that we can do effective work. Throughout this book, this truth has been frequently repeated. It is easy to accept. It is far from easy to see its full meaning—to give it the mastery over our whole beings, to live it out. This will need stillness of soul, meditation, strong faith, and fervent prayer. As it is God alone who can work in us, it is equally God alone who can reveal Himself as the God who works in us. Wait on Him, and the truth that ever appears to be beyond your reach will be opened up to you through the knowledge of who and what God is. When God reveals Himself as *"God which worketh all in all"* (1 Cor. 12:6), you will learn to believe and work according to the power of Him who works in you mightily (Col. 1:29).

God's strength can work only in weakness. It is only when we truly say, *"Not I,"* that we can fully say, *"but the grace of God...with me."* The man who said, *"In nothing am I behind the very chiefest of the apostles,"* first had to learn to say, *"though I be nothing."* He could say, *"I take pleasure in infirmities...for when I am weak, then am I strong"* (2 Cor. 12:10). This is the true relationship between the Creator and mankind, between the divine Father and His child, between God and His servant. Dear Christian worker, learn the lesson of your own weakness, as the indispensable condition of God's power working in you. Believe that to take time and to realize in God's presence your weakness and nothingness is the sure way to be clothed with God's strength. Accept every experience by which God teaches you your weakness as His grace preparing you to receive His strength. Take pleasure in weaknesses!

God's strength comes in our fellowship with Christ and His service. Paul said, *"Most gladly therefore will I rather glory in my infirmities, that the power of Christ may rest upon me"* (2 Cor. 12:9). *"I take pleasure in infirmities...for Christ's sake"* (v. 10). And he told how it was when he had besought the Lord that the messenger of Satan might depart from him, that He answered, *"My grace is sufficient for thee." "Christ* [is] *the power of God, and the wisdom of God"* (1 Cor. 1:24). We do not receive the wisdom to know or the power to do God's will as something that we can possess and use at our discretion. It is in the personal attachment to Christ, in a life of continual communication with Him, that His power rests on us. It is in taking pleasure in weaknesses for Christ's sake that Christ's strength is known.

God's strength is given to faith, and the work that is done in faith. A living faith is needed to take pleasure in weakness, and in weakness to do our work, knowing that God is working in us. The highest exercise of a life of faith is to go on in the confidence of a hidden power working in us, without seeing or feeling anything. Faith alone can do God's work in saving souls. Faith alone can persevere in prayer and labor. Faith alone can continue to labor more abundantly despite unfavorable circumstances and appearances. Let us be *"strong in faith, giving glory to God"* (Rom. 4:20). God will show Himself strong toward him whose heart is perfect with Him (2 Chron. 16:9).

Be willing to yield yourself to the very utmost to God, so that His power may rest upon you and work in you. Let God work through you. Offer yourself to Him for His work as the one purpose of your life. Count upon His working in you to equip you for His service and to strengthen and bless you in it. Let the faith and love of your Lord Jesus, whose strength is going to be made perfect in your weakness, lead you to live even as He did, to do the Father's will and finish His work.

1. Let every minister seek the full personal experience of Christ's strength made perfect in His weakness. This alone will enable him to teach believers the secret of their strength.

2. Our Lord says, "My grace, My strength." As we abide in Christ, and have Christ abiding in us in close personal fellowship and love, His grace and strength can work.

3. Hearts completely given up to God, to His will and love will know His power working in their weakness.

27
A DOER WHO WORKS WILL BE BLESSED IN DOING

*Be ye doers of the word, and not hearers only,
deceiving your own selves.*
—James 1:22

*Whoso looketh into the perfect law of liberty, and
continueth therein, he being not a forgetful hearer,
but a doer of the work, this man
shall be blessed in his deed.*
—James 1:25

God created us not to contemplate but to act. He created us in His own likeness, and in Him there is no thought without simultaneous action. True action is born of contemplation. True contemplation, as a means to an end, always causes action. There would never have been a separation between knowing and doing if sin had not entered the world. In nothing is the power of sin more clearly seen than this, that even in the believer there is such a gap between intellect and conduct. It is possible to delight in hearing, to be diligent in increasing our knowledge of God's Word, to admire and approve the truth, even to be willing to do it, and yet to fail entirely in the actual performance. Thus, James warned us not to delude ourselves with being hearers and not doers. Thus, he pronounced the doer who works as blessed in his doing.

Blessed in doing. The words are a summary of the teaching of our Lord Jesus at the close of the Sermon on the Mount: *"Not every one that saith unto me, Lord, Lord, shall enter into the kingdom of heaven; but he that doeth the will of my Father"* (Matt. 7:21). *"Therefore whosoever heareth these sayings of mine, and doeth them, I will liken him unto a wise man"* (v. 24). To the woman who spoke of the blessedness of her who was his mother, He said, *"Yea rather, blessed are they that hear the word of God, and keep it"* (Luke 11:28). To the disciples on the night before His crucifixion He said, *"If ye know these things, happy are ye if ye do them"* (John 13:17). It is one of the greatest dangers in religion that we are content with reorganizing with pleasure and approval the meaning of a truth, yet do not immediately perform what it demands. It is only when conviction has been translated into conduct that we have proof that the truth is mastering us.

"A doer of the work, this man shall be blessed in his deed." The doer is blessed. The doing is the victory that overcomes every obstacle. It brings out and confirms the very image of God, the Great Worker. It removes every barrier to the enjoyment of all the blessing God has prepared. We are ever inclined to seek our blessedness in what God gives in privilege and enjoyment. Christ placed it

in what we do because it is only in doing that we really prove and possess the life God has bestowed. When one said, *"Blessed is he that shall eat bread in the kingdom of God"* (Luke 14:15), our Lord answered with the parable of the supper (vv. 16–24). The doer is blessed. It is only in doing that the painter or musician, the man of science or commerce, the discoverer or the conqueror finds his blessedness. So, and much more, is it only in keeping the commandments and in doing the will of God that the believer enters fully into the truth and blessedness of fellowship with God and deliverance from sin. Doing is the very essence of blessedness, the highest manifestation, and therefore, the fullest enjoyment of the life of God.

A doer of *the work, this man shall be blessed in his deed.* This was the blessedness of Abraham, of whom we read, *"Seest thou how faith wrought with his works, and by works was faith made perfect?"* (James 2:22). He had no works without faith. There was faith working with them and in them all. And he had no faith without works. Through them his faith was exercised, strengthened, and perfected. As his faith, so his blessedness was perfected in doing. It is in *doing* that the doer who works is blessed. The true insight into this will make us take every command, every truth, and every opportunity to abound in good works as an integral part of the blessedness of the salvation Christ has brought us. Joy and work, work and joy, will become synonymous. We will no longer be hearers but doers.

Let us put this truth into immediate practice. Let us live for others, to love and serve them. If you think you are not able to labor for souls, begin with the bodies. Only begin and go on, and abound. Believe that *"it is more blessed to give than to receive"* (Acts 20:35). Pray for and depend on the promised grace. Give yourself to a ministry of love. In the example of Christ and in the promise of God, you have the assurance. *"If ye know these things, happy are ye if ye do them"* (John 13:17). Blessed is the doer!

28
THE WORK OF SAVING SOULS

Brethren, if any of you do err from the truth,
and one convert him; let him know, that he
which converteth the sinner from the error
of his way shall save a soul from death,
and shall hide a multitude of sins.
—James 5:19–20

We sometimes hesitate to speak of men being converted and saved by men. Scripture here twice uses the expression of one man converting another, and once of his saving him. Let us not hesitate to convert and save men, for it is God who works in us.

"Shall save a soul from death." Every workman studies the material in which he works—the carpenter the wood, the goldsmith the gold. Our *"deeds...are wrought in God"* (John 3:21). In our good works we deal with souls. Even when we can at first do no more than reach and help their bodies, our aim is the soul. For these Christ came to die. For these God has appointed us to watch and labor. Let us study the habits of these people. What care a hunter or a fisherman takes to know the habits of the spoil he seeks! Let us remember

that we need divine wisdom and training and skill to become winners of souls. The only way to get that training and skill is to begin to work. Christ Himself will teach each one who waits on Him.

The church with its ministers has a part to take in that training. The daily experience of ordinary life proves how often unexpected powers exist in a man. When a man becomes conscious and a master of the power that is in himself, he is a new creature. The power and enjoyment of life are doubled. Every believer has hidden within himself the power of saving souls. The kingdom of heaven is within us as a seed. Every one of the gifts and graces of the Spirit is also a hidden seed. The highest aim of the ministry is to awaken the consciousness of this hidden seed of power to save souls. A depressing sense of ignorance or powerlessness keeps many back. James wrote, *"Let him know, that he which converteth the sinner...shall save a soul from death."* Every believer needs to be taught to know and use the wondrous blessed power with which he has been endowed. When God said to Abraham, *"I will bless thee, and...all the nations of the earth* [will] *be blessed"* (Gen. 22:17–18), He called him to a faith not only in the blessing that would come to him from above, but also in the power of blessing that he would be in the world. It is a wonderful moment in the life of a child of God when he sees that the second blessing is as sure as the first.

"He shall save a soul." Our Lord bears the name of Jesus, Savior. He is the embodiment of God's saving love. Saving souls is His own great work. As our faith in Him grows to know and receive all there is in Him, as He lives in us

and dwells in our hearts and dispositions, saving souls will become the great work to which our lives will be given. We will be the willing and intelligent instruments through whom He will do His mighty work.

"If any of you do err from the truth, and one convert him...he which converteth the sinner...shall save a soul." The words suggest personal work. We chiefly think of large gatherings to whom the Gospel is preached. The thought here is of one who has erred and is sought after. We increasingly do our work through associations and organizations. "If *one* converts him, *he* saves a soul." It is the love and labor of some individual believer that has won the erring one back. It is this we need in the church of Christ—every believer who truly follows Jesus Christ looking out for those who are erring from the way, loving them, and laboring to help them back. Not one of us may say (as in Genesis 4:9), *"Am I my brother's keeper?"* We are in the world only and solely as the members of Christ's body, so that we may continue to carry out His saving work. As saving souls was and is His work, His joy, and His glory, let it be ours. Let each give himself personally to watch over individuals and seek to save them one by one.

"Know, that he which converteth the sinner... shall save a soul." *"If ye know these things, happy are ye if ye do them"* (John 13:17). Let us translate these Scripture truths into action. Let us give these thoughts shape and substance in daily life. Let us prove their power over us and our faith in them, by *work.* Is there a Christian around us wandering from the way, needing loving help

and willing to receive it? Are there some whom we could take by the hand and encourage to begin again? If we are truly at the disposal of Jesus Christ, He will use us to show others the right way.

If we feel afraid, let us believe that the love of God dwells within us, not only calling but also enabling us to do the work. Let us yield ourselves to the Holy Spirit to fill our hearts with that love, and to equip us for its service. Jesus, the Savior, lives to save. He dwells in us. He will do His saving work through us. *"Know, that he which converteth the sinner...shall save a soul from death, and shall hide a multitude of sins."*

1. More love for souls, born out of fervent love for the Lord Jesus—this is our great need.

2. Let us pray to love in the faith. As we exercise the little we have, more will be given.

3. Lord, open our eyes to see You doing Your great work of saving men, and waiting to give Your love and strength into the heart of every willing one. Make each one of Your redeemed a soulwinner.

29
PRAYING AND WORKING

*If any man see his brother sin a sin which is not
unto death, he shall ask, and he shall give him
life for them that sin not unto death.*
—1 John 5:16

*And let us consider one another to provoke
unto love and to good works.*
—Hebrews 10:24

These words in Hebrews express what lies at
the very root of a life of good works—the
thoughtful, loving care we have for each
other, that not one may fall away. In Galatians
6:1 we read, *"If a man be overtaken in a fault,
ye which are spiritual, restore such an one in the
spirit of meekness."* Jude wrote of Christians who
were in danger of failing away: *"Others save with
fear, pulling them out of the fire; hating even the
garment spotted by the flesh"* (v. 23). As Christ's
doing good to men's bodies always aimed at winning their souls, all our ministry of love must be
subordinated to that which is God's great purpose
and longing—the salvation unto life eternal.

Praying and working must always go together in this labor of love. At times prayer may reach those whom words cannot reach. At times prayer may chiefly be needed for ourselves, to obtain the wisdom and courage for the words. As a rule, praying and working must be inseparable—the praying to obtain from God what we need for the soul, the working to bring to it what God has given us. The words of John here are most suggestive as to the power of prayer in our labor of love. We are led to think of prayer as a personal work with a very definite purpose and a certainty of answer.

Let prayer be a personal effort. *"If any man see his brother...he shall ask."* We are so accustomed to act through societies and associations that we are in danger of losing sight of the duty resting upon each of us to watch over those around him. Let every member of our bodies be ready to serve any other member. Every believer is to care for the fellow believers who are within his reach, in his church, his house, or social circle. The sin of each is a loss and a hurt to the body of Christ. Let your eyes be open to the sins of your brethren around you. Do not speak evil or judge or helplessly complain, but love and help and care and pray. Ask God to see your brother's sin in its sinfulness, its danger to himself, and its grief to Christ. However, God's compassion and deliverance are within reach. Shutting our eyes to the sin of our brethren around us is not true love. See it, take it to God, and make it part of your work for God to pray for your brother and seek new life for him.

Let prayer be definite. *"If any man see his brother sin...let him ask."* We need prayer from a person for a person. Scripture and God's Spirit teach us to pray for all society, for the church with which we are associated, for nations, and for special areas of work. This is necessary and blessed. But somehow more is needed—to make those with whom we come into contact, subjects of our intercession. The larger supplications must have their place, but it is difficult to know when our prayers are answered regarding them. But nothing will bring God so near, will test and strengthen our faith, and make us know that we are fellow workers with God, as when we receive an answer to our prayers for individuals. It will quicken in us the new and blessed consciousness that we indeed have power with God. Let every worker seek to exercise this grace of taking up and praying for individual souls.

Count upon an answer. *"He shall ask, and God will give him* [the one who prays] *life for them that sin."* The words follow on those in which John had spoken about the confidence we have of being heard, if we *"ask any thing according to his will"* (1 John 5:14). There is often complaint made of not knowing God's will. But here there is no difficulty. *"*[God] *will have all men to be saved"* (1 Tim. 2:4). If we rest our faith on this will of God, we will grow strong and grasp the promise: *"He shall ask, and* [God] *will give him life for them that sin."* The Holy Spirit will lead us, if we yield ourselves to be led by Him, to the souls God would have us take as our special care, and for which the grace of faith and persevering prayer will be given us. Let the wonderful promise—that God will give to him who asks life for them who sin—stir us and encourage us to our priestly ministry of personal and definite intercession, as one of the most blessed among the good works in which we can serve God and man.

Praying and working are inseparable. Let all who work learn to pray well. Let all who pray learn to work well.

1. Let us pray confidently, and if need be perseveringly, for an individual who needs a close walk with God, and for the faith that we can overcome with Him.

2. In all our work for God, prayer must take a much larger place. If God is to work all, then our position is to be that of entire dependence, waiting for Him to work in us. If it takes time to persevere and to receive in ourselves what God gives us for others, there needs to be a work and a labor in prayer.

3. Oh, that God would open our eyes to the glory of this work of saving souls, as the one thing God lives for, as the one thing He wants to work in us!

4. Let us pray for the love and power of God to come on us, for the blessed work of soulwinning.

30
"I KNOW THY WORKS"

Unto the angel of the church of Ephesus...in Thyatira...in Sardis...in Philadelphia...of the Laodiceans write...I know thy works.
—Revelation 2:1, 18; 3:1, 7, 14–15

"I *know thy works.*" These are the words of Him who walks in the midst of the seven golden candlesticks, and whose eyes are like a flame of fire. As He looks upon the churches, the first thing He sees and judges is their works. The works are the revelation of the life and character. If we are willing to bring our works into His holy presence, His words can teach us what our work ought to be.

To Ephesus He says, *"I know thy works, and thy labour, and thy patience, and how thou canst not bear them which are evil...and hast borne, and hast patience, and for my name's sake hast laboured, and hast not fainted. Nevertheless I have somewhat against thee, because thou hast left thy first love....Repent, and do the first works"* (Rev. 2:2–5). There was much here to praise—toil, patience, and zeal that had never grown weary. But there was one thing lacking—the tenderness of the first love.

In His work for us, Christ gave us before and above everything His love, the personal tender affection of His heart. In our work for Him, He asks us nothing less. There is a danger of work being carried on, and our even bearing much for Christ's sake, while the freshness of our love has passed away. That is what Christ seeks. That is what gives power. Nothing can compensate for it. Christ looks for the warm, loving heart, the personal affection that ever keeps Him the center of our love and joy.

Christian workers, see that all your work be the work of love, of tender personal devotion to Christ Jesus.

To Thyatira He said, *"I know thy works, and charity, and service, and faith, and thy patience, and thy works; and the last to be more than the first. Notwithstanding I have a few things against thee, because thou sufferest that woman Jezebel, which calleth herself a prophetess, to teach and to seduce my servants to commit fornication"* (Rev. 2:19–20). Here again the works are enumerated and praised. The last had even been more than the first. But then there is one failure—a false toleration of what led to impurity and idolatry. And then He adds of His judgments, *"The churches shall know that I am he which searcheth the reins and hearts: and I will give unto every one of you according to your works"* (v. 23).

Along with much of good works, there may be some one form of error or evil tolerated that endangers the whole church. In Ephesus there was zeal for orthodoxy, but a lack of love—here love and faith, but a lack of faithfulness against error. If good works are to please our Lord, if our whole lives must be in harmony with them, in entire separation from the world and its allurements, we must seek to be what He promised to make us, established in every good word and work. In His judgment, our work will decide our value.

To Sardis His message was this: *"I know thy works, that thou hast a name...and art dead. Be watchful, and strengthen the things which remain, that are ready to die: for I have not found thy works perfect before God"* (Rev. 3:1–2).

There may be all the forms of godliness without the power and all the activities or religious organization without the life. There may be many works, and yet He may say, "I have found no work of yours fulfilled before My God, none that can stand the test and be really acceptable to God as a spiritual sacrifice. In Ephesus it was works lacking in love, in Thyatira works lacking in purity, in Sardis works lacking in life."

To Philadelphia He says, *"I know thy works... for thou hast a little strength, and hast kept my word, and hast not denied my name....Because thou hast kept the word of my patience, I also will keep thee"* (Rev. 3:8, 10).

On earth Jesus had said, *"He that hath My commandments, and keepeth them, he it is that loveth me"* (John 14:21). *"The Father himself loveth you, because ye have loved me"* (John 16:27). Philadelphia, the church for which there is no reproof, had this mark: its chief work, and the law of all its work, was that it kept Christ's Word, not in an orthodox creed only, but in practical obedience. Let nothing less be the mark and spirit of all our work—a keeping of the Word of

Christ. Full, loving conformity to His will will be rewarded.

To Laodicea Christ says, *"I know thy works, that thou art neither cold nor hot....Thou sayest, I am rich, and increased with goods, and have need of nothing"* (Rev. 3:15, 17). There is not a church without its works, its religious activities. And yet the two great marks of Laodicean religion, luke-warmness and self-complacence, may rob them of their worth. It is not only the need for a fresh and fervent love, as Ephesus teaches us, but also the need for that poverty of spirit, that conscious weakness out of which the absolute dependence on Christ's strength for all our work will grow. It will no longer leave Christ standing at the door, but will enthrone Him in the heart.

"I know thy works." He who tested the works of the seven churches still lives and watches over us. He is ready in His love to discover what is lacking, to give timely warning and help, and to teach us the path in which our works can be ful-filled before God. Let us learn from Ephesus the lesson of fervent love for Christ, from Thyatira that of purity and separation from all evil, from Sardis that of the need of true life to give worth to work, from Philadelphia that of keeping His Word, and from Laodicea that of the poverty of spirit that possesses the kingdom of heaven and gives Christ the throne of all! Workers, let us live and work in Christ's presence! He will teach, correct, and help us, and one day give the full reward of all our works because they were His own works in us.

31
THAT GOD MAY BE GLORIFIED

If any man speak, let him speak as the oracles of God; if any man minister, let him do it as of the ability which God giveth: that God in all things may be glorified through Jesus Christ, to whom be praise and dominion for ever and ever. Amen.
—1 Peter 4:11

Work is not done for its own sake. Its value consists in the objective it attains. The purpose of him who commands or performs the work gives it its real worth. And the clearer a man's insight into the purpose, the better equipped he will be to take charge of the higher parts of the work. In erecting a splendid building, the purpose of the day laborer may simply be as a hireling to earn his wages. The trained stonecutter has a higher objective—he thinks of the beauty and perfection of the work he does. The master mason has a wider range of thought. His aim is that all the masonry will be true and good. The contractor for the whole building has a higher aim—that the whole building will perfectly correspond to the plan he has to carry out. The architect has a still higher purpose—that the great principles of art and beauty might find their full expression in material shape. With the owner we find the final end—the use to which the grand structure is to be put when he presents the building as a gift for the benefit of his townsmen. All who have worked on the building honestly have done so with some true purpose. The deeper the insight and the keener the interest in the ultimate design, the more important the share in the work, and the greater the joy in carrying it out.

Peter told us what our aim ought to be in all Christian service—*"that God in all things may be glorified through Jesus Christ."* In the work of God, a work not to be done for wages but for love, the humblest laborer is invited to share in God's plans, and to an insight into the great purpose which God is working out. That purpose is nothing less than this—that God may be glorified. This is the one purpose of God, the Great Worker in heaven, the Source and Master of all work, that the glory of His love and power and blessing may be shown. This is the one purpose of Christ, the Great Worker on earth in human nature, the Example and Leader of all our work. This is the great purpose of the Holy Spirit, the power that works in us, or, as Peter said here, *"the ability which God giveth."* As this becomes our deliberate, intelligent purpose, our work will rise to its true level and lift us into living fellowship with God.

"That God in all things may be glorified." What does this mean? The glory of God is this, that He alone is the Living One, who has life in Himself. Yet not for Himself alone, but because His life is love for men as much as for Himself. This is the

glory of God, that He is the only and ever-flowing fountain of all life and goodness and happiness, and that His creatures can have all this only as He gives it and works it in them. His working all in all, this is His glory. And the only glory His creature, His child, can give Him is this—receiving all He is willing to give, yielding to Him to let Him work, and then acknowledging that He has done it. Thus God Himself shows forth His glory in us. In our willing surrender to Him and our joyful acknowledgment that He does all, we glorify Him. And so our life and work are glorified, as they have one purpose with all God's own work, *"that God in all things may be glorified through Jesus Christ, to whom be praise and dominion for ever and ever."*

See here the spirit that elevates and consecrates Christian service. According to Peter, *"If any man minister* [in ministering to fellow believers or the needy], *let him do it as of the ability which God giveth."* Let us cultivate a deep conviction that God's work, down to the details of daily life, can be done only in God's strength by *"the power that worketh in us"* (Eph. 3:20). Let us believe firmly and unceasingly that the Holy Spirit dwells in us as the power *from* on high for all work to be done *for* on high. Let us in our Christian work fear nothing so much as working in our own human will and strength, thus losing the one thing necessary in our work: God working in us. Let us rejoice in the weakness that renders us so absolutely dependent upon such a God and wait in prayer for His power to take full possession.

"Let him do it as of the ability which God giveth: that God in all things may be glorified

through Jesus Christ." The more you depend on God alone for your strength, the more He will be glorified. The more you seek to make God's purpose your purpose, the more you will be led to give way to His working and His strength and love. I pray that every worker might see what a nobility it gives to work, what a new glory to life, what a new urgency and joy in laboring for souls, when the one purpose has mastered us—that in all things God may be glorified through Jesus Christ.

1. The glory of God as Creator was seen in His making man in His own image. The glory of God as Redeemer is seen in the work He carries on for saving men and bringing them to Himself.

2. This glory is the glory of His holy love, casting sin out of the heart, and dwelling there.

3. The only glory we can bring to God is to yield ourselves to His redeeming love to take possession of us, to fill us with love for others, and so through us to show forth His glory.

4. Let this be the one purpose of our lives—to glorify God; in living to work for Him, *"as of the ability which God giveth"*; and winning souls to know and live for His glory.

5. Lord, teach us to serve in the ability that You give, so that in all things You

may be glorified through Jesus Christ, *"to whom be praise and dominion for ever and ever. Amen."*